The Politics of
Taxation in Canada

The Politics of Taxation in Canada

••

GEOFFREY HALE

broadview press

NATIONAL LIBRARY OF CANADA CATALOGUING IN PUBLICATION DATA

Hale, Geoffrey E., 1955-
    The politics of taxation in Canada

Includes bibliographical references and index.
ISBN 1-55111-300-7

1. Taxation—Canada
2. Fiscal policy—Canada
I. Title.

HJ2449.H29 2001   336.2'00971   C2001-902405-3

BROADVIEW PRESS, LTD.
is an independent, international publishing house, incorporated in 1985.

North America
Post Office Box 1243, Peterborough, Ontario, Canada K9J 7H5
3576 California Road, Orchard Park, New York, USA 14127
TEL (705) 743-8990; FAX (705) 743-8353

www.broadviewpress.com
customerservice@broadviewpress.com

United Kingdom and Europe
Thomas Lyster, Ltd. Unit 9, Ormskirk Industrial Park,
Old Boundary Way, Burscough Rd, Ormskirk, Lancashire L39 2YW
TEL (1695) 575112; FAX (1695) 570120; E-MAIL books@tlyster.co.uk

Australia
St. Clair Press, Post Office Box 287, Rozelle, NSW 2039
TEL (02) 818-1942; FAX (02) 418-1923

Broadview Press gratefully acknowledges the support of the Ministry of Canadian Heritage through the Book Publishing Industry Development Program.

Cover design by Zack Taylor.
Typeset by Liz Broes, Black Eye Design.

Printed in Canada

10 9 8 7 6 5 4 3 2 1

Contents

Acknowledgements

I wish to acknowledge with thanks the cooperation of the many people inside and outside government, including many current and former officials of the federal Department of Finance, the Prime Minister's Office, and provincial Finance and Treasury Ministries, who took the time to speak to me about their experiences in government and their perspectives on the tax policy process and to comment on different parts of this book during its writing.

I appreciate the willingness of current and former Ministers of Finance, including Paul Martin, Michael Wilson, and Marc Lalonde, to discuss the political and policy challenges of managing tax and economic policies during an exceptionally challenging period in Canada's economic history. Several former deputy ministers of finance, including Grant Reuber, Ian Stewart, Marshall Cohen, Stanley Hartt, Fred Gorbet, and David Dodge, were also generous with their time and insights, as were virtually all the assistant deputy ministers for tax policy who have held the position since the era of the Carter Commission and the Benson White Paper.

Tables 2.1, B.1, 6.2, 7.1, 8.1, 9.1, 9.6, C.1, 11.1, 12.1 and 13.4 are reproduced with the permission of the Minister of Public Works and Government Services Canada, 2001.

Sid Noel, John McDougall, and Allan McDougall provided invaluable advice during the initial stages of the development of this book while I was completing my Ph.D. dissertation at the University of Western Ontario. The Social Sciences and Humanities Research Council also provided financial assistance in the form of a graduate fellowship during that period. Don Drummond, Chief Economist of the Toronto-Dominion Bank, my colleague, Alan Siaroff, and an anonymous reviewer at Broadview Press were kind enough to read advanced drafts of the manuscript and to provide me with a number of helpful insights and critiques.

Michael Harrison, Suzanne Hancock, and Judith Earnshaw at Broadview Press have provided valued encouragement and support in seeing the book through to publication, as has my wife, Susan, whose sharing of life's journey makes it much less taxing and far more rewarding.

List of Tables and Appendices

Chapter 9

Part III: Introduction

Chapter 10

Chapter 11

Chapter 12

Chapter 13

Introduction

Money is, with propriety, considered as the vital principle of the body politic; as that which sustains its life and motion and enables it to perform its most essential function. A complete power, therefore, to procure a regular and adequate supply of revenue, as far as the resources of the community will permit, may be regarded as an indispensable ingredient in every constitution.

Alexander Hamilton[1]

The very principle of constitutional government requires it to be assumed that political power will be abused to promote the particular purposes of the holder; not because it always is so, but because such is the natural tendency of things, to guard against which is the especial use of free institutions.

John Stuart Mill[2]

Taxation is an immutable fact of life in the modern world. Most of our incomes are subject to taxation. Virtually everything we buy or sell through traditional forms of commerce is subject directly or indirectly to taxation—although governments have not yet figured out how to measure, capture, and tax the growing flows of commercial activity through the Internet. Most of our property and accumulated wealth are subject, sooner or later, to the demands of the tax collector.

Taxes are widely viewed as both a positive good and a necessary evil. They are a positive good to the extent that they pay for public services desired by citizens in a democracy—and that we as citizens have the power both to control the size of government and to ensure that we get reasonable value for our tax dollars. They are a necessary evil in that governments are made up of ambitious, self-interested human beings, as well as dedicated public servants, whose activities often seem to be motivated as much by the pursuit of political and bureaucratic self-interest as by the goal of enhancing the prosperity and security of the nation and its citizens.

The politics of taxation in Canada are largely defined by the struggle between these competing and overlapping views of reality, sometimes described by economists as the "public finance" and "leviathan" views of government,[3] and by the attempts of Finance Ministers and their officials to strike some kind of balance between them.

The political and ideological conflicts of the 1970s and 1980s—the Trudeau and Mulroney years—left Canada a bitterly divided country, deeply in debt, and struggling to adapt to a series of economic and social changes that were effectively beyond its governments' ability to control. On the surface, much of the conflict was about taxes. Depending on one's economic interests or point of view, Canada's economic problems were blamed on governments spending and taxing too much, or not using its powers to impose enough political control on powerful economic interests. The federal government was seen alternately to be indulging "corporate welfare bums," a universal subsidy of tax and spending handouts,[4] or to be beholden to the predatory ambitions of self-serving politicians and interest groups. The fair, just, and economically sound answer to these problems might be to "make the rich pay," to "run government more like a business," or to find and hold a consistent balance between the need to promote economic growth and the need to provide (or allow) all Canadians a fair share of its benefits.

These issues have often been the subject of vigorous debate and, occasionally, bitter political and ideological conflict since the mid-1960s. The conflict they triggered created political conditions that fostered chronic deficits and rapidly growing public debt for more than twenty years, undermining the federal government's capacity for economic leadership.

By the early 1990s, the failure of successive governments to come to grips with these problems and to build a national political consensus around the size and role of government had left Canada's public finances in a shambles with rising taxes, declining levels of public services, and shrinking living standards for most of its citizens. In response, a broad political and public consensus gradually emerged in support of deficit reduction and balanced budgets, more disciplined public spending (and private demands on government), and a more selective approach to government intervention in order to set Canada's economic house in order.

At the same time, governments' struggle to balance their budgets, achieve sustainable levels of public spending, and ensure the future solvency of major social programs—especially the Canada Pension Plan—resulted in 1998 in overall government revenues reaching their highest level in Canadian history as a share of national income, before starting to decline (see Table 1.1).

The tax system that has emerged from these debates at the beginning of the new century reflects a series of compromises between competing political and ideological priorities that have become embedded in Canadian political life:

> relatively high tax rates on personal income, taking effect at modest income levels relative to our major trading partners;

> relatively generous incentives for retirement, and more recently, education savings, together with a growing set of income transfer programs administered through the tax system;

> a corporate tax system with competitive tax rates favourable to the growth of manufacturing, resource, and small business sectors, but with high rates, by international standards, for most service industries;[5]

> capital gains taxes on the sale of most shares and other investments on the death of their owners, but no estate or inheritance taxes payable at death;

> relatively high sales tax levels compared to the United States to pay for Canada's higher level of public spending, offset by refundable tax credits to reduce their impact on lower-income families;

> significant increases in payroll taxes during the late 1990s, mainly to restore the Canada Pension Plan to financial solvency.

These compromises involve a balancing of the long-term interests and objectives of governments and major interests in society. They have a pervasive impact on economic and social relationships and are deeply embedded in the economic and social lives of Canadians—from the extensive use of tax measures to assist parents, reduce poverty, encourage retirement savings, foster the growth of small businesses, finance and offset the costs of education, avoid double taxation, and support a wide range of voluntary community activities and services. As a result, major changes to the tax system usually require the formal or informal approval or consent of a majority of political and economic stakeholders—not merely the government of the day.

Economists such as the American Nobel Prize winner James Buchanan have likened these structures and rules to a fiscal or economic "constitution" governing the basic economic relationships of society.[6] These durable systems of rules, which evolve over time but are rarely subject to sudden major changes, parallel the formal political constitutions that define the powers and limits on governments and the basic rules governing their operations. Any attempt to reopen these basic compromises by introducing major changes to the tax system is likely to produce much the same level of political conflict as did proposals for constitutional reform in the early 1990s.

Canada has gone through a decade of relative stability in its tax system since the introduction of the Goods and Services Tax in 1990. However, the political and economic circumstances that shape the politics of taxation have changed significantly. A steadily growing economy and rising tax revenues have generated budget surpluses at the federal level and in most provinces. Governments are facing growing political pressure to use this "fiscal dividend" to reduce taxes, increase spending on major public services such as health care, initiate new social programs, and pay down Canada's huge public debt. While governments may act boldly on one or two fronts, they cannot satisfy all these demands in the short term without risking a return to the unbalanced tax and spending policies of the 1970s and 1980s. As a result, many of the same issues that divided Canadians during this period are returning to the political forefront.

> How much should Canadians pay in taxes in order to provide the levels of public services that we want, while attempting to design tax and spending policies that enable our economy to grow in ways that will provide us with higher and more secure standards of living?

> How should governments organize our tax system to provide citizens with appropriate incentives to work, save, and invest while sharing the costs of public services in ways that recognize both individuals' ability to pay and the fairness of allowing some citizens and businesses that receive significantly greater benefits from governments to pay directly for those benefits?

> How should governments balance different considerations of fairness—not the least that tax burdens should reflect individuals' (or families') ability to pay, and that people in similar economic circumstances should pay approximately equal levels of taxation?

> Is the tax system relatively predictable and transparent in its operations, or does it lend itself to manipulation by unscrupulous tax professionals or to arbitrary interpretation by heavy-handed tax collectors?

➤ To what extent should the tax system accommodate Canadians' social goals and objectives through individual and community action—including the capacity of parents to raise their children, the support of voluntary and charitable organizations, support for political parties and other groups through which we participate in democratic debate—or are these objectives better addressed through direct government spending?

➤ How do our governments attempt to balance the desires of their citizens that our economic, social, and tax policies reflect the expectations of Canadians with the ever-present reality of international economic competition which influences our ability to pay our way in the world and to improve both our standard of living and our quality of life as a nation?

These decisions—about what is taxed, when, by how much, and by which combination of federal, provincial, municipal and, increasingly, foreign governments—are not made in a vacuum. Rather, they are the product of past political decisions, historical trade-offs among competing interests, and the continuing interaction among political and economic institutions and systems—the basic structures and laws that govern our societies and economies. The tax system reflects an often uneasy balance between political and economic considerations, On the one hand, it is shaped by the disciplines of economics—not least by an international economic system that is increasingly difficult for national governments to influence, let alone control. As such, the tax system reflects the views and values of civil servants and economists who advise politicians about the options available to them, the likely impact of their choices on ordinary citizens, and their capacity to achieve other political and policy goals. On the other hand, the tax system is also the product of a political marketplace in which politicians, interest groups, citizens, and businesses scramble to maximize the benefits they derive both from the economic system and from governments, and to minimize their costs (e.g., taxes), often by shifting them to others.

The political economy of taxation is heavily influenced by three major factors. The "idea-centred approach" reflects the belief that the activities of the modern state require a set of unifying principles that are capable of generating viable responses to the major policy challenges facing decision-makers in the public and private sectors. The institutional framework for policy-making—including the organizations, laws, and formal and informal rules that shape the decision-making process—shapes the options, priorities, and policy choices of government decision-makers in setting budgetary and tax policies. At the same time, the pursuit of consistent economic policies requires sustained political support from a wide cross-section of Canadians for whom ideas are primarily a means of promoting or protecting their interests and status. This requires the political skill to build coalitions of interests and a base of support among voters either in support of a new policy consensus or to sustain the government in the face of strong political opposition.[8]

Before exploring these issues in greater depth, it would be helpful to provide a few basic facts about the overall level and distribution of taxes paid by Canadians, the different sources of tax revenues enjoyed by different levels of government, the impact of Canada's federal system of government on the tax system, and how Canadian tax levels compare with those of other major industrial countries.

Canada's Tax Structure: A Basic Outline

Canadian governments at all levels raised more than $460 billion in 2000—about $14,960 for every Canadian—or about 44.3 per cent of national income[9] in order to pay for the wide range of services and transfers that Canadians have come to expect, along with interest charges on past government borrowing. Although governments at all levels are seeking to expand their revenue sources, most of this money comes from a wide range of taxes.

OVERALL TAX LEVELS

Overall levels of taxation can be measured in a number of ways, depending on what the observer is trying to measure. Canadian governments typically keep three sets of books: budgetary accounts, which measure their spending commitments and revenues collectable during a fiscal year (April 1–March 31), not including special "dedicated accounts" such as those for government-run businesses, arms-length agencies, and national pension plans; national accounts, which are Statistics Canada's measure of the total volume of revenue and spending accrued during a calendar year; and the Financial Management System (FMS), which measures overall government cash flow.

Governments have increased their share of national income in recent years, increasing taxes and other sources of income between 1990 and 2000, while reducing their levels of spending relative to the size of the economy in order to balance their budgets. Total government spending as a share of national income peaked at 52.4 per cent of GDP in 1992. Since then, it has declined to about 40.8 per cent of GDP in 2000, resulting in growing overall public-sector surpluses (see Table 1.1).

National and provincial governments have considerable discretion in the level of services they provide to their citizens, as well as in the level of redistribution among citizens and income groups provided through the tax system. However, the growing mobility of business and investment in regional and global economies means that governments that want to spend a higher level of their national incomes often choose to do so by imposing lower tax levels on "mobile" factors of production—especially corporate, self-employment, and investment income—and higher rates of tax on less mobile tax bases: employment payrolls and consumption of goods by their residents.

Canada's overall tax levels are slightly below the average of the major industrial countries that make up the G-7, but significantly higher in most areas than those of its major trading partner, the United States. This has influenced the recent decisions of Canadian governments to reduce personal income taxes, which now absorb a larger share of national income than any major industrial country, rather than payroll or consumption taxes, which are significantly below the levels of Canada's major industrial competitors[10] (see Table 1.2).

Table 1.1 ·· GOVERNMENT SPENDING, TAXES, REVENUES, AND BUDGET BALANCES AS A SHARE OF NATIONAL INCOME: 1970-2000 (NATIONAL ACCOUNTS BASIS)

	total public spending	total government revenues	total tax revenues	government surpluses/ (deficits)*
		AS A PERCENTAGE OF GDP		
1970	34.2	36.1	29.7	- 1.9
1980	40.8	38.1	29.4	- 4.1
1990	48.2	43.6	35.9	- 5.9
1992	52.4	44.2	36.5	- 9.2
2000[P]	40.8	44.3	37.0	+3.4

* Including capital and financial accounts.
P = preliminary

Sources: Canada, Department of Finance (2000d); Statistics Canada (2001), *National Income and Expenditure Accounts*, Cat. # 13-001 (March).

Table 1.2 •• TOTAL GOVERNMENT TAXATION IN OECD COUNTRIES—1997

	Total Tax Revenue	Taxes on Personal Income	Taxes on Corporate Income	Social Security Contributions	Payroll Taxes	Taxes on Property	Taxes on Goods and Services
				AS A PERCENTAGE OF GDP			
OECD AVERAGE	37.2	10.2	3.3	9.6	0.4	1.9	11.6
CANADA	36.8	14.0	3.8	4.9	0.8	3.7	9.0
US	29.7	11.6	2.8	7.2	na	3.2	4.9
JAPAN	28.8	5.9	4.3	10.6	na	3.1	4.8
EU AVERAGE	41.5	10.9	3.5	11.8	0.4	1.8	12.6
GERMANY	37.2	8.9	1.5	15.5	na	1.0	10.3
FRANCE	45.1	6.3	2.6	18.3	1.1	2.4	12.6
ITALY	44.4	11.2	4.2	14.9	0.1	2.3	11.5
UK	35.4	8.8	4.3	6.1	na	3.8	12.4

Source: David B. Perry (2000) "International Tax Comparisons," *Canadian Tax Journal* 48(2), 535-36.

Another way to measure tax levels is relative to individuals' overall incomes. How much disposable income do Canadians have left over after taxes and government transfers which help to redistribute income among different groups of Canadians?

BETTER OR WORSE OFF?

Canadians' support for or resentment of governments is often linked to their relative economic well-being. This can be expressed in terms either of higher disposable income—"take-home" pay—at the end of the year, or of their economic well-being relative to other Canadians, depending on their social position and political outlooks.

The federal and most provincial governments raised taxes during the 1980s in an attempt to curb chronic budget deficits, but spending—especially the rapidly rising costs of interest on growing debts—rose even faster. The tax increases and spending reductions at both federal and provincial levels during the 1990s, which largely cancelled out the small increases in personal and family incomes during this period, reflect both slow economic growth and the efforts of most governments to balance their budgets.[11] To offset the impact of these changes on lower-income earners, middle- and upper-income Canadians have paid a significantly larger share of the tax burden during the 1990s.

For lower and middle-income Canadians, the benefits received from government may significantly offset or even exceed the levels of taxes paid, creating a significant political constituency for increased public spending. While income taxes, the single largest source of federal and provincial tax revenues, rose faster than the incomes of most Canadian families between 1980 and 1997, transfer payments grew even faster for lower and middle-income families, despite the spending reductions of the 1990s.[12]

As a result, while Canadians' average "retention rate," or take-home pay, declined from 82 to 75 per cent of income between 1980 and 1998 (see Table 1.3), overall levels of economic inequality, measured in terms of incomes after taxes and government transfers, have remained relatively constant during this period.[13] Table 1.4 outlines the relative effects of the tax-transfer system on Canadians' standards of living in 1989 and 1997.

The above figures are incomplete, since current information quantifying the distribution of other forms of taxation paid by individual Canadians and

Table 1.3 ·· PRIVATE INCOME RETENTION RATE: 1970-98
(PRIVATE AFTER-TAX INCOME AS A SHARE OF TOTAL INCOME)

	Average Total Income	Average Market Income	Average Government Transfers Received	Average Taxes Paid	Average Disposable Income	Retention Rate % of total income
			1998$ PER PERSON			
1970	14,295	13,060	1,235	2,643	11,652	81.5%
% of total income		91.4%	8.6%	18.5%		
1980	20,915	18,682	2,234	3,795	17,121	81.9%
% of total income		89.3%	10.7%	18.1%		
1990	22,893	19,837	3,056	5,198	17,695	77.3%
% of total income		86.7%	13.3%	22.7%		
1998	24,246	20,546	3,700	6,000	18,246	75.3%
% of total income		84.7%	15.3%	24.7%		

Source: Statistics Canada, *National Income and Expenditures Accounts*, Cat. # 13-001; author's calculations.

Table 1.4 •• INCOME TAXES, TRANSFERS, AND THE DISTRIBUTION
OF FAMILY INCOMES (IN CONSTANT 1997 DOLLARS)

		Average Income Before Transfers	Average Transfers	Average Income Tax	Average Benefits Minus Income Taxes Paid	(As % of Income Before Taxes and Transfers)	Average After–Tax Income
Lowest Quintile	1989	10,228	9,525	1,351	8,174	79.9%	18,402
	1997	8,199	9,528	905	8,623	101.5%	16,876
Second Quintile	1989	30,986	6,729	4,917	1,812	5.8%	32,798
	1997	25,979	8,420	4,386	4,034	15.5%	30,013
Middle Quintile	1989	48,215	5,115	9,369	-4,254	(8.8%)	43,962
	1997	44,627	5,921	9,320	-3,399	(7.6%)	41,228
Fourth Quintile	1989	67,116	4,224	14,353	-10,129	(15.1%)	57,025
	1997	64,450	4,610	14,659	-10,049	(15.6%)	54,401
Highest Quintile	1989	113,140	3,998	27,768	-23,770	(21.0%)	89,370
	1997	110,113	3,836	28,432	-24,596	(22.3%)	85,516

Source: Statistics Canada (1999) *Income after Tax: Distributions by Size in Canada*, 1997, Catalogue # 13-210 (Ottawa, July).

the benefits directly received in services (including public-sector employ-ment as well as cash transfers) is not available. Nevertheless, the data clearly show that the existing tax-transfer system reinforces a strong political bias in favour of increased public spending among lower- and many middle-income Canadians.

DIFFERENT SOURCES OF TAX REVENUE

The growth of governments relative to the economy since the World War II has resulted in the creation of new taxes and other revenue sources to avoid crippling economic activity and encouraging tax resistance by imposing excessively high tax rates on any one source of economic activity.[14] As a result, the national tax system contains four major components: income taxes, sales and excise taxes, social insurance (or "payroll") taxes on employ-ment earnings, and property taxes, and a number of lesser revenue sources.

Most of these revenue sources are shared between different levels of government (see Table 1.5).

The ever-growing share of economic activity taking place in different regions and countries makes it increasingly difficult for governments to regulate, tax, and control it. As a result, governments need to coordinate the design and administration of their tax rules. This is done in order to limit "double taxation" of income or business transactions in ways that could reduce overall economic activity, and to control tax avoidance practices that result from individuals and businesses attempting to play off one government and set of tax rules against another.

Thus, the politics of taxation involves more than questions of how much governments will collect in taxes, or how the tax burden will be distributed among different groups of taxpayers, but also how governments will cooperate in managing and accommodating one another's tax policies while attempting to treat one another's citizens fairly and consistently. In Canada, this is done through a network of federal-provincial agreements, including agreements covering the design, collection, and redistribution of taxes between federal and provincial governments, and through a series of tax treaties with other countries that give Canadians living or doing business

Table 1.5 ·· DISTRIBUTION OF TAXES BY MAJOR SOURCE, LEVEL OF GOVERNMENT, 1999 (IN $ MILLIONS)

	Federal	Provincial	Local	CPP/QPP	Total	Per cent
PERSONAL INCOME TAX	81,351	52,827	—	—	134,178	37.8%
CORPORATE INCOME TAX	23,868	13,001	—	—	36,687	10.3%
SOCIAL INSURANCE TAXES	18,659	6,633	—	20,963	46,255	13.0%
CONSUMPTION/ INDIRECT TAXES	36,030	65,939	—	—	101,969	28.7%
OTHER TAXES	3,195		32,326	—	35,521	10.0%
TOTAL	163,067	138,400	32,326	20,963	354,756	100.0%
PER CENT	46.0%	39.0%	9.1%	5.9%	100.0%	

Source: Karin Treff and David B. Perry (2001) *Finances of the Nation: 2000* (Toronto: Canadian Tax Foundation), Table B-4.

abroad the same rights and responsibilities as foreign residents or businesses in Canada. While most taxes on individuals are shaped mainly by national or provincial economic and political considerations, business taxes are more heavily influenced by international considerations—especially by overall tax levels in the United States.[15]

As a result, the politics of taxation often resembles a four-ring circus. In one ring, governments try to balance the cost of financing services and benefits that their voters want or expect against the need to expand the economic pie and finance other major spending priorities. In a second, different groups of voters compete with one another to maximize their benefits from the economic system and either limit their costs or shift them to other, less organized interests. This effort may well include deficit financing to transfer the costs of current services to a future generation whose members do not yet have the right to vote, or obtaining selective tax reductions, sometimes called "tax expenditures," to support particular forms of social or economic activity. In a third, governments attempt to balance domestic concerns with the complex challenges of the international economic system. In the fourth, federal and provincial governments try to control their own fiscal and economic priorities within the complex rules of Canadian federalism that force them to share most sources of tax revenue with other levels of government.

Understanding the politics of taxation—as opposed to tax law, fiscal policy, bureaucratic politics, federal-provincial relations, domestic or international political economy—requires a set of unifying principles that help to connect these different disciplines in a more or less coherent whole. The following ten principles provide both a summary of the major findings of this book and a way of connecting theories of taxation and political economy with the practical realities of Canadian politics.

The Politics of Taxation in Canada: An Overview

1. The principles of Canada's tax system reflect a series of trade-offs between competing political philosophies and policy objectives, including the taxation of income at progressive rates[16] based on "ability to pay" and the promotion of private savings, economic growth, and wealth creation by deferring taxes on the majority of long-term savings, rather than any "grand vision" of taxation based on first principles.

The many policy objectives built into the tax system reflect a series of compromises among interests, policy objectives, and political ideologies that have accumulated over the years. The result is a hybrid tax system based on two fundamentally different concepts of taxation: "income-based" and "consumption-based." Competing economic interests and political outlooks make it virtually impossible for government to impose either system in anything resembling its "pure" form without massive political conflict.

As a result, Canada's tax system is a blend of both models. It technically defines the income tax as an income-based system imposed on all individual income over a basic threshold ($7,412 in 2001), while exempting most private investment income from taxation until it is taken into income in the form of private pensions, RRSPs, salaries paid to business owners, or capital gains from the sale of investments.[17] A series of other measures limits the double taxation of business or investment income. These trade-offs balance the processes of wealth creation (and retirement income security) through private savings and investment with income redistribution through the tax system. As a result, marginal tax rates for most Canadians are moderately high by international standards, but taxes are deferred on about 75 per cent of investment income.[18] One effect of these multiple and interconnected trade-offs is that the tax system—particularly income tax—is extremely complex.

2. The major elements of the tax structure reflect a political consensus on a nation's basic social and economic institutions, values, and priorities. For many groups in society, certain aspects of the tax system (as well as some social programs) have taken on the character of entrenched "property rights" through long usage and broad political acceptance.

Some parts of the tax system are "constitutionalized" as a result of the federal division of powers built into Canada's constitutions, federal-provincial agreements, international treaties, or the accumulation of legal precedents. Others achieve the status of an "economic right" through the passage of time. When proposed changes or tax reforms are seen to threaten those rights and entitlements, they are likely to provoke a major political backlash no matter how "rational" they may appear in light of other policy goals. Efforts to simplify the tax system through tax reforms based on first principles are generally frustrated unless they recognize and accommodate these interests. The proverbial devil is always in the details. The greater the number of principles and interests that must be accommodated in this way, the greater the likelihood that the pursuit of simplicity will be lost to the pursuit of fairness and the balancing of diverse interests.

3. The tax system is part of an economic constitution that is as durable and pervasive in its impact as the political constitution that defines and limits the powers of the state and the rights of individuals. Its size, scope, and complexity discourage radical change in the tax system.

The functions of the modern state—and its demands for revenue—are so extensive that the tax system has become deeply embedded in the economic and social lives and in the expectations of Canadians. Widespread public acceptance of the tax system as an instrument of economic and social policy gives governments substantial power to influence the choices and behaviour of Canadians. However, this also limits the autonomy of Finance Ministers, especially when they attempt to introduce major structural policy changes without a broad consensus among societal interests. As a result, the basic structures of major taxes—personal and corporate income taxes, federal and provincial sales taxes, and major social insurance taxes to finance the Canada Pension Plan, Employment Insurance or provincial Workers' Compensation systems—may evolve over time but are as resistant to large-scale changes as Canada's political constitution.

The timing, extent, and political effectiveness of tax reforms, defined as major changes in overall tax levels, structures, or the distribution of the tax burden among Canadians, depend on the capacity of the federal government, especially the Department of Finance, to achieve its fiscal and other policy objectives without excessive political and economic disruption. To do this, it must be able to package proposed tax reforms in ways that combine respect for existing economic and social relationships with adequate transitional provisions to smooth the path of change.

4. Most people are more concerned with the taxes they pay compared with their incomes (or business profits) and the services and benefits they receive from governments in return, than they are with political or economic theories of a "good tax system." Overall tax levels are as likely to reflect the political demands facing individual governments and their perceptions of citizens' willingness to pay as they are economic issues of "fairness" or "competitiveness."

Strong governments that enjoy broad public support can enforce and sustain the tax and spending levels desired by their major supporters without regard to whether these are "high" or "low" compared with neighbouring countries or provinces. Weak governments, and those whose policies lack broader public support, are more likely to balance competing economic and social pressures to preserve and expand public services while reducing or holding the line on taxes by running sizeable budget deficits. However, these policies eventually lead to a fiscal crisis, described by one economist as the "scissors crisis of public finance,"[19] in which Finance Ministers are forced to impose the tax and spending discipline needed to restore fiscal balance in order to avert economic and political bankruptcy.

5. Any proposals for major changes either in the overall level and distribution of taxes or in the basic principles which shape the design of the tax system (i.e., "tax reform") must begin with the tax system as it is, not as we might wish it to be in the best of all possible worlds.

Governments that desire to change the tax structure, overall tax levels, or their distribution among different groups of citizens without major political conflict or economic disruption would be well advised to do so in a piecemeal, incremental fashion, dealing with one major aspect of the tax system at a time. The more overloaded the agenda for policy change, the greater the likelihood a government will inflict unintended damage on enough interests to promote the creation of an alternative political coalition that will disrupt the consensus necessary to achieve politically effective (lasting) tax reform. This effect can be seen in the massive political backlash against Allan MacEachen's proposed tax reform budget of 1981 and the introduction of the Goods and Services Tax in 1990, both of which ultimately led to the defeat of the governments that introduced them.

However, successful policy changes can be introduced over several years if they are seen to be part of a coherent plan that spells out the problems and challenges to be faced, outlines a credible program to overcome these problems, and spells out the means by which these proposals will improve the economic well-being of members of most major economic groups while striking a balance between competing political and ideological objectives. These principles helped to shape Michael Wilson's income tax reforms of the late 1980s, which ushered in a long period of relative tax stability in the 1990s. This approach has also been central to Paul Martin's successful campaign to eliminate the federal deficit in the 1990s and to his medium-term tax reduction plans introduced in the budgets of February and October 2000.

6. The introduction of major changes to the principles and objectives of the tax structure requires a significant shift in the intellectual framework or "policy paradigm" guiding national or provincial economic policies.

The federal Minister and Department of Finance enjoy considerable independence in making tax policy, as long as they are successful in communicating proposals for change as logical extensions of existing policies, usually as responses to specific policy problems. Major changes to the structure of the tax system or the levels of major taxes require that political leaders build some degree of consensus on the main objectives of tax-related economic and social policies and the most effective ways of achieving these objectives. Such a consensus is often difficult to achieve unless policy-makers can convince the public that a crisis is at hand that threatens the ability of governments to fulfil their basic responsibilities.

However, crisis conditions do not guarantee the political success or durability of tax reforms or major economic policy changes. Those groups in society whose interests are set aside, or who are likely to pay a disproportionate share of the costs of "reform," will resist these changes unless they are compensated for these costs or unless they are pushed to the margins of political influence. The competitive nature of partisan politics and the willingness of many voters to change their political loyalties mean that few groups are permanently excluded from a share of power.

Indeed, those groups most adversely affected by major tax changes are likely to mobilize their members in support of political parties that offer to roll back "excessive" tax changes. This is precisely what happened following tax reforms introduced in 1969-71 and 1981-82. Large segments of the business community and the middle class refused to accept the stated principles of tax reform when faced with the prospect of significantly higher taxes for themselves. This undermined Liberal support and encouraged other parties to promise wholesale changes to the tax system—along with lower taxes—following the next election. The same pattern occurred in 1993 when both the Liberals and the Reform Party ran successful campaigns against the governing Conservatives based in part on promises to replace the hated Goods and Services Tax.

7. The political legitimacy and durability of major changes to tax levels or the tax system depend largely on the ability of governments to build coalitions in support of their proposals among those interests most likely to be affected by these changes.

The political success of major changes to the tax system depends on the ability of Ministers of Finance to build a consensus on their objectives and contents among three distinct groups: tax policy experts, major interest group stakeholders, and the general public. However, active support from the latter is vital only when the first two groups, which form the broad tax policy community, are in serious conflict. Provincial governments also must be willing to accommodate major changes in federal tax policy, especially in areas of overlapping federal and provincial tax rules.

In practical terms, the political success of major changes to Canada's tax system depends on the Department of Finance's ability to market them as a "positive-sum game" yielding economic benefits or minimal costs for most major economic and social groups, not just for "the economy as a whole." Although these changes may result in some income redistribution over time, the need for consensus effectively precludes the use of tax reform for deficit reduction or for the large-scale redistribution of wealth and income.

8. Building consensus on the objectives and details of tax reform depends in large measure on the use of a meaningful consultation process which allows policy stakeholders to "buy into" proposed changes and which identifies and overcomes potential political and institutional roadblocks.

The Minister and Department of Finance face significant constraints in introducing major changes to the tax system or overall levels of taxation. Political leaders must be able to navigate proposed reforms through the bureaucracy, Cabinet, and Parliament, and to overcome political constraints inside and outside government. To do so, Ministers of Finance must persuade cabinet colleagues, major stakeholders, and opinion-makers, including the media, that the benefits of the proposed changes outweigh their political and economic risks. A well-managed consultation process is essential to mobilizing elite and public consent to policy changes that may significantly affect their economic rights and entitlements. Both the Mulroney government's income tax reforms of 1987-88 and the Chrétien government's successful deficit reduction program in the 1990s emphasized the need for consensus-building and the accommodation of both existing business interests and social commitments within the revised tax structure. The growing use of the tax-transfer system as a vehicle for the delivery of social benefits has enabled Paul Martin to mobilize a broad consensus on the use of growing federal surpluses for tax and debt reduction as Canada enters the new century.

The Goods and Services Tax did not lend itself to this kind of accommodation, despite some of the most extensive consultations in Canadian tax history. As a result, the Mulroney government suffered the political penalty for having asked Canadians for their views and then ignoring the response: virtual annihilation in the 1993 federal election.[20] However, the survival of the GST demonstrated the ability of the Minister and Department of Finance to make mainly cosmetic changes to the hated tax so long as they were able to mobilize the support of most policy experts and major stakeholders within the tax policy community.

9. Major changes in tax policy should be consistent with broad trends in international taxation in order to maintain the competitiveness of the

Canadian economy with those of its major trading partners. This is particularly important for the taxation of business and investment income.

Canadian governments, political parties, and organized interests are more likely to adopt new policy ideas when they have been implemented with reasonable success somewhere else. The bipartisan American tax reforms in 1986 created both a visible example of tax reform and a ready-made coalition of interests to support a parallel tax reform plan in Canada. However, this demonstration effect was noticeably absent when Allan MacEachen attempted to use tax reform as a vehicle to raise personal and corporate taxes at the same time that Ronald Reagan was cutting them in the United States. The prospect of large budget surpluses and continued economic growth at the end of the 1990s made it easier for Paul Martin to package the phased reduction of corporate income and capital gains taxes to US levels, following the lead of several other industrial countries, in his pre-election budgets of 2000.

10. A key element in building consensus and diffusing opposition to major tax changes is the offer of compensation to groups whose interests may be threatened by proposed reforms, thus reducing their incentive to organize a political coalition against these changes.

Finance Ministers attempting to build a consensus in support of major tax changes are often compelled to compensate aggrieved interests, not only through "grandfathering" provisions and other transitional measures, but also through substantive changes to other tax provisions. Such trade-offs include Edgar Benson's decision to phase out federal estate taxes[21] after 1971 to offset the introduction of a new tax on capital gains, and Michael Wilson's promise of sales tax reform to diffuse big business opposition to his proposed corporate tax reforms. More recently, the federal government has allowed the provinces to set up their own tax rate structures, based on a shared definition of income to offset the revenue losses likely to result from federal tax reductions and the reindexation of federal tax brackets (see Chapter 12).

Outline of the Book

This book is intended to provide a political and economic context for a broad understanding of the principles, organization, and politics of Canada's tax system. It explains the main objectives and components, the organizational and institutional structures that define and control the tax system, and the political processes that influence and manage the process of policy change. It summarizes the evolution of Canada's tax system over the last 30 years, explains the relationship between fiscal and tax policies and the growth of federal budget deficits during the 1980s and early 1990s, and discusses the successful struggle of its governments to regain control over their finances (and ours). Finally, it examines several major issues that are helping to shape the politics of taxation in Canada at the beginning of the twenty-first century.

The Politics of Taxation in Canada is organized in three parts. Part 1—The Context of Canada's Tax System—examines the intellectual, economic, and political contexts within which Canadian tax policy is made. It outlines the major principles and objectives of the Canadian tax system, the political and economic structures that have shaped its evolution, and the tax policy processes that translate ideas for policy changes into political and parliamentary consent.

Chapter 2, "The Tax System and the Politics of Ideas," examines the major objectives of taxation as an instrument of public policy, and the relationship between economic ideas about the size and role of government and the nature of the tax system. It outlines the competing theories of "the good tax system" which have shaped the attitudes of economists and activists promoting major changes to the tax system, and summarizes the key factors that have shaped the evolution of Canada's tax system as a "hybrid" of competing concepts and objectives.

Chapter 3, "The Tax System as Economic Constitution," summarizes the major elements of Canada's tax system, along with the major structural and institutional constraints on policy-making. It discusses the political, legal, and economic structures that have shaped the evolution of Canada's tax system and that have frustrated most proposals for radical reform. It examines the ways in which the basic framework of tax laws has emerged from Canada's constitution, legal system, political compromises, and adaptations to changing social and economic realities.

Chapter 4, "The Tax Policy Community," assesses the role of the federal Department of Finance as the main "gatekeeper" of the tax policy process and the efforts of its Ministers and officials to balance competing tax and spending demands from both inside and outside government.

Chapter 5, "The Public Tax Policy Process," considers the ways in which Finance Ministers and their Departments attempt to control the economic and tax policy agendas through the budget process. It reviews Finance's relationship with competing interest groups and the methods that Finance Ministers use to mobilize consent for their policy proposals both inside the federal government and among the Canadian public.

Part II—The Politics of Taxation from Carter to Martin—examines the evolution of Canadian tax policy between the Carter-Benson Tax Reforms of 1967-71 and the largely successful efforts of federal and provincial governments to eliminate the chronic deficits that resulted from their consistent failure to balance competing demands for increased public spending and limits on taxation during the 1970s and 1980s. It provides a historical context for current tax policies and the major political battles that have shaped Canada's present tax system.

Chapter 6, "The Tax Reform Pendulum," summarizes the political conflicts over economic and tax policies during the Trudeau era, and Finance Minister Allan MacEachen's ill-fated efforts to redesign the federal tax system in his 1981 budget. It considers the swings in economic and tax policies, "the tax reform pendulum" of the Trudeau era, as rising inflation, unemployment, energy prices, and deficits destroyed the post-war consensus on economic policy and spurred the search for workable policy alternatives.

Chapter 7, "The Mulroney Legacy," examines the politics of taxation and deficit reduction during the Mulroney era between 1984 and 1993, and the difficulties of balancing the tax increases needed to contain the federal deficit with Michael Wilson's efforts to restructure the tax system. It notes Wilson's successful efforts to build consensus for his modest income tax reforms that set the pattern for federal tax policies during most of the 1990s, along with the frustration of his efforts to contain rising national deficits and debt.

Chapter 8, "The Politics of Sales Tax Reform," assesses Ottawa's repeated efforts to reform the federal sales tax system, culminating in the introduction of the Goods and Services Tax in 1989-90, as a classic example of the political risks of structural tax reforms, and explains the reasons for the survival of this highly unpopular tax despite the election of a Liberal government committed to "replace" it.

Chapter 9, "Chrétien, Martin, and the Politics of Deficit Reduction," examines the implications of the Chrétien government's successful war against the federal deficit for the distribution of power within the federal government, and the ways in which Paul Martin's skilful changes to the budget process enabled him to take firm control of its economic and fiscal policies while building a broad political consensus to support them. It also considers Martin's creative use of the tax system to coordinate economic and social policy goals while balancing the demands of business and social liberals to pursue very different policy priorities.

Part III—The Politics of Taxation in the Twenty-first Century: Balancing National, Regional, and Global Pressures—provides an overview of the effects of fiscal and tax policies on living standards and the relationship between economic and social policies as Canada enters the new century. It addresses four major sets of issues facing Canadians as they attempt to balance the competing demands for expanded spending on public services and social transfers with the promotion of economic growth and higher living standards.

Chapter 10, "Living Standards and the Politics of Personal Taxation," discusses the implications of growing budget surpluses on the politics of taxation as Canada enters the twenty-first century, and Ottawa's balancing act in managing the "fiscal dividend" to deal with competing demands for personal tax reduction and increased social spending. It considers the emerging tax reduction agenda, and the way it has been shaped to balance distributive, or "fairness," considerations with the promotion of economic growth.

Chapter 11, "Globalization, Domestic Politics, and Business Taxation," outlines the principles that are shaping the evolution of business taxation in an increasingly globalized economy, and the related trade-offs between domestic politics and international economic forces in both the level and distribution of business taxes.

Chapter 12, "Taxation, Federalism, and the Provinces," examines the evolution of provincial tax systems in response to planned reductions in federal tax rates and the growing diversity of provincial economic policies across Canada. It explains the growing diversity of provincial tax systems as a way of reducing federal-provincial conflict and accommodating different political and economic priorities within a flexible tax structure.

Chapter 13, "Taxation, the Family, and Civil Society," discusses the impact of tax policies in shaping civil society and expanding the range of choices available to families and voluntary organizations for improving their lives and contributing to communities across Canada. It notes the flexibility and the limits of tax policy as an alternative to direct government spending in accommodating different social priorities and values, and some of the options available to governments for empowering citizens to play a more active and independent role in their communities.

NOTES

1   Alexander Hamilton (1961) "Federalist # 30," *The Federalist Papers*, ed. Clinton Rossiter (New York: Mentor Books), 188.

2   John Stuart Mill (1862) *Considerations on Representative Government* (New York: Harper & Co.) 234-35.

3   Avi-Yonah (2000); Buchanan (1991).

4   Lewis (1992); Canada, Task Force on Program Review (1986).

5   Mintz (2000b); Canada, Privy Council Office (1999a).

6   Brennan and Buchanan (1980); Buchanan (1991).

7   Gillespie (1991).

8   Hall, ed. (1989).

9   Statistics Canada (2001) National Income and Expenditure Accounts, Cat. # 13-001 (March).

10 Martin (1999b).

11 For a detailed analysis of factors contributing to stagnant and declining living standards in the 1990s, see Fortin (1999).

12 Lower-income families are defined by the "lowest quintile" or 20 per cent of family incomes; middle income as the second-lowest and middle quintiles. Direct government transfer payments far outweigh income taxes payable for the lowest-earning 40 per cent of Canadian families. Statistics Canada (1999a) *Income after Tax, distributions by size in Canada*, 1997, Cat. # 13-210XPB (Ottawa, July), 30.

13 Statistics Canada (1999a), 31.

14 Bird (1970).

15 Thirsk (1993); interview, Department of Finance (ADM-II).

16 Except in Alberta's recently introduced provincial income tax system (see Chapter 12).

17 Poddar and English (1999).

18 Ibid.

19 Tarchys (1983).

20 Public support for the GST dropped from 26 per cent in early 1989 to 12 per cent in the fall of 1990. Gallup Canada (1990).

21 Technically, estate taxes are levied on the property of deceased persons before it can be distributed among their heirs. Inheritance taxes are imposed on persons receiving an inheritance from someone else. Under Canadian constitutional law, only the federal government can impose estate taxes as an "indirect tax," while inheritance taxes can be imposed by the provinces. In practice, once Alberta eliminated its inheritance tax during the 1970s, other provinces followed suit to avoid tax-induced migration.

part one

The Context of Canada's Tax System

The Tax System and the
Politics of Ideas

There is no part of the administration of government that requires
extensive information and a thorough knowledge of the principles of
political economy so much as the business of taxation. The man who
understands those principles best will be least likely to resort to
oppressive expedients, or to sacrifice any particular class of citizens to
the procurement of revenue.

Alexander Hamilton[1]

Good ideas do not always win.... To become policy, ideas must link
up with politics—the mobilization of consent for policy. Politics
involves power. Even a good idea cannot become policy if it meets certain kinds of opposition, and a bad idea can become policy if it is able
to obtain support.[2]

Most people are more concerned with their overall tax levels relative to their
incomes (or business profits) and the services and benefits they receive from
governments in return than they are with political or economic theories of a
"good tax system." However, in a democracy, ideas about taxes—how much
people should pay, who should pay them, for what purposes, and with what
impact on citizens' other economic and social activities—are closely linked
to our understanding of the appropriate size, role, and limits of legitimate
government activity.

Most citizens tend to view governments as a mix of positive good—providing valued services, along with a measure of social cohesion, security, and
responsiveness to the popular will—and necessary evil. The latter reflects
public ambivalence or cynicism about the motives and methods of politicians, interest groups, and others who seek to obtain and use the power of
government to pursue their own self-serving agendas, often at others'
expense. These views are reflected in public finance and public choice

analyses of fiscal and tax policies, respectively, that will be discussed later in this chapter.

To mobilize public opinion and political power in the pursuit of particular goals in the face of competing interests, political leaders often attempt to promote a unifying set of ideas (or "paradigm") to promote both their concept of the common good and the policies they consider necessary to move towards it. These ideas may relate to the role of government in a country's economy and society, the most effective ways of balancing the pursuit of economic growth and prosperity with a relatively equitable distribution of incomes and opportunities among its citizens, or the design of a tax system intended to support these goals.

Canada's tax system reflects a series of trade-offs between competing political philosophies and policy objectives, rather than any "grand vision" of taxation based on first principles. The balancing of these objectives, and the levels of government spending that are consistent with their attainment, are the subjects of vigorous and sometimes bitter debate among economists, interest groups, opinion leaders, and politically active citizens. The intensity of these debates grows when changing social or economic circumstances lead to a rethinking of the intellectual framework or "policy paradigm" guiding national or provincial economic policies.

This chapter examines the major objectives of taxation as an instrument of public policy along with the relationship between economic ideas about the size and role of government, desirable levels and distribution of taxes among citizens, and the basic principles that should guide the operation of the tax system. It examines the effects of these ideas on the tax reform debates of the Trudeau and Mulroney eras that helped to form most of Canada's present tax system. It also explains the dominant ideas that have shaped the evolution of Canada's tax system in recent years, and their implications for the politics of taxation in the foreseeable future.

Major Functions and Principles of Taxation

Any tax system serves a number of overlapping and often competing functions. To do so effectively, it must attempt to balance competing principles that reflect a number of different political, economic, and sometimes ideological assumptions and objectives. "Balance" is widely seen as an essential element of a good tax system—between the principles of ability to pay and benefit-related taxation, between the taxation of income, consumption, and capital, and between the demands of social egalitarianism and the pursuit of economic growth. The balance is usually the product of competing interests in the political marketplace rather than the abstract theories or scientific designs of economists.

Michael J. Boskin cites four major functions of fiscal policy and taxation in the modern economy: the financing of government expenditures, the attempted redistribution of income, the encouragement or discouragement of certain activities, and the stabilization of the overall economy.[4] Tax policies are simultaneously a form of economic regulation, a source of incentives and disincentives for economic efficiency and growth, and a tool for the micromanagement of the economy. The more objectives that the tax system pursues at the same time, the greater are the difficulties of harmonizing them or of avoiding the unintended consequences of conflicting policies.

The Income Tax Act, the single largest source of both federal and provincial government revenues, is the most politically and economically significant part of the tax system. At the risk of oversimplification, the durable core of the Act is shaped by three main principles: horizontal equity, economic neutrality (or efficiency), and vertical equity. Horizontal equity requires that individuals in similar circumstances pay similar levels of (or have similar exemptions from) taxation. Individuals or companies in different circumstances may also persuade the Department of Finance to allow them to calculate income in different ways in order to be subject to the same effective rates of taxation. This principle is reflected in provisions that enable taxpayers to carry forward (and sometimes back against previous years' earnings) capital gains and losses, contributions to retirement savings or pension funds, charitable donations, and other provisions to smooth out the annual variations in their incomes over a number of years.

Horizontal equity is often linked to the values of neutrality or efficiency—the idea that the tax system should not bias individual economic decisions in the marketplace or restrict the ability of businesses and investors to adjust to changing technologies, distribution systems, and forms of business organization. This principle reflects neo-classical economic assumptions of the superior efficiency of self-regulating markets. However, in practice, governments have often ignored this principle when it served their political and economic interests to do so.

Since their inception in Canada in 1917, income taxes have also been based, in large measure, on the principle of vertical equity or ability-to-pay, the idea that the necessary expenses of government related to provision for the common good should be distributed among individuals roughly in proportion to the economic advantages derived from their membership in society. Lars Osberg summarizes the principle of vertical equity as the principle that "the rich should pay more tax than the poor, because they can afford to. By this criterion, one of the objectives of the tax system should be to progressively increase tax rates as ability to pay increases so that the distribution of after-tax tax income will become more equal."[6]

In practice, the redistributive goals of taxation have often been modified to limit the impact of high marginal tax rates on private investment and economic growth. The higher the marginal rates of taxation, the greater the incentive to avoid taxes by shifting economic activity to activities or jurisdictions with lower tax rates, or to evade taxes altogether. In past years, the punitive effect of high marginal tax rates on economic initiative has created significant political pressure to reduce the size of the tax base by creating or extending various tax preferences, exemptions, or "tax expenditures." More recently, some governments have sought to reverse this trend, lowering tax rates and reducing the tax differences between different income groups while broadening the definitions of income subject to taxation.

As a result, the greater the state's demands for revenue relative to the size of an economy, the more likely it is to levy a wide range of taxes to diffuse the political opposition that would result from excessive reliance on any single dominant source of revenue.[7] Taxes on relatively mobile factors of production, such as capital, or goods for which lower-taxed substitutes are available are likely to be lower than taxes on other factors of production (e.g., labour income), which are relatively immobile. As a result, the level of taxation on business income is far more sensitive to tax rates in Canada's major competitors than are personal income or consumption taxes.

High marginal and/or effective tax rates lead to political pressure for the removal of tax-related barriers to various activities that are identified by various groups with the social or economic well-being of society. These may include raising children, creating employment for oneself and others, saving for a secure retirement, donating to charities and other worthy causes, investing in research and innovation, preserving family farms and businesses, and many others. While this goal may be accomplished through incidental or transitory changes to tax legislation, the larger the organized group in question—or the greater its ability to link its particular interests with the general interests of society—the more its demands are likely to become firmly entrenched within the tax system.

However, the ways in which governments pursue these objectives and manage these trade-offs are heavily influenced by the outlook of senior politicians and their bureaucratic advisors on the size and role of government within a national or provincial economy.

Taxation, Public Finance, and the Role of the State

The intensity of public debate over taxation in Canada between the 1970s and 1990s was a direct result of the rapid growth of government and the failure of established government economic policies to provide consistent prosperity, economic security, and rising standards of living for the majority of Canadians. This debate led to intense political conflict over the answer to these problems: smaller, less intrusive government; greater government control of the economy; or a more focused, disciplined government capable of providing better management of tax dollars without abandoning an active role for governments in the provision of public services and the redistribution of income. This section examines the role of ideas in shaping these debates and their implications for the tax system.

Before the Great Depression of the 1930s, governments in most English-speaking countries were small and limited in their size and functions. Taxes, levied by the consent of the governed through their elected representatives, were viewed as an exception to the rule of private property. Tax revenues provided for a limited number of essential public services, the protection of life and property, and the financing of public works considered vital to the nation's economic development or national security. Overall government spending as a share of economic activity was usually less than 20 per cent of the national income (see Table 2.1).

The massive social and economic dislocation of the Depression, the potential for governments to mobilize the economic energies of the nation to serve common purposes demonstrated by the World War that followed, and the pressing desire of politicians and opinion leaders of all classes to avoid a repetition of the economic upheavals of the 1920s and 1930s helped to create a receptive audience for the theories of British economist John Maynard Keynes. Keynes's theories of demand management offered a plausible means for governments to influence overall levels of economic activity through the use of fiscal policies—taxation, spending, and the redistribution of income—without directly intervening in the day-to-day management and investment decisions of private businesses. As a result, Keynes's theories enabled governments to strike a political balance between the expectations of business interests supportive of economic and social stability, but hostile to what they viewed as inappropriate interference in business, and the growing desire of many Canadians for governments to provide a social and economic "safety net" and a more equal distribution of economic opportunities.

All major Canadian political parties came to subscribe, in differing degrees, to the Keynesian economic doctrines that had enabled governments to play a growing role in the management of national economies after World War II. However, some economists warned that Keynes's theories

were not a magic wand that guaranteed prosperity and the automatic fulfilment of rising social expectations. A few recognized that their successful
application was largely dependent on the observance of what Schumpeter
has described as the three conditions for the effective democratic management of economic policy: "limitation of the area of effectively political
decision-making, the existence of a well-trained bureaucracy, and the exercise of political self-restraint."[8] To meet these conditions, Canadian
governments tended to centralize control over budgetary trade-offs within
authoritative Finance ministries capable of balancing competing political
and economic demands and weighing dispassionately their probable costs
and benefits. The breakdown of these institutional structures and of the
fiscal self-discipline they had promoted resulted in the increasingly erratic
management of tax and fiscal policies during the 1970s. A renewed commit-

Table 2.1 ·· GOVERNMENT SPENDING IN THE ECONOMY

| | GNP Nominal | Total Government Spending | Government Spending as Percentage of GDP** | |
| | | | FEDERAL | TOTAL |
	———MILLIONS OF $———			
1926	5,345	810	6.0%	15.1%
1933	3,492	956	12.9%*	27.3%*
1939	5,621	1,205	8.2%	20.5%
1943	11,053	5,022	—	45.4%*
1950	18,491	4,080	12.4%	21.3%
1960	38,359	11,380	17.1%	28.8%
1970	85,685	30,088	17.2%	34.9%
1980	302,064	128,008	19.8%	40.3%
1990	669,467	326,793	22.9%	46.8%
1999	957,911	404,321	18.2%	42.2%
2000[P]	1,056,010	429,714	16.9%	40.7%

*   Spending as percentage of Gross National Product
** Basic GDP measurement changed after 1970.
P = preliminary

Sources: Gillespie (1991), Appendix C; Statistics Canada, *National Income and Expenditure
Accounts*, Cat. # 13-001-XIB (Ottawa, March 2001); Canada. Dept. of Finance (2001), *Fiscal
Reference Tables*; author's calculations.

ment to these principles has been a decisive factor in restoring fiscal discipline and more coherent economic policies during the 1990s.

The relative prosperity of the "Keynesian era" that enabled governments to achieve relative social cohesion between the 1940s and early 1970s deeply influenced Canada's political culture. It helped to foster the widespread public perception of government as a benevolent, by-and-large competent overseer of the economy that could, and indeed should, play an active role in creating and sharing economic opportunities and regulating a growing range of activities in the public interest. It allowed governments to take advantage of the rapid economic growth of the 1950s and 1960s to provide a greatly expanded range of public services financed by relatively modest levels of taxation. It also created a revolution of rising expectations, in which many Canadians came to view continuing and steady improvement in their standard of living, accommodated and assisted by governments, as something approaching a national birthright.[9]

The success of Keynesian economics also helped to shape the emerging "public finance" approach to taxation and the business of government, especially within federal and provincial Departments of Finance. The dominant view of public finance is that benevolent governments seek rational public policy approaches to maximize the well-being of their citizens. Much of this intervention is based on the assumption that private markets require guidance and regulation by governments in order to correct market failures caused by self-interested economic actors and to promote a more equitable distribution of incomes and economic activities.[10] The public finance perspective further assumes that the competent, professional public servants who administer democratic governments provide levels of service consistent with public needs and wants and the efficient management of the public business. As a result, in policy terms, taxation tends to be something of a residual in that countries do not set their tax burdens or policies first, without reference to other policies. Instead, a nation first makes a whole range of social and economic choices, and then the tax system is used to finance and reinforce these policies.[11]

Canadians' optimism about their national future and the capacity of governments to create a better world through the application of "rational" and "scientific" management techniques appears to have peaked around 1967, at the time of Canada's centennial celebrations. From a tax policy perspective, this optimism was reflected in the report of the Royal Commission on Taxation, known as the "Carter Commission" after its Chairman, Kenneth Carter. The Carter Report recommended a total overhaul of Canada's tax system from first principles, exposing for the first time virtually all areas of economic activity and private property to direct taxation by the federal government. In the absence of sharply lower tax rates, the resulting windfall would have vastly expanded the capacity of governments to finance a wide range of new activities.

The Commission's proposals prompted a political backlash. This came not only from wealthy Canadians and corporate interests that would have faced tax increases of up to 40 per cent,[12] but from a broad cross-section of middle-class interests that felt that many of their most fundamental interests were threatened by Carter's proposed "reforms." The bitter political debate surrounding the tax reform bill of 1971 was followed by more than 15 years of conflict over the levels and distribution of taxes that resulted in repeated changes to tax laws.

The 1970s and 1980s also marked a period of prolonged economic instability in Canada and most other major industrial nations. The post-war economic order, based on the comfortable assumptions of Keynesian economic policies and unchallenged American economic dominance of the global economy, had broken down under the impact of rapid price inflation triggered by rising oil prices and the emergence of global capital markets beyond the control of national governments. The unexpected phenomenon of stagflation, which saw inflation and unemployment rise together, defied conventional economic theories and created a crisis of public confidence in the ability of governments to respond effectively to these changing circumstances. Some economists, such as Harvard's John Kenneth Galbraith, suggested that governments could control the emerging forces of globalization by expanding their powers to regulate national economies. Galbraith's ideas influenced Prime Minister Trudeau's experiments with wage and price controls during the 1970s, his vision of a government-led industrial strategy financed by the nationalization of windfall oil profits in the National Energy Program of 1980, and Allan MacEachen's abortive tax reform budget of 1981. This strategy, which Donald Smiley has described as Canada's "Third National Policy," sought to restore the credibility of the federal government and expand its role as a benevolent provider for Canadians by increasing the redistributive nature of the tax system and mobilizing surplus energy revenues to expand social benefits, generate massive public works, and expand business subsidies to buy the loyalty (or acquiescence) of all regions and classes of society.[13] The public credibility of the government's strategy collapsed in the face of massive business and provincial resistance, the worst recession since World War II, and the puncturing of the OPEC oil price balloon after 1983.

More influential, in the long run, were the ideas of "public choice" economists such as James Buchanan who developed their "economic theory of politics" to explain the vast expansion of bureaucratic activity in the 1960s and 1970s. Public policies are seen as the product of political exchanges among largely self-interested actors, including politicians, bureaucrats, interest groups, and the voters they seek to represent. Rather than being made up of benevolent, rational policy experts dedicated to the public good, these theories portrayed governments as "Leviathan," large bureaucratic organizations attempting to maximize their power, status, and economic well-being in cooperation with competing social and economic interest groups, often at the expense of the unorganized majority of citizens. Thus, rather than seeking to expand the size and power of governments to correct market failures, the new paradigm sought to identify the causes of "government failure" and to impose firm rules to discipline governments and limit the arbitrary exercise of state power.[14]

The influence of public choice ideas can be seen both in the neo-conservative governments of Margaret Thatcher in Great Britain and Ronald Reagan in the United States during the 1980s and in the emergence of a populist, anti-government backlash that viewed resistance to higher taxes as a means of increasing popular control over the operations of government and limiting its capacity to interfere with the lives and choices of citizens. This brand of populist neo-conservatism had limited influence in Canada since federal and provincial Conservative governments, while occasionally indulging in anti-government and anti-tax rhetoric, have tended to indulge in the same kinds of bureaucratic patronage and expansive spending on middle-class entitlement programs such as health care and education as their Liberal (or New Democratic) predecessors.

More influential—at least within most Canadian governments—was a neo-liberal ideology that emerged in response to the neo-conservative critique of large, inefficient, bureaucratic government, and its effects in undermining the economic growth necessary to finance and sustain social programs and other public services in an increasingly competitive economy. Heavily influenced by the 1985 report of the Macdonald Royal Commission, neo-liberalism accepted the need for rethinking the role of governments in response to changing domestic and international economic realities. Its most significant early achievement was to secure Canada's entry into a comprehensive free trade agreement (FTA) with the United States in 1988. The FTA, which was later expanded to include Mexico in 1994, effectively foreclosed a return to the nationalist and interventionist policies of the Trudeau era. Instead, it forced all major parties to come to grips with the realities of global economic competition, technological change, new approaches to management in both the public and private sectors, and the need to coordinate economic and social policies so that they would complement one another rather than work at cross-purposes. These changes were bitterly contested by social and economic groups—particularly unions, economic nationalists, and advocates of extended social services—that rightly saw

45

them as a threat to their status and ability to mobilize the resources of society to serve their objectives.

The Mulroney government between 1985 and 1990 introduced major changes to Canada's income and sales tax systems that sought to adapt them to the new economic and social realities. It increased overall tax levels and the use of the tax system for income redistribution, but in ways intended to target benefits more closely and limit their overall growth. These changes reflected a neo-liberal program of rationalizing tax preferences and targeting a larger share of funds available for social spending to lower- and middle-income families, including those delivered through the tax system, rather than a neo-conservative agenda of "shrinking the state," as suggested by some critics. The Chrétien government, elected in 1993, continued and extended the tax and social policies of the Mulroney government, centralizing power in the Prime Minister's Office and the Department of Finance, imposing widespread spending reductions, and making deficit reduction its major policy objective.[16] These policies were paralleled, to greater or lesser degrees, by provincial governments, so that the budgets of Canada's public sector entered into surplus by the end of 1997.

Public debate over taxation since then has focused less on the major principles of taxation, which reflect a pragmatic acceptance by most governments of existing tax structures, than on the relative importance of tax reduction in distributing the anticipated fiscal dividend resulting from renewed prosperity and continued discipline in government spending. The new consensus, such as it is, reflects a major shift in the central ideas of tax reform that have shaped the policy agenda of federal politicians and their economic advisors since the 1960s.

Competing Theories of Taxation

The importance of economic ideas is directly related to their capacity to address the major economic and social problems facing a nation without creating more problems than they solve, either politically or economically. Most policies evolve incrementally or in a piecemeal fashion as they are adapted to changing circumstances, opportunities, or political pressures. However, when these policies consistently fail to meet the major policy goals of a government or a society, pressures build up for major, not just incremental, policy change.

The economic system can absorb only a certain amount of change at any one time without triggering collective political and economic indigestion. The tax system, in particular, is so deeply interwoven with existing social and economic relationships that politicians must be able to provide taxpayers, especially those who are significant stakeholders in the existing system, with a compelling justification to obtain their support for changes that could disrupt accustomed business practices and economic expectations.

Peter Hall suggests that economic ideas capable of providing an effective rationale for policy change must meet four major criteria: economic viability (the ability to address major economic problems better than existing policies); sponsorship by senior politicians and bureaucrats capable of turning them into action; institutional capacity, i.e., the legal and political authority to translate ideas into action; and political viability, the capacity to win the support or consent of enough voters so that their advocates can win election or reelection.[17]

Large-scale tax reforms may result from efforts to consolidate many small changes to tax laws (the "tax reform cycle"), or from a comprehensive redesign of tax systems from first principles. The latter is far more likely to provoke conflict since it requires governments to override traditional political compromises built into the tax system. However, with the exception of the Goods and Services Tax, the greater the challenge posed by proposed tax reforms to traditional principles and structures of taxation, the lesser the likelihood of their political success or longevity.

This section examines the Haig-Simons model of comprehensive income taxation that was embodied in the report of the Carter Royal Commission and, to a lesser degree, in the Benson White Paper of 1969 and the MacEachen budget of 1981. It also examines the pragmatic alternatives to the idea of comprehensive tax reform that have shaped more recent tax reforms in several industrial countries, including Canada, in balancing competing political and economic goals of federal tax policies.

THE CAUSES OF TAX REFORM

The active use of tax policy as a policy instrument by governments and major societal interests has created an extensive web of obligations, interests, and expectations. Although specific policy problems may be successfully resolved by piecemeal structural changes to the tax system consistent with theoretical concepts of tax reform, too many Canadians identify their economic and social well-being with various aspects of the existing tax structure for radical changes in the basic principles of taxation to be politically viable, except in the event of a national emergency.

It is easy for politicians to seek short-term political advantage by making changes to the tax system, and they have often done so. This political approach, which is frequently shaped by cluttered political agendas and the short time horizons of election cycles, may succeed in dealing with specific issues, but often at the cost of creating further complications and problems that create pressure for further changes. The political approach tends to be heavily influenced by considerations of brokerage politics and political coalition-building, balancing the potential impact of proposed policies on different interest groups and swing voters for whose support the government and opposition are competing. Finance Ministers have often used this approach. A few examples include

> John Turner's partial indexing of personal income taxes in 1973 to offset inflation;

> Jean Chrétien's introduction of the refundable child tax credit in 1978;

> Marc Lalonde's National Energy Program (NEP) of 1980 and tax-based pension reforms of 1983-84;

> Michael Wilson's introduction of the capital gains exemption and the minimum tax in 1985, followed by the dismantling of the NEP in 1986;

> Paul Martin's withdrawal in 1994 of the capital gains tax exemption, except for owners of small businesses and family farms;

> Paul Martin's introduction of the Harmonized Sales Tax in 1997, which integrated the sales tax systems of three provinces with the federal Goods and Services Tax; and

> Paul Martin's program of up to $100 billion in personal and business tax reductions over five years, announced before the 2000 election.

The political approach may lend itself to clientele politics, in which Finance Ministers offer economic benefits to specific groups in the hope of gaining disproportionate political and/or economic benefits, to majoritarian politics, in which both costs and benefits are widely dispersed among a broad cross-section of taxpayers, or to the redistribution of income from upper- to lower-income taxpayers.

The sheer volume of incremental changes to tax laws lends itself to periodic efforts at consolidation. This is a major cause of both comprehensive and piecemeal tax reform. Allan Maslove suggests the existence of a tax reform cycle in which a consensus is reached on the nature of an appropriate tax base. This consensus is subsequently eroded by the extension of tax preferences to various groups in response to changing economic, political, and technical conditions. It then gives way to the restructuring of the entire tax system in response to a new synthesis of political and economic priorities.[18]

Academic approaches to tax reform tend to reject piecemeal changes to the tax system in favour of comprehensive restructuring based on certain normative and theoretical principles in order to make the tax system conform more closely to an ideal tax base.[19] This approach is comparable to what political scientist Peter Russell has described as "mega-constitutional reform." Such basic changes to the legal system effectively reopen basic questions of national identity, citizenship, and "fundamental principles of the body politic."[20] The Carter-Benson reforms of 1967-71 and Allan MacEachen's tax reform budget of 1981 are the clearest examples of this approach to tax reform. The Goods and Services Tax introduced in 1989-90, which broadened the sales tax base by almost two-thirds, prompted an equally vigorous public debate.

THE CARTER REPORT AND THE TAX REFORM AGENDA

Two major theories of comprehensive tax reform have challenged existing tax structures in Canada and other major industrial countries since the 1960s. The comprehensive income tax, or Haig-Simons model, provided the intellectual impetus for the 1967 Carter Commission Report on Taxation, the 1969 Benson White Paper on Tax Reform, the 1981 tax reform budget of Allan MacEachen, and the tax policy agenda of much of the Canadian left since the 1960s.[21]

A more recent model is the expenditure-based income tax system, in which current consumption rather than income would be taxed.[22] This has become the inspiration for a flat-rate income tax advocated by Hall and Rabushka in the United States[23] and popularized by Republican presidential candidate Steve Forbes during the 1996 primaries. While consumption-based income taxes are too radical a departure from existing orthodoxies to have been politically or administratively viable in Canada until now, the Carter Commission's vision inspired a generation of Finance Department officials and political activists in their effort to create "the good tax system."

The Haig-Simons model on which the Carter Report is based redefines income as any increase in a taxpayer's net wealth, hence theoretical net buying power, during a fixed period, usually a calendar year. Unlike the traditional Anglo-Canadian definition of income, it does not distinguish between various form of cash income, accrued (balance sheet) income, personal gifts, imputed (notional) income, or growth in the value of assets not readily subject to conversion into cash. Rather, it seeks to eliminate all "artificial" distinctions in income that have resulted over the years from the accumulation of legislative and judicial decisions and trade-offs, and to replace them with a comprehensive benchmark tax structure. Departures from its ideal tax base (tax preferences) were characterized as "tax expenditures," on the grounds that failure to collect taxes is the perceived equivalent of direct government transfers to the taxpayers in question.[24] This distinction was captured in the slogan "a buck is a buck" used to promote the Benson White Paper of 1969.

Carter's ideas appealed to three very different groups within the broader tax policy community. For one, libertarians and neo-classical economists, a distinct minority in the 1960s, supported the wholesale removal of tax preferences as state-imposed distortions on private economic activity. Taxing accrued and imputed income would force taxpayers to shift investments to those areas which would yield the highest returns, rather than sitting on unproductive capital to avoid taxes. Second, many public finance economists and professionals applauded Carter's proposals for returning the tax system to what they believed should be it main purpose, the collection of tax revenues, while using other policy instruments to achieve other economic and social policy objectives. According to this view, shared by many Finance Department officials at the time, substituting public grants, loans, subsidies, and regulations for tax preferences would enable governments to improve the targeting of public assistance and impose greater control and accountability over public spending.[25] Finally, social democrats applauded Carter's egalitarian goal of subjecting all forms of income to progressive tax rates, thus radically increasing the scope for the redistribution of income and wealth and the expansion of other activities by the state.[26] A 1994 study suggested that adoption of the Haig-Simons model would have increased the 1988 taxable income of families earning between $40,000 and $100,000 by an average of 28.4 per cent.[27]

The 1969 White Paper on Taxation, introduced by Trudeau's first finance minister, Edgar Benson, rejected the Carter Report's most radical recommendations, but sought to implement enough of them to promote a significant political backlash. This forced him to make significant changes, including a promise that his reforms would be revenue neutral and that the introduction of a new tax on capital gains would be offset by the elimination of the existing federal Estate Tax.[28]

Allan MacEachen's tax reform budget of 1981 sought to eliminate many of the tax preferences which had been added to the tax system during the previous decade and to extend accrual taxation to a number of areas of business and investment income. The political impetus for the 1981 tax reform budget was a looming fiscal and economic crisis. The US Federal Reserve Board had responded to high and increasing inflation with monetary shock treatment that drove Canadian interest rates over 22 per cent—more than 10 per cent after inflation. Conventional Keynesian economics called for a more restrictive fiscal policy of deficit reduction to combat inflation and permit an easing of interest rates. The Trudeau cabinet, elected on a social democratic platform of activist government, was committed to sharp increases in public spending. Finance Minister MacEachen chose to impose the resulting tax increases through a systematic attack on tax preferences rather than a general increase in tax rates.[29]

MacEachen explicitly justified his proposals by appealing to the concept of "tax expenditures" as arbitrary and unfair departures from Carter's economic ideal.[30] MacEachen's rhetoric—and that of his political opponents—ensured that the resulting political battle would be fought in the shadow of the earlier Carter-Benson proposals for reform, as well as the interventionist-nationalist goals of the National Energy Program.

This decision suited the policy preferences of many Finance Department officials who shared a deep intellectual commitment to Carter's model of tax reform. These officials tended to resent the proliferation of tax preferences during the 1970s, measures that they regarded as politically-inspired distortions of a "good tax system."[31] However, their strategy, while perhaps well-intentioned, made the fatal error of ignoring an increasingly polarized political environment. The politicization of the tax expenditure concept was a major tactical error that aggravated the ideological conflict surrounding federal economic policies and fostered a massive political backlash against MacEachen's proposed tax reforms.

Both Benson and MacEachen were forced to make major changes to their initial proposals to make them politically and economically viable. The issues of economic and political viability struck directly at the heart of the claims made for Carter's vision of tax reform, especially with Canada's growing integration into continental and global markets for goods and capital.

ECONOMIC VIABILITY

The strongest economic arguments for comprehensive income taxation are rooted in neo-classical economic theory. Economists of this school argue that high marginal tax rates, offset by an ever-growing number of tax exemptions and preferences, create incentives for taxpayers to engage in extensive tax avoidance by shifting economic activity to less heavily taxed forms of income and to lobby for even more tax preferences (rent-seeking). This in turn shifts the costs of government to less politically favoured groups, and creates economic distortions and inefficiencies which reduce overall economic welfare.

Both the Carter-Benson reforms and more recent proposals for a flat rate, consumption-based tax system were intended to remove many of these economic distortions and inequities, and to increase incentives for taxpayers to maximize their economic opportunities in the marketplace rather than through rent-seeking or tax avoidance. Moreover, Carter's proposals to tax investment income on an accrual basis would have prevented the growth of large concentrations of wealth and economic power in private hands and facilitated its redistribution by governments to less fortunate Canadians or, alternatively, its transfer to government control. These arguments appealed to the egalitarian spirit of the 1960s. The general prosperity of that period made issues of economic equality a higher economic and political priority than promoting savings, investment, or other measures to encourage economic growth. Governments still enjoyed relatively high levels of social trust.

However, critics of the Carter-Benson proposals and the 1981 tax reform budget charged that these benefits depended on other policy decisions which could not be taken for granted. First, the economic incentives of tax reform would be realized only if tax increases from base-broadening measures were offset by substantial reductions in tax rates so that all major groups in society would be better off. Second, the "fairness" of tax reform would depend on the accessibility and efficiency of direct government spending programs that replaced tax preferences. This was unlikely with many broadly-based tax measures, especially those targeted at the middle class and small businesses. The Haig-Simons model challenged a wide-range of middle-class tax benefits that allowed pension and retirement savings to accumulate tax-free, along with the equity in family homes and businesses, and that exempted many employer-paid benefits from taxation. As a result, long-term private savings would be taxed in order to promote short-term government spending.[32]

Third, the success of tax reform depended on the federal government's ability to manage international capital flows and thus reduce the effects of transfer pricing and international tax competition on business practices and investment. Canada's increasing openness to international trade and investment in the late 1960s and 1970s, although only a fraction of current levels, made such control increasingly difficult, if not economically counterproductive. Fourth, the economic effects of comprehensive income taxation were closely linked to price stability and the level of inflation. The government's single-year accounting framework took little or no account of the impact of inflation on medium- and long-term investments, a major drawback in the inflationary economy of the 1970s and early 1980s, especially on business and investment income.[33] Fifth, the administrative viability of the proposals was dependent on adequate transition and grandfathering provisions to minimize economic disruption, especially on investments made on the basis of the old tax rules. As economist Sijbren Cnossen comments,

> If normative implications of the accretion concept of income are taken seriously, much more vigorous efforts are needed to fully tax in-kind fringe benefits, to tax retirement claims on imputed (non-cash) income, to fully tax realized capital gains, to move towards an accrual tax on other capital gains, and to fully integrate the corporate with the personal income tax. *Doing so, however, invites possibly insuperable valuation, imputation and business adjustment problems.*[34]

Business criticisms of the Carter Report, the Benson White Paper, and the 1981 budget emphasized their potential for disrupting existing patterns of economic activity. The Benson White Paper was modified extensively following parliamentary hearings and business lobbying. The 1981 MacEachen budget, which sought to introduce major changes to the tax structure without benefit of prior consultation with business groups or the general public, was notable for its initial lack of transitional measures, a factor that seriously damaged its economic and political credibility.[35]

The success of tax reform's critics in the business and financial communities in calling into question its economic viability seriously undermined its political support among the majority of middle-class Canadians. The failure of its supporters to demonstrate that the proposed tax changes would not only make the system fairer, but would also lead to a stronger economy and higher living standards for most Canadians demonstrated that claims to validity in political or economic theory were no match for the politics of short-term self-interest.[36]

However, the greatest political handicap facing the Haig-Simons approach to tax reform was that large segments of the Canadian public had come to accept the idea of tax policy as an active instrument of economic and social policy, largely because they had become the beneficiaries of such tax preferences. The federal government failed to create a political constituency with a clear interest in tax reform. At the same time, interests threatened with sharply higher taxes as a result of tax reform—most notably small businesses, the investment and resource industries, and large numbers of private-sector tax professionals—organized massive political resistance.[37] These groups succeeded in persuading the parliamentary opposition, several provincial governments, large segments of the mass media, and the general public that the proposed reforms threatened their economic well-being.

These tax reforms largely failed the test of economic and, more importantly, political viability. The political backlash they triggered, not just from the rich and powerful, but from thousands of middle-class Canadians, demonstrated that any politically viable approach to tax reform must begin with the tax system as it is, not as we might wish it to be in the best of all possible worlds. This insight is the key to the "pragmatic" approach to tax reform during the 1980s of governments throughout the English-speaking world and the persistence of Canada's "hybrid" tax system.

The Goods and Services Tax debate also illustrates the challenge of attempting to rely on theoretical economic arguments to justify major changes to tax policies to the general public, particularly when these result in new or increased taxes. The GST was a logical response to the erosion of the old Manufacturers' Sales Tax base during the 1980s as a result of a series of court rulings that undercut federal efforts to stem large-scale tax avoidance. It also eliminated the MST's taxation of exported goods, which would have been economically perverse after Canada signed a free trade agreement with the United States in 1988.

However, by subjecting most services—about two-thirds of economic activity—to direct sales taxation for the first time and expanding the number of tax-collecting businesses from about 60,000 to almost 2 million, the GST's political sponsors left many Canadians with the firm impression that they were imposing a huge new tax burden on the country, instead of just replacing one consumption tax with another, more efficient one. Although the Mulroney government forced passage of the GST despite overwhelming public opposition (as much as 88 per cent in published polls), its subsequent destruction in the 1993 federal election left little doubt that, once again, comprehensive tax reform had failed to pass the test of political viability.

THE PRAGMATIC APPROACH TO TAX POLICY

The major alternative to academic ideas for comprehensive tax reform is a pragmatic approach that accepts the tax system as one policy instrument among many that governments may use to promote various policy objectives and societal goals. The cumulative effect of using tax policies to pursue a variety of economic and social policy objectives is that tax considerations become deeply embedded in the fabric of national life.

Governments must still collect taxes to finance valued public services. Promoting economic efficiency is also an important, though often neglected, goal of economic and tax policies. However, these policies do not exist in a vacuum. Rather, they reflect a broad range of political commitments and cultural expectations about the role of the state and relationships between state and society. Since Confederation, governments have played an active role in promoting economic development, growth, and capital formation—"the promoter (or developmental) state"—and in protecting Canadians against external economic forces and, increasingly, domestic social conditions, in response to demands from voters and organized interests—"the protective state." This approach to public policy is consistent with public choice analyses of the policy process, such as those of Hartle and Savoie, that emphasize the institutional interests of policymakers and their desire to protect and promote the interests of the groups or institutions they represent.[38]

Advocates of the pragmatic approach to tax policy and tax reform may explicitly reject the normative assumptions of comprehensive income taxation as the dominant principles of tax policy, believing that they should be subordinated to the political objectives of the state. Alternatively, they may believe that whatever their conceptual virtues, these ideals can only be implemented piecemeal, while balancing competing policy goals. Such a balance is seen as necessary to achieve legitimacy for fiscal and tax policies through the accommodation and conciliation of social and economic interests. In either case, this approach, which David Good labels "the politics of accommodation,"[39] lends itself to brokerage politics and incremental policy change.

Maslove has noted that the pragmatic approach to tax policy carries with it a periodic need for tax reform, if only to rationalize the large number of policy changes since the previous restructuring.[40] Piecemeal changes to the tax structure are preferred to large-scale or comprehensive change because they are easier to implement without creating serious economic disruption or political controversy. Piecemeal changes, such as the indexing of personal income taxes in 1973 (and again in 2000) or their partial deindexing in 1982 and 1985, may be implemented unilaterally through the budget process. However, in recent years, they have usually been the product of a consensus-building process including formal and informal consultations between the federal Minister and Department of Finance and a number of governmental and societal interests. (This process is discussed further in Chapter 5.)

Perhaps the most important reason for the persistence of the pragmatic approach to tax policy as an alternative to comprehensive tax reform is the flexibility it offers to politicians, major economic interests, and ordinary taxpayers in promoting their perceived interests through the political process. Ministers of Finance, however, value the use of tax preferences to balance the political and economic claims of competing interests within society. This enables them to respond to different economic concerns without having to create new bureaucratic instruments for the delivery of public services or direct subsidies for the promotion of economic development. It also enables them to maintain more direct control over the policy process than would comparable expenditure programs overseen by another federal department or level of government. However, critics of the pragmatic approach argue that as tax expenditures become entrenched as fiscal entitlements rather than discretionary expenditures, they become demand-driven and power is lost by Ministers of Finance as well.

The pragmatic approach to tax policy lends itself to piecemeal responses to policy problems and challenges. Tax policy is used to encourage or discourage certain social activities, or to mitigate the effects of external economic forces that threaten the security of individual citizens or major societal groups. Recent examples include the increased use of targeted tax credits to deliver tax reductions to lower- and middle-income families with children, to increase the accessibility and affordability of education, and to promote private support for non-profit and charitable activities.

In Canada, the pragmatic approach to tax policy has often had a bias toward accommodating business practices that give private businesses and investors considerable discretion in pursuing their economic interests without the detailed bureaucratic supervision typical of many regulatory structures or of direct government subsidies. To the extent that investments in particular sectors or regions offer higher levels of risk or require longer periods before reaping a competitive rate of return, tax preferences offer both politicians and business interests a convenient way to diffuse risk, harness private capital to promote economic development, and create a mutually beneficial political environment. To the extent that potential tax revenues are reduced by such policies, business interests can often point to higher levels of job-creating, revenue-generating economic activity and a reduced potential for (or dependence on) direct state control. At the same time, the widespread availability of tax preferences lends itself to competitive rent-seeking by business and other societal interests.

These features, while attractive to politicians, bureaucrats, and interest groups whose outlook on the role of the state is shaped by the ideology of business liberalism, are usually anathema to those with a social democratic, Marxist, or statist outlook, who tend to view tax preferences as tax expenditures involving the alienation of discretionary economic power from the state to private interests. This tends to make the state more dependent on the cooperation and goodwill of bourgeois interests, thus reducing its power to implement structural economic and social change over the long term.[41]

Taxation and the New Economy

The effects of globalization—particularly the integration of Canada's economy into the North American and global economies, and the impact of rapid technological change on economic organization, business practices, and financial markets—have also created significant new challenges for national tax policies. They reflect many of the same debates over the distribution and limits of taxation and the role of the state in adapting to economic change. However, they also reflect a growing awareness of the dynamics of the new knowledge-based economy and the implications of the new technological revolution for economic development and the role of government.

Those critical of the global marketplace and its tendency to undermine the ability of national governments to regulate capital flows and transnational corporations whose operations transcend national boundaries, have largely abandoned the pursuit of self-sufficient national economic policies. Instead, they advocate the creation of international governmental and nongovernmental agencies to regulate economic activity, manage the social and environmental consequences of economic change, and restrict levels of international tax competition.[42] Such rules, particularly in international taxation, may be used to harmonize international tax laws or, at a minimum, to limit the emergence of international tax havens that enable corporate and financial investors to minimize the tax burden on capital income.

Critics also argue for a continued emphasis on the redistributive functions of Canada's tax system, both in maintaining public services in an aging society and in limiting the inequality resulting from unequal access to opportunities in the new economy. These arguments reflect the social democratic elements of Canada's political tradition and a strong emphasis on state leadership and control in both economy and society.

Neo-liberal critics of this approach contend that it fundamentally misjudges the character of the emerging knowledge-based economy and the factors necessary for promoting the development of an entrepreneurial culture for technological innovation, adaptation, and leadership in the new economy. While recognizing that competitive tax policies, especially for business and investment income, are only one element of the "new growth economics," they contend that international tax competition actually promotes economic growth and increased prosperity by linking taxes on capital to the economic benefits received by businesses. They point to lower levels of taxation as one of four key elements in attracting and retaining investment, particularly in the high-technology sectors that have driven increases in economic efficiency and productivity in recent years, reducing inflationary pressures, and promoting extensive job creation and higher standards of living.[43] Other major factors in this process include a strong physical and technical infrastructure, usually, though not always, financed by tax dollars; a strong education system capable of producing large numbers of skilled workers; an entrepreneurial class capable of organizing and mobilizing people and resources to take advantage of new and changing economic opportunities; and a flexible, transparent regulatory framework capable of adapting to changing circumstances.

Neo-liberal critics also note that changing investment patterns by pension funds and growing personal investments in mutual funds have significantly broadened the ownership of corporations, resulting in significant increases in average household wealth and a wider distribution of the benefits of corporate profitability.[44] Supporters of the "new growth economics" argue for significant reductions in the taxation of business and investment income in order to attract highly mobile capital and the skilled entrepreneurs and knowledge workers whose innovations drive the process of economic change and growth.[45]

These arguments have been accepted implicitly in recent years by neo-liberal and even some social democratic policy-makers, as industrial nations from Australia to Scandinavia have sharply reduced taxes on business and capital income rather than attempting to tax them at high marginal rates. The Chrétien government's decision in its 2000 budget to equalize corporate income taxes for all industries at rates comparable to those of the United States, even though phased in over five years, reflects this trend. So do recent changes deferring capital gains taxation on employee stock options—a growing compensation tool for employees in high technology industries—and on "rollovers," in which up to $2 million in profits from the sale of one business may be reinvested tax-free in another eligible business.

Most economic observers agree that national governments have greater flexibility in taxing less mobile factors of production—especially social insurance taxes on earnings and consumption taxes—depending on their capacity to deliver tangible benefits and services to citizens in return. However, while labour is less mobile than capital, the greater mobility of highly skilled technical workers, professionals, managers, and entrepreneurs has raised questions about the degree to which relatively high personal income tax rates affect Canada's ability to retain its most capable "knowledge workers."[46] This has led to growing debates in recent years about whether governments should take advantage of growing tax revenues and emerging fiscal surpluses to provide their citizens with significant, broadly-based tax reductions, thus contributing to higher living standards and stimulating further economic growth, or whether a higher priority should be given to the expansion of spending on public services, including, but not limited to, increased access to health care and education. (These issues are addressed in greater detail in Chapters 10 and 11.)

These debates, at one level, involve competing economic ideas about how to expand the general prosperity and ensure that most citizens have the opportunity to participate in it, particularly in response to the effects of the new "knowledge-based economy" on earnings opportunities and the distribution of work. However, contests over economic ideas also involve a continuing political struggle for political and economic power among competing interests inside and outside government.

Conclusion

Major changes to tax policy do not occur in an intellectual vacuum. Rather, they reflect the spread of ideas that offer economically credible responses to significant policy problems that cannot be resolved by existing policy structures or concepts. However, by themselves, ideas for major policy change have limited influence. They must enjoy the sponsorship of authoritative political figures. They must be capable of implementation within existing political institutions and be adaptable both to a country's dominant political culture and to the interests of the governing party and its supporters.

Edgar Benson's proposals for tax reform were not excessively radical in the context of the late 1960s. However, like Allan MacEachen's proposed tax reforms in 1981-82, they succeeded in alienating much of the governing Liberals' support among business groups and professionals by confronting them with the prospect of significantly higher taxes without corresponding benefits.

Michael Wilson was successful in promoting tax reform as long as he could point to the precedents of relatively successful tax reform programs in the United States and Great Britain and offer significant benefits (or minimal costs) to the majority of the government's business and middle-class supporters. But Wilson's idea of a joint federal-provincial sales tax, while probably the technically soundest, most politically marketable idea for sales tax reform advanced during the 1980s, fell by the wayside in the absence of provincial support. Wilson's fall-back proposal for sales tax reform, the Goods and Services Tax, enjoyed the support of large elements of the tax profession and the corporate establishment, which it compensated for the corporate tax increases he had used to finance personal tax cuts in his 1988 income tax reform package. Unlike most previous large-scale tax reforms, the GST survived intact the fall of the Mulroney government because its critics, including the governing Liberals, could not agree on any politically or economically feasible alternative.[47]

The political success of Wilson's changes to the income tax system can be seen in their wholesale adoption by his Liberal successor, Paul Martin. Martin has expanded the Child Tax Credit, which Wilson used to replace a wide range of grants and tax benefits for families, to respond to demands by Liberal colleagues for increased social spending, while controlling costs and delivering benefits directly to Canadians, rather than creating major new children's services bureaucracies, as demanded by some social policy advocates. While broadening the business tax base as part of his attack on the deficit during the mid-1990s, Martin has also announced plans to reduce differences in the tax levels of different business sectors and to move corporate tax rates closer to levels in the United States, another key objective of Wilson's tax reforms.

Ideas may contribute to the legitimization of proposed policy changes, for example, by linking them credibly to larger societal objectives that already enjoy broad popular acceptance or support. However, the Canadian public has shown a limited tolerance for abstract ideas as a justification for policy change when these appear to threaten their individual or group interests, or when they become associated in the public mind with failed policy initiatives in other areas or countries. Efforts to build a consensus on tax reform in a society as diverse as Canada are likely to involve a balancing of competing economic, social, and political objectives, and a blurring or diffusion of theoretical precision and ideological rigour. Consensus is more easily achieved through the processes of piecemeal tax reform, in which specific problems can be addressed with the cooperation of a narrow range of interests.

The problem with any comprehensive theoretical framework for tax reform in a decentralized political and economic system such as Canada's is that it reopens all the established economic and political relationships of society, not just the dysfunctional ones. While this may be intrinsically attractive to the ideologically-minded, it also guarantees tremendous political and economic disruption as established social and economic relationships are subordinated to the service of an abstraction. The potential for disruption guarantees political resistance which is unlikely to be overcome unless the majority of organized interests and politically attentive citizens can be convinced that tax reform can be a positive-sum game, positive, that is, both for society and for their own interests.

In this view, the ideal of a fully rational, neutral tax system is utopian. The income tax, reflecting the basic compromises of Keynesian political economy, reconciles within itself the policies accommodating the creation of new wealth and economic activity by private businesses and investors and the redistributive functions of the modern state.[48] The coordination or reconciliation of these objectives takes place within a series of institutional and political constraints that are central to the political calculus of tax policies and tax reform.

NOTES

1 Alexander Hamilton (1961) "Federalist # 35," *The Federalist Papers*, ed. Clinton Rossiter (New York: Mentor Books), 216-17.

2 Gourevitch (1989), 87-88.

3 Bossons (1969); Goodman (1988a); Head and Bird (1983), 5.

4 Boskin (1978), 2.

5 Bossons (1969).

6 Osberg (1993), 75.

7 Bird (1970), 463-69.

8 Brittan (1977), 46.

9 For a broader discussion of this phenomenon in a North American context, see Bell (1974) and O'Connor (1973).

10 Buchanan and Musgrave (1999).

11 Brown (2000), 71.

12 MacDonald (1988), 360-61; Bossons (1969); Bird (1970).

13 Smiley (1987); Axworthy and Trudeau eds. (1990); Milne (1986).

14 Buchanan (1999); Brennan and Buchanan (1980); Buchanan and Musgrave (1999), 107-28.

15 Courchene (1991).The Chrétien government's blueprint for this coordination was the 1994 "Purple Paper," Canada, Department of Finance (1994a).

16 Savoie (1999).

17 Hall, ed. (1989).

18 Maslove (1989), 16-20.

19 Canada, Royal Commission on Taxation (1967); Surrey (1973); St. Hilaire and Whalley (1985), 195-96.

20 Russell (1993), 75-76.

21 Lewis (1972); National Council of Welfare (1976); McQuaig (1987).

22 Meade (1978).

23 Hall and Rabushka (1985).

24 Surrey and McDaniel (1985); Brooks, ed. (1979); Smith (1988).

25 Interviews, Department of Finance officials (ADM-1; ADM-2; FO3; FO4).

26 Brooks (1988).

27 Vermaeten, Gillespie, and Vermaeten (1994), Tables A3, A4, A5.

28 Benson (1970); Bukovetsky and Bird (1972), 39.

29 MacEachen (1981c); interview, former Deputy Minister of Finance (D3); see Chapter 6.

30 MacEachen (1981c); Canada, Department of Finance (1981a).

31 Interviews, former Liberal MP (MP3), Assistant Deputy Ministers (ADM-2, ADM-3), current and former officials of Tax Policy—Legislation Branch (FOI, FO3, FO4).

32 Kesselman (1988), 289-300, 318.

33 Helliwell (1970); Jenkins (1977); Bossons (1980).

34 Cnossen (1988), emphasis added.

35 Maslove and Eicher (1987).

36 Robertson (1988), 47.

37 Maslove (1988); Maslove and Eicher (1987).

38 Hartle (1982); Hartle (1988a); Savoie (1990).

39 Good (1980).

40 Maslove (1988); Maslove and Eicher (1987).

41 Woodside (1983); McQuaig (1987); Panitch (1993).

42 Avi-Yonah (2000).

43 Lipsey (1996); Fortin (1999); Kesselman (2000).

44 Poddar, Neubig, and English (2000), 111-12; Blackwell (2000).

45 Fortin (2000); Mintz (1999); Mintz (2000a).

46 Most studies conclude that tax rates are only one major factor in the so-called "brain drain," which is also influenced by differences in earnings and career opportunities, access to a supportive work environment, and quality of life.

47 Ironically, the Liberal plan to "replace" the GST evolved into a variant of Wilson's federal-provincial sales tax when Paul Martin negotiated a "Harmonized Sales Tax" with three Atlantic provinces to be administered by Ottawa.

48 Bird (1970), 445ff; Bukovetsky and Bird (1972), 439; Feldstein (1976); Aaron, Galper, and Pechman, eds. (1988), 1-3.

THREE

The Tax System as Economic Constitution

Tax policy is one of the central and most comprehensive expressions of the relationship between citizens' ordinary lives and the role of governments. Indeed, in many ways, the tax structure is to economic life what the formal political constitution is to civic life—an elaborate framework of rights, rules, and responsibilities that reflects the basic compromises of Canada's economic and social order.

The four major components of the national tax system—personal and corporate income taxes, general sales taxes, and social security taxes—involve a balancing of the long-term interests and objectives of major state and societal actors. Their pervasive impact on economic and social relationships make it exceptionally difficult to change their basic objectives, principles, and structures without major political and economic disruption. Although the annual budget process results in dozens of changes to tax legislation every year, the major features and objectives of the income, sales, and social security tax systems have remained relatively stable over the years. Every 15 to 20 years, however, the accumulated annual amendments, particularly to the Income Tax Act, have made it unwieldy enough that Ministers attempt to rationalize and streamline it through a process of comprehensive tax reform.

However, this process has the potential to reopen debate on the underlying principles of tax laws and, with it, what Buchanan and others have called the "economic constitution"[2]—the major legal and economic institutions and durable policy instruments which provide a stable framework for the economic behaviour of individuals, businesses, and government. As such, the process enables certain groups to obtain or enhance legal recognition of their central interests, values, and policy goals. It also poses a potential threat to the positions of groups whose "constitutionalized" interests may come under renewed scrutiny and possible attack.

This chapter applies the concept of an economic constitution to the major structural components of Canada's tax system and summarizes their evolution since the 1967 report of the Royal Commission on Taxation. It identifies the major factors that help to embed the tax system in the daily economic lives of Canadians, and outlines the practical political steps that must be taken by any federal minister of finance wishing to introduce tax reforms or major changes to the tax system and carry them to a successful conclusion.

Recognizing the Economic Constitution

Two major purposes of political constitutions are to define the powers available to governments and to provide the means to limit the use of those powers.[3] Political constitutions contain several elements. These may include one or more written documents that define and limit the powers of governments toward their citizens and, in a federal system, their relationship with one another. They may also include legal precedents and institutional arrangements established either by binding agreements among governments or by judicial rulings. However, constitutions are also bodies of legal custom, tradition, convention, and precedent, "the living constitution" that embodies the fundamental social and political institutions and values of a society.[4]

Peter Russell notes the existence of two distinct Anglo-American constitutional traditions. The British parliamentary or Burkean tradition is the product of "organic development ... the collection of laws, institutions and political practices that have survived the test of time and are found to be useful by a people."[5] Constitutional change in this tradition may be implemented by parliamentary changes to framework economic legislation or by international agreements confirmed and accepted by subsequent governments. The substantial constraints imposed on Canadian governmental powers by the Canada-US Free Trade Agreement and subsequent international trade treaties, though deeply contested at the time, are a significant example of this kind of constitutional change. Others relevant to Canadian tax policies include major structural income tax reforms in 1971 and 1988, and the introduction of the federal Goods and Services Tax in 1990.

Alternatively, constitutional change may take place gradually and incrementally, through the accretion of judicial or quasi-judicial rulings and the widespread acceptance of innovative economic practices. Broad shifts in regulatory policies, such as economic deregulation of previously regulated industries or the cumulative effects of trade tribunal rulings in constraining governments' use of protectionist regulatory and trade policies, are examples of the latter. So are the successive incremental changes to Canada's Unemployment Insurance system between 1988 and 1996, which had the cumulative effect of restructuring the objectives and entitlements associated with one of Canada's largest tax-based social programs. Support for families' child-rearing expenses by governments has undergone a series of changes since the 1970s, moving from a universal system of family benefits and tax preferences to a system of narrowly targeted refundable tax credits in the early 1990s, and back to a quasi-universal system with most benefits targeted to lower and middle-income families in the early twenty-first century.

The other tradition, "Lockean constitutionalism," is based on "the perception of the written constitution as a comprehensive statement of the basic principles of government and the rights of the people."[6] Amendment may take place either through a stringent process of securing an extraordinary majority for proposed changes or through a shift in the philosophy of judicial interpretation, often driven by political competition to secure control of the courts.[7] Reg Whitaker notes that, in Canada before 1982, written constitutions were intended primarily to define relationships between governments rather than citizen-state relationships.[8] The 1982 Constitution, particularly the Charter of Rights and Freedoms, reveals the growing influence of American constitutional ideas in Canada, especially for the protection of the prescriptive rights of individuals affirmed or created by judicial action against the intrusions of increasingly remote and bureaucratized governments. It also reveals a trend toward the more widespread constitutionalization of interests—the formal recognition of group aspirations and entitlements as formal rights in the constitution in ways that may pre-empt the normal competition of interests through the political process—although such practices have existed from the earliest days of Canadian constitutional history.[9]

Buchanan describes the basic economic institutions of a liberal democratic society as part of its economic constitution in the sense that "a constitution is conceived as a set of rules, or social institutions within which people operate and interact with one another ... rules (which) set boundaries on what activities are legitimate."[10] These rules or institutions may come to be seen as legitimate through a number of different processes. These include discussions leading to formal agreement among major political and economic stakeholders, the gradual development of a normative or ethical consensus between these groups and their attentive publics, or the generalized application of legal and administrative precedents over an extended period.[11] Major changes to these rules, affecting not only the details of policy but their basic conceptual and institutional framework, usually can be achieved only with the consent of major stakeholders or through a substantial shift in the social and political consensus.

Such rules or institutions may be generalized to the whole of society, such as widespread rights of private property ownership, the predominance of market capitalism, the provision of a social safety net through the major components of the welfare state, or the expectation of comprehensive taxpayer-funded medical services. C.B. Macpherson identifies such "entitlements" as a form of private property.[12] Other institutions central to the interests of major economic and social groups have become entrenched in public policy. These include supply management in agriculture, collective bargaining and a variety of legal immunities for organized labour (at least in the private sector), and generalized provisions for small business in federal and provincial tax legislation. Still others may be embedded in numerous federal-provincial agreements and the conventions of regional economic redistribution. Buchanan notes that the retrenchment of these rights frequently requires some form of compensation for those whose "property rights" have been infringed upon as a result of changes in their settled economic expectations.[13]

The detailed rules of the economic constitution are largely defined by "framework legislation" that codifies, creates, or radically changes the institutional structure governing the legal, economic, or social status of large segments of society, and whose application is interpreted primarily by the courts or by independent regulatory agencies. Canadian examples include the Income Tax Act, the Excise Tax Act, the Canada Labour Code (and parallel provincial statutes), the Canada Business Corporations Act, the Competition Act, the Bank Act, the Bankruptcy Act, legislation creating systems of supply management for various agricultural sectors, the Employment Insurance Act, and the Criminal Code. Although governments may introduce piecemeal policy changes and technical amendments from time to time, the institutional structures created by such legislation tend to be extremely durable and resistant to large-scale change. While the Bank Act is subject to parliamentary review every ten years, most other economic framework legislation is effectively subject to major structural change only with the consent of Parliament and major stakeholder groups.

Buchanan, Mancur Olson, and Douglas Hartle argue that the growth of government intervention in the economic and social life of most industrial nations since World War II has led to an increase in "rent-seeking" by organized groups, i.e., the capture or preservation of economic advantages conferred by preferential state actions. The greater the extent of government intervention in economy and society, the greater the incentives for organized groups to engage in rent-seeking or rent-avoidance.[14] The success of certain groups in obtaining institutional recognition and protection of their distinctive identities and interests in framework economic or fiscal legislation creates precedents for other groups to follow in staking their claims to political, economic, and social recognition. These include both economic interests such as small business, organized labour, organized agriculture, and the oil industry, and new social movements described as "equity-seeking groups" who have pursued competing agendas while attempting to create or capture government institutions capable of promoting their interests.

The spread of neo-liberal perspectives and policies in Canada and other industrial democracies since the early 1980s may have provided a means for governments to challenge the legal and institutional privileges of many entrenched economic interests. However, this has merely changed the terms on which groups seek recognition, support, and protection from the state, not the inherent nature of political and interest group competition. Therefore, just as political constitutions evolve over time as the result of formal amendment, judicial interpretation, and the rise of new constitutional conventions which reflect changes to the social and political balance of power, an economic constitution may evolve through changes in the structures of taxation, forms of property ownership, or broadly based income transfer and other entitlement programs which reflect the shifting balance of political and social forces.

The generalized application of the tax system and its ability to influence the distribution of economic opportunities and rewards for an entire society lends itself not only to the log-rolling and rent-seeking activities of politicians and interest groups, but also to the "constitutionalization of interests," the transformation of the political discourse of interests competing for benefits within the political system to the constitutional language of rights and entitlements.[15] However, to understand the Canadian tax system as a constitutional instrument, we must first identify its main components and locate it in relation to the formal constitutional framework.

The Tax System as Economic Constitution

The political economy of taxation in Canada is shaped by four basic institutions. Federalism—the relationship between federal and provincial governments—is central to the division of power over various forms of taxation and public spending, and the ways in which governments institutionalize cooperation and manage conflict. The growing integration of North American and global economies both constrains policy choices available to federal and provincial governments and encourages the harmonization of economic policies with Canada's major trading partners. The dominance of market capitalism as the major source of domestic investment, employment, and economic growth on which governments rely for electoral success both encourages a measure of cooperation between governments and a diverse business sector and sets limits on overall tax levels in Canada's relatively open economy. A relatively egalitarian culture committed both to government respect for individual rights and to the use of government policies to reduce social and economic inequalities imposes limits on the arbitrary design or application of tax laws and encourages governments to use tax measures to further a wide range of economic and social goals.

THE CONSTITUTIONAL DIVISION OF POWERS

The Constitution Act, 1867, as interpreted by the courts, has resulted in shared federal-provincial jurisdiction over 90 per cent of federal revenue sources and almost three quarters of provincial revenue sources in recent years.[16] Section 91(3) permits the federal government to raise money "by any Mode or System of Taxation." Ottawa has exclusive control over customs and excise duties, indirect taxation, and Employment Insurance. Federal tax legislation must originate in the House of Commons and is not legally binding until passed by Parliament, although this convention has been increasingly ignored in recent years.

Provincial governments control "direct taxation within the province," expressed primarily through retail sales taxes. Their "primary jurisdiction over resource taxation" was confirmed following a bitter conflict between federal and provincial governments and resource industries over energy revenues in the 1970s and early 1980s.[17] In recent years, provincial governments have taken an increasing share of property tax revenues—traditionally a preserve of local governments—usually in conjunction with increased provincial control over education funding.

Other relevant constitutional rules include Section 121 (1987), which provides for free trade among all provinces in goods produced in any province; Section 125, which exempts both federal and provincial Crown property from taxation;[18] and Section 8 of the 1982 Charter of Rights which guarantees individuals the right "to move to and take up residency in any province" and "to pursue the gaining of a livelihood in any province."[19]

The Constitution's assignment to the provinces of primary responsibility for such major areas of public spending as education, health care, social services, and intra-provincial transportation has contributed to a significant fiscal imbalance since the Great Depression of the 1930s. This has led to a half-century of federal-provincial revenue-sharing agreements, culminating in the formal constitutionalization of equalization payments in 1982. Section 36(2) of the revised Constitution commits the federal government "to the principle of making equalization payments to ensure that provincial governments have sufficient revenues to provide reasonably comparable levels of public services at reasonably comparable levels of taxation."

The federal government's historic fiscal advantage in administering the Personal Income Tax in nine provinces (all except Quebec) has given it significant political leverage over the tax policies and spending priorities of the provinces. However, in recent years, Ottawa's need to limit its spending to reduce its deficits has led to the decentralization of power over both tax and spending policies to the provinces and reduced federal leverage over the fiscal policies of the larger provinces (see Chapter 12).

✓ Provincial "own-source" tax revenues steadily increased from 29 per cent of federal revenues in 1960 to 74 per cent in 1980 and 87 per cent in 1995 before declining slightly in the late 1990s (see Table 3.1). Profits from provincial Crown corporations, especially those managing gambling and liquor distribution, have given the provinces greater overall revenues than

Table 3.1 •• THE CHANGING FEDERAL-PROVINCIAL-LOCAL DISTRIBUTION OF TAX REVENUES: 1950-2000

	Federal (%)	Provincial (%)	Local (%)	CPP/QPP (%)	% of GDP	Provincial Revenues as a % of Federal Revenues
1950	69.0	18.7	12.4	—	21.4	27.0
1960	64.8	18.2	17.0	—	23.7	28.1
1970	52.3	30.3	13.5	3.9	30.1	57.9
1980	48.3	36.0	11.8	3.9	29.4	74.5
1985	48.4	37.1	10.7	3.8	31.4	76.7
1990	46.2	39.2	10.3	4.2	35.9	84.8
1995	45.3	39.3	10.4	5.0	35.6	86.8
2000[P]	46.3	38.6	8.6	6.5	37.5	83.4

P = Preliminary

Sources: Treff and Perry (2001), Table B-4; Statistics Canada (2001) *National Income and Expenditure Accounts* (Ottawa, March).

the federal government since 1993. However, the distribution of these revenues is heavily skewed between "have" and "have not" provinces. For this reason, much of the "constitutional" structure governing Canadian tax policies is the product of federal-provincial executive agreements.

QUASI-CONSTITUTIONAL ARRANGEMENTS: EXECUTIVE AGREEMENTS AND INTERNATIONAL TREATIES

The main components of the national tax system in Canada are income and excise taxes, Canada/Quebec Pension and Employment Insurance premiums, and the federal tax collection agreements. Of these, the Income Tax Act, the Federal-Provincial Tax Collection Agreements, and agreements governing equalization are the most financially significant elements.

Personal income taxes (PITs) are the largest source of both federal and provincial revenues. Federal PIT revenues grew from 28 per cent of total federal revenues in 1966 to 48 per cent in 1999.[20] PITs generated 35 per cent of provincial government revenues, not including federal transfers, in 1998-99, up from 12 per cent in 1963-64, largely due to a shift of taxing powers from the federal government in return for a slower rate of growth in federal transfers to the provinces.

The national tax system became highly centralized during the 1940s, reflecting federal fiscal dominance during and after World War II. This centralization also reflects the adoption of Keynesian economic policies and the use of fiscal policy for national economic stabilization after 1945.[21] Although federal dominance has declined and the tax system has become more decentralized since the 1960s, the tax collection and revenue-sharing agreements remain critical vehicles for national economic integration.[22]

The Federal-Provincial Tax Collection Agreement, originally concluded in 1957, is a major pillar in Canada's economic union. It provides for

> ➤ tax harmonization—a common federal-provincial tax base, defined by the federal government, applying to nine provinces (except Quebec) for personal income taxes and seven provinces for corporate income taxes;[23]

> ➤ federal administration and collection of income taxes for these provinces;

> ➤ limited provincial discretion in defining income subject to taxation, although recent changes will provide provinces with greater flexibility[24] (see Chapter 12);

➤ a short-term federal revenue guarantee to offset revenue losses to the provinces resulting from changes in federal tax rates or changes in the tax base.

Changes to the federal-provincial tax collection agreements negotiated in 1998 provide for provincial governments to set their own personal income tax rate structures independently of those of the federal government, effective in 2001. Unilateral changes by the federal government or major provincial governments to their tax bases can significantly affect the revenues of the other level of government. For this reason, changes to federal policies affecting major provincial industries can provoke serious political reactions from provincial governments.[25] The National Energy Program of 1980, like its predecessor, the Oil Export Tax of 1973, was intended to divert windfall revenues triggered by OPEC price increases from provincial to federal coffers. Federal tax reductions, such as those contained in 1988 tax reform legislation, also cut into provincial revenue projections, prompting several provincial governments to offset federal measures with tax increases of their own. Similarly, provincial tax changes, such as the adoption and extension of payroll taxes to finance burgeoning health and social insurance costs during the 1980s, which had the effect of reducing the federal tax base, prompted the federal government to limit the deductibility of increased payroll taxes against federal tax payments. Tax rate reductions by the largest provinces can also affect revenues of their smaller neighbours by reducing the tax base on which federal equalization payments are calculated.

Canada's status as a relatively open economy, largely dependent on international trade and capital flows, also imposes a range of formal and structural constraints on the taxing powers of the federal government. Canada has entered into a network of bilateral tax treaties with most of its major trading partners that typically define who is subject to taxation and provide for reciprocal, non-discriminatory tax treatment of nationals and non-nationals. These treaties also permit withholding of taxes on income earned by foreign residents, and allow credits on foreign income taxes paid to avoid double taxation of cross-border income and capital flows.[26] Parallel rules govern taxation of the foreign source income of Canadian residents.

CONTINENTALISM, GLOBALIZATION, AND THE CANADIAN TAX SYSTEM

The Canadian economy and, to a lesser extent, the politics of taxation have been transformed during the last 25 years by their growing integration into the North American and global economies. Canadians now have a larger financial stake in the rest of the world, through corporate foreign investment and the investment of our private savings, mutual, and pension funds, than foreigners have in Canada.[27] More than 40 per cent of the goods and services produced in Canada are exported to foreign countries. In 1999, 85.9 per cent of Canadian merchandise exports went to the United States. Seven out of ten Canadian provinces depend more on foreign trade for their prosperity than on sales of goods and services to neighbouring provinces. Canadians are free to purchase a rapidly growing range of goods and services from anywhere in the world over the Internet, rather than dealing with local or national suppliers. Growing numbers of both foreign and Canadian businesses increasingly have the option of basing their operations in whatever province or country makes the most business sense, rather than being constrained by regional or national boundaries.

Government policies can shape the direction of these market forces to some extent and make them work to the benefit of Canadians. However, few Canadians still share the illusion that governments can contain international economic forces outside our national borders or ignore the pressures of global economic realities in making domestic policy. While we still have the freedom to choose a more extensive range of public services than our American neighbours and to levy higher taxes to pay for them, the way we do this will have a major impact on our ability to sustain these services, support an aging population, and maintain or improve our standards of living as individuals and as a nation.[28]

Canadian economic development and tax policies have long reflected an uneasy balance between what Neil Bradford describes as liberal continentalist and interventionist nationalist policies.[29] The former have been used to attract and retain large amounts of foreign investment, particularly in the development of Canada's resource-rich western and northern regions. The latter have usually sought to foster the development of Canadian-controlled industries within protected domestic markets and to strengthen the independent policy-making capacity of the federal government. Domestic political support for these often-competing policy perspectives has depended largely on whether various political and societal interests are more reliant on export markets (or strategic alliances with foreign multinationals) or on protected domestic markets.

Since World War II, Canada's growing integration within the North American economy has limited the federal government's capacity to pursue economic and tax policies that place Canadian businesses at a serious competitive disadvantage compared with their American competitors, or that impose significant restrictions on the operation of North American capital markets. While this has not prevented Canadian governments from regulating foreign investment or giving preferential treatment to Canadian

companies in several industries, such intervention has usually required substantial and continuing support from large segments of the Canadian
business community to become institutionalized. However, since the mid-
1980s, most Canadian governments have retreated from interventionist
nationalism in favour of a trade-driven industrial strategy of closer integration with North American and international markets.

As a result, a series of international treaties such as the GATT and free trade
agreements with the United States, Mexico, and other countries has placed
progressive limits on the rights of both federal and provincial governments to
impose discriminatory tax and regulatory provisions on non-residents.
Finally, Canada's relatively high dependence on foreign investment and borrowing for economic development, public finance, and the major investments
of Canadian corporations in other countries has placed significant limits on
the federal government's ability to impose or enforce taxes on capital income
that are significantly higher than those imposed by its major trading partners
or that hinder international capital flows.[30]

Globalization and Canada's trade-driven industrial strategy have contributed to two other major shifts in Canada's tax structure in recent years: the
introduction of the Goods and Services Tax to replace the old Federal Sales
Tax in 1991, and the progressive shift since the early 1980s in the incidence of
business taxation from profit-sensitive taxes to profit-insensitive taxes.[31]

THE TAX SYSTEM, MARKET CAPITALISM, AND PERSONAL
ECONOMIC SECURITY

Two other central institutions in Canada's economic constitution which
have a pervasive influence on the tax structure and the politics of tax policy
are the government-fostered role of market capitalism in promoting economic development, growth, and individual opportunity, and egalitarian
liberalism. These objectives may complement or conflict with one another,
both in shaping government policies and in legitimating or challenging
those policies in the highly political marketplace of public opinion.

The institutions of market capitalism have evolved over time, along with
forms of business organization, cultural norms, access to capital and technology, and government attitudes toward business. In Canada, these have
come to include broadly diffused ownership of property, including business
ownership; relative freedom of investment and capital movements; relative
freedom of private contract and security of property; and the preponderance
of private business corporations—large and small—as the main vehicles of
economic activity, job creation, and economic growth.

Michael Bliss has noted that major structural changes in framework legislation that shapes the legal terms and conditions under which various economic sectors or industries conduct their business generally reflect political pressures from organized segments of the business community.[32] Such demands for supportive government intervention have often taken a mercantilist form. They have included the high tariff National Policy of the late nineteenth century, demands for the nationalization of major public utilities and infrastructure to provide low-cost power and rail freight in the early twentieth century; and the spread of economic regulations intended to restrict competition and maintain producer prices, of which agricultural marketing boards are the most prominent relics. They have also included restrictions on foreign ownership, particularly in the banking, cultural and, for a time, energy sectors, and a wide range of preferential tax policies, particularly for small businesses.

Since the mid-1970s, Canada's growing dependence on international markets, growing awareness of the costs of economic inefficiencies created by fiscal and regulatory restrictions on competition, and the effects of rapid technological change have led to new coalitions of producer and consumer groups pursuing a neo-liberal economic agenda. These have successfully pressured governments for economic deregulation, a retreat from interventionist nationalism, government initiatives to promote more rather than less competition, and a trend away from preferential tax treatment for particular industries.

The tax structure has often been used as an instrument to combine the promotion of business development with capital accumulation by individuals and smaller businesses. Governments have institutionalized a wide range of tax preferences for small businesses and family farms, eliminated wealth and inheritance taxes in favour of capital gains taxation (except for owner-occupied homes, smaller businesses, and family farms), and encouraged widespread private capital formation through RRSPs, pension plans, and other institutionalized savings vehicles. During the 1990s, these policies have resulted in Canada becoming a net exporter of capital, and in the broadening of corporate share ownership to include the majority of middle-class Canadian households.

By systematically promoting personal business and property ownership, these policies have contributed to a broader distribution of the economic benefits of market capitalism and to the creation of political counterweights to economic domination by governments or large corporations. Since the mid-1970s, small businesses and, more recently, own-account self-employment have been the largest sources of job creation, offsetting job losses from the rationalization of larger firms and reducing political pressures for the expansion of the state sector as a large-scale employer of last resort.

EGALITARIANISM, REDISTRIBUTION, AND FOSTERING
OPPORTUNITY

The tax system has been used not only as a means of fostering equality of
economic opportunity through widespread business ownership and capital
accumulation, but as a means of redistributing economic opportunity in different ways. Both supporters and critics of the existing tax system appeal to
different concepts of "tax fairness" in promoting their economic and ideological agendas:[33]

> horizontal equity—the concept that individuals with similar
  incomes and in similar circumstances should pay similar amounts
  of tax;

> equity in diversity—taxpayers in significantly different circum-
  stances should be subject to different tax treatment, particularly if
  the imposition of a uniform tax structure would impose economic
  hardship or deprive certain groups of economic and competitive
  opportunities enjoyed by other taxpayers;

> vertical equity—a progressive tax rate structure that imposes
  higher marginal tax rates as income levels increase;

> procedural equity—taxpayers should have the same protections
  against governmental abuses of power, such as retroactive or retrospective tax laws and the presumption of innocence in tax disputes,
  as in other areas of law; in recent years, this concept has been
  expanded to limit creative tax avoidance through the unintended
  use of various tax preferences;

> generational equity—limiting the ability of one generation to shift
  excessive financial and tax burdens to its successors through sys-
  temic deficit financing for current expenditures or the underfund-
  ing of public pensions.[34]

Canada's income tax system has promoted the redistribution of incomes
through a progressive rate structure since its introduction during World
War I. Since the Carter Commission report of 1967, a gradual flattening of
the rate structure has been accompanied by the broadening of the personal
tax base, thereby attempting to reconcile the goals of horizontal and vertical
equity. During the 1990s, the federal government greatly expanded its use of

refundable tax credits as a method of income redistribution, effectively integrating federal tax and transfer systems.

Canada's top personal income tax rates—ranging from 39.0 per cent to 48.7 per cent in 2001,[35] depending on provincial tax rates and surtaxes—are significantly higher than comparable rates in the United States and are applied at much lower income thresholds: $100,000 in Canada, compared with about $420,000 in the United States. In 1986, the federal government introduced a system of alternative minimum income taxes (AMTs) on upper income earners to limit the pyramiding of tax preferences to avoid taxes. However, despite the efforts of more ardent redistributionists, the system has been designed to minimize its effects on the legitimate use of tax preferences such as carry-forwards of business losses against other income, thereby recognizing the principle of equity in diversity.

Since the collapse of federal efforts to create a guaranteed annual income in the 1970s, governments have reshaped the tax system to deliver a variety of income support measures to lower- and middle-income families, including the Child Tax Credit (now the National Child Benefit), the Goods and Services Tax Credit, and provincial property tax credits. Statistics Canada reported in 1995 that tax and transfer programs have reduced the income differences between high- and low-income families from 23:1 on a pre-transfer basis to about 5:1 on an after-tax basis.[36]

Tax reforms during the 1980s also attempted to reduce disparities in effective tax rates imposed on various kinds of businesses through the reduction of tax preferences for manufacturing and resource industries and the extension of federal sales taxes to the services sector. However, since corporate revenues, cost structures, and profitability vary widely from one industry to another, these reductions have been used to justify significantly different tax regimes for capital-intensive and labour-intensive industries, seasonal and cyclical industries, and export-dependent firms compared with those facing mainly domestic Canadian competition. Recent changes introduced to their Corporate Income Tax systems by the federal and Ontario governments will phase out most differences in marginal tax rates between manufacturing, resource, and service sectors by 2005, although effective tax rates will still vary depending on the effects of other tax measures.

Income tax policy and legislation are the responsibility of the federal Department of Finance. The Canada Customs and Revenue Agency (formerly Revenue Canada) administers and collects all federal taxes and most provincial income taxes under various tax collection agreements.

THE LEGISLATIVE FRAMEWORK: INCOME, EXCISE, AND SOCIAL INSURANCE TAXES

Although the first Income Tax Act was passed as a temporary wartime measure in 1917, the basic structure of Canada's Income Tax Act was introduced in 1949. Separate income tax rules apply to individuals (the personal income tax), corporations (the corporate income tax), different kinds of corporations, trusts, non-profit organizations, and foreign-source income.

The Income Tax Act has a "progressive" rate structure, with marginal rates on individuals increasing with levels of taxable income. Since 1949, there has been a trend toward expanding the definition of taxable income while lowering marginal tax rates, the rate applied to each additional dollar of taxable income. The top personal marginal tax rate was lowered from 84 per cent in 1949 to 61.34 per cent in 1973 and 51.0 per cent in 1987, although the income levels at which these rates were applied have been reduced significantly.[37] In 2001, top marginal rates ranged from 39.0 per cent in Alberta to 48.7 per cent in Quebec. However, the broadening of the tax base and the introduction of a variety of refundable tax credits for lower- and middle-income taxpayers has made effective income tax rates much more sharply progressive in recent years, resulting in many middle-income families who earn $30,000–$40,000 paying marginal tax rates in excess of 60 per cent.[38] This has led both federal and several provincial governments in recent budgets to reduce tax rates for citizens earning between $30,000 and $100,000. While personal income tax is normally levied on the annual incomes of individuals rather than households, as in the United States, the income tax system has come to recognize the increasing diversity of economic and social arrangements through a wide range of tax preferences and adjustments.

The 1949 Act sharply limited ministerial discretion in the interpretation of the Income Tax Act, created an independent Tax Appeal Board, and established many of the current concepts and definitions of personal and corporate income, including those providing for the partial integration of personal and corporate income taxes to limit double taxation of capital income.[39] Major changes were made to the Act in 1971, following the report of the Carter Royal Commission, a White Paper, and extensive public debate. Tax rates were lowered, many tax preferences were modified or abolished, and income taxes were extended to capital gains for the first time.[40] A number of piecemeal changes to the tax structure during the 1970s and 1980s introduced new concepts, including partial inflation indexing, refundable tax credits for lower- and middle-income taxpayers, and expanded recognition of multi-year income patterns for business and investment income and retirement savings. The 1987-88 tax reform legislation further broadened the tax base, lowered marginal rates, and converted a number of traditional deductions into tax credits. Most of these changes, while important, have resulted in the gradual, piecemeal evolution of an existing tax structure rather than large-scale structural change.

Historically, consumption taxes have provided the second largest source of both federal and provincial revenues (see Table 3.2). Indirect taxation—excise and other consumption taxes levied prior to the retail level—is reserved for the federal government under the constitution. Both federal and provincial governments may levy direct taxes on consumers.

The Excise Tax Act historically provided for three forms of taxes: customs duties on imported goods, excise taxes on specific goods such as gasoline, alcohol, and tobacco, and a general sales tax. Consumption taxes of all kinds accounted for 20.5 per cent of federal revenues in 1999 and about 18 per cent of provincial own-source revenues.

The Federal (or Manufacturers') Sales Tax (FST) was levied on domestic and imported manufactured goods between 1924 and 1990. The FST was the federal government's second largest source of revenue during the 1970s and 1980s. Efforts to replace it with a Wholesale Tax in 1975-77 and 1982-83 failed as a result of massive resistance from business groups.[41] After several false starts, the FST was replaced in 1990 by the Goods and Services Tax, a value-added tax on most goods or services sold in Canada, imposed at each level in the production and distribution chain.

Table 3.2 ·· CONSUMPTION TAXES AS A SHARE OF FEDERAL REVENUES

	General Sales Taxes*		Customs & Excise		Total Consumption Taxes	
	$ MILLION	%	$ MILLION	%	$ MILLION	%
1965-66**	1,917	21.6	1,428	16.1	3,345	37.7
1975-76[†]	3,610	10.4	4,560	13.1	8,170	23.5
1985-86	9,583	11.5	7,877	9.5	17,460	21.0
1995-96	19,174	15.2	10,912	7.7	30,086	23.4
1999-2000	22,790	13.8	10,096	6.1	32,886	19.8

*   Manufacturers Sales Tax to 1990; Goods & Services Tax after 1990.

** Includes sales tax revenues dedicated to Old Age Security tax

†   Includes Oil Export Tax.

Sources: *The National Finances*, 1967-68; *The National Finances*, 1978-79, 28, 98; *Finances of the Nation*, 1997: A-7; *Annual Financial Report* (Ottawa, Dept. of Finance, September 2000), Table 2.

The federal government has consistently attempted to persuade the provinces to integrate their retail sales taxes with the GST into a single "Harmonized Sales Tax" (HST), but with limited success. The Mulroney government negotiated a partial merger of the two taxes with the Government of Quebec in 1991, although some differences remain. Three other provinces—Newfoundland, Nova Scotia, and New Brunswick—entered into a harmonized sales tax agreement with the federal government in 1996.[42]

Payroll taxes to finance health and social insurance programs, primarily Canada Pension and Employment Insurance at the federal level, have been the fastest growing source of federal revenues in recent years. This field of taxation is also shared with the provinces, although in 1993 the federal government announced it would limit the deductibility of provincial payroll and capital taxes against federal income taxes, effectively capping provincial rates in these areas. All provinces impose payroll taxes to finance their Workers' Compensation systems. Newfoundland, Quebec, Ontario, and Manitoba impose general payroll taxes to support provincial medicare systems. Table 3.3 summarizes the federal and provincial payroll taxes as a share of overall revenues.

The tax structure reflects the policy and legislative framework designed by the Department of Finance (except in the case of Employment Insurance, in which jurisdiction is shared with Human Resource Development Canada) and approved by Parliament. However, the actual interpretation of tax laws is the responsibility of the courts.

CONSTITUTIONAL AND COMMON LAW PRECEDENTS

Historically, the role of the courts in shaping the economic constitution has fallen into three main categories: jurisdictional boundary maintenance, individual tax litigation, and, since 1982, the application of specific Charter rights to the administration and, more recently, the design of the tax system.

Traditionally, the federal courts have carried out "boundary maintenance" between federal and provincial tax jurisdictions. This has often led to a certain degree of legal arbitrage as individual and corporate taxpayers attempt to use the federal-provincial division of powers to limit federal or provincial fiscal innovations seen as inimical to their interests.[43] The courts have also imposed strict procedural requirements on the revenue-raising activities of governments. As Krishna states "It has been well established since Magna Carta that there is no common law authority to levy taxes; income tax can only be levied under the authority of specific fiscal legislation."[44] The constitutional doctrine of "no taxation apart from law" has resulted in strict legal limits on retrospective taxation, legislation which "creates new obligations, imposes new duties or attaches new disabilities in respect of past events or transactions."[45] The doctrine has also reinforced the constitutional role of the courts in applying common law rules of statutory interpretation.

The role of the courts is amplified by several factors. Rather than applying a single set of rules to all forms of income derived from all sources, Anglo-Canadian traditions of tax law provide for separate rules and principles of taxation for different "sources and types of income," such as employment and investment income, capital gains, and several distinct kinds of business income recognized by Parliament.[46]

Historically, the courts have ruled that tax laws must be applied exactly as enacted by Parliament in order to minimize the level of bureaucratic discretion in seizing the property of individuals for use by the state. The doctrine of "strict construction" provides for the courts to interpret tax laws in accordance with the plain and established meanings of its language,[47] although the technical drafting required to restrict the unintended uses of many tax provisions is far from being either plain or transparent to non-experts. While this doctrine can work both for and against the interests of individual taxpayers, it has also contributed to a system of competitive tax avoidance in which many taxpayers and their professional advisors go to great lengths to minimize their taxes within the law. The basic principle of taxpayer rights in common law was summarized by Lord Tomlin in *I.R.C. v. Duke of Westminster* (1936): "Every man is entitled, if he can, to order his affairs so that the tax attaching under the appropriate Acts is less than it otherwise would be. If he succeeds in ordering them so as to secure this result ... he cannot be compelled to pay an increased tax."[48]

Table 3.3 ·· HEALTH AND SOCIAL INSURANCE TAXES AS A SHARE OF FEDERAL AND PROVINCIAL REVENUES (IN $ MILLION)

	Federal* ($)	%	Provincial** ($)	%	Total ($)	%
1975-76	2,039	6.4%	1,046	3.3%	3,085	4.6%
1986-87	9,558	11.1%	7,649	9.6%	17,207	10.4%
1996-97	19,816	14.1%	11,859	8.4%	31,675	11.2%
1999-2000	18,512	11.2%	8,273	5.4%	26,785	8.5%

*   CPP/QPP premiums and benefits not included in budgetary revenues

**   Excluding federal transfers

Sources: *The National Finances*, 1978-79; 1987-88; *Finances of the Nation*, 1997, A8-9; Public Accounts 1996-97, 3:3; Provincial budgets 2000; Canada, *Annual Financial Report*, Sept. 2000.

In response to such rulings legitimizing specific tax avoidance tactics, Finance Ministers introduce annual legislative changes to Parliament, including anti-avoidance rules. In recent years, the courts have imposed stricter limits on tax avoidance by taking into account the purpose or intent of tax laws, not only their literal wording.[49] This "purposive approach" to interpreting tax laws has been reinforced since 1987 by Parliament's approval of General Anti-Avoidance Rules (GAAR) which have vastly expanded bureaucratic discretion in the administration and enforcement of tax laws.[50]

Since the Charter of Rights came into legal effect in 1985, the federal courts have applied its provisions to tax policy primarily in matters relating to enforcement and the rights of the accused.[51] Although the courts have been somewhat reluctant to apply the equality provisions of the Charter to substantive matters of tax policy, their recent willingness to entertain such cases on issues dealing with general equality and family status suggests that a new set of constitutional issues may be introduced into the balance of economic and social interests through the tax system.

Economic Rights, Conventions, and the Constitutionalization of Interests

A major challenge in defining the theory of an economic constitution is to distinguish "constitutional" structures and processes from the ordinary competition of interests and the policy processes that characterize the day-to-day practice of politics. "Constitutional" measures transcend ordinary changes in two basic ways. One is procedural: a higher degree of public consensus is required to introduce, implement, and sustain such changes. The other is substantive: proposed changes face a widespread public perception that they are conferring or withdrawing significant rights or entitlements of citizenship.

The major difference between statutory and constitutional law is that the former may be changed at the discretion of the government of the day, subject to the approval of Parliament or legislature; changes to the latter require a substantial and ongoing shift in the consensus of major social and political actors over the distribution of power and the ideas that govern its use. This may take the form of systematic public and stakeholder consultations to develop a measure of consensus over time, the use of a plebiscite or referendum to ratify a major shift in public policy within the term of a government, or an appeal for an electoral mandate to ratify (or reject) a major policy initiative, such as the federal "Free Trade" election of 1988.

The longer a particular principle, feature, or convention of tax law remains in effect, the greater the number of taxpayers that benefit from such provisions. The greater its relative importance to the economic well-being of a cohesive, well-organized economic group, the more likely this principle or convention will be regarded as an acquired property right which secures the ability of individuals or corporations to produce revenues as a direct result of government policy or legislation.[52] Consequently, the right usually cannot be withdrawn without some form of compensation, usually in the form of lower tax rates and/or transition rules to ease taxpayers' collective burden of adjustment to the new system.

The following tests may be used to distinguish tax measures that have achieved "quasi-constitutional" status from normal, everyday legislative measures:

i) Generalized Application to Large Numbers of Taxpayers

The institutional or legal structure should be general in application, so that it has a pervasive influence on the economic decisions and status of a broad cross-section of individual or business taxpayers. Major changes to such provisions should cause economic dislocation sufficient to disrupt the political balance of power and threaten the survival of the offending Minister or government. For example, the backlash against tax reform legislation in both 1971 and 1981 was such that Prime Minister Trudeau replaced his Finance Ministers with successors willing to reverse many of their policies. Conversely, Michael Wilson acknowledged this principle during the mid-1980s when he made only relatively minor changes to general tax preferences benefiting large numbers of taxpayers while curtailing a large number of narrowly targeted tax preferences benefiting specific groups.

Examples of such generalized features of the tax system include the taxation of individual rather than family (or household) income,[53] the small business deduction for small Canadian-controlled private corporations, the capital gains exemption for owner-occupied homes, and the taxation of most capital gains upon realization rather than on an accrual basis.[54]

Finance Ministers may succeed in removing or curtailing general tax preferences providing significant benefits to large numbers of taxpayers. However, this usually requires implementation in smaller, incremental steps over a number of years or compensation through tax reductions in other areas. Examples of this approach include the elimination of the general deductions for parents of dependent children in several steps between 1987 and 1993.

ii) Broad Perception of an Economic Right among Beneficiaries

The institution or legal structure should have acquired the normative status of an "economic right" through the passage of time or long-standing legitimization through the political process. Such economic rights may be linked to the fulfilment of societal norms and responsibilities; for example, tax deductions and credits that recognize the personal responsibility, within limits, to care for one's family, save for one's retirement, or contribute to the well-being of one's community through contributions to charitable organizations. Such norms may convey either a presumed right to state assistance or to non-interference in the fulfillment of such obligations.

Other "rights" are linked to principles of natural justice: the avoidance of double taxation, protection against retroactive taxation, or the right to deduct the costs of earning income. The proliferation of such rights, whether established as formal matters of law or convention, may create serious problems in balancing competing rights and concepts of rights, such as the competing concepts of equity noted earlier.

iii) Comparable Social and Economic Status

Economic demands and interests of major social groups become institutionalized as rights within the tax system when organized interests succeed in demonstrating the validity of comparisons between related forms of economic or social activity, some of which already benefit from tax preferences. These changes may be the result of legal action or the political process.

Major examples include income tax amendments providing for equal tax treatment of married and common-law (and more recently same-sex) couples; equivalent tax treatment for employment pensions and RRSPS introduced in the 1984 budget; and comparable treatment extended to farms and small businesses. The principle of horizontal equity is often used by the courts to extend tax preferences beyond the limits originally set by Parliament. However, the same principle may be used to increase tax liabilities if the minister of finance can persuade Parliament and other interest groups that a particular group's tax privileges give it an unfair economic advantage not available to others.

A review of personal and corporate tax preferences reveals the extent to which various interests have secured entitlements to income tax exemptions, deferrals, deductions, or credits. These include special provisions for "culture and recreation, education, farming and fishing sectors, general business and investment, small business, resource sector," families and child care, private health insurance, lower-income groups, retirement savings and pensioners, aboriginal peoples, homeowners, and the recognition of the multi-year character of business and investment income and expenses.[55]

iv) Relative Economic Impact

"Constitutionalized" elements of the tax structure are sufficiently important to the economic welfare of a major segment of Canadian society to require compensation in the event of major changes. As with generalized individual tax benefits, compensation normally takes the form of offsetting tax reductions in other areas, substantial transitional provisions, or both.

Tax preferences of vital importance to small, cohesive economic groups are often preserved when tax reform deprives larger, more diverse groups of tax preferences which give them only marginal benefits. For example, cohesive sectoral interests such as charities, the insurance industry, and the oil and gas industry frequently succeed in watering down or eliminating major changes to their tax structures. Such groups are most likely to succeed when they can demonstrate a disproportionate economic burden or major competitive disadvantage from proposed changes resulting in business failures, politically significant increases in unemployment, or a large-scale shift of investment and economic activity to neighbouring jurisdictions. For example, the political backlash against the introduction of a capital gains tax in 1971 from farmers, small business owners, and investment dealers was sufficient to force Finance Minister Edgar Benson to introduce generous transition provisions and to eliminate federal estate taxes as partial compensation for the new tax.

Allan Maslove has suggested that for a comprehensive tax reform program to be politically viable, the government must demonstrate to significant majorities of most major socio-economic groups that they will be better off as a result of tax reform.[56]

v) Disproportionate Importance to Major Provincial Economies

Major changes that threaten to disrupt the economies or tax bases of provinces or regions are often subject to implicit provincial consent. Federal-provincial revenue sharing agreements have explicit provisions for a one-year revenue guarantee to cushion provincial revenues against the effects of unilateral federal changes. Provincial governments have often lobbied effectively against federal tax changes that threaten to have a disproportionate impact on major provincial industries or major income transfer programs. However, the federal government may choose to ignore provincial objections if the proposed changes are vital to its own fiscal stability.

The unilateral federal imposition of the National Energy Program in 1980, while offset to a degree by subsequent federal-provincial negotiations, prompted a long-term political backlash that led to the policy's reversal after the 1984 election. Although the federal government offered significant compensation to Atlantic Canada and other areas of chronically high unemployment for changes to the Employment Insurance program introduced in 1995-96, continuing protests from the regions most affected resulted in a partial rollback of these changes before the 2000 federal election.

vi) Mobility of Capital or Economic Activity

The mobility of goods, services, and capital gives consumers, businesses, and investors who have the capacity to transfer significant levels of economic activity to neighbouring jurisdictions the power to impose serious constraints on government policy. Individual and business taxpayers who can readily avoid taxes by transferring or converting politically-valued investment and other economic activities to less heavily-taxed jurisdictions are more likely to obtain recognition of their interests through the tax system than those with limited mobility.[57]

Canadian businesses and investors often attempt to use the threat of capital flight to fend off proposed tax increases or to obtain reductions in their tax burdens relative to Canada's major competitors. In recent years, many Canadians have shown a willingness to challenge high prices and taxes on consumer goods. Large-scale smuggling of cigarettes to evade the substantial difference between Canadian and American excise taxes prompted the federal and Quebec governments to make major reductions in their cigarette taxes in 1994, leading several other provinces to follow suit.[58] Subsequent increases in American cigarette taxes and prices have prompted Canadian governments to reverse these tax reductions.

However, the impact of foreign precedents can cut both ways. Major changes to British and American tax laws in the mid-1980s, while resulting in a general lowering of income tax rates, also resulted in significant increases in the overall tax burden on many kinds of investment income. Canada's adoption of the Goods and Services Tax between 1985 and 1990 reflects a conscious effort to remove barriers to international trade and investment while retaining the freedom to finance differences in the level of public services between Canada and its major trading partners.[59]

Conclusion

The constitutional traditions of parliamentary sovereignty and responsible government place few formal limits on governments' ability to legislate within their own jurisdictions on major issues of economic policy. However, major structural changes to framework economic legislation such as the Income or Excise Tax Acts, the Competition Act, and the Bank Act or the Bankruptcy Act affect such a wide range of public and private economic transactions that they virtually compel adherence to certain quasi-constitutional conventions.

The study of federal tax politics and policies during the past thirty years suggests that there is a process closely akin to an "amendment procedure" that Finance Ministers must observe in order to be successful in implementing major tax reforms. The most important requirement is that formal and informal consultations with tax experts and affected interests be used to test the economic, political, and administrative viability of proposed changes. These usually involve the publication of proposed changes in a White Paper and formal parliamentary hearings involving experts and major interest groups. Maslove and Eicher suggest several other necessary components of the process: a commitment not to increase overall tax levels through tax reform; the need to ensure that a majority of socio-economic groups are economic "winners"; and some form of compensation for groups that may pay significantly higher taxes as a result of structural changes to the tax system.[60] Other traditional conditions include the avoidance of retroactive changes and the provision of adequate transitional measures to facilitate economic adjustment. Failure to comply with these procedural requirements may fatally undermine parliamentary and public support for tax reform or result in its reversal by subsequent governments or Ministers of Finance.

The choice of an incremental, piecemeal approach to tax reform permits the gradual introduction of new ideas, policy objectives, and procedural changes through the normal budgetary process. This process may create both internal and external constituencies for further change. It allows potentially controversial structural changes to evolve gradually through the normal processes of policy development, brokerage politics, and administrative trial and error. Such incremental changes—for example, the gradual replacement of universal family benefits and tax deductions with a system of targeted tax credits between 1978 and 1993—are far less challenging to existing structures, processes, and interests than a large-scale constitutional change such as the introduction of a guaranteed annual income through the tax system.

The balancing of these policy objectives and the management of the tax policy process are controlled, at the federal level, by the Department of Finance. The Department and its officials are the "guardians" of both the federal tax policy process and its impact on other economic policies.

NOTES

1 Other forms of taxation, particularly residential and commercial property taxes, may perform a similar function. However, since these vary widely in rates and structures from one province to another and are not integrated with federal tax policies, they are beyond the scope of this study.

2 Brennan and Buchanan (1980); Buchanan (1991).

3 Brennan and Buchanan (1980), 4-5.

4 Dicey (1915), 21-29; Fuller (1969). For discussions of the nature and role of constitutional conventions, see Geoffrey Marshall and Graeme Moodie (1959) *Some Problems of the Constitution* (London: Hutchinson) and Heard (1991).

5 Russell (1993), 10.

6 Russell (1993), 9.

7 David M. O'Brien (1993) *Storm Centre*, 3rd ed. (New York: W.W. Norton); Edward Erler (1991) *The American Polity* (New York: Crane Russak).

8 Reg Whitaker (1983) "Democracy and the Constitution," in A. Keith Banting and Richard Simeon, eds., *And No One Cheered: Federalism, Democracy and the Constitution Act* (Toronto: Methuen), 240-60.

9 Alan C. Cairns (1990) "The Minorization of the Constitution," in David C. Leslie and Ronald Watts, eds., *Canada: The State of the Federation, 1990* (Kingston: Institute for Intergovernmental Relations); Peacock, ed. (1996).

10 Brennan and Buchanan (1980), 3.

11 James M. Buchanan, "Interests and Theories in Constitutional Choice," in Buchanan (1991), 51-64.

12 Macpherson (1978), 8.

13 Buchanan (1985), 178-85.

14 Buchanan (1980); Olson (1982); Hartle (1988a).

15 For other discussions of the "rights explosion" in political discourse, see Cairns (1990 [see n. 9 above]), Mary Ann Glendon (1991) *Rights Talk* (New York: The Free Press), and Peacock, ed. (1996).

16 Treff and Perry (1997) *Finances of the Nation, 1997* (Toronto: Canadian Tax Foundation, 1997); Canada (1997a) *Public Accounts of Canada, 1996-97*, 3.3. This includes shared jurisdiction over personal and corporate income taxes, general sales taxes, payroll taxes, and product-specific taxes on alcohol, tobacco, and gasoline.

17 Section 92A, *Constitution Act*, 1982; Marsha A. Chandler (1986) "Constitutional Change and Public Policy: The Impact of the Resource Amendment, (Section 92A)," *Canadian Journal of Political Science* XIX:1 [March], 103-26.

18 Krishna (1993), 6-7.

19 Sheppard (1986).

20 Canada, Department of Finance (2000b).

21 Perry (1989).

22 For a summary of the evolution of federal-provincial revenue sharing, see Boadway and Hobson (1993), 35-75.

23 While Ontario, Alberta, and Quebec have separate corporate income tax systems, the first two provinces have tended to parallel changes to federal corporate tax provisions.

24 Canada, Department of Finance (2000a). These changes provide provinces with the option to levy personal income tax rates on the same principle as provincial corporate income tax rates, as a percentage of the taxpayers' taxable income, not federal taxes payable.

25 For example, see Bukovetsky (1975); Doern and Toner (1985).

26 Bird and Mintz, "Introduction" to Bird and Mintz, eds. (1993), 11.

27 Statistics Canada, *Canada's Balance of International payments*, Cat. # 67-001 (annual).

28 Watson (1998).

29 Bradford (1998).

30 Stein, ed. (1988); Thirsk (1993).

31 Canada, Department of Finance (1997b), Chapter 2.

32 Michael Bliss (1987) *Northern Enterprise: Five Centuries of Canadian Business* (Toronto: McClelland and Stewart).

33 Maslove, ed. (1993); Canada, Department of Finance (1997), 145-71.

34 Corak, ed. (1998), *Government Finances and Generational Equity* (Ottawa: Industry Canada, February).

35 Provincial budgets, 2001-02.

36 Based on differential between top 20 per cent and lowest 20 per cent of family incomes. Statistics Canada (1995) "Income after tax: 1993," *The Daily* (Ottawa: Statistics Canada, June 14), 3-4.

37 Treff and Perry (1997), 3:5, 3:19.

38 Davies (1998); Wilson (1999).

39 Perry (1990), 19.

40 Bird (1970); Bukovetsky and Bird (1972); Macdonald (1985).

41 Hartle (1985).

42 Canada, Department of Finance (1996).

43 McDougall (1985); Thorburn (1985).

44 Krishna (1993), 39.

45 Ibid., 53.

46 Perry (1990), 33-39.

47 Krishna (1993), 41-47.

48 [1936] AC 1 at 19-20, 19 TC 490 at 520 (House of Lords). Krishna cites a number of legal authorities on the legal principles of tax avoidance and tax planning, along with legal doctrines that have evolved to limit abuses of these rights. Krishna (1993), Chapter 26, "Tax Avoidance."

49 Krishna (1993), 47-52. The watershed case in this regard was *Stubart Investments Ltd. vs. the Queen* [1984].

50 Krishna (1993), 1113-68; Robert D. Brown, et al. (1990), "The GAAR and Tax Practice: More Questions than Answers," in *Report of Proceedings of the Forty-First Tax Conference* (Toronto: Canadian Tax Foundation).

51 Vercheres and Bernier (1987).

52 Macpherson (1978).

53 A fairly recent exception to this principle involves the taxation of family-related tax preferences and transfers on the basis of household incomes.

54 Capital gains taxes on most assets are levied upon their sale or, for farms and small businesses, as payment is received over a limited number of years. Taxes on accrued gains would apply on the annual increase in the value of the asset, whether or not it is realized in cash.

55 Canada, Department of Finance (1993) *Personal and Corporate Income Tax Expenditures* (Ottawa: the Department, December), Table 1; Canada, Department of Finance (1998b).

56 Maslove (1988); Maslove and Eicher (1987).

57 Thirsk (1993).

58 "High taxes feed defiance of law,"
   The Globe and Mail, 26 January 1994;
   "Cigarette taxes cut," *Toronto Star*,
   9 February 1994, A10, 11.

59 Wilson (1987b), 11-18; interview, Stanley
   H. Hartt; see Chapter 12.

60 Maslove and Eicher (1987).

The Tax Policy Community:
Institutions and Processes

The tax policy process may be divided into two very different processes: internal and external. The design and implementation of tax policy and tax reform in Canada are mainly the responsibility of the tax policy community within the Department of Finance. Although it may respond to policy suggestions from outsiders, including the federal cabinet, parliamentary committees and interest groups, the Department has a virtual monopoly on federal tax policy through the budget process.

Ideas may be an important component of policy change. But policy champions such as Ministers of Finance and their senior officials are usually necessary to convert those ideas into significant changes in tax policies, or in the overall levels and distribution of taxation. Even then, they must be navigated through the often complex political and administrative processes of the federal government. Internal policy processes powerfully influence the timing, direction, and extent of major policy changes.

This chapter analyses the institutional framework for tax policy within the federal government and the internal, largely bureaucratic process of tax policy formation within the Department of Finance. It also examines the institutional constraints on the Minister of Finance in making major changes to tax policy, and the ways in which these may affect the policy process. Chapter 5 will examine the process of legitimating the Department's proposals for structural and policy change as they are translated into law, political, and public support.

Tax Policy: The Institutional Framework

Institutional analyses of tax reform and other major shifts in economic policy stress the importance of government policy-makers as independent actors in the introduction of major policy change, and of state institutions as "the organizational channels through which political actions must pass."[1] Institutions may be conceived in a number of ways: as formal legal structures—constitutions, legal precedents, and formal government organizations—or as political, legal, social, and administrative conventions: systems of rules that govern the relationships of individuals, groups, and organizations within a political or economic system.[2]

The Department of Finance dominates the formation of federal economic policies and enjoys a virtual monopoly over matters of tax policy.[3] However, these policies also reflect a political and economic context that is shaped by the interaction and competition of a number of political and bureaucratic decision-makers, not just organizations, seeking to influence and control policy priorities and choices. This process is subject to change rather more frequently than the formal structures of government, leading Hall to define institutions as "the formal rules, compliance procedures and standard operating practices that structure the relationships between individuals in various units of the polity and economy. As such, they have a more formal status than cultural norms, but one that does not necessarily derive from legal, as opposed to conventional, standing."[4]

As noted in Chapter 3, the institutions influencing tax policy and tax reform are partly economic—for example, market capitalism as a major organizing principle of the Canadian economy and Canada's integration into international capital markets—partly a function of Canada's constitutional blend of federalism and Westminster-style parliamentary institutions, especially cabinet government, and partly a system of rules and conventions devised by central agencies to coordinate the budgetary processes of the federal government and ensure their accountability to cabinet and Parliament through the Minister and Department of Finance.

THE TAX POLICY COMMUNITY WITHIN THE DEPARTMENT OF FINANCE

The formation and evaluation of Canadian tax policy is the direct concern of the Minister of Finance and his officials. David Good identifies the tax policy community within Finance as the Minister, Deputy Minister, the Assistant Deputy Minister, Tax Policy and Legislation, and a number of senior and middle managers in the Tax Policy and Federal-Provincial

Relations Branches—about 25 people in the late 1970s[5] (see Table 4.1). Since then, the institutionalization of budget and tax reform consultations has resulted in the creation of a Consultations and Communications Branch headed by an Assistant Deputy Minister, the expansion of the tax policy branch, and the enhancement of its position within the Finance hierarchy. Staff levels in the Tax Policy Branch, which averaged 120 in the early 1990s and reached almost 150 by 2000, grew by more than 60 per cent between the mid-1970s and mid-1980s and again in the late 1990s as the federal government considered different options for tax reduction and tax reform (see Table 4.2).

Good distinguishes between the tax community as a group of insiders within the Department of Finance which closely guards its monopoly control over the tax policy process, and what he calls the "attentive actors"—members of the federal cabinet, the Revenue Canada officials called upon to enforce tax laws, officials of other affected federal departments, and Members of Parliament.

> In Canada, tax policy is made in one place, the tax community. Other agents in the process, standing outside the community, influence tax policy in subtle and indirect ways.... Outsiders are taken into account before tax proposals are put forward and decisions announced. The tax community anticipates the reactions of attentive actors. Tax policy is made not through the centre bargaining with the periphery but rather by accommodating some of the outsiders' concerns within the tax decisions that it makes.[6]

This outlook is confirmed by the comments of a senior participant in the tax policy process, who notes that the Department deals with most interest groups on its own terms, testing ideas, examining the practical "real world" implications of various policy options, but maintaining firm control over the policy process: "I would not consider anybody to be particularly influential.... We talk to a lot of people. It is a serious mistake to make tax policy in a vacuum. You have to talk to everybody. When you have consulted with everybody, then you make tax policy."[7]

Although the Department regularly defers the implementation of complex tax changes, particularly as they relate to complex business transactions, to allow for technical fine-tuning, interviews with Finance officials at all levels suggest that Good's description is as true of issues within federal jurisdiction in the 1990s and early years of the twenty-first century—especially income tax legislation—as it was during the 1970s. If anything, the demands of government restructuring and deficit reduction during the 1990s, and the management of fiscal policy to balance the competing political demands for

Table 4.1 ·· THE TAX POLICY COMMUNITY
IN THE DEPARTMENT OF FINANCE

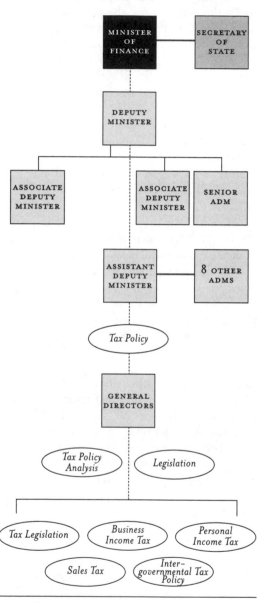

Source: Finance Canada (2000) *Structure and Role*
(Ottawa)

debt reduction, tax reduction, and new government spending have given Finance greater influence and authority over economic policy and spending priorities within the federal government than at any time since World War II. As one former senior official put it, "Finance always had control of the agenda."[9]

At the same time, senior Finance Department officials have sought to build cooperative relationships with their provincial counterparts through the Federal-Provincial Committee on Taxation, which is made up of senior tax officials from both levels of government. Since the late 1990s, federal officials have used the committee as a vehicle to solicit provincial views on needed changes to the federal tax system and to sound out their provincial counterparts on possible changes in their annual fall meetings. Senior provincial tax officials also are given advance notice of federal tax changes affecting their jurisdictions.[10] However, while this consultation process is intended to encourage greater federal-provincial cooperation, neither level of government is likely in the foreseeable future to sacrifice the autonomy necessary for joint decision-making in tax policy .

The "attentive actors" of the broader tax policy community also include taxation interest groups heavily weighted toward the business community, selected

Table 4.2 •• TAX POLICY AND LEGISLATION BRANCH STAFF LEVELS[8]

Fiscal Year	Number of Staff	Fiscal Year	Number of Staff
1983–84	95	1991–92	122
1984–85	107	1992–93	120
1985–86	113	1993–94	122
1986–87	102	1994–95	123
1987–88	111	1995–96	116
1988–89	130	1996–97	114
1989–90	127	1997–98	127*
1990–91	117	1998–99	134*
		1999–2000	149*

* Full-time equivalents (rounded); actual staff levels vary slightly.

Sources: Dept. of Finance, *Estimates, Part III* (Ottawa, 1983-84 - 1998-99); Financial Services Branch, Department of Finance.

academic specialists, and tax professionals. The latter's views are often moderated through professional associations such as the Canadian Institute of Chartered Associations, the Canadian Bar Association, and the Canadian Tax Foundation.[11] During the 1980s, the federal cabinet played an active role in considering strategic issues of policy change. Although the details of income tax reform in 1981-82 and 1987-88 were primarily the responsibility of the Minister of Finance and his officials, a Special Cabinet Committee on the Goods and Services Tax was struck to provide direct political oversight of this highly charged issue.[12] The Chrétien Government struck a special cabinet committee on program review, largely driven by the Minister of Finance and his officials, to evaluate proposed spending reductions during the fiscal crisis of 1994-95.[13] Before the 1999 Throne Speech, which defined the Chrétien government's priorities during the second half of its term, Finance coordinated a committee of senior officials from economic and social policy ministries to discuss the relationship of tax policies to the federal government's overall agenda in the medium term.[14]

Although the policy process has become more transparent and consultative in recent years, with department officials making public a much greater range of economic data to encourage policy proposals based on shared economic assumptions,[15] an understanding of the tax policy community must still begin with key actors within the Department of Finance.

THE ROLE OF THE TAX POLICY BRANCH

> ... undertakes analysis of and makes recommendations relating to tax policy, and is responsible for maintaining a tax system which raises revenue in a fair and efficient fashion and effectively targets incentives to meet governmental goals; seeks to develop tax policies consistent with the government's objectives in other areas: social, cultural, economic, political, regional and inter-governmental; and develops legislation and regulations necessary to implement federal tax measures.
>
> *Department of Finance 1997-98 Estimates*

The Tax Policy Branch (formerly Tax Policy and Legislation) of the Department of Finance is the professional heart of the tax policy community. Since the 1970s, the Branch has been divided into staff and line functions, with increasing degrees of specialization. Separate divisions for Personal Income Tax, Business Income Tax, and Sales Tax (formerly Commodity Tax) are responsible for assessing the economic impact of existing policies and proposed changes to tax laws through the budget process. The Intergovernmental Tax Policy Group is responsible for advising the Minister on proposed changes to provincial tax laws requiring federal action and on tax issues related to First Nations' emerging institutions of self-government. The Tax Legislation Division is responsible for the specific wording of legislative changes, adapting and responding to changes in the legal environment, and adapting policy decisions into the precise legal language of statute law, in cooperation with the Tax Counsel Division and the Department of Justice.[16]

The Assistant Deputy Minister and the two General Directors periodically set up task forces or project groups to examine specific policy areas. Each division is subdivided into a number of specialized sections dealing with individual elements of the tax structure.

The Tax Policy Branch is managed by two General Directors, one responsible for the legislative, the other, the tax policy aspects of budgetary changes. These positions have traditionally been filled by career Finance Department officials, often for long periods. For example, Alan Short was General Director, Tax Policy from the mid-1960s until 1993. The General Directors and directors of individual branches are responsible for identifying major technical and policy problems within the tax system, filtering proposals for change into budgetary and technical streams, screening out proposals which may be technically flawed or economically ill-advised, and advising the Assistant Deputy Minister (and often, the Minister), on the structuring of budgetary proposals.

The Tax Policy Branch is part of a self-conscious professional elite within the Department and the profession, cultivating an ethic of public service and "guardianship" over the tax base and the integrity of the tax system.[7] One official comments, "it's a bit like the US and the rest of the world.... We've got the power and they [other departments] have to deal with that."[18] The Tax Policy Branch maintains close relations with senior members of the legal, accounting, and economics professions, although relatively few outsiders develop relations of close mutual trust and professional respect with the career professionals who dominate the management ranks of the Branch.[19]

ATTITUDES TOWARD TAX POLICY

"One of the most important norms that tax policy officers learn is that their job is to defend the tax system against forces that would erode its legitimacy and its revenue base."[20]

Interviews with current and former officials of the Department suggest that a relatively stable consensus has emerged regarding the character of Canada's tax system and its capacity to generate needed government revenues to accommodate the government's economic and social policy objectives. One senior observer comments that "there is much less divergence within the group [the broader tax policy community] than within the Canadian people as a whole." Another suggests that "there seems to be a fairly uniform consensus on what tax policy should be within the department."[21]

This consensus tends to reflect what one former Deputy Minister describes as a "pragmatic" view of tax policy that attempts to reconcile the political priorities of the government with the constraints of economic and administrative viability. In this view, ministers and governments are elected to govern and to set the priorities and objectives for public policies. It is the function of civil servants to advise ministers of the likely consequences of proposed policies, to devise the means of balancing competing objectives and, once decisions are made, to attempt to maximize the benefits and minimize the disruptions resulting from policy decisions made by ministers and the Department's senior management.[22]

The "pragmatists" tend to assess tax preferences according to their relative efficiency in achieving a range of policy goals, and the likelihood of potential abuse, revenue losses, or economic disruption. Proposals for tax reform tend to be judged in terms of their administrative and economic viability and the difficulties involved in achieving a transition to the new system, rather than by reference to an abstract ideal. At the same time, the current tax consensus, drawing on ongoing economic research into the effects of taxation on work incentives and economic efficiency, tends to favour more generalized tax preferences intended to achieve particular economic objectives over narrowly targeted ones, which may have the effect of substituting bureaucratic discretion for generalized market rules.

This consensus stands in sharp contrast to the divisions within the tax policy community during most of the 1980s over the extent to which the tax system could or should be used as an effective instrument of economic and social policy. Interviews with current and former officials of the Department strongly suggested the existence of debate and conflict between the "pragmatists" and what some described as "purists" who were committed to the classical public finance view of the tax system and to the systematic reduction of tax preferences and tax expenditures as an extension of this outlook.

A former Deputy Minister labels the latter group the "golden truthers."[23] Initially dominated by economists schooled in the traditions of the Carter Commission, most were intellectually and ideologically committed to a systematic application of the tax expenditure concept, to resisting the addition of new tax preferences to the tax structure, and to removing as many existing preferences as possible as illegitimate intrusions into the public domain. Some sought to use their influence and expertise to promote large-scale economic and social change through fundamental changes to the tax structure, regardless of the potential for short-term economic disruption in the transition to a fairer tax system. Others were incrementalists, attempting to apply Carter's principles of equity to individual segments of the tax structure as circumstances permitted. A third group within the Department, the "technicians," focuses primarily on issues of policy implementation rather than on ideological debate.

Good comments that "the tax officer is the victim of conflicting norms and must play conflicting roles," on the one hand, protecting the integrity of the tax system, and serving the Minister's broader policy and political needs on the other.[24] In effect, an ongoing tension exists and is necessary between the political and technical requirements of tax policy, between theoretical concepts of "good tax policy" and "what is practical" in terms of its political and economic impact.[25] Ultimately, the role of the Department's senior management is to referee these debates, to strike a balance among the competing views of tax policy, and to reconcile the demands of sound tax and economic policies with the government's broader political objectives.

THE ROLE OF THE ASSISTANT DEPUTY MINISTER

The Assistant Deputy Minister (ADM)-Tax Policy provides overall direction for the development of tax policy. He is responsible for coordinating and shaping budgetary proposals for consideration by the Department's senior management and the Minister, setting priorities for the Branch, and for managing major problems that have arisen within the tax system.[26] The ADM-Tax Policy may champion ideas for piecemeal structural change and promote them through the policy process. Although decisions to initiate major changes to the tax system are the Minister's prerogative, the ADM-Tax Policy is responsible for developing and implementing the reform proposals and for providing the detailed economic and technical justification necessary to support the Minister's proposals before Parliament.

Unlike most other managers in the Branch, who tend to be career Finance Department professionals, tax policy ADMs are sometimes tax policy experts drawn from outside the Department. Marshall ("Mickey") Cohen (ADM, 1972-77; Deputy Minister, 1982-85) was a senior tax lawyer before joining Finance in 1970. Glenn Jenkins (ADM, 1981-84) was a leading tax economist at Harvard. David Weyman (ADM, 1984-86) and Kevin Dancey (ADM, 1993-96) were senior partners with leading accounting firms. In recent years, however, tax policy ADMs have typically been recruited from within the Department. Three of the four most recent ADMs, David Dodge (ADM, 1986-92; Deputy Minister, 1992-97), Don Drummond (ADM, 1996-98) and Munir Sheikh (ADM 1998-2001), have been economists and career Finance Department officials. All three previously served in the fiscal policy branch before taking responsibility for tax policy. This has contributed to a high degree of continuity in policy and intellectual outlook on economic and tax policies since the mid-1980s.[27]

Assistant Deputy Ministers may be policy entrepreneurs, aggressively promoting their own policy ideas to the Deputy Minister and the Minister, or consensus-builders, seeking to shape a corporate view of "good tax policy" consistent with the most current economic policy research. The ADM's background and outlook is often vital in shaping the "tax policy culture"—the ideas, values, and objectives that will be promoted and downgraded in budgetary suggestions to the Minister.[28] Cohen, in particular, was known for his activist approach to the use of tax policy as a tool of economic and social policy. Jenkins, who helped to design the largely abortive 1981 tax reform budget, leaned strongly in the other direction, seeking to protect the tax base and promote a more rigorous approach to "neutrality" in taxation. David Dodge, who managed both the government's Income Tax and Sales Tax reform projects between 1987 and 1991, helped to shape the tax policy consensus of the 1990s as a pragmatic mixture of the two approaches, pursuing greater neutrality in business taxation while expanding the use of the personal income tax system as a vehicle for integrating the government's economic and social policies within a coherent policy framework.[29] Recent ADMs, recognizing the constraints imposed by the government's fiscal framework, have emphasized the need to focus policy changes on areas in which marginal tax rates create significant distortions in individual and business behaviour or are uncompetitive with those of Canada's major trading partners.[30]

THE ROLE OF THE DEPUTY MINISTER

The Deputy Minister is the Chief Operating Officer of the Department. He is responsible for coordinating the wide range of fiscal and economic policy issues facing the government and advising the Minister on how to balance the competing political and policy demands of his position. In addition to the formulation of tax policy, the Department of Finance's responsibilities include the coordination of fiscal and budgetary policy, negotiations with other federal departments on policy issues with major tax or spending implications; monetary, exchange rate, and other international economic policies (in cooperation with the Bank of Canada); federal-provincial fiscal relations; the negotiation of tax treaties with other countries; and the regulation of banking and financial institutions. Douglas Hartle comments that "the very character of the Department as a whole may depend on the Deputy Minister."[31] Indeed, Finance's growing influence and scope during the 1990s as the dominant economic policy ministry of the federal government has created an additional layer of management, since recent Deputies have delegated significant responsibility for particular files to two Associate Deputy Ministers with broad management experience within the Department, particularly when they involve issues that cut across the jurisdictions of different Finance Department branches or other federal ministries.[32] The degree to which Deputy Ministers delegate responsibility for budget coordination or the management of major issues is a function of their management styles. Some Finance Deputies, like Marshall Cohen in the 1980s and David Dodge in the 1990s, play a strongly hands-on role in the policy process. Others are more strategic in their involvement, delegating broad responsibilities to Associate Deputy Ministers and other senior officials.[33]

The Deputy Minister's appointment is a political statement. Deputy Ministers are chosen by the Prime Minister and are accountable not only to their own ministers, but also to the Prime Minister through the Clerk of the Privy Council. In recent years, Finance Deputies usually have been drawn from the senior ranks of the Department, although Trudeau, Clark, and Mulroney all appointed outsiders, sometimes from the ranks of the Privy Council Office, sometimes from outside government, to ensure greater consistency with their priorities.[34]

The Deputy's role in tax policy is to "balance the demands of good tax policy with the political necessities of the day."[35] Deputies' participation in the details of tax policy depends on their personal background, inclinations, and the salience of tax issues to the government's political standing.[36] The comparatively long tenure of David Dodge as Deputy Minister of Finance under both Conservative and Liberal governments between 1992 and 1997, followed by his "protégés" Scott Clark and Kevin Lynch during the Chrétien government's second term, was a major factor in giving Canada's tax system a rare degree of continuity and stability during the 1990s.[37] Associate Deputy Minister Don Drummond, who coordinated the preparation of the 1999 and 2000 budgets, had previously headed branches responsible for Economic and Fiscal and Tax Policies.

THE ROLE OF THE MINISTER

The Minister of Finance is the bridge between the internal policy processes of the Department of Finance and, by extension, of the federal cabinet and government, and the external (or public) policy process by which the federal government seeks to define its political agenda, "sell" it to the Canadian public, and adapt it in response to interest group pressures and public opinion. This requires a juggling of political and policy considerations, "balancing aspirations and reality [and] reconciling infinite wants and needs."[38]

The Minister of Finance largely directs the federal government's economic agenda through his responsibility for preparing, presenting, and promoting the federal budget. In recent years, the Minister has also reasserted Finance's traditional role as the federal government's chief economic policy ministry, using the budgetary process to coordinate economic, social, and budgetary policies and to increase the government's political and fiscal discretion in responding to a variety of political and policy demands. Without this kind of centralized control, exercised in close cooperation with the Prime Minister and his senior advisors, it is unlikely that the federal government would have been able to eliminate its chronic deficits, balance its budgets, and pursue a relatively coherent set of economic and social policies.

The power of the Minister and Department of Finance in setting and enforcing policy and budgetary priorities has fluctuated significantly during the past thirty years, depending on the policy priorities of the Prime Minister and his senior advisors, their willingness to delegate responsibility for setting budgetary priorities to their Finance Minister, and the Minister's political skills in maintaining Prime Ministerial support and political credibility both in financial markets and with the general public.

While he controls virtually all tax policy decisions included in the budget and subsequent tax legislation,[39] the Finance Minister's influence and independence in directing federal fiscal and economic policies depend largely on his relationship with the Prime Minister and his ability to maintain the latter's support against the competing claims of cabinet colleagues. As a former ministerial aide from the Mulroney era put it, "the Finance Minister has 38 natural enemies in cabinet. The prime directive is to maintain a close relationship with the Prime Minister.... Every minister has a natural relationship with the Prime Minister and will use it to protect his own turf."[40]

The power of the Finance Minister also depends on the Prime Minister's interest in economic policy issues and his leadership style, particularly in managing competition among cabinet colleagues. Prime Minister Trudeau's direct involvement with economic issues was intermittent. He usually left their management to trusted senior ministers, particularly Allan MacEachen (until the 1981 budget backlash) and Marc Lalonde.[41]

Brian Mulroney was much more involved in the brokerage of policy decisions, especially between 1984 and 1986. Herman Bakvis has described Mulroney's early leadership style as "transactional," lending itself to policy deals with individual ministers, often with little regard for the cabinet hierarchy or the fiscal framework. Mulroney's management style forced a much closer liaison between the Minister of Finance and the Prime Minister on budgetary and tax issues in order to limit the political conflict that surfaced soon after his election.[42] Mulroney would often communicate directly with Deputy Ministers of Finance on current issues, bypassing formal communications channels.[43]

Prime Minister Chrétien, the only former Finance Minister in modern Canadian history to be elected Prime Minister, worked very closely with his Finance Minister, Paul Martin, in imposing unprecedented fiscal discipline on his cabinet colleagues during his first two terms in office, although this relationship cooled noticeably after 1998.[44] A long-time Liberal strategist comments:

> In all my years in Ottawa, I don't think you've ever seen as close a relationship and as much support between the Prime Minister and the Minister of Finance. It goes back to August 1978 when the Prime Minister was Minister of Finance. It is his view that there must not be any light between himself and the Minister of Finance. It doesn't mean they always agree. They debate on substance. But at the end of each meeting, there is consensus.[45]

Savoie suggests that Chrétien's decision to eliminate the Priorities and Planning Committee—the so-called "inner cabinet" of previous governments—in 1993, along with his tendency to delegate extensive responsibility to senior ministers, enabled Finance to regain the power over government spending it had exercised before the 1970s, as well as the revenue side of the budget process.[46] The ability to control overall spending levels and to build in various budgetary "cushions" which shifted control over discretionary spending from cabinet to the Finance Department gave Martin the power to reduce overall tax levels without resorting to deficit financing for the first time since the late 1960s.[47]

The Minister's political and communications skills and his capacity to develop an independent political base within the government party are also vital factors in his ability to wield a measure of independent political power in setting the government's policy agenda. This involves the capacity to manage the internal levers of political power, to maintain a strong core of supporters within the government's parliamentary caucus, and to develop a credible public image with the media, the electorate as a whole, and the financial community, which tends to view the Finance Minister as "its" representative within the federal cabinet.

Marc Lalonde, as Trudeau's former Principal Secretary and undisputed head of the Liberal Party organization in Quebec, wielded enormous power over the government's overall party agenda as Finance Minister. Paul Martin, while capitalizing on the budgetary crisis of the mid-1990s to assert his control over the government's agenda, succeeded in maintaining his control over the budgetary process and winning policy battles with cabinet and caucus colleagues long after he succeeded in balancing the budget.[48] By contrast, despite Michael Wilson's long tenure as Minister of Finance and his widespread support in the business community, he was able only rarely, in the absence of an independent political base, to dominate the government's policy agenda.

Finance Ministers' approaches to tax policy vary widely, depending on the political priorities of the government, the Minister's background and ideological outlook, his political experience, management style, and relations with department officials. As the political head of the Department, the Minister is expected to set strategic directions for policy. Some ministers, most notably Paul Martin and Michael Wilson, have taken a hands-on approach, becoming directly involved in the discussion and development of policies. Others, like Marc Lalonde, have set clear political objectives for policy and left the details to Department management and staff. Still others, most notably Allan MacEachen, have been relatively remote (or even hands-off).[49]

However, the Minister's role is not limited to setting policy priorities or to balancing the political and economic trade-offs inherent in the budgetary process. It also involves the framing of public expectations, the selling of the government's main policy goals, the balancing of competing interests, and the building of public support for the government's fiscal and tax policies. (This process will be discussed in Chapter 5.)

Managing Change in Tax Policy: Processes and Constraints

Finance Ministers seeking to restructure the tax system or make major changes to levels of taxation have a number of options. They can introduce proposed changes within the framework of a single budget, or signal proposed changes to the public and interest groups through the publication of a White Paper, followed by extended public and/or private consultations and, ultimately, legislation. In recent years, Finance Minister Paul Martin has used his annual fall "Economic Update" to signal the government's financial expectations and policy priorities within a two- to five-year fiscal framework, while introducing policy changes through annual budgets with two-year fiscal projections to maintain a measure of policy discretion.

Maslove, Prince, and Doern note that federal budgets are major goal-setting and tactical occasions for the federal government, allowing them to showcase their fiscal and economic priorities and their skill in dealing with economic issues.[50] The adversarial culture of Parliamentary debate also gives opposition parties and interest groups with a high profile opportunities to attack (or more rarely, to applaud) the government's priorities and actions.

The budgetary approach to tax reforms allows the government to take advantage of the tradition of budget secrecy to seize the political initiative before interest groups can mobilize to defend their interests. However, this approach to complex tax changes has largely fallen into disuse as a politically high-risk strategy that reduces the government's ability to cultivate public opinion and to adapt proposals in response to public comment and the technical advice of tax professionals. Budgetary approaches are usually most practical when introducing piecemeal changes to tax reform. These may be politically popular measures, such as the re-indexation of income tax brackets and credits to inflation or the overall tax reduction strategy outlined in the February and October 2000 budgets, or more controversial measures involving a limited range of societal actors, such as the National Energy Program of 1980.

Allan Maslove has argued that the Canadian government's ability to introduce tax reform is directly linked to its ability to build distributive coalitions of economic winners, and to mollify potential losers through a combination of financial compensation for lost tax breaks and transitional measures to ease the difficulties of adjusting to a new tax structure.[51] The consultative approach offers the opportunity to test market ideas in greater detail, discard those found to be politically or administratively unworkable, and provide stakeholders in the tax system with the chance to buy into a consensus on proposed policy changes.[52] It lends itself to coalition-building and the co-opting of major interests into the policy process. However, it also exposes the government to the risk of losing control of the policy process. The political assault mounted by the business community and the provinces on the White Paper on Tax Reform in 1971, and the generally antagonistic relationship between the Trudeau Government and these groups in 1981 argued strongly for Finance Minister MacEachen to introduce tax reform through the budget process.[53] While the consultative approach enables the government to demonstrate its responsiveness to public concerns, as in the case of Paul Martin's withdrawal of the proposed Seniors' Benefit in the late 1990s, it may also backfire politically if the government persists in forcing through major changes in the face of widespread public opposition, as it did with the introduction of the Goods and Services Tax in 1989-90.

Both the budget and consultative processes take place within a broader framework of institutional constraints that lend themselves to incremental changes in the tax structure rather than a comprehensive restructuring of the tax system.

INSTITUTIONAL AND POLITICAL CONSTRAINTS

As noted in Chapter 3, a purposeful, piecemeal approach to incremental tax reforms (or restructuring) over a number of years is likely to be more effective and durable than a comprehensive effort at system-wide reform involving the full range of personal, corporate, capital, excise, estate, and social security taxes.

Richard Bird suggests a number of practical constraints on the government's capacity to introduce large-scale policy changes at one time. These include limits on the staff resources needed to ensure the technical benefits of change in several areas simultaneously and the need to avoid "collective political indigestion" among interest groups and taxpayers with too many changes to absorb in a short time.[54] The greater the degree of proposed change, the greater the political wisdom of phased introduction in several stages, with provisions for widespread public consultation, the development of transitional measures to reduce avoidable disruption, and the use of policy trade-offs to compensate "losers" and ease the political and economic pain of adjustment.[55]

Three other structural constraints help define the "limits of the possible" for tax reform in Canada: the political requirement for revenue neutrality (or, since the emergence of regular budget surpluses, a "balanced" program of tax reduction, debt reduction, and selective spending increases); the demands of international competitiveness, especially in comparison to the United States; and respect for provincial sovereignty.

The principle of revenue neutrality in tax reform implicitly recognizes that the state is engaged in an adversarial relationship with taxpayers. From the perspective of the taxpayer whose income, assets, or status relative to others are potentially threatened by new or higher taxes, "all taxes are bad taxes."[56] Most federal and provincial governments evaluating in recent years the prospects for a "fiscal dividend" and lower taxes, following the elimination of years of deficit financing, have gone to considerable lengths to ensure that lower- and middle-income earners receive a disproportionate share of the benefits of tax relief, in order to maintain the political support of groups accustomed to the benefits of public spending financed largely by other people's taxes.[57]

The principle of international competitiveness in tax policy—at least with respect to business taxation—is enforced by Canada's dependence for its prosperity, as an open economy, on international trade and investment. Wayne Thirsk has suggested that specific issues of tax competitiveness are largely issues of the relative mobility of capital (for business taxation), of consumers (for commodity taxes), and of labour (for income and social insurance taxes).[58] However, the implications are most significant for business taxation, particularly for those industries most directly exposed to international competition. The central role of multinational corporations in Canadian manufacturing and resource industries and the competitive pressure of marginal and effective US tax rates on the Canadian tax system have made it difficult for the federal government to introduce principles of taxation that place Canadian companies at a competitive disadvantage relative to their US counterparts. This reality has surfaced in several ways over the years. Most recently, the growing integration of service-sector firms into global markets has prompted the decision of the federal, Ontario, and Alberta governments to phase in major tax reductions for service industries in order to approximate or undercut effective rates in the United States and to match Canadian tax rates for manufacturing and resource industries.[59]

Provincial governments, especially those of Ontario and Quebec, have strongly resisted any federal intrusion into provincial jurisdiction and revenue shares in direct taxation and revenue resources. They have also led political counter-attacks against federal tax measures that threaten the economic well-being of important provincial industries.[60] More recently, the Ontario government has attacked the federal government over its alleged reluctance to accommodate the use of provincial tax systems to deliver a variety of economic and social policy initiatives, as well as over the timeliness of federal payment of taxes collected for the provinces.[61] The shift in 2000-01 of provincial tax systems from calculating their personal income tax rates as a percentage of the federal taxes payable to separate and distinct provincial tax rate structures was intended, at least in part, to give the federal government greater flexibility in reducing its own tax rates without triggering offsetting provincial tax increases such as those that followed the federal tax reforms of 1987-88.

Table 4.3 ·· BACKGROUNDS OF DEPUTY MINISTERS OF FINANCE: 1970-2000

Prime Minister	Deputy Minister	Tenure as Deputy	PREVIOUS EXPERIENCE			
			in Finance	D.M. of Other Dept.	in PCO	Outside Gov't
TRUDEAU	Simon Reisman	1970-75	YES	YES	NO	NO
	Thomas Shoyama	1975-78	YES	YES	YES	NO
	William Hood	1978-79	YES	NO	NO	NO
CLARK	Grant Reuber	1979-80	Economist / Banker			YES
TRUDEAU	Ian Stewart	1980-82	NO	YES	YES	NO
	Marshall Cohen	1982-85	YES*	YES	NO	NO**
MULRONEY	Stanley Hartt	1985-88	LAWYER	NO	YES	YES
	Fred Gorbet	1988-92	YES	NO	YES	NO
	David Dodge	1992-97	YES*	NO	NO	NO
CHRÉTIEN	Scott Clark	1997-2000	YES	NO	NO	NO
	Kevin Lynch	2000 -	YES	YES	NO	NO

*   Former ADM–Tax Policy, Department of Finance

**   Tax Lawyer in Private Practice before 1970

The cumulative impact of these constraints is to increase the potential political costs of major changes to federal tax policies, especially when they result in increased taxation for particular segments of society. Although federal Ministers of Finance have considerable power in pursuing their policy objectives, particularly during periods of majority government, their ongoing political effectiveness depends on their ability to mobilize widespread political support for their policies from engaged interest groups and in the court of public opinion.

Conclusion

In a narrow sense, the tax policy process is controlled by the Minister and Department of Finance. However, their autonomy in making major changes to tax policies, the tax structure, or overall levels of taxation is limited by a series of constraints imposed by both the political and economic constitutions: Prime Ministerial and cabinet government, the parliamentary system, fiscal federalism, and, since 1982, the legal guarantees of the Charter, domestic entitlements, and the international economic system.

Thus, the process of managing structural policy change involves not only the formal institutional powers of ministers and governments, but also the "external" tax policy process: the mobilization of support and consent among attentive actors among the tax professions and members of advocacy groups who make up the broader policy community, as well as the general public.

NOTES

1 Steinmo (1989), 501; Nordlinger (1981); Hall, ed. (1989); Peters (1991).

2 Steinmo (1989), 502.

3 Doern (1985), 1-109; Gillespie (1991); interview, Dept. of Finance (ADM-11).

4 Hall (1986), 23.

5 Good (1980), 45-78.

6 Ibid., 79.

7 Interview, senior Finance Department official (ADM-11).

8 Since these figures include support staff, they are not directly comparable to Good's measurement of the tax community.

9 Interview, former senior tax policy official (FO3).

10 Interview, senior Finance Department official (ADM-12).

11 Good (1980), 79-97.

12 Interviews, former cabinet ministers, deputy ministers, and PMO/PCO officials.

13 Greenspon and Wilson-Smith (1998).

14 Canada, Privy Council Office (1999a); interview, Department of Finance (F12).

15 Interview, senior Finance Department official (ADM-12).

16 Canada, Department of Finance. On internet at: www.fin.gc.ca/toce/1998/sr-e.html

17 Interviews, current and former Department officials (ADM-1, FO1, FO3, FO4, FO5); Good (1980), 50. Savoie (1990) developed the concepts of "guardians" and "spenders" in *The Politics of Public Spending in Canada*.

18 Freeman (1992).

19 Interviews (ADM-11, FO1, FO5, P6).

20 Good (1980), 50.

21 Interview, senior tax policy advisor, Department of Finance, (P6); senior Finance Department official (ADM-11, ADM-12).

22 Interviews (D5, ADM-3, FO7). One former Deputy Minister puts it more bluntly: "Our role as officials was to devise and execute what the government of the day wanted to do" (D5).

23 Interview, former Deputy Minister (D5). Another senior official concurred, with the comment that some of these officials "had an almost moral-religious view of the good tax system" (ADM-3).

24 Good (1980), 55.

25 Interview, former Assistant Deputy Minister (ADM-3).

26 Good (1980), 62-65; interviews, Department of Finance (ADM-11).

27 Interview, Department of Finance (ADM-12, F11).

28 Good (1980), 62-63; supported by comments of present and former tax policy officials interviewed (ADM-3, FO3, FO4).

29 Interviews, Department of Finance (ADM-11).

30 Interviews, Department of Finance (ADM-11, F12).

31 Hartle (1982), 37.

32 Interview, Department of Finance (ADM-12, F11).

33 Interview, senior Finance Department official (ADM-12).

34 Interviews, former PMO officials (PMO-1, PMO-2). Although Chrétien's appointment in March 2000 of Kevin Lynch, a former Deputy Minister of Industry and senior Finance official, as Deputy Finance Minister prompted some public comment, it has not resulted in significant policy changes.

35 Interview, former Deputy Minister (D5).

36 Hartle (1982), 37. Interviews, former Finance Department officials (D1, D2, D4, D5, D8, ADM-3, FO2, FO5).

37 Interview, senior official, Department of Finance (ADM-11).

38 Long-time federal Deputy Minister Arthur Kroeger, quoted in Savoie (1999), 157.

39 There are three exceptions to this rule: first, the Prime Minister may pre-empt his Finance Minister, publicly, as was the case with Prime Minister Trudeau's August 1978 surprise announcement of tax and spending changes and Prime Minister Mulroney's public endorsement of the minimum personal income tax in 1984, or privately, as was the case with Mulroney's prior insistence on revisions to the 1985 budget and Prime Minister Chrétien's refusal to accept proposals for a reduction in federal seniors' benefits as part of the landmark deficit reduction budget of 1995. [Chrétien (1994), 117-18; interview, senior PMO official (PMO-1); Savoie (1999), 187.]

40 Interview, Department of Finance (FO2).

41 Interview, senior PMO official (PMO-3). For discussion of Trudeau's approach to tax reform and economic policy, see John N. McDougall (1993), *The Politics and Economics of Eric Kierans: A Man for All Canadas* (Montreal-Kingston: McGill-Queen's University Press), 106-16; McCall-Newman (1980); McCall-Newman and Clarkson (1994); and Johnston (1986).

42 Interviews, former PMO, PCO, Finance officials (PMO-1, D7, FO2). After 1986, much of the management of cabinet business was delegated to Don Mazankowski as Deputy Prime Minister and chair of its Operations Committee. The result was more centralized control of the budgetary process, particularly on issues on which "Maz's" and Finance Minister Wilson's views coincided. Bakvis (1991), 262-64; interviews, Hon. Michael Wilson, former PMO officials (PMO-1).

43 Interview, senior Finance Department official (ADM-12).

44 Interview, senior Finance Department official (ADM-12).

45 Interview, senior PMO advisor (PMO-11). See also Savoie (1999), 156. However, by mid-2000, amid continuing press reports of Martin loyalists pressing for Chrétien's retirement and Chrétien's semi-public criticisms of his minister, senior officials described the relationship between the two men as "virtually nonexistent."

46 Savoie (1999), 170.

47 For a discussion of Martin's budgeting practices, see Hale (2000a).

48 See Greenspon and Wilson-Smith (1998) for a first-rate analysis of budgetary politics during the Chrétien government's first term. More recently, Martin's ability to enforce his tax reduction agenda despite serious internal pressures for massive spending increases indicated his skill in using the available levers of power [Hale (2000a)].

49 Interviews, former Ministers of Finance, Finance Department officials (M3, ADM-3, ADM-11, ADM-12, F1, FO2, FO3).

50 Maslove, Prince, and Doern (1986), Chapter 2.

51 Maslove (1989).

52 Gillespie (1983); interviews, Department of Finance (ADM-11, F11).

53 Gillespie, (1983); Bukovetsky and Bird
(1972), Milne (1986), 36ff.

54 Bird (1970), 454-55.

55 Gillespie (1983), 193-97.

56 Hartle (1988a), 35-45; Robertson (1988),
49.

57 Hale (2000a, 2000b).

58 Thirsk (1993).

59 Dodge (1989), 37; Canada, Department
of Finance (2000b); Ontario (2000)
Ontario Budget 2000 (Toronto: Ministry
of Finance, May 2).

60 The most notable examples include
Ontario's defence of its mining industry
during the tax reform debate of 1971, and
the efforts of western energy-producing
provinces to revise the National Energy
Program after 1980. A.R.A. Scace (1970)
"Ontario Proposals for Tax Reform,"
Canadian Tax Journal 18(4) [July-
August], 310-18; Doern and Toner
(1985).

61 Courchene (1999). For the federal
government's rebuttal, see Canada,
Department of Finance (2000a).

The Public Tax Policy Process:
Agenda-Setting, Interest Groups, and Public Opinion

> The structure of taxes is created by the process of a very political marketplace, where groups of politicians compete against each other for the votes of the electorate which will bestow the prize of political power.
>
> *Irwin Gillespie*[1]

The Minister and Department of Finance may control the details of tax policy. But the overall level of taxation and the distribution of taxes among various groups of Canadians and different kinds of economic activity are very much the product of a political process.

Every government attempts to balance the challenge of designing effective economic policies to promote growth and employment with the expectations of its constituents for public services and the protection or improvement of their standards of living, along with other social and economic objectives. In Canada's parliamentary system, the annual budget speech provides a vehicle for Ministers of Finance to demonstrate economic "leadership"—or at least an agenda capable of demonstrating a capacity to address the economic challenges facing Canadians and of promoting their economic well-being and "quality of life."[2]

However, the budget speech is only the culmination of a year-round process. This process involves the balancing of competing interests within governments, the juggling of competing groups of voters and related interest groups and their agendas, and the mobilization of consent for government policies through various consultation processes and efforts at media and news management. These processes, likened earlier to a four-ring circus, are separate but interrelated. The ability of governments to manage their policy agendas depends increasingly on their ability to integrate the processes of policy development with the communication of those agendas, while conveying the perception that they are listening and responding to the concerns and interests of an increasingly fragmented electorate.[3]

The success of governments' efforts in recent years to regain control of their fiscal and economic agendas has largely depended on their ability to gain and hold the political initiative in the face of competing and often contradictory demands from interest groups and politically engaged citizens. As a result, they have attempted to develop strategic economic plans that enable them to withstand competing interest group pressures and to coordinate fiscal, economic, and social policies in a reasonably coherent manner. These plans are partly a means of managing public opinion and partly a means of allowing governments to respond to its general direction. The ability to mobilize broad, if superficial, public support for these plans has become a key factor in enabling Finance Ministers to impose priorities on their cabinet colleagues and to manage interest group pressures within the boundaries established by their fiscal frameworks.

Such "plans" may be outlined in an election platform, such as the federal Liberals' "Red Book 11" in 1997 which promised a "50-50" division of projected surpluses between new spending on one side, and a combination of debt repayment and tax reduction on the other. Sitting governments may resort to a White Paper or a broad statement of economic priorities, such as Paul Martin's so-called "Purple Book"[4] of 1994, which largely defined the federal government's subsequent deficit reduction plan and economic strategy. Alternatively, they may use a pre-election budget to spell out such a strategy, such as Martin's February and October 2000 budgets which spelled out a five-year plan for tax reductions and increased social spending, much of it to be delivered through the tax system. A number of provincial governments have pursued similar approaches, with intermittent success. Most notable of these were the Ontario Conservative government's *Common Sense Revolution* platform of 1995 and its 1999 pre-election budget, both of which outlined detailed tax and other policy commitments.

The political success of major changes to tax rates and the tax structure has largely depended on the ability of Ministers of Finance (and their departments) to market them as "positive-sum games" yielding economic benefits or minimal costs to most major economic and social groups. While such tax reforms or restructurings may contribute to a small-scale redistribution of incomes, such a process effectively precludes the use of tax reforms as an instrument for raising taxes, reducing deficits, or redistributing income and/or wealth on a large scale.

Public acceptance of, or acquiescence to, major changes in tax policies also depends on the government's ability to mobilize sustained political support from a cross-section of organized interests that reflect, or can influence, large segments of public opinion. The interaction of governments and interest groups vitally affects the ultimate political success or failure of tax reform initiatives. However, during the 1990s, governments at all levels, aided by growing technological and marketing sophistication, have attempted to reach beyond organized interest groups to communicate directly with members of the public.

This chapter examines the nature of the *public* tax policy process, defined as the process of reconciling government policy objectives with the political and economic expectations of various societal interests or, in other words, as an exercise in securing political legitimacy and public support. The chapter will examine the relationship between the Department of Finance and the various groups that make up the broader tax policy community, most notably interest groups and interested Members of Parliament. It also assesses the role of the general public and public opinion on ministers, their decisions, and their "non-decisions."

Tax Reform and Coalition-Building

Proposals for major changes to the tax system must win support in a competitive political marketplace. Governments attempt to maximize the political benefits of government spending (and of selective tax concessions as a form of spending) and to minimize the political costs of taxation for groups of voters whose support is critical to win and retain political power.[5] Governments that have ignored these constraints in introducing major changes to tax systems usually have lost subsequent elections, despite such expedients as changing ministers or attempting to offset the impact of proposed policy changes on selected groups.

Before the massive political backlash triggered by the 1981 tax reform budget, efforts at coalition-building by the Minister and Department of Finance were usually of an ad hoc nature, modifying tax laws through the annual budget cycle in an effort to deal with pressing political problems and to correct inequities that had arisen as a result of previous tax changes.[6] This process was usually reactive, with governments responding to outside pressures. The result was often the unraveling of previous tax reform initiatives and the systematic erosion of the tax base as Finance Ministers, particularly John Turner in 1972-75 and Marc Lalonde in 1982-84, scrambled to recover the political support lost by their predecessors' efforts to introduce large-scale policy changes.

Since 1981, the Department of Finance has recognized the need to cultivate a broader degree of consensus in developing and marketing its fiscal and economic policies, particularly when these involve significant policy changes. During the 1990s, this effort has emphasized the integration of policy development with the marketing of those policies.[7] This process takes place on several levels, including consultations with cabinet and caucus colleagues, meetings with interest groups, and ongoing polling to test public opinion on key priorities, proposed policy initiatives, and responses to suggested budget themes and messages.

The consensus-building process involves three major elements. First, it addresses the substance of economic and tax policies in an effort to formulate or refine policies based on broadly shared values and policy objectives. Second, it involves the process of policy change, the manner in which changes are introduced and refined in response to public consultation and debate. Finally, it takes careful account of economic and symbolic outcomes—who wins or loses economically and politically as a result of major changes to tax levels or the tax system. Most tax reform initiatives are likely to be heavily contested unless they involve a reduction in taxes for most major social and economic groups rather than simply a restructuring and redistribution of tax burdens.

As a result, governments need to build a political consensus at two levels. Policies must be packaged in ways that will secure broad, if sometimes superficial, public acceptance, or at least acquiescence. Major interest groups, which are more interested in the practical details of policy, seek a public acknowledgement of their concerns and a sense that "their issues" are being addressed in ways that will result in practical benefits for their members. The integration of these objectives in order to win the acceptance or support of multiple constituencies is sometimes known as "political triangulation."

The Public Tax Policy Process

The general direction of tax policy and overall levels of taxation are political matters reflecting "the political and economic environment for particular policies, the volume of demands on government and the real or perceived urgency of these problems."[8] These demands and the options for balancing and responding to them are weighed by the Minister and Deputy Minister of Finance. They involve formal and informal consultations with the Prime Minister, cabinet colleagues, central agencies, and other Deputy Ministers, and sometimes with major national interest groups with interests in specific areas of fiscal and tax policy.

During the 1990s, the enormous political and administrative effort required to eliminate the federal government's huge deficit (and those of several provinces) and to coordinate fiscal, economic, and social policies with limited resources has greatly increased the power of ministers and the Department of Finance over federal and provincial budget priorities. It has also contributed to a decline in the traditional collective decision-making role of the federal cabinet and resulted in an unprecedented centralization of control over fiscal priorities and policy decisions in the hands of the Prime Minister and a limited number of trusted advisors, especially the Minister of Finance.[9]

Coleman identifies the traditional process of tax policy formation as part of a "pressure pluralist" network in which largely autonomous state agencies—in this case, the Department of Finance—make policy at arm's length from, but in ways responsive to, the competing political pressures of a wide range of interest groups.[10] This view is confirmed by a senior participant in the budget process, who emphasizes that the Department may listen to outside views, but that groups that ignore or reject its broad fiscal and policy framework are likely to have minimal influence on the policy process:

> We tell the organizations ... "tell us what your issues are." We tell them where we are coming from.... We ask them to respond based on what is happening in the real world and taking into account the constraints we are facing. [But] there is no point in talking to someone who hasn't read the fall update.[11]

Finance Minister Paul Martin and his officials took this process two steps further during the 1990s in meetings with groups seeking to influence budgetary policy. The first step was to give groups a detailed outline of existing government spending, and then to invite specific proposals for changes to spending priorities. The second step was to provide detailed projections on the revenues to be gained or lost from a wide range of specific tax changes, and then to invite groups to come up with specific tax changes that could be accommodated within the government's overall budget targets:

> It imposed a great deal of discipline on the groups by making the numbers add up. They were quite important in generating a common view within the business community. We used to have spread sheets with the name of each association on the top and all the specific tax parameters recommended by each group.... We spent a lot of time with those groups.[12]

Finance's proactive approach to the budget consultation process enables the Minister and senior officials to shape the terms of public and interest group debate by developing a shared set of economic and fiscal projections in cooperation with leading private sector economists, which then can be used by interest groups seeking to develop alternative policy agendas.

On more technical issues, Hartle has noted that well-organized interests can extract major policy changes on issues that have relatively little importance or visibility to the broad majority of voters, either by focusing public debate on the potential effects of tax changes in disrupting economic activity or by persuading the government that the proposed policies will be counterproductive to achieving its declared policy goals.[13] While the general public is not directly involved in policy decisions over the general direction of tax policy (or tax levels), policy debates at this level must take public opinion into account, as either an enabling or a limiting factor in the debate.

The federal budget process currently has four major stages. The first, beginning immediately following the previous year's budget (usually delivered in February), involves an assessment of major policy pressures, the financial resources available to meet them, and initial discussions with the Prime Minister's Office and cabinet colleagues. Different factions in the government caucus, usually linked to organized social and economic interests, may use parliamentary committee hearings to discuss particular issues and to produce reports intended to promote their agendas. Finance also commissions public opinion research to gauge public expectations and how they coincide (or conflict) with the government's own policy priorities. This stage usually concludes in late June or early July when senior officials present the outline of what one described as their "perfect budget" to the Minister.[14]

The second stage involves a more formal assessment of priorities through discussions with cabinet and caucus colleagues and the floating of policy "trial balloons" through the media by ministerial offices or senior officials. In recent years, Finance Minister Martin has asked cabinet and caucus colleagues to submit their priorities for new spending and tax initiatives prior to their respective summer retreats. However, this process often generates an ill-coordinated grab bag of wish-lists, leaving the Minister of Finance and Prime Minister with considerable discretion in setting their priorities.[15] These political discussions are reinforced by negotiations between Finance Department officials and their counterparts in spending ministries concerning the ways in which ministry priorities can be accommodated within the budget process without disrupting the fiscal framework. By the end of September or early October, Finance officials will have prepared a set of fiscal projections based on updated economic forecasts which can provide a framework for political debate, and the Minister of Finance will have come to an agreement with the Prime Minister on the broad outline of the budget's priorities.

The third stage usually begins in late October or early November with the presentation of the Minister of Finance's fall Economic Update and a series of pre-budget hearings by the Commons Finance Committee. In addition to public hearings, which involve academic economists, representatives of think-tanks, and advocacy and interest groups, the Minister and Department officials may meet with representatives of various groups. However, the private consultation process is not as intensive as it was during the 1980s, when ministers might meet with 60 to 70 interest groups during the annual budget cycle.[16] The Economic Update is an agenda-setting exercise that summarizes the government's economic forecasts and fiscal targets, outlines its priorities, and poses major questions to be addressed during the pre-budget debate. Finance's demonstrated capacity to define and enforce its fiscal framework, while entertaining extensive debate over the details of proposed policies, has generally constrained the demands of various interest groups in recent years. At the same time, Finance marginalizes groups that ignore or disregard the Department's fiscal framework in their demands for substantially higher (or lower) taxes or spending.[17]

This stage usually concludes with the presentation of the Finance Committee's pre-budget report in early December. The Committee's recommendations reflect both the broad policy framework outlined in the Economic Update and the political response of government MPs to the recommendations of policy experts and interest groups during the public hearings. While opposition MPs suggest that the Committee tends to mirror the government's policy agenda, participants on the government side argue strongly that MPs seek to use their independent judgment to balance feedback received from public hearings with their understanding of the government's policy objectives.[18]

The final stage involves the eight to ten weeks between the release of the Finance Committee report and the presentation of the budget. This stage involves the resolution of any remaining disputes, the introduction of new tax or spending measures in response to changing political conditions or the revenues projected by new economic forecasts, and the fine-tuning of key budget themes and messages based on current public opinion research. It may also incorporate the outcomes of federal-provincial negotiations over fiscal transfers that have become in recent years an increasingly sensitive part of the budget process. If the previous year's budget seriously underestimated government revenues—a fiscal management technique that most governments now use to increase their policy discretion—the weeks prior to the budget might also feature a series of announcements of future spending commitments financed from the current year's fiscal "windfall."

In sharp contrast to the older tradition of making all major budgetary initiatives closely guarded secrets until the Minister rose in Parliament to deliver his budget speech, the budget's agenda-setting function is now reinforced by weeks of media speculation, often encouraged by "trial balloons" circulated by Finance Ministers and "informed sources." These are intended to shape public expectations so that relatively few of the policies announced on budget day will come as a surprise to outside observers. The only major federal budget initiatives of recent years that have not been leaked to the media in one form or another were Paul Martin's decisions of February 2000 to reintroduce inflation indexing to the Personal Income Tax and to embark on a five-year corporate tax reduction program.

Agenda-Setting, Interest Group Competition, and the Public Budgetary Process

The annual budget speech is the focal point of the federal government's efforts to define and mobilize public support for its fiscal and economic agenda. As such, it is an opportunity for the federal government to define its priorities, exercise leadership, and obtain legal and political support for its policies, through both the formal processes of Parliament and direct appeals for public support. The process of securing political legitimacy is complicated by the need to create a community of shared values on two levels: between the Department of Finance and attentive actors in the tax policy community on the one hand, and between the Minister of Finance and the politically attentive electorate (estimated at about 30 per cent of the population)[19] on the other.

Finance Ministers actively seek to shape public opinion through the budget process, both to increase public support by demonstrating the government's capacity to provide policy leadership, and to respond to public priorities and diffuse potential opposition to its policies. However, while Finance Ministers take public opinion into account in setting the general direction of tax policy, most voters pay little attention to budget policies and demonstrate little interest in their details as opposed to the major themes and direction of the budget.[20]

Instead, the public debate over budget and tax measures tends to be dominated by a relatively small number of interest and advocacy groups, most of which focus their lobbying and public relations efforts on relatively narrow policy areas. Some advocacy groups, such as the C.D. Howe Institute and the Caledon Institute, have helped to shape the intellectual environment for changes to economic and social policies related to the tax system. However, the more public the lobbying activities of interest and advocacy groups or the more vocally they dissent from the fiscal and policy framework outlined by the Department, the less likely they are to influence bureaucratic decisions.[21]

The practical details of policy development and the translation of technical policy proposals into legislative language are often the product of consultations between different parts of the Tax Policy Branch and individual businesses, technical experts, and tax professionals, particularly when these involve the development of detailed rules with specific application to a particular industry sector. Since the fiasco of the Scientific Research Tax Credit of 1983-85, which saw more than $2 billion in tax credits siphoned off for unintended uses, this process has involved an increasing number of contacts between Department officials and individual businesses to test the practical impact of proposed changes on actual business operations.[22]

"Political" consultations are usually kept separate from technical consultations, in which Finance officials seek out individuals or groups with specialized policy knowledge. The consultative process within the broader tax policy community gives Finance an opportunity to "sell" its general policy objectives to representatives of key societal interests. However, the Department's objective is to maintain control so that the Minister will be able to lead the policy process rather than being guided primarily by the reactions of interest groups or the general public. Outside interests may influence the technical application of tax laws when they interfere seriously with business decision-making. The more complex, technical, and specialized the issues at stake, the more likely it is that outside tax professionals will be asked to participate in the fine-tuning of specific measures.[23] However, senior Finance Department officials suggest that outside tax professionals have rather less influence over basic policy decisions.

In specialized policy areas, such as retirement savings, small business taxation, energy taxation, or corporate taxation, Finance has succeeded in maintaining the initiative over policy by focusing its dealings on selected representatives of each segment and using them as a sounding board for possible changes to the system. Occasionally, industry representations may result in significant policy changes, such as the government's decision to withdraw the revised "Seniors' Benefit" proposed in the 1996 budget, based on the massive reaction of the financial services industry against its impact on private savings incentives. Expertise, mutual respect, and absolute discretion are the major criteria for continuing involvement in these specialized policy communities.[24]

Private-sector representations concerning tax policy tend to be rather industry-specific, with few, if any, organizations paying close attention to the broad range of tax policy and tax administration issues. Those which are most prominent or most vocal include major "horizontal" business groups such as the Business Council on National Issues and the Canadian Federation of Independent Business, and sectoral associations, including the Alliance of Canadian Manufacturers and Exporters, the Canadian

Construction Association, the Investment Dealers' Association of Canada, the Canadian Mining Association, and the Canadian Labour Congress and its largest national member unions, which are all regular participants in the policy process. The influence of these groups on tax policy tends to be limited. In recent years, most business groups have sought to influence Finance Minister Paul Martin's fiscal priorities at the margin, rather than launching a direct challenge to his tax and spending priorities.

On social issues, a number of social policy groups, such as the National Council of Welfare, the National Anti-Poverty Organization (NAPO), and the Caledon Institute have also emerged to promote the use of the tax system as an instrument of income redistribution, especially for lower-income families. Although social policy groups rarely were able to win in direct confrontations with business groups over general policy objectives during the 1970s and 1980s,[25] they were able to convince the Department of Finance to introduce refundable tax credits for lower-income families. They also influenced Finance's decision in the income tax reforms of 1987-88 to convert many personal income tax deductions to credits, mainly targeted at lower- and middle-income earners. This was part of a deliberate government strategy to broaden support for tax reform by appealing to as many Canadians as possible in the year before a general election.[26] In the 1990s, the Caledon Institute played a leading role in persuading the federal government to convert family allowances and universal tax allowances for dependent children to the Child Tax Benefit, a tax transfer payment targeted at lower- (and later middle-) income families.[27] The National Child Benefit, expanded after the 1997 budget as part of an agreement with the provinces, has become the federal government's largest tax transfer program, valued at over $7 billion per year.

Selected "equity-seeking" groups have received federal funding that enables them to influence the public policy process, although the Department of Finance itself was not part of this process. The National Council of Welfare sought to popularize the concept of tax expenditures during the 1970s, and advocated the introduction of the alternative minimum tax as a fiscal "antidote" to legal tax avoidance measures during the 1980s. LEAF, the Legal Action and Education Fund, has used public funding successfully to address specific tax-related issues through the courts, particularly with respect to the deductibility of family support payments. The Department of Indian and Northern Affairs has financed the Assembly of First Nations and other representative groups in the slowly evolving process of developing a framework for the sharing of tax revenues and taxing authority between federal and provincial governments and First Nations.[28] However, the funding of advocacy groups generally has been incidental to the broad process of policy formation and political brokerage associated with tax policy.

The relationship between the Department of Finance and major interest groups has evolved significantly since the 1970s. Most business groups and senior tax professionals viewed the economic policies of the Trudeau government with ill-disguised hostility. This attitude came to be reciprocated by many Finance officials who saw themselves as trying merely to recover a series of overly generous tax breaks given away during the 1970s. After the political fiasco of the 1981 budget, both ministers and senior officials came to see such overt conflict as detrimental to the country's political and economic stability.[29] This resulted in significant changes, both to the public policy process and to the Finance Department's attitude towards consultation.

The consultation process has enabled Ministers of Finance to mobilize public consent to policy changes by explaining policy problems that require changes to the tax system or the use of public funds before introducing legislation, rather than being perceived as dictating changes that could adversely affect the livelihoods of many individuals or important economic sectors. The consultation process contributes to the government's credibility by allowing Finance Department officials to test their policy assumptions in public and in informal discussions with those most likely to be affected before firmly committing themselves to a specific policy.

Consultation also provides a face-saving way around the rigid partisanship of the parliamentary process by allowing ministers and MPs to discuss the objectives and rationales of proposed policies and possible alternatives before their formal introduction as budget legislation or a White Paper in Parliament. The result has been the frequent use of discussion papers to introduce new policy initiatives, both as part of the budget process and independently of it. This expanded consultative process has helped to expand public awareness of fiscal and tax policy options to the extent that there has been comparatively little public pressure for major change to either the income or sales tax systems since the early years of the Chrétien government.[30]

CONSENSUS-BUILDING AND PARLIAMENTARY POLITICS

Canada's single member plurality, or "first-past-the-post," electoral system allows a political party to form a majority government with a minority of the popular vote, and to wield largely unrestricted power as long as it respects the boundaries set by the Constitution, the courts, and the conventions of federalism.

However, the intensely partisan climate of parliamentary politics gener-ally promotes conflict and policy instability rather than consensus and continuity.[31] This means that opposition parties frequently have an incen-tive to overturn the policies of their predecessors in order to reward the "losers" in previous policy disputes for their support. This result can be seen in the policy swings that followed the election of the Clark government in 1979, the "Trudeau Restoration" of 1980, the revenge of the Mulroney Conservatives in 1984, and the election in 1993 of the Chrétien Liberals on a platform of replacing the hated Goods and Services Tax. Ironically, the deficit crisis of 1994-95 and the Chrétien/Martin government's conversion to the policies of spending restraint, deficit reduction, free trade, and market economics advocated by the Conservative and Reform/Alliance opposition has produced the longest period of relative stability in federal tax policies since the 1950s.

Although Parliament as an institution has become largely a rubber stamp for most government decisions, including the formal budget process, three groups within Parliament play a significant advisory role in the policy process: the government caucus, the Commons Finance Committee, and the Senate Banking Committee.

Under the Trudeau Liberals, the role of caucus was mainly reactive, serving as a lightening rod for public and interest group reactions on issues such as the 1978 reforms to Unemployment Insurance and the 1981 tax reform budget.[32] Prime Ministers Mulroney and Chrétien have both used their cau-cuses as a political "reality check" on major policy initiatives.[33] Cabinet and caucus resistance to proposed sales tax reforms during the Mulroney era delayed the introduction of the Goods and Services Tax by more than two years and forced Finance Minister Wilson to cultivate caucus as part of his consultation process. Faced with a large, diverse parliamentary majority in their first term and some backbench unrest after 1997, Chrétien and Martin have used caucus and parliamentary committees as safety valves for internal policy debates—particularly the political and financial trade-offs associated with internal demands for tax reduction and increased funding for children's services as part of the National Children's Agenda.[34]

The Commons Finance Committee, as noted earlier, has served as the principal vehicle for the Chrétien government's consultation and agenda-setting process on budgetary and tax policies. While rigidly partisan, it has served as an effective sounding board for government MPs—particularly the "business Liberals" who have historically dominated the economic decision-making of Liberal governments. This stands in contrast to the Finance Committee's role during the late 1980s, when long-time Tory backbencher Don Blenkarn used it to build an all-party consensus on the broad outlines of Michael Wilson's income tax reforms. However, this consensus was destroyed during the bitter partisan debates surrounding the introduction of the Goods and Services Tax and has never really recovered given the strong mutual dislike and ideological aversions of Liberal and opposition members since 1993.

Under the long chairmanship of tax lawyer Salter Hayden (1951-83), the Senate Banking Committee exercised the most important parliamentary oversight of tax policy issues. Hayden was probably the most influential figure of tax policy issues outside the Department of Finance during this period. He initiated "pre-study" of tax bills by the Committee prior to their receiving Second Reading in the House of Commons during the 1970s. Hayden also secured the services of experienced tax advisors to brief Senators, prepare questions and cross-examine witnesses. Unlike the Commons Finance Committees of the 1970s and early 1980s, which were comparatively inexpert and under tight political control, the Banking Committee regularly demanded changes to budgetary tax bills, receiving written commitments from Ministers of Finance that the required changes would be made in their next budget.[35] While the Senate Committee's influence declined after Hayden's retirement in 1983, it continues to serve as a strong and occasionally effective advocate of business liberalism within the federal government.

Tax Policy, Tax Reform, and Public Opinion

The management and accommodation of public opinion are major factors in the budget process—and in the ability of Finance Ministers to win the cooperation, however grudging, of interest groups and parliamentary colleagues. The views of the average taxpayer, who is seen to be relatively disengaged and uninformed of the details of economic and budgetary policies,[36] have traditionally held minimal weight on detailed tax issues. However, public opinion becomes the court of appeal when political and economic elites are divided over the feasibility or desirability of major changes to tax policies and tax levels.

The role of public opinion is strongest in influencing the general direction and trends of tax policy—particularly on issues with a high public profile or symbolic importance. Public opinion may be assessed (and often manipulated) through mass media coverage of tax issues, the number and intensity of interest group members and ordinary voters who contact their Members of Parliament, or through polls and focus groups commissioned by central agencies, political parties, and interest groups.

The Department of Finance regularly commissions public opinion research—two to four times during each budget cycle in recent years—to test for public perceptions of government economic policies, responses to possible policy options and budget themes. Survey results clearly influence the themes and priorities stressed in the Minister's public statements—even though their direct impact on specific policy decisions may be relatively small. These studies point to three overriding priorities in public views of tax policy and periodic proposals for major changes to the tax system. Not surprisingly, public opinion on tax policy appears to be closely tied to financial self-interest—particularly with the maintenance of after-tax living standards. Public dissatisfaction with government priorities tends to increase when the average standard of living is seen to be eroded by inflation, taxes or both—as it was for most Canadian families during the 1990s. Finance Department surveys suggest that the average citizen appears to be less interested in tax reform than in tax limitation.

However, this does not automatically result in widespread support for tax reduction. Public views of taxation are heavily affected by voter perceptions of the relationship between benefits and services financed from taxation and the costs directly borne by individuals and families. Research conducted by the Fraser Institute suggests that families with total incomes below $40,000, about half of Canadian families, tend to receive significantly more in government benefits and services than they paid in taxes.[37] Such voters tend to favour targeted tax reductions that benefit them directly (i.e. to lower and middle income taxpayers) but not at the expense of priority public services such as health care and education.[38] There is a growing fragmentation of public opinion, varying widely by region, income level, source of income, and relative dependence on governments as opposed to the private-sector economy for its economic opportunities and security.

The public's view of governments' budgetary and tax policies between the mid 1980s and the late 1990s appears to have been one of overwhelming skepticism—whether of governments' ability to reduce public deficits, limit tax burdens or increase the fairness of the tax system. During the late 1980s, tax reform was perceived as a contest between "us" (average taxpayers, small businesses, and farmers, who are often seen as neighbours, sources of economic opportunity, and fellow-victims of the tax system) and "them" (the government, large corporations, and a few wealthy taxpayers with access to benefits not available to average citizens).[39] Taxes were seen as "too high," typically having increased faster than benefits received from governments. The federal government was seen as something "created unnecessarily by government waste and inefficiency."[40] During the late 1980s, tax reform was widely, if incorrectly, perceived as a vehicle to increase taxes for the average person with little prospect of improvement in

the overall fairness of the tax system, whatever the government's pro-
claimed objectives.[41]

Thus, public resentment over the cumulative tax increases of the 1980s
constrained most governments in the options available to them in confronting their record deficits during the early 1990s. Both federal and
provincial governments tended to respond by taking advantage of "stealth"
taxes—particularly the de-indexation of personal income tax brackets and
credits to generate higher revenues from the effects of inflation, increasing
the progressivity of their tax systems through the use of "temporary" or
"deficit reduction" surtaxes for middle and upper income individuals and
corporations, and, for a brief period, making significant reductions to
spending on government administration and federal-provincial transfers.[42]

Secondly, Canadians' views of the tax system and their support for tax
reforms have been largely contingent on perceptions of equity and fairness:
that those less well-off than themselves should pay lower taxes, that their
own taxes should increase only a little or not at all, and that those better off
than themselves, especially large corporations, should pay more.[43] Public
support for NDP proposals for a minimum tax prompted Prime Minister
Mulroney to adopt this proposal in 1984, despite significant reservations
among tax professionals and the Department of Finance.[44] These factors,
reinforced by the Mulroney government's low standing in the polls in early
1987, seem to have played an important factor in the fateful decision to separate income and sales tax reforms into separate stages to be implemented
before and after the 1988 election.[45] While Finance Minister Wilson ultimately introduced and forced through the Goods and Services Tax despite
massive public opposition, the Conservatives ultimately paid a serious political price for this decision.

Public opinion has heavily influenced, if not controlled, the design and
marketing of Paul Martin's budgets since the mid-1990s. The targeting of
tax reductions to lower- and middle-income families, the expansion of the
Child Tax Benefit, the emphasis of tax reductions on personal income taxes,
and the government's reluctance to reduce tax rates for upper-income
earners all reflect the perceived self-interest of a large majority of taxpayers.
While only a small fraction of taxpayers actively supported Martin's decision to implement corporate tax reductions in his 2000 budget, these were
packaged in such a way that personal tax cuts accounted for more than 80
per cent of his five-year tax reduction package.[46]

The Canadian public's third persistent concern is that tax and economic
policies promote, or at least do not impede, economic growth. Tax policy
changes that can be sold to the general public as facilitating economic
growth and job creation are likely to win popular support, whether or not
they are rooted in rational economic policies. Conversely, tax policy changes

that are seen to limit growth or reduce employment—particularly during times of economic uncertainty—may create significant political difficulties for a government. Public support for more redistributive tax and spending measures appears to grow during periods of relative prosperity and decline during periods of economic stagnation. This suggests, if nothing else, that resistance to taxation (and support for tax reduction) reflects a "political business cycle" that gives business groups their greatest influence during periods of economic difficulty, but largely takes economic growth for granted during periods of relative prosperity.

Conclusion

The public tax policy process reflects the continuing efforts of Finance Ministers to direct and coordinate the federal government's economic and social policy agendas within the broad constraints of public expectations and public opinion. The federal government's efforts to introduce a greater appearance of openness to the budget process in recent years has masked a systematic effort by both federal and provincial governments to shape the terms of public debate and to focus that debate on the evaluation of a limited range of options consistent with their broad policy objectives.

The government's discretion in setting its priorities and designing the details of tax and related budgetary policies depends on its capacity to maintain a broad sense of public trust and project a sense of direction while appearing responsive to the general priorities and concerns of citizens and a cross-section of interest groups. Maintaining this level of trust provides it with a margin of flexibility in dealing with specific policy problems, adapting the tax system to changing circumstances or the specific concerns of particular interest groups, or in taking selective policy risks to shift the balance of taxes and benefits for particular groups.

Generally, the more technical or specific the application of a particular policy, the more likely its discussion is to be restricted to those interest groups most directly affected. While interest groups attempt to influence the climate of public opinion, their actual influence on the tax policy process is limited by their ability to work within the constraints of the broad fiscal and policy frameworks outlined by Finance Ministers and their officials, and to demonstrate that their proposals for policy change will advance the broad objectives set out in the policy framework.

However, the capacity of governments to dominate the policy process in this way is closely tied to their success in promoting economic growth and a rising standard of living for most social and economic groups. Governments that are seen to fail as "economic managers"—or to allow external economic forces to undermine the living standards and economic security of large numbers of Canadians—open themselves to serious political challenges from opportunistic political rivals and from organized economic and social interests who perceive their vital interests to be threatened by either the government's actions or its neglect.

Governments that lose the political initiative in this way may or may not lose office. However, they become increasingly vulnerable to the pressures of competing interest groups and to losing the ability to balance competing demands in the pursuit of a broader public interest. The public treasury may become little more than a cash register that competing groups inside and outside government seek to raid to maximize the benefits they receive from governments while minimizing their own costs—often by shifting them to others. The result is a kind of fiscal anarchy that undermines the ability of governments to perform their basic and necessary functions—and the political legitimacy and trust needed to do so without major social and political conflict.

The politics of taxation between the 1970s and the mid-1990s reflected this breakdown of social and political trust and the search for a workable consensus on the role and limits of government—and the kind of tax system that would finance its operations while allowing for the growth and adaptation of its economy to a changing world. Rebuilding and retaining that trust has been critical to the ability of both federal and provincial governments to implement coherent economic and social policy agendas that can improve both Canadians' standard of living and their quality of life.

NOTES

1 Gillespie (1991).

2 Earnscliffe Research and Communications (1999c).

3 Elly Alboim, remarks on Public Policy and Communications, Canadian Centre on Management Development conference, May 2000 (notes shared with author). Alboim's firm, Earnscliffe Research and Communications, has provided polling, policy, and communications advice to Finance Minister Paul Martin on an ongoing basis.

4 Canada, Department of Finance (1994).

5 Gillespie (1991), Chapter 2.

6 The 1969-71 White Paper on Tax Reform involved widespread public consultations prior to the introduction of legislation. However, the Trudeau government rapidly lost control of the political agenda and was forced to react to a series of political attacks from both enraged economic interests (especially business groups) and alarmed members of its own parliamentary caucus. Macdonald (1985).

7 Alboim (see n. 3 above); interviews, current and former Finance Department officials.

8 Cohen (1978), 10.

9 Aucoin (1995); Savoie (1999).

10 Coleman (1988), 47-50.

11 Interviews, senior Finance Department official (ADM-11).

12 Interviews, senior Finance Department official (ADM-12).

13 Hartle (1985, 1988a, 1993).

14 Interview, Department of Finance (ADM-12).

15 Paul Wells (2000), "How the cabinet neutered itself", *National Post*, 19 February, F3; Interviews, Department of Finance, Liberal caucus. [M12; MP12]

16 Interviews, Department of Finance (F14, F16).

17 Interviews, Department of Finance (ADM-11).

18 Interviews, current and former Finance Committee chairs (M12).

19 Alboim (see n. 3 above).

20 For example, 51 per cent of voters surveyed in May 1999, 15 months after the federal government announced that it had balanced the budget, thought that the "deficit is large; little progress is being made." Earnscliffe Research and Communications (1999b). A comparison of post-budget survey responses between 1998 and 2000 showed that, on average, only 22 per cent of respondents paid "a great deal of attention" to annual federal budgets, while a third paid little or no attention to them. Public awareness of twelve major budgetary actions contained in the 2000 budget averaged 36 per cent–ranging from 22 per cent for corporate tax reductions to 49 per cent for increased spending on health care. Earnscliffe Research and Communications (2000b).

21 Interviews, senior Finance Department officials (F1, ADM-11*)*.

22 Interviews, Department of Finance (F07, F08, F11). For a detailed discussion of the STRC affair, see Hale (1996), Chapter 10.

23 Interviews, Department of Finance (F01, P6, F11).

24 Interviews, Department of Finance (FO1, FO5, FO6, P3, P6, F12). One highly connected professional comments in this context that "they won't consult people who won't keep their mouths shut" (P6).

25 Social policy groups attempted in the late 1970s to make "tax expenditure analysis" a major tool for income and wealth redistribution. While this was a major theme of the 1981 MacEachen budget, it prompted a large enough backlash among business groups and tax professionals to discredit the concept as an ideological weapon. Other direct confrontations between social policy and business groups over the expansion of the public pension system and the creation of a Minimum Tax suggested that the former's influence was limited to those objectives that could be achieved through piecemeal changes to the tax system.

26 Interviews, Don Blenkarn, MP, senior Finance Department official (D1).

27 Ken Battle, Caledon Institute, letter to the author.

28 Austin (2000); Chief C.T. (Manny) Jules (2000) "Responses to Challenges: The Future of the Indian Taxation Advisory Board," Canadian Tax Journal 48(5), 1470-95.

29 Interviews, Hon. Marc Lalonde; tax policy officials, Dept. of Finance (FO1, FO3, FO4).

30 Earnscliffe Research and Strategy, polling results released by Department of Finance, 1994–2000.

31 Steinmo (1989), 527-32.

32 Interviews, former Liberal MPS (M4, MP3); Paul Thomas (1985) "Role of National Party Caucuses" in Peter Aucoin, ed., Party Government and Regional Representation (Toronto: University of Toronto Press).

33 Interviews, senior PMO and Finance Department officials (PMO-1, D4, FO2, MI2, MPI2).

34 Hale (2000a); interviews, federal Liberal caucus (MPII, MPI2).

35 Hayden was appointed to the Senate by Prime Minister MacKenzie King in 1940. Interviews, Thomas S. Gillespie (former Senate Committee counsel); senior Finance Department official (FO1). Examples of Banking Committee Reports that extracted promised changes in future budgets were those on Bill C-37 (1978), Bill C-17 (1979), and Bill C-48 (1981).

36 Studies conducted for the Department of Finance during the 1990s suggest that no more than 30 per cent of Canadians pay consistent attention to politics and public affairs, and that a significant majority have little idea of the government's financial position on all but the most publicized details of budget speeches. Earnscliffe Research and Communications, surveys and focus groups conducted for the Department of Finance, 1994-2000; Alboim (see n. 3 above).

37 Walker (1999).

38 Earnscliffe Research and Communications (1998, 1999a, 2000a); Chwialkowska (1999a); Ekos Research Associates (1999); Angus Reid Associates (2000).

39 Decima Research Ltd (1985, 1987); Angus Reid Associates (1988).

40 Decima (1985), 23-26; Decima (1987), 20-25.

41 Gallup Canada (1990).

42 Hale (2000b). See also Chapter 8.

43 Decima (1987), 15-17, 31; Earnscliffe (1998, 1999a, 1999b, 2000a, 2000b).

44 Canada, House of Commons, Debates, (1984) 33rd Parliament, 1st session, Nov. 22, 490-91; Huggett (1986).

45 Interviews, former Deputy Ministers (D1, D4). A March 1987 Angus Reid poll found that 63 per cent of respondents were opposed to the introduction of a Value-Added Tax to replace the Federal Sales Tax, with only about one in four supporting the proposal. Hoy (1987), 128.

46 Earnscliffe (1999b); Canada, Department of Finance (2000b). Public response to corporate tax cuts after the budget was modestly supportive, perhaps reflecting limited awareness and the far greater emphasis placed on personal tax reductions. Earnscliffe (2000b).

part two

The Politics of Taxation from Carter to Martin

Introduction

Part II, The Politics of Taxation from Carter to Martin, examines the evolution of Canadian tax policy between the Carter-Benson Tax Reforms of 1967-71 and the largely successful efforts of federal and provincial governments to eliminate the chronic deficits that had resulted from their consistent failure to balance competing demands for increased public spending and for limits on taxation during the 1970s and 1980s. Part II provides a historical context for current tax policies and the major political battles that have shaped Canada's present tax system, and outlines the ways in which past political decisions and historical events have shaped both today's tax system and Canadians' attitudes towards it.

The 23 years between the publication of the Carter Commission Report on Tax Reform in 1967 and the passage of the Goods and Services Tax in 1990 witnessed the greatest peacetime expansion of government spending in Canadian history, largely transforming the nature of Canadian society in the process. The rise of federal and provincial taxes over this period, while significant, failed to keep pace with spending levels. Chronic deficits and rising debt, especially at the federal level, drove a wedge between the cost of taxes and the benefits received in public services for most citizens. As a result, pressures for deficit reduction dominated the Canadian political agenda and the politics of taxation during the 1990s. Government spending declined in most jurisdictions, not only as a percentage of national income, as occurred during the boom years of the late 1980s, but in actual dollar terms.

The evolution of the Canadian tax system during this era reflected several underlying factors:

> ➤ the internal struggle within and between governments for control over Canadian fiscal and economic policies, in response to the rapid growth of government and the unsustainable growth of public expectations that followed it;

➤ the response of governments and the tax system to inflation and its effect on public-sector budgets, tax levels, and citizens' living standards;

➤ the effects of chronic deficits on governments' ability to balance their promotion of economic growth, the provision of high levels of public services, the redistribution of income, and the maintenance of the living standards of most Canadians during a period of rapid economic change;

➤ the pursuit of tax reform as a means of balancing the efficient raising of government revenues with the use of the tax system to promote major economic and social goals.

Many of the tax policy decisions made during this period, whether in accommodating, balancing, or resisting the demands of social and economic interests for recognition within the tax system, have become deeply entrenched within the structures of Canadian tax law and the Canadian economy. As such, they reflect not only historic trade-offs among competing interests and policy considerations, but have become deeply embedded in the social and economic expectations of Canadians, whether in adapting to inflation, saving for retirement, building family farms and small businesses, or delivering government transfer payments to lower- and middle-income families. Some of these trade-offs were deeply rooted in the tax system even before the bitter tax policy debates of the 1970s and early 1980s. Others were specific responses to the social and economic pressures of the Trudeau and Mulroney eras.

Controlling Fiscal and Economic Policy

Canadian economic policy between the end of World War II and the mid-1970s largely reflected Keynesian ideas of economic management. However, the Keynesian consensus collapsed during the 1970s under the weight of political pressure for increased spending, limits on taxation, and protection against inflation and rising energy prices. The Minister and Department of Finance, while still controlling federal tax policies, faced increasing competition from the Prime Minister's Office and spending departments for control over spending and other areas of economic policy. The absence of consistent Prime Ministerial support often undermined the ability of Finance Ministers to pursue coherent fiscal and economic policies between the mid-1970s and early-1990s, or to impose coherent spending priorities on the federal government.

Federal spending grew by almost 50 per cent as a share of the national economy between 1966 and 1984, before systematic efforts at deficit reduction during the 1990s (see Table B.1).

Provincial expenditures more than doubled with the expansion of provincial health, education, and social services. The status and economic well-being of virtually every citizen and business corporation came to depend to some degree on government action or forbearance.

This expansion was in part the product of social pressures experienced throughout the industrial world—growing urbanization, rapid population growth, and the expansion of public services by means of a burgeoning welfare state. It also reflected an initial optimism about the capacity of governments to manage stable economic growth, eliminate disparities of income and wealth, and provide a broader distribution of economic opportunity and security, without interfering unduly with the freedom of citizens functioning within a market economy and an open society. At the same time, the expansion created the conditions for a widespread public backlash against the intrusion of government into the rights and accustomed privileges of individual citizens and organized groups.

The post-war consensus on economic policy and the role of government in the economy fell apart during the 1970s. This resulted from several major economic and political challenges that undermined the basis for the

Table B.1 •• THE GROWTH OF GOVERNMENT: 1966-2000
(PERCENTAGE OF GDP)

	Federal Revenue	Federal Spending	Federal Surplus/ (Deficit)	TOTAL GOVERNMENT		
				Revenue	Spending	Surplus/ (Deficit)
1966	14.9	15.2	- 0.3	30.9	27.6	3.3
1975	18.0	20.6	- 2.6	38.0	39.4	- 1.3
1984	16.5	23.0	- 6.5	40.2	46.2	- 6.0
1993	17.7	23.1	- 5.3	43.5	51.5	- 8.1
1998	18.3	18.3	0.0	44.4	44.4	0.0
2000	18.4	16.9	1.5	44.3	44.7	3.4

Sources: Canada. Dept. of Finance (2001). *Fiscal Reference Tables;* Statistics Canada, *National Income and Expenditure Accounts;* author's calculations.

Keynesian consensus that had united most liberals, conservatives, and social democrats. The revolution of rising expectations that characterized the 1960s and 1970s ran aground on the economics of fiscal restraint, as rising rates of inflation and unemployment defied conventional economic theories.[1] A series of international economic shocks, such as the sudden rise of world oil prices in the 1970s, underlined the emerging reality of globalization. Major industrial and resource-based economies were becoming increasingly interdependent, thus limiting the policy-making discretion of national governments. Fiscal measures taken during the 1970s to stimulate growth and help taxpayers adjust to inflation contributed to what has been described as the "scissors crisis" of chronic budget deficits and to the "fiscal crisis of the state."[2]

The growing impact of government spending and regulation on economic and social life contributed to intensified political competition within and among both governments and societal interests to protect or enhance their relative political, economic, and social positions.[3] This competition was reflected in frequent changes to the tax system as governments responded to pressures to provide comparable tax treatment to members of different groups. The election of a separatist government in Quebec and the absence of effective representation of western regional interests within the federal government for most of the period between the mid-1970s and the mid-1980s provoked a series of federal-provincial confrontations that challenged the legitimacy of federal economic leadership.

Both the Mulroney and Chrétien governments struggled to come to grips with these issues, to reduce public expectations of what governments could achieve, bring public-sector revenues and spending commitments more closely into balance, and create the conditions for the sustainable economic growth necessary to finance the preservation of public services in an aging society. The contrast between Ottawa's approach to tax issues during most of the Trudeau era and since 1984 can be clearly seen in its approach to the problem of inflation and its relationship with the tax system.

INFLATION, TAX LEVELS AND LIVING STANDARDS

Canadian politics during most of the period since 1968 has been cautiously reformist, conforming to T.C. Douglas's caustic description of middle-of-the-road populism: "getting money from the rich and votes from the poor by promising to protect each from the other."[4] Tax policy was intended to finance modest levels of income redistribution through income transfers and public services, while enabling middle-class Canadians to enjoy a rising standard of living and a measure of financial security through tax-sheltered savings. The persistence of historically high rates of inflation during the 1970s and 1980s made it increasingly difficult for governments to meet these competing expectations (see Table B.2).

The problem of inflation and the tax system was closely related to the issue of whether governments should "profit from inflation" at the expense of their citizens, or take advantage of it to finance a growing public sector. During the 1970s, governments accommodated inflation within the personal income tax system, as well as tying increases in many spending programs to inflation. The uneven distribution of the benefits of growth among Canada's regions and income groups created political pressures for ever-greater levels of federal government intervention in the economy.

Table B.2 •• INFLATION RATES AND THE VALUE OF A DOLLAR

	Average Inflation Rate (CPI)	Decline in value of $1
1966-70	3.8%	17.1%
1971-75	7.4%	29.9%
1976-80	8.8%	34.2%
1981-85	7.5%	30.0%
1986-90	4.5%	19.6%
1991-95	2.2%	10.5%
1996-2000	1.7%	8.2%

Sources: Canada (1996), *Economic Reference Tables* (Ottawa, Dept. of Finance, August); Statistics Canada, CANSIM, Matrix 9957.

By separating the perceived benefits of public spending from the visible costs of the taxes needed to pay for them, a "revolution of rising expectations" contributed to chronic deficit spending during the 1970s and 1980s,[5] and undermined the efforts of federal governments to regain control over their finances, whether through higher taxes, reduced federal spending and transfers, or a combination of both.

The Mulroney and Chrétien governments responded to these problems by imposing a series of "stealth taxes" to reduce the political costs of reducing deficits through increased taxation. Michael Wilson limited indexing to annual inflation levels over 3 per cent after 1985, yielding a cumulative inflationary windfall to the federal government of between $750 and $900 million every year in what became known as "bracket creep."[6] He also imposed annual tax increases to sustain the underfunded Canada Pension Plan after 1986, and began the process of applying surplus Unemployment Insurance taxes to other government activities. All these policies were exploited and extended by Paul Martin in the 1990s.

These changes recognized that the living standards of Canadians could not be maintained indefinitely in the face of chronic deficits. Balancing public-sector budgets became an indispensable condition of maintaining public services and creating the conditions for sustained economic growth. However, winning public support for these policy changes would require a fundamental shift in the attitudes and expectations of both politicians and voters.

TAXATION, FISCAL LIMITS AND THE POLITICS OF THE DEFICIT

The public perception of government intervention as "a moral imperative" in "an inherently unstable economy" made governments in the 1970s the prisoners of their own policy assumptions. O'Connor attributed the growing "fiscal crisis" of chronic deficits to the increasing inability of Keynesian economic policies to satisfy growing public expectations that the state would facilitate both "accumulation," the process of private capital formation necessary for wealth creation in a capitalist society, and "legitimation," the provision of public needs and private wants through an expanding system of public services and income transfers.[7]

A multitude of interest groups emerged to seek the protection of government and, in some cases, protection from government. The increasing power of the political system to confer benefits or impose penalties on private economic and social activities had encouraged competitive political activity by interest groups in efforts to maintain or improve their economic power and social status. This process of "rent-seeking" blurred traditional distinctions between public and private spheres, and between public needs and private wants. In Canada, this dilemma was reflected in trends towards higher overall government spending, both real and nominal, in growing public resistance to parallel increases in taxation, and in a rapid increase in federal deficits between 1975 and 1984. Its political result was to force the governments of most Western industrial democracies to impose a variety of economic disciplines on their citizens to force their adjustment to changing economic conditions.

The politics of restraint made the tax system an increasingly important source of political benefits for organized interests, which lobbied for selective tax reductions or exemptions—sometimes described as "tax expenditures"—as an alternative to direct government spending. However, it also led to calls for tax reform and the elimination or reduction of tax expenditures in order to achieve greater fairness in the distribution of the growing tax burden. However, this could not be done without increasing the tax burden on the middle-class majority that was the beneficiary of most tax preferences, thereby undermining the credibility of governments as effective managers of the economy.

The Mulroney Government succeeded in introducing an economically rational set of tax reforms during the late 1980s. It lowered tax rates for individuals and, to a lesser extent, for businesses, and broadened the tax base by reducing special tax preferences for particular groups. Most controversially, it converted the antiquated Federal Sales Tax to a Goods and Services Tax in the aftermath of the Canada-US Free Trade Agreement of 1988. However, public and interest group resistance precluded the use of tax reform as a means of coming to grips with chronic budget deficits and rapidly growing debt levels. The Mulroney government slowed the rate of spending growth during its nine years in power. However, after 1988, the rising costs of interest on the federal debt swallowed up annual tax increases imposed in its efforts to reduce the deficit. These measures contributed to growing tax fatigue, an intense political backlash against the introduction of the GST, and, ultimately, the near destruction of the Conservatives in the election of 1993.

However, the measures also helped to set the scene for Paul Martin's successful efforts to eliminate the $42 billion deficit he inherited from the Conservatives in 1993 and to balance the federal budget. During his first term, Prime Minister Chrétien restored to Martin and the Department of Finance the power to control the federal budget process that had been undermined under Trudeau and Mulroney. Martin reduced federal spending in actual terms—not just as a share of GDP—so that most of the revenue windfall from economic growth actually could be applied to deficit reduction, rather than to new spending initiatives.

THE TAX REFORM PENDULUM AND THE ROLE OF THE TAX SYSTEM

Between the mid-1960s and the mid-1990s, the federal government introduced four major efforts at tax reform, along with a series of smaller, piecemeal initiatives. The first two reform initiatives—Edgar Benson's 1969 White Paper on Tax Reform and Allan MacEachen's budget of 1981—proved so politically controversial that the Trudeau government was forced to retreat from many of their provisions. This cycle of base-broadening tax reforms, followed by policy retreats and the active use of the tax system to pursue a wide range of social and economic policy objectives, might be described as the "tax reform pendulum."

Although tax experts were often critical of the multitude of "tax expenditures" introduced into the tax system to serve a variety of policy (or political) objectives, business groups and many middle-class taxpayers proved highly resistant to proposed changes that threatened to increase their taxes in the name of greater "fairness," or to the increased redistribution of incomes by governments.

The reaction against Trudeau-era tax reforms forced the Department of Finance to pursue a more consultative, if not particularly transparent, approach to major policy changes during the 1980s and early 1990s: cultivating public opinion and attempting to accommodate the concerns of major interest groups. The political fiasco of the MacEachen tax reform budget, which had been intended to reduce the deficit by broadening the tax base, discouraged his successors from linking tax reform to higher taxes or deficit reduction. As a result, income tax reforms introduced by Michael Wilson between 1985 and 1988 were characterized by extensive consultations and efforts to provide modest tax reductions to a majority of taxpayers in all income groups. However, rising deficits precluded Wilson from using his sales tax reforms of 1989-90 to finance a similar tax cut.

Wilson's tax policies laid the foundations for Martin's successful deficit reduction campaign by broadening the tax base, expanding the range of economic activities subject to taxation, and allowing governments once more to reap an annual inflation windfall from "bracket creep." While these changes forced all income groups to pay higher taxes during the 1990s, they also increased the redistributive character of Canada's tax system, both at the federal level and in most provinces.

Outline of Section

The next four chapters summarize the evolution of Canada's tax system between the 1960s and the 1990s and the political and economic context of these policy changes. Chapter 6 assesses the political battles over taxation and the role of government during the Trudeau era. It discusses the fluctuations in government policies and Ottawa's efforts to regain control over the federal tax base that led to the tax reform pendulum of the 1970s and early 1980s. Chapter 7 reviews the politics of taxation in the Mulroney era, particularly the federal government's unsuccessful efforts to control the deficit, the influence of international economic forces on the evolution of tax policy, and Michael Wilson's income tax reforms of 1987-88. Chapter 8 examines Ottawa's repeated efforts to reform the federal sales tax system, culminating in the introduction of the Goods and Services Tax in 1989-90 and the Chrétien government's efforts to replace it with a harmonized federal-provincial sales tax after 1993. Chapter 9 outlines the factors that contributed to the relative stability of tax policy during the 1990s, and Finance Minister Paul Martin's successful efforts to balance the federal budget.

Table B.3 •• FEDERAL MINISTERS OF FINANCE SINCE 1968

Minister	Tenure in Office	Party	Province	CABINET EXPERIENCE Before Finance	After Finance
HON. EDGAR BENSON	Apr. 20, 1968 – Jan. 27, 1972	LIB	Ontario (Kingston)	3.8 yr.	8 mos.
HON. JOHN TURNER	Jan. 28, 1972 – Sept. 9, 1975	LIB	Ontario (Ottawa)	7 yr.	3 mos.*
HON. CHARLES DRURY (Acting)	Sept. 10, 1975 – Sept. 25, 1975	LIB	Quebec (Westmount)	13.5 yr.	1 yr.
HON. DONALD MACDONALD	Sept. 26, 1975 – Sept. 15, 1977	LIB	Ontario (Toronto)	7.5 yr.	—
HON. JEAN CHRÉTIEN	Sept. 16, 1977 – June 3, 1979	LIB	Quebec (St. Maurice)	10.4 yr.	12.8 **
HON. JOHN CROSBIE	June 4, 1979 – Mar. 2, 1980	PC	Nfld. (St. John's)	—	8.8 yr.
HON. ALLAN MACEACHEN	Mar. 3, 1980 – Sept. 9, 1982	LIB	N.S. (Cape Breton)	16.3 yr.	2 yr.
HON. MARC LALONDE	Sept. 10, 1982 – Sept. 16, 1984	LIB	Quebec (Outremont)	9.1 yr.	—
HON. MICHAEL WILSON	Sept. 17, 1984 – Apr. 20, 1991	PC	Ontario (Toronto)	9 mos.	2.3 yr.
HON. DONALD MAZANKOWSKI	Apr. 21, 1991 – June 25, 1993	PC	Alberta (Vegreville)	7.3 yr.	—
HON. GILLES LOISELLE	June 25, 1993 – Nov. 4, 1993	PC	Quebec (Quebec City)	4.5 yr.	—
HON. PAUL MARTIN, JR.	Nov. 4, 1993 –	LIB	Quebec (Montreal)	—	n/a

* Prime Minister, June–September 1984

** Through September 2001—Prime Minister: 1993-

Source: Library of Parliament.

NOTES

1   Bell (1974), 39-40; McCall-Newman (1980), 241-321.

2   Tarchys (1983); O'Connor (1973).

3   Crozier, et al. (1975); Olsen (1982).

4   David C. Mitchell (1983) *W.A.C. Bennett and the Rise of British Columbia* (Vancouver, Douglas and McIntyre), 391.

5   Bell (1974), 38.

6   The February 2000 federal budget restored the indexing of personal income tax rates and credits.

7   O'Connor (1973).

The Tax Reform Pendulum:
The Politics of Taxation during the Trudeau Era

The four governments of Pierre Elliott Trudeau spanned a tumultuous period in Canada's political and economic history. Trudeau's six Finance Ministers, Edgar Benson (1968-72), John Turner (1972-75), Donald Macdonald (1975-77), Jean Chrétien (1977-79), Allan MacEachen (1980-82), and Marc Lalonde (1982-84), presided over two major efforts at comprehensive tax reform, along with a series of smaller, but significant, changes to the Canadian tax system. These changes coincided with significant political and ideological conflict over the role of government in the economy, conflict that centred in part on the size and costs of government, but also on the relationship between governments and the private sector.

However, although Trudeau presided over a significant expansion in the size of the federal government during his career, the period of his political leadership was characterized by a series of fiscal and economic policy shifts in response to changing circumstances that left two competing legacies. Much of the Canadian public came to look to governments, as never before, to provide them with increased economic security and opportunities, along with a greater degree of equality. But Trudeau's chequered economic track record left many others, particularly in the corporate and small business sectors, with a deep suspicion of large-scale government intervention and a burning desire to reduce the size and power of governments.

These shifts in economic policy were matched by wide swings in tax policies that could be described as the "tax reform pendulum." Following the Carter Commission Report, Ottawa introduced a major expansion of the tax base, only to see it eroded as various economic interests challenged the impact of the government's policies on their competitiveness and economic well-being. Later on, the Finance Department attempted to stem, and then reverse, the erosion of the federal tax base by introducing major new tax reforms, only to provoke another round of conflict and policy retreats. Taxation and economic policies were means to other ends for

Trudeau, as for many of the governmental elites of his day, who sought to use the growing powers of government to build a "just society" that would combine prosperity, national sovereignty, and a more equal distribution of income, opportunity, and wealth. However, the force of economic circumstances and the growing political polarization over the role of government and its relationship to the economy resulted in a series of abrupt policy shifts over 16 years.

Trudeau came to power in 1968, months after the Carter Royal Commission on Taxation released its controversial report. Trudeau's first Finance Minister, Edgar Benson, spent most of the government's first term between 1968 and 1972 trying to adapt its proposals into a politically and economically viable set of tax reforms. Benson's successor, John Turner, dismantled much of his handiwork between 1972 and 1975, while attempting to come to grips with a rising wave of inflation, spurred by global oil price increases, inconsistent monetary policies, and growing public sector deficits that were destabilizing economic policies in most of the industrial world. The politics of taxation were dominated for most of the next decade by the interrelated issues of inflation, deficits, and energy prices.

After Turner's resignation as Finance Minister in October 1975, his successors, Donald Macdonald and Jean Chrétien (the first French-Canadian Minister of Finance in Canada's history), attempted to control the rising tide of inflation and the growth of government spending while seeking to stimulate economic growth with a series of selective tax reductions for individuals and businesses. These policies sparked a bidding war between the Liberals and opposition Conservatives to offer the most generous tax breaks to middle-class Canadians.

The politics of energy and inflation helped to undermine the short-lived minority government of Joe Clark in 1979-80, which failed to reconcile the competing demands of energy-producing and energy-consuming provinces over how to deal with the skyrocketing prices of oil and natural gas induced by the OPEC cartel. It also prompted another swing in the tax reform pendulum, as Finance Department officials attempted to regain control over fiscal policy and federal finances.

Trudeau's return to power in the election of February 1980 resulted in an all-out effort to expand the federal government's control over the economy in what has been described as a "Third National Policy."[1] This effort was intended to harness revenues from rising world energy prices, thereby enabling the federal government to balance its budgets, expand the welfare state, and introduce a new national industrial strategy as an expression of Canadian economic nationalism and federal power. Its initial products, the National Energy Program and Allan MacEachen's tax reform budget of 1981, were deeply controversial. They resulted in a polarizing of the tax and economic policy processes as the federal government sought to impose its vision of the national interest on a deeply divided society. This agenda was resisted by business and financial communities bitterly opposed to what they viewed as wrong-headed and ideologically-driven government inter-ference in the economy.

The recession of 1981-82 triggered the final swing of the tax reform pen-dulum during the Trudeau years, as Trudeau replaced MacEachen at Finance with Marc Lalonde. Lalonde once again sought to accommodate the business community with a series of tax concessions to speed economy recovery and give the Liberals a chance to recover public support before the 1984 election. More significantly in the long term, Lalonde also introduced a series of reforms to private-sector pensions and RRSPs that significantly expanded incentives for private retirement savings. Ultimately, these mea-sures helped to finance the stock market boom of the 1990s and to help Canada become a mature, capital-exporting economy.

The Trudeau era marked the end of the post-war consensus on Keynesian economic policies that had resulted in the rapid expansion of governments' role in the economy. It demonstrated, however unwillingly, the limits to state control over a modern industrial economy, and the growing dependence of national government policies on the global market-place for goods and capital. The economic and political failure of Trudeau's Third National Policy forced a systematic rethinking of Canadian economic policies and the emergence over time of a new style of business liberalism under the Mulroney and Chrétien governments.

This chapter will examine the politics of taxation during the Trudeau era, and the swings of the tax reform pendulum from the Carter-Benson reforms of 1969-71 to the retreat from Allan MacEachen's tax reform budget of 1981.

THE CARTER REPORT AND THE TAX REFORM AGENDA

Comprehensive tax reform has provoked raucous political debates on the three occasions it has been attempted since the 1960s. The tax reform debates have reflected a broader contest over the role of government within the economy and society. Would the design of the federal tax system limit or expand the fiscal powers of governments to manage the Canadian economy? Opposition to the Carter-Benson-MacEachen message of tax equity was largely expressed in the language of resistance to higher taxes and the need for limits to the expansion of governmental power.

The political impetus for the 1960s round of tax reform had been the fear of many tax professionals that the federal courts were gradually moving in the direction of a redefinition of income that could subject many upper-income taxpayers to huge *retroactive tax* liabilities at high marginal rates of income tax.[2] Harvey Perry notes that the risks of unfavourable tax rulings on disputed taxes were magnified by marginal tax rates of up to 80 per cent, compared with about 50 per cent in the post-1971 tax system.[3] However, Carter's recommendations exceeded their worst fears, arguably doing more to create a political crisis for the Pearson government than to resolve one. Rather than merely tidying up the anomalies and inconsistencies of the existing tax system, the Commission's five volume report, released in 1967, proposed a root-and-branch restructuring of the income tax system involving major philosophical and structural departures from the existing system and tax increases averaging 40 per cent for many upper-income taxpayers.[4] Although these proposals were generally welcomed at the time by orthodox Keynesian economists, they posed a serious enough threat to existing economic relationships to promote massive political resistance from the tax and business communities, even after substantial revisions by Finance Department officials.[5]

Carter's proposals for a radical restructuring of the tax system owed more to 1960s optimism over governments' capacity to manage the economy than to any widespread public sense of crisis over the shortcomings or inadequacies of the tax system. The political viability of the Haig-Simons model of tax reform hinged on the ability of would-be reformers to convince a majority of Canadians to accept two ideas. Its advocates believed that the ability of upper-income Canadians to take advantage of many gaps in the taxation of income imposed a serious injustice on other taxpayers and reduced revenues otherwise available for redistribution by governments. They developed the concept of *tax expenditures:* the idea that any deviation from the benchmark tax base is an implicit subsidy by the state to taxpayers whose incomes, as defined by Carter, are not subject to the fullest possible degree of taxation.[6]

However, any concept of tax expenditures based on the idea of comprehensive income taxation carries with it an implicit assumption that the state has first claim on a society's income and wealth.[7] This radically different concept of income—and taxation—would have forced large numbers of middle-class taxpayers to face major reductions in their disposable incomes. This might have been a small factor to academic economists, but it became a major consideration to politicians seeking re-election.

The second concept underlying Carter's proposed reforms was pragmatic. The lower tax rates possible with a restructured tax system would benefit a majority of taxpayers and the Canadian economy as a whole. But many advocates of tax reform also saw it as an opportunity to replace tax preferences, whose use was largely at the discretion of individual taxpayers, with government programs in which benefits were to be targeted and distributed at the discretion of government officials. This reinforced the view of many business interests that tax reform was intended as a vehicle for the expansion of state control of the economy, and that instead of reducing tax levels, comprehensive income taxation would shift economic discretion and power from individual and business taxpayers to the state.[8]

Finance Minister Edgar Benson's White Paper on Taxation, released in early 1969, rejected the Carter Report's most radical recommendations. However, it sought to implement enough of them—including the taxation of capital gains in addition to the existing Estate Tax, the elimination of the low tax rate for small business, the integration of personal and corporate income for tax purposes, and increased taxes on resource industries and intergenerational gifts and transfers—to promote a significant political backlash. Former Deputy Finance Minister Robert Bryce believes that these four measures were the key political weaknesses that made the Carter Report and the White Paper politically unacceptable.[9] Benson later commented that "the White Paper ... was released, I am told, on the anniversary of the Russian revolution and was received in much the same way by many members of our affluent society."[10]

Benson referred the White Paper to parliamentary committees that conducted extensive public hearings and published reports sharply critical of many of its features. The heated public debate surrounding the White Paper was marked by the emergence of a number of organizations which served as focal points for the anti-tax, anti-big government protests of the 1970s, including the National Citizens' Coalition, led by insurance broker Colin Brown, and John Bulloch's Canadian Federation of Independent Business.

As a result of the public outcry, Benson promised that tax reform would be revenue-neutral, linking the phase-in of the White Paper measures to a phased reduction in corporate income tax (CIT) rates. Benson also eliminated the federal Estate Tax to avoid double taxation of capital gains, and made extensive revisions to the White Paper that brought the design of Canada's tax system much closer to that of the United States than to Carter's blueprint.[11]

The Legacy of Benson's Tax Reforms

Benson's amendments enabled the government to push through its tax reform bill at the end of 1971, after a running parliamentary battle of almost three years. However, the ink on the new Income Tax Act was barely dry when Trudeau replaced his embattled Finance Minister. Benson's successor, John Turner, sought to appease taxpayer resentment and rebuild Liberal ties with the business community by presenting a series of budgets dominated by the political need to accommodate a broad cross-section of economic and social interests at the expense of the short-term fiscal demands of the public sector.[12] As a result, federal revenues were allowed to lag behind the rapid growth of spending for most of the 1970s. This led to growing federal deficits, and with them an impending crisis in fiscal policy.

The tax reform debates of 1969-71 left behind a legacy of mutual suspicion between much of the business community, large and small, and the federal government. David Wolfe comments:

> In spite of the clear victory they had won, the entire (tax) reform process had left a bitter taste in the mouths of the business community and a legacy of bad feeling between it and the [Trudeau] government.... [Turner's] reliance on corporate tax incentives to promote economic growth served as a political device to repair the damage caused by other policy initiatives.[13]

In the short term, the effects of rising inflation rates made taxes and popular perceptions of wasteful government spending major issues in the 1972 election, which left the Trudeau Liberals with the narrowest of margins in the House of Commons. NDP leader David Lewis challenged the growth of corporate tax breaks and government hand-outs to business, while PC leader Robert Stanfield made major gains by attacking abuses of the recently-expanded unemployment insurance program and promising to index both public pensions and personal income taxes.[14] In the longer term, the bitter debate undermined the traditional Liberal party coalition of business and social liberals, laying the foundation for a series of bureaucratic battles to control fiscal and economic policies. This led to persistent conflict during the 1970s between Trudeau's economic advisors in the rapidly-growing Privy Council Office and the Department of Finance over fiscal and spending priorities that reflected very different views of the federal government's role in the economy.[15] Both opposition parties made use of these divisions to exploit taxpayer resentment of eroding standards of living and higher levels of unemployment in promoting their very different political agendas.

INFLATION, STAGFLATION, AND TAX POLICIES

Inflation remained the most intractable economic problem facing the federal government between the 1972 election and the summer of 1982, when Finance Minister Allan MacEachen partially de-indexed personal income taxes as part of a broader program of public-sector controls. Inflation and the policies intended to constrain it destabilized the political and intellectual consensus surrounding economic and tax policies, bringing into the open a wide range of competing public expectations that were unsustainable in the absence of the surpluses created by real economic growth. Without adequate growth to generate higher government revenues, the deficit reduction policies necessary to help contain inflation resulted in growing political competition to reallocate income and wealth among different functions and sectors. Numerous interest groups mobilized to protect themselves from potential changes in the balance of political and economic power.[16]

The indexation of personal income tax rates, exemptions, and selected transfer programs by Finance Minister John Turner in 1973, followed by repeated tax policy changes to offset the effects of inflation on taxes, were meant to eliminate the hidden or inflationary component of tax increases and to reduce the political incentive to allow inflationary increases in federal spending.[17] The Finance Ministers of the 1970s and their officials considered it their responsibility to restrain federal spending in order to control inflation while selectively easing tax burdens on business so that the private sector could generate employment for a rapidly growing labour force and maintain its competitive position in world markets.

Turner's decision to introduce partial inflation indexing in 1973 was strongly influenced by his belief that he could only constrain his colleagues' spending by slowing the growth of federal revenues. This decision was also intended to curb the effects of inflation and progressive tax rates on middle-class living standards. Indexation was accompanied by a series of tax concessions and reductions for individuals which removed 750,000 lower-income Canadians from the tax rolls altogether. Turner also proposed, in measures held over from the 1972 budget, corporate tax cuts of 20 per cent for manufacturers and small businesses.[18] As a result of these and other measures, the number of non-taxable individual tax returns increased from 16.8 per cent to 35.5 per cent in 1979 (see Table 6.1). These policies were immensely popular, and arguably helped the federal government avoid the middle-class anti-government backlash embodied in the tax revolts of California's Proposition 13 and its imitators in the United States in the late 1970s. However, without effective political constraints on the growth of

Table 6.1 ·· NON-TAXABLE PERSONAL TAX RETURNS AS A PERCENTAGE OF TOTAL TAX RETURNS: 1970-79

1970	16.8%
1971	22.7%
1972	22.2%
1973	22.8%
1974	23.0%
1975	29.2%
1976	28.6%
1977	30.4%
1978	38.5%
1979	35.5%

Source: *Taxation Statistics, 1972-81* (Ottawa: Revenue Canada); author's calculations.

spending, indexing contributed to the steady growth of the federal deficit during the 1970s by limiting the growth of federal revenues, the so-called "scissors crisis of public finance"[19] (see Table 6.2).

The cabinet committed the government to numerous social policy initiatives, both before and during the minority government of 1972-74, when the Liberals were dependent on NDP support. Although Turner resigned from cabinet over his disagreement with the imposition of wage and price controls in September 1975, his successor, Donald Macdonald, followed much the same course, using a growing number of tax preferences to stimulate economic activity, but within a fiscal framework in which tax and spending policies were coordinated only in the sense of "giving with both hands."[20]

The burdens of progressive income tax rates were offset by the rapid growth of tax preferences for middle- and upper-income Canadians. During the 1970s, while the federal tax base grew at an unprecedented rate, the total volume of tax preferences grew along with it. Total personal exemptions and deductions claimed from taxable income were 31.8 per cent of assessed income in 1970 and remained virtually constant around 34 per cent of assessed income between 1975 and 1984.[21] Indexation was only one of a number of broadly-based tax measures introduced or expanded during the 1970s to facilitate private savings and capital formation.

Between 1973 and 1979, Ministers of Finance introduced more than 500 changes to the Income Tax Act to promote competitiveness and growth, limit the impact of tax-based inflation, and minimize inequities within the tax system. Some of these changes reflected pressures from the business community to increase its competitiveness with Canada's major trading partners and offset the punitive effect of inflation on business and capital gains taxation. Even so, John Bossons estimated that 44 per cent of federal corporate tax revenues in 1978-79 were the result of the inflation-induced overstatement of taxes.[22]

Others reflected the desire of Finance Department officials to use tax measures as a creative substitute for government spending, while generating political credit among business and professional groups increasingly critical of the government.[23] This trend was reinforced by federal efforts to restrain the growth of direct spending after the federal government imposed a system of wage and price controls between 1975 and 1978. Viewed from this perspective, the use of tax preferences (or tax expenditures) as an instrument of industrial strategy, regional development, or job creation could be seen as a systematic effort by the Department of Finance to reassert its authority within a federal government seriously divided over its approaches to economic management and political strategy.

The politics of tax preferences benefited virtually all Canadians in some way. Based on a model of theoretical tax "purity," the volume of personal income "tax expenditures" rose from 13.6 per cent of federal revenues in 1972 to 20.5 per cent in 1977, compared with 11.6 per cent and 13.3 per cent respectively for corporate tax preferences[24] (see Table 6.3). Business groups, in particular, preferred tax measures to direct subsidies because they provided a greater level of discretion in the timing and purpose of investments, and because they minimized the need for contact with a federal bureaucracy whose alien ways they neither understood nor appreciated.

However, this policy ultimately proved self-defeating. The paradox of the "embedded state"[25] is that the ability of governments to make independent decisions based on a shared view of the common good is undermined in proportion to the level of their direct intervention in the lives of citizens. The greater the number of social and economic objectives to be achieved by

Table 6.2 ·· THE SCISSORS CRISIS IN CANADIAN PUBLIC FINANCE: 1974-81

	1974	1975	1976	1977	1978	1979	1980	1981
INFLATION (CPI) (%)	10.7	10.9	7.5	7.8	9.0	9.2	10.1	12.4
GROWTH IN REAL PER CAPITA GDP (%)	6.4	0.2	5.9	0.9	0.7	3.6	0.6	0.9
REAL PER CAPITA FEDERAL SPENDING (1973=100)	115.3	127.6	128.4	132.3	133.4	132.1	137.4	142.2
REAL PER CAPITA FEDERAL REVENUES (1973=100)	117.2	111.5	114.4	107.9	102.3	106.6	110.3	124.9
FEDERAL SPENDING AS A PERCENTAGE OF GDP	18.8	20.8	19.6	20.3	20.3	19.1	19.8	20.3
FEDERAL REVENUES AS A PERCENTAGE OF GDP	19.6	18.6	17.9	16.9	15.8	15.7	16.4	18.3
SURPLUS/DEFICIT AS A PERCENTAGE OF GDP	0.8	-2.2	-1.7	-3.4	-4.5	-3.4	-3.4	-2.1

Sources: Canada, Department of Finance (1996a, 2000d); Statistics Canada.

Table 6.3 ·· PERSONAL AND CORPORATE TAX EXPENDITURES: 1972-78[26]

	PIT EXPENDITURES		CIT EXPENDITURES	
	% growth vs. previous year	*% of total revenues*	*% growth vs. previous year*	*% of total revenues*
1972	—	13.6	—	13.6
1973	25.3	13.3	71.2	15.4
1974	47.5	15.1	39.1	16.6
1975	28.8	17.5	6.3	15.9
1976	15.4	18.6	- 14.6	12.5
1977	13.0	20.5	9.3	13.3
1978	35.0	26.3	n/a	n/a

Source: Maslove, Prince, and Doern (1986), 87.

manipulating the tax system, the more likely policies are to conflict with one another. This, in turn, creates new anomalies and inequities which trigger political demands for "equitable treatment"—whether in the payment of taxes or protection from taxes—of all income groups and most kinds of economic activity so that tax policies reflect the complexity and diversity of Canada's economy and society.

As the number and cost of tax preferences grew, supporters of expanded government services began to challenge what they saw as a double standard between persistent restraints in direct federal spending and the rapid growth of "tax expenditures."[27] Finance Department officials shared these concerns. They sought to curb the expansion of tax preferences by regaining control over the tax system against demands for further tax concessions. Under these circumstances, the tax expenditure concept was a useful way to quantify the costs of new tax preferences and reassert the concepts of economic neutrality and equity in tax policies that had been championed by Carter and the 1969 White Paper.[28] However, the economy's sluggish growth, a volatile electorate, and the imminence of a federal election in 1978 and early 1979 made it difficult to separate tax policy from the demands of brokerage politics.

Taxation and the Politics of Deficit Reduction:
1978-80

The Trudeau government, which was trailing in the polls as it approached the end of its mandate in 1978, faced difficult political choices in attempting to control inflation, promote economic growth, and curb the growing federal deficit. These issues could be dealt with in several ways: by pursuing a more restrictive fiscal policy involving higher taxes, more rigid spending constraints, or a combination of both; by attempting to protect selected groups either with targeted tax preferences or more comprehensive indexation; or by a more comprehensive system of regulatory controls, including a tax-based incomes policy (TIP).

The Liberals' emphasis on deficit reduction through spending cuts, although short-lived, was abruptly introduced by Prime Minister Trudeau in a nationally televised speech in August 1978. Trudeau's speech, prepared without consulting his cabinet or any but his closest personal advisors, announced plans for $2 billion in spending cuts—much of it in reduced Unemployment Insurance benefits—as part of a broader set of initiatives. Finance Minister Jean Chrétien considered resigning after his humiliation by the Prime Minister, but remained in office after demanding and getting a free hand in preparing a new budget to implement the changes in November 1978. [29]

The Conservative opposition responded to Trudeau's speech by adopting a quasi-Keynesian agenda of budgetary stimulus and direct appeals for public support through a series of targeted and general tax reductions, most notably, the promise of mortgage interest and property tax deductibility. These were unveiled before a series of by-elections in October 1978. The Tories' proposals were carefully targeted at groups with large numbers of middle-class swing voters. Although specific tax measures are rarely considered politically significant in the sense of shifting large numbers of votes, Tory strategists attributed a swing of 3 per cent of voters in the close 1979 election to the mortgage interest promise. [30]

When the Tories took power as a minority government in April 1979, the economic promises that had been so appealing on the campaign trail were put on hold in response to Finance Department warnings about a worsening deficit, a new round of OPEC-driven oil price increases, and cabinet's unwillingness to risk the political dangers of major spending reductions. [31] The debate over new tax incentives led to serious conflict between the new government and Finance Department officials, whose views of tax policy were sharply at odds with those of Prime Minister Clark and his senior advisors. [32] However, the Clark government's freedom of action on fiscal and budgetary policy was shackled by the rapid escalation of world energy prices in mid-1979 which triggered a three-cornered conflict with the governments of Alberta and Ontario over energy pricing and revenue-sharing. Clark's seeming inability to strike a balance between energy producers and consumers eroded his popularity and perceived competence as an economic manager. Long, drawn-out negotiations with Alberta prevented Finance Minister Crosbie from introducing a budget until December. This left the impression of political dithering. Meanwhile, the Bank of Canada raised interest rates from 12 to 15 per cent between May and December 1979 in response to rising inflation, increasing US interest rates, and Canada's growing balance of payments deficit. Under these circumstances, the "feel-good" economic policies that had helped the Tories to win the 1979 election went out the window, to be replaced by warnings of the need for further economic restraint and new tax increases.

Pierre Trudeau's announcement in November 1979 of his retirement as Leader of the Opposition appeared to give Crosbie an opportunity to bring in a deficit-reducing budget including higher gasoline taxes, despite the government's minority status in Parliament. Clark, Crosbie, and their advisors did not expect a leaderless Liberal opposition to provoke an election over the budget, even with the government trailing by 20 per cent in the polls.[33] They were wrong. Crosbie's December 1979 budget championed deficit reduction, economic restructuring, and energy development under the pithy slogan "short-term pain for long-term gain." Its most visible measure, an 18 cent-per-gallon increase in the excise tax on gasoline, was intended to fund a National Energy Bank to finance new energy projects and related infrastructure development.[34] However, these proposals became a dead letter when the three opposition parties combined to defeat the budget in the House of Commons.

While the higher energy taxes were a major issue in the resulting election campaign, issues of leadership and ideology loomed even larger. Trudeau seized on the conflict between Alberta and the federal government to highlight the differences between his centralized "nation-building" concept of federalism and the more decentralized "community of communities" advocated by Clark and the Conservatives. The Liberals proposed an expansion of federal fiscal and regulatory powers as a direct response to the centrifugal forces of regionalism and Quebec separatism. These proposals to shift the economic balance of power paralleled Trudeau's long-standing commitment to repatriate and reform the Canadian Constitution.[35] The fiscal and economic crisis that faced the revitalized Liberal government in 1980 offered a political opportunity to introduce radical changes to the economic constitution. These changes, embodied in the National Energy Program of 1980 and the tax reform budget of November 1981, were not long in coming.

The Third National Policy and the National Energy Program

The multiple crises facing the re-elected Trudeau government in 1980 have been described as the "non-military equivalent of a five front war."[36] These included high and persistent inflation, spiraling world energy prices, and steadily growing deficits resulting from previous federal efforts to mitigate the impact of these and other economic problems on Canadians. The energy stand-off with Alberta, the looming Quebec sovereignty referendum, and Trudeau's own proposals for unilateral constitutional change led to federal-provincial confrontations on an even broader range of issues. The government's efforts to come to grips with these problems during a period of declining economic growth inevitably conflicted with a wide range of societal interests which believed that the government could not pursue its declared objectives without incurring unacceptable costs to their social and economic well-being.

The Liberal platform of 1980 was a striking attempt to mobilize the powers of the federal government to resolve the challenge of managing major economic change in a society in which competing interests had mobilized to defend their various economic advantages or "entitlements," enjoyed directly or indirectly as a result of government policies. Partisan political competition during this period both fed and responded to public expectations that governments could and should spend more and more money on public services and income transfers in order to protect Canadians from economic uncertainty.

When the Liberals returned to power in 1980, Trudeau and his advisors interpreted the election results as a repudiation of their previous restraint policies and a mandate to carry out a program of centralizing political and economic power in the hands of the federal government.[37] Donald Smiley has described this strategy as a Third National Policy, paralleling the nation-building efforts of Sir John A. Macdonald in the nineteenth century and the efforts of post-World War II Liberal governments to lay the foundations of the welfare state. Bruce Doern called the 1980 Liberal program "the most coherent exercise of political belief and principle by the Liberals since the early years of the Pearson government."[38] Trudeau and his advisors viewed the separatist movement in Quebec, the "province-building" economic strategies of other provincial governments, and the resistance of business groups to increased government control of the economy in much the same light, as the encroachment of narrow interests on Ottawa's ability to pursue policies in the interests of the nation as a whole.[39]

The National Energy Program of 1980 and the 1981 tax reform budget were conceived as efforts to break out of the dilemmas of slow economic growth, fiscal constraints on government, and institutional deadlock. As outlined in the 1980 Throne Speech, "Canada's resource-base" was to become the foundation of "a vigorous industrial policy" that would "provide jobs, spur growth, improve regional balance and improve Canadian owner-ship and control of the economy."[40] It linked "security of energy supply at a fair price for all Canadians" with the nation-building railway policies of the 1880s, evoking images of the original National Policy.[41] This commitment was intended to finance a megaprojects-based industrial strategy that could, in its formative stages, be used to justify the wholesale rationalization of tax incentives and subsidies as part of a comprehensive process of tax reform. Fiscal surpluses from new energy pricing and revenue-sharing arrangements would give Ottawa the leverage to direct public and private investment to areas with potential for long-term growth. The tax reforms would also enable the federal government to develop a more direct economic relation-ship with Canadians in all regions of the country.[42] This vision was aggressively articulated by Liberal strategists such as Jim Coutts and enjoyed considerable support from the left wing of the Liberal cabinet. However, it lacked support from the senior officials at the Departments of Finance and Regional Economic Development whose responsibility it would be to implement such a policy.[43]

Instead of creating the basis for a new consensus on economic policy, these proposals led to an intense political confrontation with business and the provinces. The government failed to create the effective coalition of interests necessary to win public support in the midst of economic upheaval unprecedented since the Great Depression.

ENERGY TAXES AND THE NATIONAL ENERGY PROGRAM

Liberal energy policies were intended to favour the energy-consuming provinces—especially Ontario and Quebec—which had voted against higher oil prices and taxes in the 1980 election. Although cloaked in the lan-guage of "sharing" and "national unity," these policies were clearly intended to shift the balance of political and economic power from the provinces and the private sector to the federal government.

Energy taxation and development policies in the 1970s had attempted to balance the interests of energy-producing and consuming provinces, while respecting traditional federal and provincial jurisdictions over trade and resource development, respectively. When world oil prices increased from about US$2.59 per barrel to US$11.65 per barrel after the 1973 Arab-Israeli war, the federal government used its powers over interprovincial trade to set a blended price for oil and natural gas well below the world price. It also levied an export tax on crude oil and natural gas, using the proceeds to subsidize purchases of imported oil in Quebec and Atlantic Canada.[44] When Ottawa attempted to limit the deductibility of increased provincial royalties from income taxes and to reduce other industry tax write-offs, the resulting drop in exploration and development forced both levels of governments to reduce their tax demands.[45]

Between 1975 and 1979, the federal government allowed the Canadian price of oil and gas to increase gradually to about 80 per cent of the world price in response to pressures from oil-producing provinces and to the growing costs of its Oil Import Compensation Fund. However, when oil prices shot up from US$14.20 in January 1979 to US$29.27 per barrel a year later, Canadian energy policies became financially untenable, especially after the Carter Administration persuaded the US Congress to deregulate oil and natural gas prices.

The energy price shocks of the 1970s led to a massive redistribution of wealth and income within Canada from the energy-consuming provinces of Atlantic and Central Canada to the oil and gas-producing provinces of British Columbia, Saskatchewan and, especially, Alberta (see Table 6.4). Under pre-1980 energy pricing and taxation rules, the federal government was limited to less than 10 per cent of government revenues from oil and gas production, while it carried the major share of economic adjustment costs. The federal government's "energy deficit" increased from $331 in 1975-76 to $2.6 billion in 1980-81 (see Table 6.5).

The giant, foreign-owned firms that dominated the refining and distribution of oil and gasoline at the time and the "blue-eyed sheiks" of the Alberta government who had received the lion's share of economic rents from high world oil prices were convenient political targets under such circumstances. However, the federal government's half measures in adapting

Table 6.4 ·· CHANGES IN RELATIVE PROVINCIAL GDP: 1971-86
(CANADA AVERAGE = 100)

	Quebec	Ontario	Sask.	Alta.	B.C.
1971	90.1	117.8	84.4	106.4	105.1
1974	86.6	112.3	99.9	134.1	106.6
1978	89.5	106.8	96.6	142.1	108.9
1981	86.2	102.6	104.3	156.2	111.6
1986	90.7	111.2	86.3	122.2	98.7

Source: Canada, Department of Finance (1996a), 16.

to high world oil prices during the 1970s left both energy-producing and consuming provinces bitterly dissatisfied. The Clark government's difficulties in brokering a new energy pricing and taxation agreement satisfactory to both Alberta and Ontario were central to its loss of political credibility and to the Tories' subsequent defeat in the 1980 federal election.[46]

The Liberals' new Energy Minister, Marc Lalonde, was one of the few cabinet ministers of the Trudeau "restoration" who had taken the time while in opposition to develop detailed policy alternatives and to build support for them with the Prime Minister, his caucus colleagues, and the Liberal Party as a whole.[47] After the 1980 election, Lalonde and a small handful of officials fleshed out the details of a comprehensive energy strategy that would combine the Liberal campaign promises of greater Canadian ownership, oil and gas prices lower than those contemplated by the Clark government, a larger federal revenue share, and long-term security of supply.[48]

The National Energy Program (NEP), unveiled in Finance Minister Allan MacEachen's budget of October 1980, sought to generate additional revenues to finance economic restructuring and deficit reduction, becoming a model and impetus for the government's national economic strategy.[49] It combined a series of tax, spending, and regulatory measures intended to assert federal control over the price of oil and gas, the balance of federal and provincial revenues, the economic incentives for energy exploration and development, and the ownership of the Canadian oil industry. Although Lalonde expected that negotiations with Alberta and other producing provinces would be necessary to implement the government's agenda, he sought to strengthen his bargaining position by taking a preemptive strike in the hope of controlling the public agenda.

The NEP anticipated a steady series of increases in world oil prices that would permit Canadian oil prices to double within five years, while still maintaining a discount of almost $20 per barrel from world oil prices. The budget also introduced a range of new taxes, mainly the Petroleum Gas Revenues Tax (PGRT) and the Natural Gas and Gas Liquids Tax (NGGLT), which were excise taxes on production revenues rather than income taxes levied on corporate profits. This was a direct attack on provincial jurisdiction that led Alberta to impose production cuts on the industry as a way of enforcing its fiscal and regulatory authority.[50]

Federal estimates projected a doubling of the federal share of energy revenues, from an average of 9.6 per cent in 1979-80 to an average of 22 per cent between 1981 and 1986. However, other studies estimated that this figure would be closer to 32 per cent of revenues, 47 per cent if the federal subsidy on world-priced imports was counted as a federal "tax ... on domestic producers to pay foreign oil producers."[51] Lalonde had also intended to shift the balance of pricing and tax incentives for oil exploration and development

Table 6.5 ·· FEDERAL ENERGY TAX REVENUES AND EXPENDITURES:
1973-85 (IN $ MILLIONS)

	energy revenues	energy–related expenditures	surplus/ (deficit)
1973-74	286	555	(269)
1974-75	1,669	1,656	13
1975-76	1,488	2,297	(809)
1976-77	1,261	1,738	(477)
1977-78	960	2,073	(1,113)
1978-79	844	1,676	(1,769)
1979-80	1,571	3,244	(1,673)
1980-81	2,902	5,709	(2,807)
1981-82	7,082	5,752	1,330
1982-83	8,784	6,736	2,048
1983-84	5,951	5,449	502
1984-85	6,675	6,445	230

Source: *Public Accounts of Canada; The National Finances* (Toronto: Canadian Tax
Foundation, 1973-74–1984-85).

toward Canadian-owned firms and away from foreign-owned multinationals in order to cultivate political support among energy industry groups.
Instead, the NEP disrupted the cash flow of many Canadian-owned inde-
pendents and led to sharp drop in drilling activity, in the process
undermining much of the government's economic credibility.[52]

After a ten-month stand-off, the federal and Alberta governments
arrived at a compromise agreement that made some technical changes to the
NEP, allowing Alberta to claim that it had protected its jurisdiction, yet
meeting most of Lalonde's original objectives through the expedient of a
faster move towards world oil prices. However, a slackening of world oil
prices and a drop in domestic oil and gas production led to a number of concessions to industry cash flow needs in the so-called "NEP Update" of May
1982 and in a further series of tax concessions in June 1983.[53]

The National Energy Program was a calculated effort to redesign fundamental political and economic relationships within Canada. By replacing
direct federal subsidies to oil and gas producers with tax preferences and
federal-provincial transfers, the Liberals sought to extend the power of the
federal government over economic development and to finance the creation

of a new political coalition. The expected energy windfall was intended to pay for a series of resource-related megaprojects and, in the process, create new client groups for the federal government along with a stronger Canadian-owned energy sector.

The actual results turned out rather differently. Ottawa was forced to compromise with the provinces for control over energy resources as a condition of its constitutional patriation agreement of 1982, a clear example of the imposition of institutional constraints over policy change. The government's planned industrial strategy collapsed amid bureaucratic infighting and business skepticism. The decline in drilling activity and the sharp drop in world oil prices after 1982 forced additional tax concessions to the oil industry.

Ironically, it was Canada's vulnerability to the same international economic forces that had made the NEP seem politically and economically feasible that ultimately proved its undoing when its forecast of higher world oil prices failed to materialize. But more importantly, the NEP aroused a deep ideological loathing of the Trudeau government in large segments of the Canadian business community, and fostered a growing coalition against its policies. The NEP's reversal became a key political priority of the Alberta government, much of the oil industry, and a federal Conservative opposition seeking to capitalize on western business alienation from the Trudeau government. This provided the core of the political coalition that swept Brian Mulroney and the Conservatives to power in 1984 and within two years reversed most of the NEP's provisions.

In the short term, the substance of the National Energy Program and the unilateral, confrontational process by which it was introduced virtually guaranteed that any serious attempt at tax reform would be met with unreserved hostility by the business community. In November 1981, that is exactly what happened.

The MacEachen Budget of 1981: How Not To Do Tax Reform

The 1981 federal budget was an unprecedented attempt to impose large-scale changes on Canada's tax system, paralleling the government's initiatives in the fields of energy policy and constitutional repatriation. It introduced a far-reaching set of tax reforms to the federal income and sales tax systems and the principles of taxation underlying them. These proposals, while understandable in the political and economic context that helped to create them, deeply undermined the political and economic credibility of the Trudeau government. This section examines the context for the 1981 tax reform budget, the deeply flawed policy process that produced it, and the political fallout that resulted from it.

THE CONTEXT OF TAX REFORM

The political decision during the summer of 1981 to pursue tax reform was the by-product of other pressures. These including the need to pay for the government's election promises of increased social spending, record interest rates spilling over from the United States (see Table 6.6) which made deficit reduction an urgent necessity, and cabinet's decision to impose fiscal restraint through tax increases rather than limits on spending.[54] The decision to introduce comprehensive tax reform also reflected the strongly-held views of Finance Department officials, many of whom saw in the government's growing financial needs an opportunity to restructure the tax system to reflect their theoretical and ideological concepts of a "good tax system."

The possibility of tax reform was signalled by Deputy Finance Minister Ian Stewart in May 1980[55] and later by MacEachen in his October 1980 budget speech. However, cabinet did not agree on the fiscal framework for his next budget until September 1981. The serious effort to design a detailed strategy for tax reform and base-broadening began only about two months before the budget.[56] This left little time to plan for either the practical implementation or the political marketing of these reforms. It also left the Department no time to locate the staff necessary to wrestle with the proposed reforms *and* the large number of issues left over from the previous budget.[57]

Finance Minister Allan MacEachen used his budget speech to justify his proposed income tax reforms to promote "restraint, equity and economic renewal" in ways that sought to combine his egalitarian principles with the logic of market economics. Restraint was justified in terms of deficit reduction and the need for tax increases to support the anti-inflation policies of the Bank of Canada. Economic renewal would result from lower inflation, lower interest rates, and the results of the consultation paper on a new economic strategy tabled with the budget. MacEachen also used the Department's tax expenditure budget to justify his claims that his proposed tax increases served the interests of equity. The result was a budget that combined an appeal to populist resent-

Table 6.6 •• AVERAGE
PRIME LENDING RATES:
1977-84*

1977	8.5%
1978	9.7%
1979	12.9%
1980	14.3%
1981	19.3%
1982	15.8%
1983	11.2%
1984	12.1%

* Average of monthly bank prime lending rates.

Source: Bank of Canada.

ment of "the rich" and their easy access to tax "loopholes" with an appeal to business and professional taxpayers based on the prospect of a simpler, more market-oriented tax system.

This outlook was reflected in the highly partisan *Tax Expenditure Analysis* tabled with the 1981 budget. This strategy, while perhaps well intentioned, reflected a total lack of understanding of the increasingly polarized political environment. The politicization of the tax expenditure concept was a major tactical error that drove a wedge between the Department of Finance and the broader policy community of tax professionals, aggravating the ideological conflict surrounding federal economic policies and the operation of the tax system, and reinforcing the mistrust of many taxpayers in the good faith of the federal government.

A FLAWED PROCESS

The government's rush to respond to the growing economic crisis caused by the rapid rise of interest rates led to a serious management breakdown in the preparation of the budget. This haste, and the Finance Department's commitment to its tradition of rigid budget secrecy in dealing with "outsiders," short-circuited the political warning lights that normally would have alerted the Minister and Deputy Minister to the political dangers lurking in the budget's proposed overhaul of tax preferences and warned the Prime Minister and cabinet colleagues in time to head off a political backlash.[58]

The Deputy Minister was fully absorbed in the challenges of implementing the government's broader fiscal and economic strategy.[59] The new Assistant Deputy Minister for Tax Policy, Glenn Jenkins, arrived from Harvard in August 1981 to inherit a budget process that had already developed a momentum of its own.[60] Although a strong supporter of comprehensive tax reform, Jenkins paid little attention to the short-term economic impact of reversing policy measures that had encouraged businesses and investors to carry out various tax-favoured activities in the first place, hoping that the budget would generate enough short-term revenue for both federal and provincial governments to permit a significant reduction in interest rates and to offset MacEachen's planned reductions in transfer payments to the provinces.[61] Many budgetary and technical proposals, some of which had been submitted to and rejected by senior officials during the previous ten years, were churned through the system with little effort to determine their potential effect on various economic interests.[62] This created business chaos in the days after the budget, especially in the residential rental construction sector, which suspended much of its activity until the uncertainties created by poor budget planning had been resolved.

These technical flaws were magnified by the outlook of a Minister who tended to see the tax system mainly as an instrument of raising revenues and redistributing income, rather than as a vehicle for economic development. This led him to ignore or dismiss the possible disruption that his proposals might cause to different industry sectors in the absence of adequate transitional measures. Since tax increases were necessary as part of the "difficulty and unpleasantness caused by the need to moderate inflation," MacEachen thought it preferable to reduce tax preferences for the relatively affluent and increase spending on vulnerable groups "to ensure that policies of restraint are borne equitably by all Canadians."[63]

The secrecy and haste with which the budget was prepared, the failure to prepare public opinion for a major shift in policy, or to include measures capable of generating a supportive constituency for the budget, and the refusal of senior management to accept the advice of their officials to build in transitional measures, were major errors in political judgment. MacEachen was handed a ticking time bomb, prepared by relatively junior officials without adequate senior management review. Rather than solving the government's economic problems as intended, the budget magnified its political problems as the economy headed into a deepening recession.[64]

THE TAX REFORM PENDULUM REVISITED

Hidden in the fine print were the most fundamental proposals for restructuring the tax system since Edgar Benson's White Paper of 1969. While base-broadening (or "loophole closing," depending on the audience) and rate reduction were designed for popular consumption, the fine print contained a series of conceptual changes in tax policies designed to make major changes in the definition of income and the concept of tax preferences.

The budget papers contained 162 separate tax measures and a series of statistical analyses to justify them, on grounds either of distributive justice or of cost savings to the federal government. It was claimed that the budget would generate $5.7 billion in new tax revenues over two years resulting from its trimming of tax preferences, while returning $2.4 billion through rate reductions and about $200 million in new federal spending.[65] However, instead of a fairer tax system and firm government leadership in economic policy, MacEachen's tax increases came to be associated both in media commentary and the public mind with massive economic dislocation and the 1981-82 recession. In essence, the budget declared war on a number of entrenched economic interests without developing any constituency for the proposed reforms. As Bruce Doern has noted,

The Budget purported to tax the rich by closing off lucrative tax expenditures and distributing the benefits to as many as twelve million Canadians in the form of reduced taxes. This proposal provided for an infinitesimal gain to the members of a dispersed constituency of largely middle class and upper-income Canadians. It provided for losses to powerful and cohesive economic interests. It rightfully earned the Liberals little support and much criticism.[66]

The Department was forced to make repeated changes to the budget that placed it on the political defensive. The extent and suddenness of the proposed reforms, combined with the overall shift in federal economic policies, aroused a broadly based chorus of criticism.

The central issue in the first stage of the tax reform debate was the retrospective application of many of the tax changes. Unlike previous structural or technical tax changes which were usually designed to minimize their impact on business decisions taken under existing rules, senior tax professionals claimed that at least 35 of the 162 tax measures in the budget were retrospective, if not retroactive in effect. Since most tax professionals did not make this distinction, the attack on *retroactive taxation* became a rallying cry for many opponents of the budget.[67]

MacEachen began to revise the budget within five days of presenting it. The next day, budget provisions affecting corporate reorganizations were revised to avoid gutting the $700 million purchase of Hudson's Bay Oil and Gas by Dome Petroleum. The Liberals had actively promoted this takeover to encourage greater Canadian ownership of the oil industry under the NEP. Industry statistics compiled by Vancouver MP Pat Carney indicated that construction had ceased on 12,916 rental housing units within a week of the budget, prompting another major change.

These mishaps prompted a series of scathing editorials from newspapers across the country calling for a major overhaul of the budget.[68] Even commentators well disposed to the government concluded that instead of attacking the rich, the budget constituted a broad swipe at the middle classes while cutting taxes for upper-income groups.[69] The life insurance industry, the small business lobbies, and the Automobile Dealers' Association launched major publicity and lobbying campaigns against the budget that had a major impact on the Liberal caucus. Business groups began to coordinate their activities in a loose coalition that grew from 23 organizations in early December to more than 50 by the spring of 1982.[70] On the left, the Canadian Labour Congress organized a massive demonstration on Parliament Hill that attacked the government's economic policies for leading Canada into a recession.[71]

The cumulative impact of this uproar was to create the widespread impression that the budget was the result of poor planning, and that wealthy and influential interests were able to obtain changes in the budget while large numbers of middle- and working-class taxpayers were left to pay the costs of the government's restraint program. Rather than tax reform, critics charged, the government had engaged in a tax grab that would drive the economy deeper into recession.[72]

Six weeks after the budget, MacEachen initiated a major effort at damage control, introducing 18 amendments, most of them transitional measures designed to mitigate many of its retrospective provisions. Five policy measures were referred to parliamentary committees for further study[73] and a number of other measures were deferred.[74] However, these changes did little to mitigate business hostility. The Department of Finance was forced to fight a series of rearguard actions, sector by sector, to preserve the major thrusts of its tax reform plan and the principles on which they were based. The debate over tax policy largely disappeared from the public eye, reverting to a series of compartmentalized debates with selected interest groups and interested tax professionals. Many of the budget's provisions were effectively reversed or neutralized over the next two years, particularly after MacEachen's replacement as Minister of Finance by Marc Lalonde in September 1982 and the appointment of Marshall Cohen as Deputy Minister of Finance.

THE TAX REFORMS OF 1981: THE AFTERMATH

The fiscal and tax policy situation faced by Allan MacEachen in January 1982 was little short of a disaster. Yet, the canny Finance Minister succeeded in holding on to many of the financial gains from his November 1981 budget[75] and in securing political breathing space for the Trudeau government in the middle of the worst recession to hit Canada in fifty years.

Projected income and sales tax revenues dropped by almost $8 billion between November 1981 and June 1982 as a result of the growing recession (see Table 6.7). The government faced major pressures to abandon its anti-inflation campaign in order to counter rising unemployment. MacEachen's White Paper on Sales Tax Reform, released in March 1982, ran into stiff opposition from both manufacturers and retailers, leading the minister to defer and later shelve its application[76] (see Chapter 8). Negotiations dragged on with the insurance industry and other groups with which the government had agreed to review budget proposals, with the result that it took

Table 6.7 ·· BUDGET FORECASTS: 1982-83 (IN $MILLIONS)

	November 1981	June 1982	October 1982	1982-83 Actual
REVENUES	$64,960	$58,600	$55,660	$55,123
% DIFFERENCE	—	- 9.8%	- 14.3%	- 15.1%
EXPENDITURES	$75,450	$78,100	$79,210	$79,776
% DIFFERENCE	—	+ 3.5%	+ 5.0%	+ 5.7%
DEFICIT	$10,490	$19,600	$23,550	$24,653
% DIFFERENCE	—	+ 86.8%	+ 124.5%	+ 135.0%

Sources: The National Finances, 1981-82, 1982-83, 1983-84; MacEachen (1982c), 2-3.

more than eight months to table enabling legislation from the November 1981 budget.

To head off his critics, MacEachen tabled a new budget in June 1982. Borrowing liberally from his critics, he introduced a handful of spending measures to counter the recession, while introducing public-sector wage and price controls in the hope of limiting inflation. The "Six and Five" program was a continuation of the government's efforts to reduce inflation, but by other means. MacEachen had rejected both a *tax-based incomes policy* and comprehensive wage and price controls before his 1981 budget.[77] The June 1982 budget tacitly acknowledged critics' charges of a double standard in curbing public expectations. The tax increases contained in the November 1981 budget and their effect in deepening the recession had reduced private-sector incomes without meaningfully reducing inflation or constraining the growth of the federal public sector. Even so, increased stimulus seemed to defy economic logic when inflation remained untamed at 11.6 per cent in the middle of a major recession. Instead, MacEachen slapped controls on wages, salaries, and administered prices in the federal public sector and encouraged the provinces and the private sector to follow his example. In a related move, he capped the indexing of personal income tax rates and major deductions at 6 per cent in 1983 and 5 per cent in 1984. The $1.1 billion in additional revenue forecast in 1983-84 more than offset the impact of deferring or cancelling even more measures from the 1981 budget.[78]

The June 1982 budget, unlike the November 1981 budget, was the product of a cabinet consensus carefully orchestrated by Trudeau and his economic advisors in the Privy Council Office. The Prime Minister's Office conducted a comprehensive public relations campaign to prepare public opinion and then to sell the 6&5 package.[79] Although public and media reactions to the budget were mixed, the government succeeded in recovering some business support, isolating organized labour politically, and reversing the Liberals' slide in the polls.

The emphasis on public-sector wage restraint and the political outcry from organized labour that resulted also helped to camouflage a series of deferrals and reversals of the budget's tax reform measures affecting the insurance industry, small business, restricted investment expenses, and corporate reorganizations. MacEachen also showcased a new consultation policy, which had been announced earlier in the year, and set up a series of consultations on proposed tax policy changes.[80] These changes represented an explicit opening of the budget process, under controlled circumstances, and an effort by MacEachen and his senior officials to regain the confidence of senior private-sector tax professionals that had been seriously damaged by the content and process of the 1981 tax reforms. These changes, partly intended to co-opt his critics, also reflected a political recognition that, during a recession, the price of encouraging business and investor confidence was to allow selected representatives of these groups increased access to the policy process.

THE LEGACY OF TAX REFORM

The 1981 federal budget attempted to make the most comprehensive changes to the personal and corporate income tax systems since Edgar Benson's tax reforms of 1971. Driven by a mixture of economic necessity and ideological conviction, Finance Minister Allan MacEachen sought to force through his tax reforms in the same unilateral, confrontational fashion in which his government had imposed both its energy policies and its proposals for constitutional repatriation. This produced a predictable political backlash.

The *Tax Expenditure Analysis* tabled with the budget provided MacEachen with an intellectual and ideological rationale for raising taxes by eliminating or pruning tax preferences. However, his decision to emphasize the connection between the tax expenditure concept and income redistribution polarized the tax reform debate without convincing most taxpayers either that the tax system would be fairer or that they would be better off. While organized business interests were almost unanimously opposed to the budget, MacEachen, in the face of a deepening recession, was unable to assemble an alternative coalition of interests supportive of his tax reform proposals. As a result, tax reform failed the tests of both political and economic viability.

The three formal sets of budget revisions made in the year following the budget represented the biggest setback for a Minister of Finance since the ill-fated Gordon Budget of 1963. These changes set the effective political limits for tax reform for most of the 1980s and heavily influenced the style and substance of both Marc Lalonde's short tenure as Minister of Finance and Michael Wilson's eventual income tax reform program of 1985-88. Nevertheless, the 1981 budget demonstrated that a determined Finance Minister, backed by a parliamentary majority, could introduce both major tax increases and structural changes to the tax system despite widespread public opposition. MacEachen succeeded in defending most of his tax-raising measures despite massive opposition because of the highly disparate nature of the coalition against him and the mutually antagonistic and inconsistent nature of their policy alternatives. However, the recession did force the government to abandon its broader economic strategy and to reach an accommodation with its business critics.

After MacEachen's departure in September 1982, the Department of Finance quietly moved away from its emphasis on tax expenditure analysis as a catalyst for major policy change, and toward an emphasis on the comparability of *effective* tax rates for different groups of individual and business taxpayers.[81] The Department sought to pursue its objective of a streamlined tax system through a series of incremental, piecemeal policy changes combined with extensive political and technical consultations designed to build consensus. Building on the lessons of 1981, the Department came to recognize that major tax changes could not be imposed on an increasingly skeptical public, but had to be marketed as a positive-sum (or "win-win") game in which potential winners could be cultivated and potential losers compensated in other areas. This involved a major change not only in the policy process but in the policy-making culture. These changes would be the major tasks of the new Finance Minister, Marc Lalonde, and his Deputy Minister, Marshall Cohen.

Marc Lalonde and the Politics of Accommodation

Good budgets must be based on a high degree of consensus in order to be effective budgets. The point is not to ensure the popularity of budgets but to build the essential level of public support to make them work. A full and effective two-way consultation process is the vital foundation.

Marc Lalonde[82]

Mon cœur à gauche, ma tête au centre; je suis un pragmatiste dans ce sens là.[83]

Virtually every major tax reform initiative in Canadian history has been followed by a shuffling of Finance Ministers and a change of emphasis in the tax policies of the federal government. The new Minister attempts to make a distinct political impression by conciliating major interests antagonized by his predecessor, reversing or mitigating some of his more controversial measures, and introducing at least one major structural change to the tax system.

Marc Lalonde's tenure as Minister of Finance between September 1982 and the Liberal government's defeat in September 1984 is an excellent reflection of this pattern. Lalonde expanded the tax policy consultation process as part of Ottawa's attempt to conciliate major business and other groups alienated by the 1981 tax reform budget. He reversed several of its more controversial measures and introduced changes to simplify the small business tax system, reaching out to some of his most vehement critics. Lalonde's pre-election budget of February 1984 also introduced an overhaul of the retirement savings provisions of the Income Tax Act, a major departure from the Trudeau government's previous approaches to social policy.

Canadian tax policy in 1983-84 can be understood as part of a broader political and economic strategy aimed at the Liberals' re-election under a successor to Pierre Elliott Trudeau. The political recovery of the Liberal Party was directly related to its success in promoting economic recovery. Lalonde, in his frequent speeches to business groups, emphasized the language of business-government partnership and a private sector-led recovery. However, he also pursued economic and industrial policies designed to direct extensive financial support to key industries and regional development projects in areas of high unemployment, especially Quebec and Atlantic Canada, areas critical to Liberal re-election prospects.

The recession of 1981-82 was the sharpest and deepest economic decline to affect Canadians since the Great Depression. Canada's GDP dropped 5.5 per cent between the growth peak of 1981 and the second quarter of 1982, the sharpest drop of any major industrial country.[84] The national unemployment rate rose to 12.8 per cent by the end of 1982.[85] Lalonde's instincts, reinforced by his economic advisors and the political interests of the Liberal Party, were to emphasize selective economic stimulus, not deficit reduction, in shaping his economic strategy. The result was a separation between federal tax and spending decisions that left a legacy of massive deficit financing to his successors.

MacEachen's anti-inflationary policies during the 1981-82 recession had seriously divided the government and the Liberal Party. Social democratic nationalists had argued for cushioning the shock of economic change through a combination of a centralized industrial strategy, a more redistributive tax system, and an expanded welfare state. More traditional, business-oriented Liberals had emphasized policies to encourage economic growth and wealth creation as a necessary precondition to improvements in income transfers and public services.[86]

Lalonde attempted to bridge the gap between the two groups. In taking over the management of economic policy at the depths of both the 1982 recession and the political fortunes of the Liberal government, Lalonde and his Deputy Minister, Marshall (Mickey) Cohen, took the same pragmatic course that John Turner, Simon Reisman, and Cohen had taken a decade earlier. His political strategy had three main parts: restoring business confidence in the government by accommodating business interests within its economic strategy; maintaining and expanding job creation and income transfer programs expected by the Liberal social policy constituency; and using all the policy tools at his disposal to maintain the federal Liberals' Quebec support in their protracted struggle with the separatist government of René Lévesque.

Lalonde had several advantages as Minister of Finance. Prime Minister Trudeau's unquestioning support gave him considerable leverage in dealing with cabinet colleagues. As head of the Liberal organization in Quebec and the mentor of most of its rising parliamentary stars, he also enjoyed great personal authority within cabinet and caucus. An experienced cabinet minister, he knew how to use his power to provide effective direction to his senior officials.[87]

Lalonde's partner in this process was his Deputy Minister, Marshall Cohen. While Lalonde provided the political leverage to restore the Department's power over federal economic policies, Cohen provided an extensive knowledge of tax policy and an unparalleled flair for bureaucratic politics. One of the most visible and controversial mandarins of the Trudeau era, Cohen was responsible for developing the detailed policies necessary to carry out Lalonde's political vision. This involved the active stimulation of the economy, using both direct spending programs and a range of tax incentives.

Lalonde's budget of April 1983 attempt to promote economic recovery by "shifting demand forward" through a combination of enhanced investment incentives for business, public works programs, and federal spending on key industries within federal jurisdiction. The budget contained $470 million in tax reductions ($770 million in 2000 dollars) and $1.3 billion in new spending ($2.2 billion in 2000 dollars), mainly on direct job creation and capital projects.[88] Investment Tax Credits were enriched. Corporate loss transfer provisions were enhanced to ease the cash flow positions of both large and small firms. A new system of Research & Development Tax

Credits was also proposed to stimulate an increased inflow of R&D investment, especially into smaller, innovative companies. The budget was
generally welcomed by business groups as a "return to sanity"[89] after almost
three years of conflict and mutual suspicion. However, this rosy fiscal forecast was seriously damaged by the decline in world oil prices during 1983
and the vanishing of surpluses forecasted in the National Energy Program
(see Table 6.8).

Lalonde also maintained the Liberals' traditional commitments to social
programs and the alleviation of regional disparities in regular gestures to the
party's left wing, even at the cost of significantly higher budget deficits.
Beginning with his economic statement of October 1982, he began to shift
federal spending to localized job creation programs, often subject to the
influence of local members of Parliament. This policy was expanded in 1983
with large investments in local development programs, public works, and
subsidies to major industries. Lalonde's strategy complemented his role as
senior political minister for Quebec by strengthening Liberal efforts to
secure the loyalty of key interest groups in the highly partisan struggle with
the Parti Québécois government of René Lévesque.[90]

However, economic recovery still took precedence over the pursuit of the
Liberal left's social policy agenda. Lalonde deflected proposals by Health
and Welfare Minister Monique Bégin to require the indexing of private
pensions and to double benefits under the Canada Pension Plan, along with
the higher taxes needed to pay for them. Instead, he supported a bipartisan
initiative to expand contribution levels for RRSPs, equalize tax rules governing employment pension plans and RRSPs, and target increases in public
benefits at lower-income seniors.[91]

Pension reform was the centrepiece of Lalonde's February 1984 budget.
He proposed to equalize the tax treatment of Registered Retirement

Table 6.8 ·· ENERGY REVENUES AND SPENDING: 1981-82–1984-85
(IN $MILLIONS)

	Revenues	Spending	Surplus
1981-82	$7,082	$5,752	$1,330
1982-83	$8,784	$6,736	$2,048
1983-84	$5,951	$5,449	$502
1984-85	$6,675	$6,445	$230

Source: *The National Finances: 1982-83 - 1985-86*, (Toronto: Canadian Tax Foundation);
author's calculations.

Savings Plans and employment pensions by phased increases over four years in the maximum RRSP deduction from $5,500 to $15,500. The budget also included measures to encourage "gains sharing" through company profit-sharing and employee share ownership plans.[92] Changes to simplify the small business tax system addressed a number of grievances left over from the 1981 budget.[93] This was followed in April 1984 by an announcement of changes to Revenue Canada's administration of the tax system, which had prompted widespread accusations of abuse of power in the House of Commons and the news media.[94] Most of these policies were continued or extended after the Liberals' defeat in the 1984 election by the Progressive Conservatives led by Brian Mulroney.

Marc Lalonde's achievements as Minister of Finance were mixed. His policies reflected a pragmatic approach both to tax policy and to strengthening the leadership of the Department of Finance in setting the framework for both federal economic and social policies. His two budgets continued the unravelling of the MacEachen tax reform proposals of 1981. They further entrenched the principle of the income tax system as a hybrid income-consumption tax by using a series of tax measures to encourage private savings, capital formation, and a wide range of social and economic activities, not least the rapid expansion of private retirement savings that ultimately made possible the stock market boom of the 1990s.

By his own standards, Lalonde succeeded in his objectives. He diffused many of the conflicts that threatened to derail economic policy. He presided over the beginnings of a sustained recovery and left the Finance Department in a stronger position to direct federal economic policy. The consultation process that matured under his leadership established a model for federal policy-making that contributed to the political success of Michael Wilson's tax reform initiatives in 1986-88. However, Lalonde was less than successful in the legacies of increasing deficits and debt left to his successors. The federal Conservatives outbid the Liberals for business and middle-class support in the 1984 federal election. While two of Lalonde's innovations, pension reform and small business tax simplification, became the basis for a bipartisan federal policy for the next decade, another, the Scientific Research Tax Credit, opened the door to some of the largest tax frauds in Canadian history.[95] Federal spending decisions were effectively disengaged from tax policy decisions. The rest of the 1980s were spent in a largely fruitless effort to reestablish contact between the two.

The Trudeau Era in Retrospect

The economic legacy of Pierre Trudeau and his impact on the Canadian tax system were far more ambiguous than his constitutional or political legacies. The Trudeau Liberals fostered increased public expectations of activist government without being willing or able to mobilize the financial resources to pay for them. Indeed, opposition to the Carter-Benson-MacEachen message of tax equity was largely expressed in the language of resistance to higher taxes and the need for limits to the expansion of government power. Trudeau's six different Finance Ministers pursued widely varying fiscal and tax policies between 1968 and 1984, including two efforts at large-scale tax reform in 1971 and 1981 that largely came unravelled under sustained pressure from the business community, large and small. The frequent turnover of Finance Ministers suggests many of the difficulties of managing economic policy during the Trudeau era, as the Keynesian consensus of the 1960s came unravelled without being replaced by coherent or consistent fiscal policies.

Trudeau's early efforts at collegial decision-making were replaced by a growing centralization of power in the Prime Minister's Office during the 1970s, a trend bitterly resisted by Finance Department officials protective of their traditional role of overseeing economic policy. The Trudeau Restoration after 1980 was driven by the grand strategic vision of the Third National Policy. This resulted in dramatic policy departures, particularly the National Energy Program and Allan MacEachen's tax reform budget of 1981, which sought to expand the fiscal, regulatory, and redistributive powers of the federal government relative to the provinces and the private sector. However, these policies ran aground with the deep recession of 1981-82 and the collapse of global oil prices, forcing Trudeau and Marc Lalonde to return to the politics of interest group accommodation that had characterized Liberal policies in the mid-1970s. The result was a series of massive budget deficits, combined with a deeply entrenched public sense of entitlement that was to hinder the efforts of their successors to bring government finances under control.

Ironically, it was the 1985 report of a Royal Commission on the future of the Canadian economy, chaired by Trudeau's former Finance Minister, Donald Macdonald, that enabled the Mulroney government to reverse many of the policies of the Trudeau era, and to negotiate a comprehensive free trade agreement with the United States that would make it virtually impossible for future governments to pursue the kinds of policies that Trudeau had attempted to implement through his "Third National Policy."

The failures of the Trudeau era to redesign the tax system from first principles—particularly the principles of the Carter Commission and the

National Energy Program—reinforced the critical role played by the tax system as an instrument of social and economic policy. These failures demonstrated the political futility of attempting to redesign the income tax system from first principles. They also highlighted the political risks of pursuing fundamental policy changes without serious efforts to build a stakeholder consensus through extensive consultation. Instead, by aggravating the ideological conflict over federal economic policies and the workings of the tax system, the government evoked a climate of fear, mistrust, and ideological antagonism that seriously undermined its capacity to provide effective leadership.

The failures of the Trudeau era in economic management underlined the need for centralized political control over the budgetary process in order to coordinate economic and social policies, and to bring tax and spending policies into some kind of balance. Restoring this control, given the federal government's huge structural deficit and conflicting public expectations of the role of government, would be the biggest challenge facing Trudeau's successors and their Ministers of Finance.

NOTES

1 Smiley (1987).

2 Hartle (1988b), 401; McDonald (1988), 352-54; McDonald (1985), Chapter 2.

3 Perry (1989), 279-83.

4 McDonald (1988); Bossons (1969); Bird (1970).

5 Bird (1970) 452; Asper (1967), 1-8; MacDonald (1985); Benson (1969).

6 Brooks (1981); *Canadian Taxation* 1(1) [Spring 1979].

7 Asper (1967); Kristol (1974), 14-15.

8 Woodside (1983).

9 Bryce (1988). For detailed comparisons of the Carter and White Paper proposals, see Bukovetsky and Bird (1972), 15-20.

10 Hon. Edgar J. Benson, "Attempts to Further the Goals of the Carter Report: The White Paper on Tax Reform," in Brooks, ed. (1988), 53.

11 Benson (1970), 8023; Bukovetsky and Bird (1972), 39.

12 According to Turner, they "reflect[ed] a decision to roll back unworkable sections of 'tax reform.' It was a deliberate decision." Hartle (1982), 22.

13 Wolfe (1988), 360, 364.

14 Lewis (1972); L. Watkins (1972) "NDP's Corporate Ripoff Campaign...," *The Globe and Mail*, 6 October, 8.

15 Hartle (1982), note opposite 33, 67; McCall-Newman (1980); Savoie (1990), 75.

16 MacEachen (1981a); Lester Thurow (1980) *The Zero-Sum Society* (New York: Penguin); Stewart (1990).

17 This outlook was reinforced by Turner's belief that economic growth, job creation, and the future success of the Liberal Party could be achieved most effectively through cooperation between business and government. Cahill (1986), 154-55, 168-69, 178-79; Allan, Dodge, and Poddar (1974); Hartle (1985), 151-78.

18 Turner (1973); Cahill (1986), 164-68.

19 Tarchys (1983), 205-24.

20 Hartle (1988a), 223-25; Savoie (1990), 134.

21 *Taxation Statistics* (Ottawa, Revenue Canada, annual).

22 Bossons (1980), 32-33.

23 Interview, former Finance Department official (F03).

24 Maslove, Prince, and Doern (1986), 87; Allan, Poddar, and LePan (1978).

25 Alan C. Cairns (1986) "The Embedded State," in Keith Banting, ed., *State and Society* (Toronto: University of Toronto Press), 54.

26 These calculations are based on a comprehensive tax base, including such items as inflation indexing, accrued capital gains, and imputed income from owner-occupied homes in their list of tax expenditures.

27 National Council of Welfare (1976); Woodside (1983).

28 Hartle (1982), 15; interview, senior Finance Department official (ADM-1).

29 Canada, Prime Minister's Office (1978); McCall-Newman (1980), 236-37; Chrétien (1994), 117-19; Interview, former PCO official (D3).

30 Interview, Dr. Jim Gillies, senior advisor to Prime Minister Joe Clark.

31 Simpson (1980), 210-31.

32 Much of this conflict and the resulting mutual suspicion could be traced to the Conservatives' view of the appropriate role of a civil service allegedly "politicized" by the Trudeau Liberals and the Finance Department's proud tradition of independence and control over economic policy advice to cabinet. It was reinforced by two key events: the dismissal of Deputy Minister William Hood in July 1979, and the Department's resistance to mortgage interest and property tax deductibility on groups of equity and cost [interviews, PMO, Department of Finance (PMO-2, ADM-1)]. The property tax measures were introduced in September 1979 as limited tax credits, rather than deductions, but died with the defeat of the Clark government in the 1980 election.

33 Interview, former PMO official (PMO-4).

34 Crosbie (1979). For a discussion of the energy pricing and taxation negotiations leading to the budget, see Simpson (1980), 178-205.

35 *Toronto Star*, 26 January 1980, 1. The ability of Liberal strategists to exploit the energy issue and the Ontario Conservative government's harsh criticisms of the federal energy plan for failing to protect the interests of Ontario consumers were central to the Liberals regaining 20 of 23 Ontario swing seats lost in the 1979 election. Doern and Toner (1985), 5; Milne (1986), 23-34.

36 Smiley (1987), 183.

37 Johnston, (1986).

38 Doern (1982), 1.

39 Milne (1986).

40 Smiley (1987), 6.

41 House of Commons, *Debates*, 14 April 1980, 4-5; Smiley (1987), 178-84.

42 Doern (1982), 14; interview, former Deputy Minister of Finance (D3).

43 Interviews, former Deputy Ministers (D3, D5); McCall and Clarkson (1994), 217-23.

44 Perry (1982), 133.

45 *The National Finances, 1980-81* (Toronto: Canadian Tax Foundation, 1981), 2.

46 Doern and Toner (1985), 5; interview, Dr. James Gillies.

47 Interview, Hon. Roy MacLaren; McCall and Clarkson (1994), 148-57.

48 Doern and Toner (1985), Chapter 2.

49 MacEachen (1980); Canada, Dept. of Energy, Mines and Resources (1980).

50 Doern and Toner (1985), 266-75; McCall-Newman and Clarkson (1994), 177-81.

51 Doern and Toner (1985), 337-41.

52 Drilling activity dropped from a peak of 425 rigs in 1979-80 to about 200 in 1984. Doern and Toner (1985), 347.

53 Canada (1981); Lalonde (1982).

54 MacEachen (1981a, 1981b); interviews, Department of Finance (PMO-3, D3, ADM-3, ADM-8, FOI, FO4).

55 Ian A. Stewart (1980), *Minutes and Proceedings*, Standing Committee on National Finance (Ottawa: The Senate, 27 May), 26-27.

56 Interviews, Finance Department officials (D3, ADM-3, FOI, FO4).

57 "Understaffed department prepared budget–official," *The Citizen* [Ottawa], 26 November 1981, 15.

58 No advance warning was given to the Prime Minister's Office to alert it of the need for a major effort to shape public opinion prior to the budget. Interview, Prime Minister's Office (PMO-3).

59 Interviews, senior Finance Department official (D3, ADM-4).

60 Interviews, senior Finance Department officials (ADM-2, ADM-3, FOI).

61 Interviews, tax policy officials (ADM-2, ADM-3, FO4); McCall-Newman and Clarkson (1994), 237.

62 Interviews, Department of Finance (M4, FOI). One senior official commented that "we were trying to do ... a numbers exercise; there was no attempt to make a qualitative assessment of the numbers."

63 MacEachen (1981b), 8. One tax policy official was more direct: "He [MacEachen] wanted to make sure that there were enough screams to make sure that he wasn't accused of catering to big business" (interview, FOI).

64 Interviews, Prime Minister's Office, Department of Finance (PMO-3, FOI, FO4).

65 *The Budget in More Detail*, 12 November 1981, 11, 50. Finance Department officials later discovered they had underestimated the impact of budget changes by more than $700 million, 28 per cent of the original first year changes.

66 Doern (1982), 10.

67 *Canadian Tax News* (Toronto: Coopers & Lybrand, 18 November 1981), 66-71. The Senate Banking Committee Report on the 1981 Budget distinguishes between retroactive and retrospective taxation: "A retroactive status [is] 'one that operates at a time prior to its enactment.... A retrospective statute is one that operates forward, but it looks backwards in that it attaches new consequences for the future to an event that took place before the statute was enacted." *Report of the Standing Committee on Banking Trade and Commerce*, Issue # 114, Dec. 1, 1982, 10. Senator Salter Hayden and the Banking Committee were jealous guardians of this principle, having often throughout the 1970s forced amendments to tax legislation.

68 Patricia Lush (1981), "Soft cost deduction changes jeopardize 20,000 rental units," *The Globe and Mail*, Nov. 17, B2. T. Walkom (1981), "Return of tax breaks allows Dome to proceed with HBOG share bid, *Toronto Star*, 19 November, B1; "Still not right," *Vancouver Sun*, 20 November 1981, A4; "Budget needs a massive rewrite," *The Citizen* (Ottawa,

Nov. 18, 1981), 7; "Scrutiny by the elected," *The Globe and Mail*, 18 December 1981, 6.

69 Eric Kierans (1981), "A sermon misdirected," *Vancouver Sun*, 17 November, A6; Richard Gwyn (1981a), "Big tax hurdle sure to stymie the small businessman," *The Toronto Star*, 19 November, A10; Richard Gwyn (1981b), "The very rich look at the budget and chortle," *The Citizen* (Ottawa, 24 November), 8.

70 Stanbury (1986), 380.

71 Hugh Patterson (1981), "Angry thousands scorn budget, interest rates," *The Citizen* (Ottawa, 23 November), 1.

72 "Social group sizes up MacEachen budget: a Robin Hood he isn't," *The Globe and Mail*, 18 November 1981, 7; W.A. MacDonald (1981), "Push for economic renewal lost in rush for revenue, *Financial Post*, 21 November, 13; "Crowd's anger justified," *The Citizen* (Ottawa, 24 November 1981), 8.

73 Taxation of life insurance policies, charitable foundations, corporate reorganizations, professional work-in-progress, and retirement allowances.

74 MacEachen (1981d); Canada, Department of Finance (1981b).

75 The "half-year rule" for depreciation ($1.1 billion/year) which cut in half the first year write-off on new capital investments; and the elimination of Income Averaging Annuity Contracts ($895 million/year) which had allowed taxpayers with highly volatile incomes to "average" their incomes, usually at lower tax rates. *The National Finances 1982-83* (Toronto: Canadian Tax Foundation, 1983). The deferral or elimination of other revenue sources from the budget cost the government about $670 million in 1983-84 (*Minutes and Proceedings*, Senate Committee on Banking and Commerce, Issue # 113, 9 December 1982, 9-11).

76 MacEachen announced plans to defer his proposed wholesale tax in March 1982 and, later, in the face of continuing political and professional opposition, in his June 1982 budget. His successor, Marc Lalonde, appointed an advisory council under prominent Toronto lawyer Wolfe Goodman, which urged him to shelve the idea altogether.

77 Barry Critchley (1981), "What MacEachen says about the economy and the issues facing him," *Financial Post*, 17 October, 2.

78 Finance officials estimated the total cost of budget rollbacks at about $269 million in 1982-83 and $685 million in 1983-84. Nick LePan (1982), Senate Banking Committee, *Minutes*, Issue # 113, 9 December, 9-11.

79 This process is described in McCall-Newman and Clarkson (1994), 249-59; interview, senior PMO official (PMO-3).

80 MacEachen (1982c); Hale (1986), Chapter 9; MacEachen (1982a).

81 Sargent (1988), 19.

82 Lalonde (1984a), 1.

83 Hon. Marc Lalonde, interview with author.

84 Wilson and Dungan (1993), 29.

85 Seasonally adjusted data. Using "unadjusted data," unemployment peaked at 13.9 per cent in March 1983. Statistics Canada (1989), *Historical Labour Force Statistics*, Cat.# 71-201 (Ottawa), 214.

86 Johnston (1986); Roy MacLaren (1986), *Honourable Mentions* (Toronto: Deneau); McCall-Newman and Clarkson (1994).

87 "It's the Minister's job to set out the broad strategic goals, and leave the administration of the Department to Deputies.... When bureaucrats make policy, it is usually because there is a vacuum [and] the Minister doesn't know where he wants to go." Interview, Hon. Marc Lalonde.

88 Lalonde (1983), 3-6, 11-13; Wilson and Dungan (1993), 46-47.

89 Marianne Tefft (1983), "'Return to sanity,' says small business," *The Financial Post*, 23 April, 7.

90 Hon. Marc Lalonde, interview with author; Minister's speeches—Releases # 83-144, 83-162, 83-168, 84-53, 84-69 (Ottawa, Dept. of Finance, October 1983–May 1984).

91 Hale (1997).

92 Lalonde (1994c). These proposals were quietly shelved following the 1984 federal election.

93 The budget proposed the elimination of the Cumulative Deduction Account for about 280,000 small businesses, effectively reversing the most complex and controversial tax increase on small businesses contained in the 1981 budget. Lalonde (1984b).

94 "Tax quotas termed bankruptcy cause...," *The Globe and Mail*, 23 January 1984, 5; Beatty (1984); Hale (1984).

95 The Finance Department projected the anticipated cost of the SRTC program at $185 million in 1983-84. However, even before the Mulroney government took office in September 1984, Finance officials estimated the costs of the program had ballooned to more than $2 billion. The program was cancelled in the May 1985 budget, but not before it had cost $2.8 billion, including an estimated $925 million in uncollectable legally required repayments. Hale (1996), 315-17.

The Mulroney Legacy:
Tax Reform, Free Trade, and the Deficit Trap

You have to take a pragmatic approach to these things. One of the most important considerations in the development of tax policy we have followed during our term in office is an evolutionary way, rather than a revolutionary way, so that you gradually move in certain directions. We have indicated what those directions are; as we move in steps, we achieve the goals, but not in a way that leaves people with major adjustments to make in their after-tax income.

Michael Wilson, April 22, 1986 [1]

The Mulroney government of 1984-93 presided over a wide range of structural changes to economic policy that involved the most thoroughgoing revisions to Canada's economic constitution since the end of World War II. The most prominent of these changes was, of course, the negotiation of the Canada-US Free Trade Agreement in 1988, followed by its extension to Mexico in 1992-94, and the application of many of its principles in the global trade talks that ultimately produced the World Trade Organization. Other changes included significant changes to Canada's Competition and Bankruptcy Acts, along with full or partial economic deregulation of several industries, including transportation, telecommunications, and financial services.

Most significantly for this study, Finance Minister Michael Wilson won parliamentary approval for significant tax reform programs which made substantial changes to the corporate and personal income tax systems between 1985 and 1988, and, in 1989-90, replaced the antiquated Federal Sales Tax with a much more broadly based Goods and Services Tax. By reducing the inflation indexing of income taxes after 1985 and targeting the delivery of many family and social benefits through the income tax system, Wilson also laid the fiscal foundations for his successors' successful deficit reduction program of the mid-1990s.

With the exception of free trade—a non-issue in the 1984 election which became the centrepiece of its economic strategy after the release of the Macdonald Royal Commission Report of 1985[2]—the government's fiscal and economic policies often resembled a process of trial and error in assembling a giant jigsaw puzzle whose final dimensions were at first only vaguely understood. Many parts of the puzzle proved a difficult "fit" with Canadians' conflicting expectations of governments, leading to the political destruction of the federal Progressive Conservative Party in the 1993 election. However, after 1993, the adoption and systematic extension of Mulroney's policies by the Chrétien government, despite their initial unpopularity, suggests a pragmatic adaptation to changing economic circumstances that had passed the test of time.

When he took office in 1984, Mulroney's overriding goal was to win a second successive majority government and to establish the Conservatives as Canada's national governing party.[3] To do this, he had to "reinforce his core supporters" and "look different from the previous government," while trying to build a consensus in support of moderate change.[4] This effort involved trying to manage the conflicting public expectations created in winning an overwhelming parliamentary majority in the 1984 election and "redefining the political centre" in the manner of the pragmatic, non-ideological Conservative governments that ruled Ontario between the 1940s and the mid-1980s. Journalist Paul Wells has noted the contradictions between the tactics Mulroney used to assemble his enormous majority—and the challenges of maintaining policy coherence with such a disparate coalition:

> Mulroney seized power by doing what Liberals do: coldly analyzing the electoral map and promising whatever it took to build a workable majority. The policy rationale behind the fabled "Mulroney coalition" of rural Maritimers, Quebec nationalists, thrifty Ontario suburbanites and Western individualists was, to say the least, hardly self-evident.[5]

As a result, Mulroney lacked both the confidence in his electoral mandate and the firm core of principle necessary to introduce the major policy changes needed to come to terms with the economic legacy of the Trudeau government during his first term.[6] This legacy included large, chronic budget deficits, extensive dependence on government subsidies and protective regulation, and a culture of entitlement that led many Canadians to expect high levels of services and transfers from governments while deeply resenting the taxes needed to pay for them. Political resistance to spending restraint led the Tories to choose the soft option of trying to grow their way out of the deficit. Their lack of political confidence, reinforced by the government's declining popularity between late 1984 and mid-1987, became the overriding political constraint on Michael Wilson's ambitions for deficit reduction and tax reform. The government's 1988 election agenda, based largely on free trade, the Meech Lake constitutional agreement, and tax reform, was the product of tactical adaptation and improvisation in response to unforeseen events rather than of any strategic plan visible in 1984.[7] Nowhere is this tactical improvisation clearer than in its handling of tax policy and tax reform.

The Mulroney government's second term, 1988-93, was dominated by three imperatives: coming to grips with the federal deficit, managing the structural economic changes necessary for Canada to make the transition to free trade, and surviving the rigours of the 1990-91 recession. However, its failure to capitalize on the 1980s economic boom to reduce the deficit left it few options but to impose a series of tax increases that coincided with the introduction of the Goods and Services Tax in 1989-90. Although Mulroney and Wilson felt they had no alternative but to ride out the political backlash that resulted from this extremely unpopular measure, the high interest rates imposed in response to rising inflation wiped out their progress in deficit reduction and triggered a sustained recession in 1990-91. Economic recovery came too late to salvage voter confidence. In the federal election of September 1993, the Conservatives were reduced to two seats in the House of Commons.

This chapter examines the efforts of the Mulroney government to balance competing public expectations and demands while introducing the most significant policy revolution in recent Canadian history. The chapter assesses the approaches to deficit reduction and the tax reforms introduced by Michael Wilson between 1985 and 1991 in response to globalization, fiscal limits, and the pressures of free trade. Finally, it evaluates the legacy of the Mulroney years in shaping the Canadian economy of the twenty-first century.

Managing Conflicting Expectations

In putting together his platform, Mulroney had not promised the moon, but he had come very close.[8]

John Sawatzky

The Progressive Conservatives who took office in September 1984 had become a party of perpetual opposition, of interests left out or neglected by previous Liberal coalitions. During the 1984 election campaign, the new government promised simultaneously to reduce the deficit, cut taxes, reduce government regulation and red tape, increase opportunities for business growth and job creation, and preserve and even expand income transfer programs and public services. These promises, whose cumulative price tag was estimated at more than $20 billion,[9] both reflected and promoted unrealistic public expectations of a government that was spending $154 for every $100 collected in revenues the year the Tories returned to power.

Like the Liberal government it succeeded, the new Conservative government rapidly divided into competing wings. One emphasized government retrenchment and market-oriented reforms to economic and social policies; the other stressed the need to build a durable electoral coalition of groups benefiting from large-scale government spending and/or selective tax reductions. To complicate matters, the new government inherited a record deficit that reached $38.5 billion in 1984-85, despite spending cuts announced in Wilson's *Economic Statement* of November 1984.

It took the government almost four years to resolve these internal conflicts. Prime Minister Brian Mulroney's approach to government reflected a combination of managerial pragmatism, learned from his career as a management-side labour lawyer, and an instinctive leaning toward brokerage politics.[10] The result was the worst of both worlds: imposing politically unpopular spending restraints and tax increases, but not enough to make meaningful reductions in the federal deficit during his first term, and arousing public expectations (and fears) of large-scale policy change, but without many practical results to show for it.

The 1984 *Economic Statement* clearly articulated Wilson's main economic policy goals. It promised to make major reductions to the federal deficit, primarily through spending reductions rather than tax increases. It committed the government to reducing excessive government spending, taxation, and regulation on Canadians, thus increasing their capacity to generate economic and employment growth, and to fostering private-sector productivity and competitiveness.[11] The government also promised major changes in energy and foreign investment policies, reforms at Revenue Canada, and a review of social programs. The Neilsen Task Force was set up to oversee a wide-ranging review of spending programs.[12] Later, the Western and Atlantic Accords began the process of dismantling the National Energy Program. But Wilson's preference for an absolute reduction in the public sector appears to have been a minority taste within cabinet.[13]

Most of the first Mulroney cabinet was firmly committed to the active use of government intervention to support economic development in their regions or areas of responsibility. The major difference from Trudeau-era intervention appears to have been a general preference for federal policies to complement market forces and support business rather than an attempt to anticipate or dictate to them. In this sense, Mulroney's policies were much closer to the traditional business liberalism of post-World War II Canadian governments than to the anti-government neo-conservatism of Margaret Thatcher and Ronald Reagan, despite what this rhetoric might have suggested at times.

During his first years in power, Mulroney appeared to be committed more to changing the style and process of government than its substance. The Prime Minister's commitment to "style" was visible in expanded public consultations, efforts to impose a centralized public relations "spin" on all initiatives, and an apparent preoccupation with polls and appearances. Mulroney's commitment to changing the *process* of government was reflected in three areas: efforts to win provincial cooperation for federal policy initiatives; substantive consultations with organized interests on key issues; and the appointment of ministerial chiefs of staff in the hope of providing political balance to the policy advice of Deputy Ministers still presumed to be oriented toward a "Liberal" way of doing things.

Mulroney's commitment to change was weakest in the area of substance. According to senior government officials, the Prime Minister had little interest in the substance of policy, concentrating instead on its political implications for the government and its standing in the country. While this approach left senior ministers with considerable independence at times, conflicting cabinet priorities were often resolved by *ad hoc* decision-making and the personal influence of individual cabinet ministers with the Prime Minister until a reorganization of the Prime Minister's Office imposed greater discipline on the process. Don Mazankowski's appointment as Deputy Prime Minister in June 1986 allowed Mulroney to distance himself from day-to-day management issues and take a more strategic approach instead.

A key factor in the evolution of the Mulroney government's economic policies was the evolution of the Prime Minister's relationship with his Minister of Finance, Michael Wilson. During his six-and-a-half years at Finance, Wilson emerged as a competent, hard-working minister with a strong grasp of the strategic and technical details of policies presented to cabinet.[14] However, it was some time before he was able to exercise political influence consistent with his position as the government's senior economic policy minister. This was due often to his inability to maintain the support of the Prime Minister in setting and holding firmly to his policy priorities.[15] One official comments that "what distinguished Wilson from others in the Finance portfolio was that he was willing to settle for half-a-loaf year after year in the knowledge that if he was able to keep gnawing at spending ... he would be more effective than taking a frontal assault that Mulroney and the cabinet were not prepared to countenance."[16]

Wilson's political credibility was undermined during the 1985 budget debate when he was forced to withdraw a proposal to reduce inflation protection for seniors' benefits after Mulroney was humiliated in a televised exchange with an irate senior citizen. The resulting backlash from seniors' groups began a long slide in the government's popularity. The Prime Minister's contradictory promises of lower taxes, lower deficits, and the protection of universal social programs as a "sacred trust" returned to haunt him. The public's response demonstrated its limited concern for deficit reduction and eroded the government's political will to engage in further spending reductions. After this incident, Wilson's strategy in dealing with cabinet was to avoid pushing decisions to confrontations with colleagues "unless he was sure of winning." As a result, apart from 1985-86, Wilson was able only to slow the rate of growth of government spending during his tenure as Finance Minister, rather than to reduce it as originally intended.

Wilson's growing political influence with Mulroney after 1986 was reflected in his extensive participation in non-Finance issues (e.g., free trade) and his appointment as political minister for Ontario to deal with party people and patronage issues. Wilson gradually gained the Prime Minister's confidence to the point of winning his support for a series of bitterly unpopular policies after the 1988 election, notably the Goods and Services Tax and the zero-inflation policies that deepened the 1990-91 recession.[17] However, the price of winning this confidence—and with it, the power to control the government's economic policy agenda—was Wilson's step-by-step approach to rebuilding the government's political credibility by means of his incremental policy reforms of the first term.

This policy of gradualism meant that, except for its controversial decision to negotiate a Free Trade Agreement with the United States, the Mulroney government during its first term tended to steer away from highly controversial decisions. This approach changed significantly after the 1988 election, which convinced Mulroney that, given a clear policy focus, he could mobilize public opinion in support of the government's policies. Increasingly confident in the logic of the government's emerging agenda of economic restructuring and shifting from universal to more targeted social programs, Mulroney demonstrated a much greater willingness to take political risks in pursuit of his objectives. However, although historians are beginning to view his record with greater favour,[18] the accumulation of controversial policy decisions during his second term proved to be too great a legacy for his successor, Kim Campbell, to overcome.

Ironically, after the Conservatives' near destruction in the 1993 federal election, the Liberals adopted and implemented most of their policies, confirming Mulroney's initial belief that style and process are often as important to the political success of governments as the actual substance of their policies. Nowhere did this reality emerge more clearly than in the two governments' handling of the federal deficit.

Taxation and the Politics of the Deficit

The Mulroney government failed to pursue consistent deficit reduction policies during the economic expansion of 1984-89. Although it succeeded in reducing federal spending slightly during its first term, after discounting for inflation, its fragile electoral coalition was too diverse to enable it to pursue strong or consistent enough tax or spending measures to reduce the *structural deficit* without alienating significant groups of its supporters. Unbudgeted increases in federal revenues after 1986 were rapidly spent by a cabinet apparently incapable of living up to its own rhetoric on fiscal self-discipline.

Wilson's tax policy agenda of 1984-86 sought to balance four major political economic priorities in what might be described as a process of "coordinated incrementalism." First, it addressed the grievances of major constituencies—especially the energy and small business sectors—which resulted from the tax policies of the previous Liberal administration. Second, it took advantage of a growing economy to raise taxes and reduce the deficit through a combination of federal income surtaxes, partial deindexing of personal income tax brackets and transfer payments, and the reduction of corporate tax breaks. Third, it began the process of targeting federal income support programs to lower- and middle-income earners, and away from universal tax and social benefits. Finally, it introduced a series of proposals for structural change in the tax system to reduce economic distortions and to respond to major structural changes in the economy.

However, Wilson rapidly discovered the limits to change. Late in 1984, the government blundered into a debate on the universality of social programs for which it was clearly ill-prepared. Wilson and Health and Welfare Minister Jake Epp appeared to be publicly at odds over limits to universality. In trying to quell the debate, Mulroney effectively foreclosed the option of major changes to universal social programs, at least during the government's current mandate.[19] This action undercut Wilson, and left the government vulnerable to attack when he limited the indexing of seniors' pensions in the May 1985 budget.[20]

Wilson introduced a series of tax increases and spending reductions in his 1985 budget. The most controversial measure was his decision to de-index both the federal tax system and a number of income transfer programs, including Old Age Security (OAS) and family allowances. The new indexing formula was based on the Consumer Price Index (CPI) less three per cent. Although GIS pension for low-income seniors was exempted, the measure prompted an intense political backlash. When even business groups questioned the wisdom and fairness of the measure, an angry Wilson restored full pension indexing and increased the income surtax on high-income earners and corporations to make up the budgetary shortfall.[21]

The major spending reductions recommended by the Neilsen Task Force were watered down by cabinet or absorbed by new spending commitments after 1986.[22] A commission headed by former Quebec cabinet minister Claude Forget proposed a thorough overhaul of the Unemployment Insurance system, but its proposals for major changes received little public support and vanished in cabinet.[23]

Mulroney's desire for federal-provincial cooperation to ease first the negotiation and then the ratification of the Meech Lake constitutional accord also precluded Finance from reducing transfers to the provinces as part of its deficit control program during Mulroney's first term. Although this would have been a standard Finance Department negotiating tactic in the 1970s, a senior Finance Department official comments that it was "contrary to Mulroney's philosophy of federal-provincial relations" during this period.[24] Although Wilson succeeded in holding spending increases for government programs near or just below the rate of inflation in five of his last six budgets, the tyranny of compound interest on the federal debt prevented annual deficits from dropping below $27.7 billion, even at the peak of the 1980s boom. Wilson's deficit reduction program was left to stand on a combination of tax increases, reduced tax preferences, and accounting sophistries (see Table 7.1).

A key element in this process was the progressive shifting of tax benefits and income transfers from middle- and upper-income to lower-income families. In 1985, Wilson increased the child tax benefit by one-third, while reducing the tax exemption for dependent children.[25] In 1987, his White Paper on tax reform proposed the replacement of a large number of tax deductions, increasing in value with the taxpayer's income, with tax credits that provided the greatest relative benefit to taxpayers earning less than $30,000. Faced with rising deficits as a result of the recession, Wilson's final budget in 1991 eliminated family allowances and universal tax preferences for children and replaced them with an enriched refundable Child Tax Credit targeted at lower-income families earning less than $20,000. Bracket creep—the effects of inflation on reducing the value of tax preferences and forcing taxpayers into higher tax brackets—provided a fiscal windfall to the provinces.

However, Wilson did not rely only on stealth taxes in his effort to reduce the deficit. The 1986 budget contained $3.9 billion in tax increases over two

Table 7.1 ·· LOSING THE DEFICIT BATTLE: 1984-93
(IN MILLIONS OF 1992 DOLLARS)

	Budgetary Revenue	Program Spending	Interest on Debt	Deficit	PERCENTAGE INCREASE/ ——(DECREASE) IN REAL——			
					Revenue	Program Spending	Debt Interest	Deficit
1984-85	71,056	87,100	22, 393	-38,437	—	—	—	—
1985-86	76,933	86,106	25,422	-34,595	4.1	-5.0	9.1	-13.5
1986-87	85,931	90,005	26,668	-30,742	7.3	0.4	0.7	-14.7
1987-88	97,612	96,453	28,953	-27,794	8.9	2.7	4.0	-13.4
1988-89	104,067	99,688	33,152	-28,773	2.5	-0.7	10.0	-0.5
4 YEAR AVERAGE					5.7	-0.6	6.0	-10.5
1989-90	113,707	103,948	38,759	-28,930	4.1	-0.7	11.4	-4.2
1990-91	119,353	108,765	42,588	-32,000	0.1	-0.1	4.8	5.5
1991-92	122,032	115,215	41,174	-34,357	-3.2	0.3	-8.4	1.7
1992-93	120,380	122,576	38,825	-41,021	-2.8	4.8	-7.1	17.6
4 YEAR AVERAGE					-0.4	1.1	0.2	5.2

Highlighted areas indicates election year.

Source: Canada, Department of Finance (2000d); author's calculations.

years. In addition to increased corporate income taxes, personal income tax surtaxes on individuals earning over $40,000 were replaced by a 3-per-cent "deficit reduction" surtax on all taxpayers. Federal sales taxes rose to 12 per cent, and alcohol and tobacco taxes were increased. By way of compensation, Wilson eliminated the 12.5-per-cent surtax on small business dividends left over from the MacEachen budget of 1981 and hinted at the replacement of the Federal Sales Taxes with a new Value Added Tax that would enable the government to eliminate the surtaxes.

However, Wilson was not able to meet his 1986 deficit reduction projections. High interest rates, a sharp drop in oil prices and revenues, and a growing agricultural trade war resulted in lower federal revenues and higher spending than earlier projected. Wilson's limited success at deficit reduction is also attributed by staff and colleagues to the ability of senior cabinet colleagues to make an end-run around spending restrictions by appealing to the Prime Minister.[26] Early proposals for a Business Transfer Tax to replace the Federal Sales Tax met a similar fate,[27] as the government's standing declined steadily in public opinion polls until the Tories fell into third place below the New Democrats.[28]

Although Wilson was prepared to invest a large part of the government's remaining political capital in the tough decisions necessary to implement his economic reforms by mid-1986, Mulroney and his cabinet colleagues were not.[29] As a result, the tax reforms of 1987-88 were used to return to Canadians a portion of the tax increases imposed since 1985, and concerted action on the deficit had to wait until after the 1988 election. By that time, the government was approaching the end of the long economic expansion of the 1980s. The effects of tax increases and greater spending discipline in reducing the deficit were offset by the effects of rising interest rates on government borrowing costs in 1989 and 1990. By the end of 1990, a growing recession began to push the federal and provincial deficits steadily higher. As the national unemployment rate rose from 7.5 per cent in 1989 to 11.3 per cent in 1992, the budgetary deficit rose from $29 billion in 1988-89 and 1989-90 to $41 billion in 1992-93.

Wilson's ability to sell his agenda for tax reform and deficit control hinged largely on his ability to win and maintain the confidence of the Prime Minister on major political decisions. Although he was able to do this on a number of major initiatives, including income tax reforms and the Goods and Services Tax, Wilson did not win Mulroney's support in his fight against the deficit until the economic consequences of previous policy decisions had made it impossible to reach his goals. The structural changes introduced by Wilson at such political cost would accrue to the benefit of his Liberal successor, Paul Martin, who enjoyed a level of prime ministerial and popular support in cutting spending that the former Finance Minister could only have dreamed of.

Taxation and the Politics of Economic Adjustment

The Mulroney government when it was elected in 1984 had no intention of embarking on major tax reforms. Early in his term, Michael Wilson all but ruled out large-scale tax reforms as likely to disrupt private business activity and confidence.[30] However, as was the case with free trade, the government's decision to launch tax reforms was made in reaction to unforeseen circumstances.

US tax reforms in 1986 that sharply reduced marginal tax rates for individuals and corporations forced Wilson to respond with comparable measures. At the same time, he recognized that tax reforms, whether intended to increase or reduce taxes, would be politically saleable only if his policies tilted the distribution of income and payroll taxes away from lower- and middle-income Canadians, and toward upper-income earners. Ironically, despite the sometimes venomous political attacks of opponents for its allegedly "heartless" policies, Canada's tax system became significantly more progressive in its impact on various income groups between 1984 and 1993 (see Table 7.2).

These changes began as a series of piecemeal policy changes designed to sort out much of the unfinished business left by the Trudeau government. Wilson's first budget, in May 1985, attempted to lay the foundations for long-term policy changes, while paying a number of political debts left over from the 1984 federal election. The budget's political centrepiece was the introduction of a lifetime exemption of up to $250,000 of taxable capital gains for individuals, to be phased in between 1985 and 1990. Wilson promoted the exemption as a symbolic, high-profile incentive for individuals to invest and take economic risks, not just save. In practice, it merely offset the effects of inflation in eroding the value of long-term investments, especially small businesses and family farms. Other campaign promises addressed in the budget included the dismantling of most of the National Energy Program, provisions allowing RRSP and pension fund investments in small businesses, a revised Research & Development tax credit to replace the dis-

Table 7.2 ·· DISTRIBUTION OF TAXPAYERS, INCOMES, AND FEDERAL INCOME TAXES PAID—LOWER-, MIDDLE-AND UPPER-INCOME TAXPAYERS: 1985, 1993

1985	Under $20,000	$20,000–$40,000	Over $40,000
NUMBER OF TAXPAYERS	46.9%	40.0%	13.1%
TOTAL INCOME ASSESSED	24.0%	44.2%	31.7%
FEDERAL TAX PAYABLE	13.1%	42.6%	43.0%
TAX AS % OF ASSESSED INCOME	6.7%	11.6%	16.6%
1993	Under $25,000	$25,000–$50,000	Over $50,000
NUMBER OF TAXPAYERS	45.0%	39.2%	15.8%
TOTAL INCOME ASSESSED	21.3%	40.8%	37.8%
FEDERAL TAX PAYABLE	11.8%	37.8%	50.3%
TAX AS % OF ASSESSED INCOME	7.2%	12.0%	20.3%
% INCREASE: 1985–1993	7.5%	3.4%	22.3%

Source: *The National Finances, 1987–88* (Toronto: Canadian Tax Foundation, 1988), Table 7:25; *1995 Taxation Statistics on Individuals* (Ottawa: Revenue Canada, 1995), author's calculations.

credited Scientific and Research Tax Credit, and a tax break for venture capital funds sponsored by organized labour.[31]

CORPORATE TAX REFORMS

The 1985 budget also included proposals for corporate tax reform. These were introduced through a Discussion Paper in the May 1985 budget, implemented in 1986, and extended further during the 1987-88 tax reform process. Many of Wilson's corporate tax changes could claim inspiration, if not direct parentage, from the tax reform measures introduced by Allan MacEachen in 1981. However, while MacEachen's tax increases had prompted massive business criticism, Wilson managed to raise business taxes with minimal political cost. How did Wilson succeed in his corporate tax reforms where MacEachen had failed? Perhaps the best answer can be found in the five Cs of tax reform: credibility, conceptualization, consultation, compensation, and circumstances.

Wilson enjoyed one enormous advantage in winning business confidence over Allan MacEachen, and indeed, over most Liberal finance ministers of the Trudeau era. He was perceived as "one of them." A former executive of Dominion Securities before entering politics in 1979, Wilson enjoyed an unmatched reputation within the business and financial communities as *the* champion within cabinet of fiscal responsibility and pro-business economic policies. A decade later, Paul Martin would earn a similar reputation relative to Prime Minister Jean Chrétien, but only after imposing the kinds of drastic spending reductions that Wilson never was able to extract from his cabinet colleagues.

From the earliest days of the Mulroney government, Wilson promoted corporate tax reforms, arguing that business and investment decisions should be made on the basis of sound economic criteria, and not distorted by tax considerations. This principle has become conventional wisdom for his successors. Different industrial sectors should be subject to roughly equivalent effective tax rates. Government support for business should be delivered through broadly-based tax or spending programs, whichever might be more cost effective, but not both.[32] The other major argument made in favour of corporate tax reform proposals was the need to reduce competitive tax avoidance and the adversarial "tax dance" between Finance officials attempting to maximize tax revenues and tax professionals attempting to minimize their clients' taxes within the law.[33]

Finance officials also worked to convince business interests that the wide disparities in effective tax rates in different industry sectors, which reflected very different access to tax preferences, should be narrowed.[34] They proposed that marginal tax rates and overall tax burdens should be competitive with those of Canada's major trading partners. Between 1985 and 1992, corporate income tax rates were reduced from 36 to 28.8 per cent for large corporations, from 32 to 23.8 per cent for manufacturers, and from 15 to 12.8 per cent for small businesses, with lower tax rates offset by a major reduction in corporate tax preferences[35] (see Table 7.4). All these arguments had been made in defence of the MacEachen budget of 1981, but were drowned out by the general backlash to the budgets and by business reaction to the lack of prior consultation and adequate transitional measures. Wilson's systematic consultation with business groups and their tax advisors ensured that the technical details of his proposals would be consistent with the political objectives outlined in his public statements.

Wilson balanced his business tax increases of 1985-88 with a series of trade-offs to reduce business opposition through promises of compensation in other areas. Tax increases of $785 million contained in the 1986 budget were phased in over three years. Small businesses, the most numerous, vocal, and anti-government sector of the business community, received preferential treatment throughout the Mulroney government's first term.[36] The oil industry, hit hard by falling oil prices, received a cash flow boost in 1986 with the elimination of the Petroleum and Gas Revenues Tax.[37] However, the key factor in muting corporate grumbling was the implicit promise of imminent reform of the Federal Sales Tax, especially changes that would be of particular benefit to manufacturers and exporters.[38] These groups saw major benefits in a Value-Added Tax that would refund to them sales taxes paid on exports and business purchases, especially with the prospect of a free trade agreement with the United States then under negotiation.

Finally, the marketing of these changes was made significantly easier by the actions of other major industrial nations, especially Britain and the United States, which introduced similar tax reforms between 1984 and 1986. Few business people were likely to criticize a policy enjoying bipartisan support and copying the example of Ronald Reagan. Unlike the tax reform debates of 1971 and 1981, the US tax reforms of 1986 set clear limits on the ability of Canadian corporate and financial interests to block major policy changes by pointing to their potential impact on Canadian competitiveness.

The bipartisan US tax reform bill created a tremendous political momentum for tax reform in Canada. Shifting a part of the tax burden onto large corporations would enable the Mulroney government to finance a modest reduction in personal income taxes in 1987-88, just before an anticipated federal election, thereby giving its tax reform program a mildly populist aura. Facing the imminent polarization of the electorate over free trade, an issue on which most business executives passionately supported the Mulroney government, modest increases in corporate taxes were a small price to pay for business to help re-elect the most sympathetic federal government in twenty years. Furthermore, for many corporate executives, the benefits of promised sales tax reforms would more than offset the costs of higher corporate taxes.

PERSONAL INCOME TAX REFORMS

Wilson's personal income tax reforms, introduced through a White Paper in June 1987, were passed by Parliament in September 1988, just before that year's "free trade" election. Unlike MacEachen's tax reforms of 1981, Wilson's program was relatively uncontroversial and received parliamentary approval with a minimum of partisan or interest group conflict. This lack of controversy can be traced to a process of careful political management and consensus-building by the Minister and the Department of Finance. Wilson avoided direct challenges to entrenched economic interests and minimized specific tax increases for particular groups, while returning to Canadians about \$2.1 billion of the tax increases he had imposed since 1985.[39] He also engaged in extensive consultation with major interest groups from across the political spectrum, and sought to reinforce the impression of policy continuity with his piecemeal tax changes of the mid-1980s.[40]

Tax reform provided an opportunity to link several separate elements of the government's overall economic strategy, and to give a clear sense of political direction to a government that appeared to be drifting halfway through its electoral mandate.[41] The biggest initiative on the federal agenda, the proposed Canada-US Free Trade Agreement, was intended to promote the competitiveness of Canadian industries in an increasingly interdependent continental and global economy. US tax reform, which was working its way through Congress during the summer of 1986, promised to make major cuts in marginal tax rates for both corporations and individuals. Canada, reliant on US markets for 80 per cent of its exports, could not hope to compete for private investment and production facilities if its corporate tax rates were 50 per cent higher than American rates. This message was repeated constantly by business groups in their meetings with the government.[42]

Canada followed the pattern of American tax reforms in several important areas. It financed part of its personal tax reduction by shifting part of the tax burden to large corporations and investment income. Wilson increased the share of capital gains subject to taxation, or "inclusion rate," from 50 to 75 per cent, and announced his decision to cap the lifetime capital gains exemption at \$100,000, except for family farms and small businesses.[43] This still appeared generous compared with the US Congress decision to tax 100 per cent of nominal capital gains.[44] Wilson also followed the US example in reducing deductions for business travel and entertainment, capital cost allowances, and other tax preferences that, under other circumstances, would doubtless have provoked savage criticism from business and financial interests. Wilson used these tax increases to finance personal tax reductions for most income groups, thus allowing him to market tax reform as a net benefit for the average taxpayer.

However, despite Finance's tradition of controlling the tax policy process, Wilson had to build a consensus with his cabinet and caucus colleagues on the proposed reforms. A senior Finance official comments that, although Mulroney consistently supported Wilson's policy proposals after the pension indexing retreat of 1985, the timing and form of these proposals were often dependent on Wilson's capacity to convince and persuade cabinet and caucus colleagues of their soundness. "On virtually every controversial issue, [Mulroney] wouldn't go ahead until he was certain he had caucus behind him.... The details of policy were left to ministers. But caucus was his reality check. Holding the caucus together was the key to Mulroney's political style."[45]

The government's steady decline in the polls throughout 1986 and much of 1987, and the likelihood of an election in 1988 limited cabinet's willingness to take political risks with tax reform. A former PMO official comments that "Mulroney wanted good news, not bad news in

Table 7.3 ·· FLATTENING THE TAX RATE STRUCTURE (IN 2000 DOLLARS)

1984	
BASIC PERSONAL EXEMPTION*	$5,934
SPOUSAL DEDUCTION*	$5,194

Federal Tax Rate on Taxable Income

FIRST $1,949	6%
$1,950 – $3,897	16%
$3,898– $7,793	17%
$7,794 – $11,691	18%
$11,692 – $19,486	19%
$19,487 – $27,280	20%
$27,281 – $35,075	23%
$35,076 – $54,560	25%
$54,561 – $93,530	30%
OVER $93,531	34%

1988	
BASIC PERSONAL CREDIT**	$8,029
SPOUSAL CREDIT**	$6,691

Federal Tax Rate on Taxable Income

UP TO $36,801	17%
$36,801 – $73,605	26%
OVER $73,605	29%

* Deduction from taxable income

** 17% of this amount deducted from federal tax payable.

Source: *The National Finances, 1987-88*, Tables 7:4, 7:5; author's calculations.

the twelve months before the election ... good news and spending.... He also wanted to get tax rebates out before the 1988 election so that tax reform would be seen as good news."[46] As a result, tax reform in 1987-88 was packaged in a simple, coherent message: "tax reform equals lower taxes." The marketing of the new tax reform strategy began in July 1986 with Wilson's statement to the House on "options for tax reform." This was followed by a *Guidelines for Tax Reform* discussion paper in October 1986, spelling out nine main policy objectives to be reconciled as part of the reform process:

> ➤ Fairness—the fair sharing of the tax burden among taxpayers

> ➤ Balance—reduced federal reliance on personal income tax revenues

> ➤ Revenue stability and certainty

> ➤ Revenue neutrality

> ➤ International competitiveness

> ➤ Recognition of special regional needs

> ➤ Encouraging economic efficiency and growth

> ➤ Appropriate transitional provisions.

> ➤ Broad consultation prior to the introduction of final legislative proposals.[47]

These proposals were followed by formal consultations by the Commons Finance Committee and Senate Banking Committee, the 1987 budget, a White Paper tabled in June 1987, more parliamentary and informal consultations, and the introduction of draft legislation in December 1987. The final tax reform bill passed in September 1988 to take effect in January 1989.

Proposed changes were intended to increase tax relief for lower-income taxpayers and shift the benefit of several major tax preferences from upper- to lower-income taxpayers by converting them from deductions to non-refundable tax credits. Rather than lowering the *income* subject to tax, the White Paper sought to *equalize* the value of tax preferences to individual taxpayers above the basic tax threshold. The tax benefit of these deductions, except for charitable contributions, would be calculated on the value of the lowest PIT rate (17 per cent) rather than increasing with marginal tax rates. As a result, the government would be able to use the added revenues to reduce tax rates for all income groups. Tax reform also reduced the number of tax benefits and shelters available to upper-income earners and profitable corporations without interfering with normal business practices. As a result, it increased the progressivity of the income tax system for all but the very top income earners[48] (see Tables 7.2, 7.3).

Other major changes to the personal income tax structure in the White Paper included the lowering and flattening of the tax structure. The number of tax brackets was reduced from ten to three: 17 per cent for Canadians with taxable incomes below $27,500, a 26-per-cent marginal rate on incomes between $27,500 and $55,000, and a top 29-per-cent tax rate for incomes over $55,000 (see Table 7.3). This would mean an initial reduction in the top federal-provincial marginal tax rate from about 50 per cent to about 44 per cent.[49] However, these rate reductions proved to be short-lived, since both the provinces and the federal government subsequently increased taxes on the broader base. Revenue losses from rate reductions were offset by a number of base-broadening measures.

Corporate tax changes were intended to reduce tax deferrals and to bring the taxable profits of corporations more closely into line with profits reported in financial statements. White Paper measures brought corporate tax rates closer to post-reform levels in the United States, while reducing capital cost allowances for several sectors, and limiting the preferred tax status of resource industries and financial institutions[50] (see Table 7.4).

Wilson sought to take control of the policy agenda and to shape public opinion by initiating a systematic speaking and public relations campaign that took him to every province. He presented his tax reforms as a non-ideological package, consistent with the economic and social objectives of his audiences, stressing competitiveness and balance to business audiences, fairness to social policy groups, and regional concerns outside of Ontario.[51]

This strategy allowed Wilson the luxury of building a constituency for tax reform on a sector-by-sector basis, rather than facing an angry coalition of aggrieved interests. Free trade and the promise of sales tax reform largely neutralized potential corporate opposition. Free trade and the rollback of the National Energy Program did the same for the energy sector. The rhetoric of fairness, the introduction of a minimum tax, and the promise to convert many tax deductions to credits won the acquiescence of the social policy community, if only as a "second-best" strategy. Although the left dismissed Wilson's attack on "tax expenditures" as minimal, he easily brushed off its calls for a corporate minimum tax.[52]

The Commons Finance Committee also served as a major instrument for the legitimation of tax reform. It provided a vehicle for consensus-building and the constructive involvement of both government and opposition members in the design of legislation. Don Blenkarn, the Committee's colourful

Table 7.4 ·· TAX REFORM 1987–CORPORATE TAX RATE CHANGES

	Pre-reform Rates	Proposed New Rates 1988	Proposed New Rates 1991	Actual Rate 1991
GENERAL BUSINESS	36	28	28	28.84
MANUFACTURERS	30	26	23	23.84
GENERAL SMALL BUSINESS	15	12	12	12.84
SMALL MANUFACTURERS	10	12	12	12.84

Source: *The National Finances: 1987-88, 1991* (Toronto: Canadian Tax Foundation).

and capable chairman, worked closely with opposition critics to improve the proposals. Blenkarn demonstrated that a well-run parliamentary committee could manage to transcend the normal partisanship of the House of Commons. The Committee also provided a forum for many interest groups to make their case, demonstrating that tax reform could pass the test of organized public opinion.

Following the negotiation of the Canada-US Free Trade Agreement in 1987, the public spotlight shifted away from tax reform. However, by then Wilson had established control over the policy agenda. Discussion was largely confined to questions of detail, largely in meetings with the tax practitioners and interest groups that dominate the broader tax policy community.

AFTER TAX REFORM

The income tax reforms of 1987-88 were the first attempt at large-scale tax reform in forty years to achieve a broad, if grudging consensus generally acceptable to tax professions, the business community, the news media, and the general public.[53] This represented a more or less consensual effort by the federal government, the parliamentary opposition, major interest groups, and the tax community to lower marginal tax rates and broaden the tax base in the wake of similar reforms in the United States.

By avoiding the bitter political battles triggered by proposed tax reforms in 1967-71 and 1981-82, Wilson's tax reforms were enough of a political success that they were virtually ignored during the bitter debates over free trade in the 1988 election campaign. By taking a non-ideological approach to tax reform, consulting broadly on its details, and avoiding major challenges to entrenched economic interests, Wilson was able to ensure that virtually all the ideas contained in his White Paper became familiar and relatively unthreatening to both business and social policy groups.

Wilson's political caution resulted in the deferral or avoidance of several major issues that could have shattered the fragile consensus on which tax reform was built. He postponed his stated goal of restructuring the sales tax system at the same time as income tax reform, and separated his deficit reduction goals from the tax reform process, thus avoiding challenges to tax reform as a zero-sum or negative sum game. Instead, he increased taxes in 1985, 1986, and 1989. Thus, income tax reform can be seen as a temporary rebate against a larger backdrop of rising taxes.

Wilson's final "fudge" on tax reform was equally important. The federal promise that tax reform would mean lower taxes largely depended on provincial governments exercising self-restraint by harmonizing their tax policies with those of the federal government. Since he would have to depend on provincial goodwill to sell the idea of a National Sales Tax to replace both federal and provincial sales taxes (see Chapter 8), he refused to link tax harmonization to the one major fiscal policy lever at his disposal, the maintenance of federal transfers to the provinces. Thus a series of provincial tax increases between 1989 and 1993, especially in Ontario, made the benefits of Wilson's tax reductions rather short-lived in most parts of the country.

Some risks, however, could not be deferred indefinitely. Unable to win provincial support for sales tax reform, Wilson acted unilaterally in 1989-90 to introduce the Goods and Services Tax. Without the sweetener of income tax reductions, which had already been offset by provincial tax increases, the federal government's popularity plummeted from 43 per cent in the election of 1988 to below 20 per cent through most of 1991 and 1992. The cumulative impact of a general recession, the difficult adjustment to free trade, the GST, and battles over constitutional change aroused enough voter resentment to shatter the Conservative Party in the 1993 federal elections.

Unlike previous tax reform programs, the 1987-88 reforms were not followed by a serious erosion of the tax base. This was partly due to the growing pressures of the deficit, which forced governments to maximize revenues. However, Wilson was successful enough in building consensus on his income tax reforms that no coalition of interest groups emerged to demand major changes.

Most post-reform changes introduced by Wilson himself, his immediate successor Don Mazankowski (1991-93), and Liberal Paul Martin (since 1993) have generally followed the broad outlines of policies introduced between 1985 and 1988. These changes include the imposition of a Large Corporations Tax integrated with the corporate income tax (1989); the consolidation of most family-related transfers and tax preferences into a more

Table 7.5 ·· FEDERAL AND PROVINCIAL PROGRAM SPENDING AND
FEDERAL-PROVINCIAL TRANSFERS

	PER CAPITA PROGRAM SPENDING GROWTH	
	1984/85 – 1989/90	*1989/90 – 1994/95*
FEDERAL	11.3%	9.6%
FEDERAL CASH TRANSFERS TO PROVINCES	18.0%	0.1%*
PROVINCIAL AVERAGE	32.3%	14.0%

* Federal per capita cash transfers increased 10.8% between 1989-90 and 1992-93, then declined to 1989-90 levels between 1992-93 and 1994-95.

Sources: *Canadian Tax Notes* (Toronto: Canadian Tax Foundation, July 18, 1995), 18; Canada (1996) *Economic Reference Tables*; Hon. Paul Martin (1995) *Budget Speech* (Ottawa: Department of Finance, February).

generous tax credit, targeted exclusively to lower- and middle-income families (1992-93); and the gradual phasing out of the capital gains exemption for all taxpayers except farmers and small business owners (1992-94). On this level, Wilson can claim to have left his successors both a stable tax base and the least hospitable political climate for special interest pleading on tax issues in many years. The introduction of the National Child Benefit in 1997, which has since grown to become the federal government's largest tax transfer program, was a direct extension of Wilson's policies. Federal tax reductions introduced in the 2000 budgets, while reversing or mitigating some of these measures, did so in ways that were broadly consistent with the pattern established by Wilson in the late 1980s.

Although the long-term effects of inflation de-indexing pushed up average federal tax levels by 20 per cent between 1989 and 1997, the largest change to overall tax rates and to the progressivity of the tax structure came from changes to provincial income taxes and surtaxes. This change was mainly due to fiscal competition between Ottawa and the provinces, sometimes characterized as "deficit offloading." Most provinces declined to curb the rapid growth in their spending to accommodate the modest tax reductions contained in federal tax reforms. This trend was reversed only after the huge deficits arising from the 1990-91 recession forced most provinces to put their fiscal houses in order (see Table 7.5).

The provinces opted instead to levy comparable or higher tax rates on the new, broader federal tax base, thus increasing total provincial revenues. When Wilson retaliated in 1990 by freezing per capita transfers to the provinces, several provinces opted for further tax increases, sometimes by levying substantial surtaxes on middle- and upper-income taxpayers.

Public resentment of Wilson's tax measures during the early and mid-1990s focused on the Goods and Service Tax. During the 1993 election, the opposition parties all promised to reduce, "replace," or eliminate the tax. However, the victorious Liberals discovered that most of the proposed alternatives were fiscally, administratively, or politically unworkable, and settled for largely cosmetic revisions in 1996.

Building to Last: Wilson's Legacy

The Mulroney government inherited a country deeply divided over the political and economic legacies of the Trudeau Liberals, and a government with a massive and unsustainable deficit. It presided over a series of major policy changes that left Canadians united, if only superficially, in frustration and anger at the economic dislocation that accompanied the transition to North American free trade, a more sustainable level of government spending, and the technological revolution that was transforming the Canadian economy. However, these changes—however difficult and controversial at the time—laid the foundation that made possible the balancing of the federal budget and Canada's return to prosperity during the late 1990s.

Michael Wilson's tax reforms of 1987-90 set the pattern for federal tax policies during most of the 1990s. Ironically, for a minister who persuaded Canadians to support his policies based on the slogan "Tax reform means lower taxes," Wilson imposed some of the most significant tax increases in post-war Canadian history, and subjected middle-income Canadians to annual inflation-driven tax increases through de-indexation and bracket creep. By 1993, the cumulative effect of de-indexation amounted to an annual income tax increase of at least $8 billion, or 11 per cent, since 1986.[53] Combined with his introduction of the intensely unpopular Goods and Services Tax, Wilson's policies contributed to a climate of tax fatigue among middle-class Canadians that made it easier for his successor, Paul Martin, to impose significant reductions on federal spending as part of his successful deficit reduction campaign of the 1990s. However, unlike previous efforts at tax reform, Wilson's policies were adopted and reinforced by his Conservative and Liberal successors, resulting in the greatest stability in the major elements of Canadian tax policies of any decade since the 1950s.

Wilson's rhetorical campaign against the deficit was more successful than were his efforts to make lasting reductions in the deficit. The failure of annual tax increases to have any significant impact on federal deficits convinced a majority of Canadians, in the absence of significant spending reductions, that more drastic action was necessary, though not in time to save the Conservatives from electoral destruction in the 1993 election. This part of Wilson's legacy was enthusiastically embraced by the new Reform Party, which replaced the Tories after 1993 as the leading voice of fiscal conservatism and free-market economics in the House of Commons. It also forced the Chrétien government to rethink the gradualist platform of deficit reduction on which it was elected in 1993, and to centralize control over budgets and policy coordination in the hands of Finance Minister Paul Martin and his department to a degree not seen since the 1950s. These changes forced Chrétien and the federal Liberals to develop a new style of liberalism capable of balancing the competing expectations and demands of global economic competition, domestic politics, and the operations of government.

NOTES

1 Hon. Michael H. Wilson (1986) Testimony to Commons' Finance Committee, *Minutes and Proceedings*, Issue # 10 (Ottawa: House of Commons, 22 April), 10.

2 Canada. Royal Commission on the Economic Union and Development Prospects for Canada, *Report* (1985).

3 Bercuson, Granatstein, and Young (1986), 27; interview, senior Finance Department official (D4).

4 Interview, political staff, Department of Finance (F02); "Speech from the Throne," Canada, House of Commons, *Debates*, November 5, 1984, 5-8. Public documents in 1984-85 repeatedly referred to "national reconciliation," "consultation," and "consensus."

5 Paul Wells (2001) "How Stock Happens," *National Post*, 28 April.

6 A senior government official comments that Mulroney and his closest associates regarded the 1984 election results more as a rejection of the previous Trudeau government than as a popular mandate for major political change under the Tories, and were therefore much more cautious about introducing major policy changes than they were in their second term. Interview, senior government official (D4).

7 Doern and Tomlin (1991) argue strongly that cabinet's acceptance of the Free Trade option was the result of protectionist pressures in the United States and policy entrepreneurship in the public service rather than any deep-seated ideological conviction.

8 Sawatzky (1991), 548.

9 Ibid.

10 Aucoin, Bercuson, Hoy, and others argue that Mulroney was not driven by a clear ideological agenda. This is confirmed by discussions with senior government officials (PMO-1, D4, ADM-9). Aucoin (1986); Bercuson, et al. (1986) 27; Hoy (1987).

11 Wilson (1984).

12 Hon. Erik Neilsen (1985) *New Management Initiatives: Initial results from the Ministerial Task Force on Program Review* (Ottawa: Supply & Services Canada, May); Canada, Task Force on Program Review (1986).

13 Bercuson, et al. (1986), 46-47.

14 Virtually all officials interviewed regarded Wilson as the Finance Minister with the best technical grasp of tax policy issues since the 1971 tax reform bill.

15 Interviews, former PMO, PCO, and Finance Department officials (PMO-1, D7, F02).

16 Interview, Department of Finance (F02).

17 Interviews, Department of Finance (D4, F02).

18 Velk and Riggs (2000).

19 Bercuson, et al. (1986), 102-09; Lipsey and Purvis (1985). Several observers have attributed Mulroney's apparent overreaction to the universality debate as a combination of inexperience and a lack of political confidence, rather than a deliberate decision to undercut Wilson. (Interviews, Privy Council Office, Department of Finance [D1, D7]). However, the political effect was still devastating.

20 For a detailed discussion of the universality debate and the government's policy incoherence, see Bercuson, et al. (1986), 52, 93-120.

21 "Tories retreat on de-indexing pensions," *The Globe and Mail*, 28 June 1985, 1. Senior Finance Department officials had recommended that Wilson offset the impact of de-indexing on the elderly poor by "super-indexing" the GIS. Wilson rejected their proposal, apparently because it would have cost the government $860 million of the $1.6 billion saved annually by benefit de-indexation. Bercuson, et al. (1986), 112-13; interview, Finance Department official (D8).

22 Savoie (1990), 132-42; Hartle (1988a), Ch. 10.

23 The Forget Report, released in November 1986, recommended that UI benefits be fully funded by employee and employee premiums, that regional and sectoral subsidies be eliminated, and that an "experience-rated" system of premiums be instituted, based on employer and industry employment and layoff patterns. Other social objectives were to be integrated into other government programs paid from general tax revenues. The only major recommendation implemented was the cut-off of UI benefits from persons quitting their jobs without just cause—in December 1992! Canada, Commission of Inquiry on Unemployment Insurance (1986).

24 "There was tremendous pressure on us in budgets not to cut federal-provincial transfers." Former Deputy Minister, Department of Finance (D4). This policy changed significantly after the 1988 election.

25 Wilson (1985b), 12-13.

26 Interviews, former minister, departmental official (M6, FO2).

27 See Chapter 8.

28 Tory popularity dropped from the 42-43 per cent range in mid-1985 to the 31-34 per cent range in mid-1986. It bottomed out in the range of 22-26 per cent through the spring and summer of 1987. *Toronto Star*, 2 September 1986, A8; Don McGillivray, "NDP may have room to grow," *The Gazette* [Montreal], 3 June 1987, B1; K. MacQueen, "NDP surge may have peaked," *The Gazette* [Montreal], 4 September 1987, B4.

29 Interview, former cabinet ministers (M2, M6).

30 Wilson (1985b), 15.

31 Wilson (1985b), 7. This tax preference was largely a symbolic measure designed to complement Quebec incentives for the Solidarity Fund set up by the Quebec Federation of Labour. Mulroney and Wilson were anxious to encourage organized labour to adopt a stakeholder attitude toward capitalism and business investment, rather than the largely adversarial approach of the Canadian Labour Congress. Ontario subsequently set up a similar measure to take advantage of the dual initiative.

32 Wilson (1985a), 8.

33 Weyman (1986), 5-6.

34 The ratio of taxable to book income ranged from 47 per cent in mining and 55 per cent in the transportation and utilities sectors to 87 per cent in retail and 94 per cent in construction. Manufacturing (70 per cent) and oil and gas (67 per cent) were roughly in the middle of this range. Weyman (1986), 5:3.

35 A corporate income surtax of 0.84 per cent was imposed as a deficit reduction measure in 1989.

36 Small business opposition to the proposed Business Transfer Tax, an initial
version of the Goods and Services Tax,
was a major factor in cabinet's decision
to defer sales tax reform and pursue a
joint sales tax reform program with the
provinces.

37 The Petroleum and Gas Revenues Tax
was a federal excise tax on well-head revenues over a basic threshold, introduced
in the National Energy Program of 1980.
According to the Western Accord of
1985, it was to have been phased out by
the end of 1988. The PGRT was not
price-sensitive during a period of sharply
falling oil prices. Energy Minister Marcel
Masse negotiated the September 1986
elimination of the tax in return for
matching royalty reductions by Alberta.

38 Deputy Finance Minister Stanley Hartt
promised at least one national business
organization that he would expedite sales
tax reform as a trade-off for corporate tax
increases during the 1986 pre-budget
consultations (interview, AE-2).

39 Maslove (1989).

40 Speeches, unpublished Department
of Finance archives.

41 Interview, senior PMO official (PMO-1).
In mid-1986, there were 386 separate
cabinet documents at various stages of
the policy process. The Prime Minister
had just reshuffled his cabinet. In a
words of a senior PMO official, "there
was a need for a renewed sense of direction." Wilson himself commented
that "the whole ... government was
involved on a whole range of issues.
It was a bloody waste of time. We than
[after mid-1986] set up a lot of ad hoc
committees with only two or three
ministers, which allowed us to deal
with issues in a lot speedier manner."
(Interview, Hon. Michael Wilson).

42 Task Force on Taxation Policy (1986);
Brown (1987).

43 The original $500,000 lifetime
exemption was phased in for family
farms and small businesses and remains
in place at time of writing (2000). While
Paul Martin considered its elimination
when he ended the $100,000 capital
gains exemption for other investments
in 1994, the decisive argument was the
tendency of many farmers and small
business owners to defer income or
reinvest it in their businesses—which
then became their *de facto* pension plans.

44 By the late 1990s, Congress had increased top marginal tax rates—but cut
the tax on long-term capital gains to
a flat 20-per-cent rate.

45 Interview, former Deputy Minister of
Finance (D4).

46 Interview, former PMO official (PMO-1).

47 Canada, Department of Finance (1986).

48 Maslove (1987), 52-53; Vermaeten,
Gillespie, and Vermaeten (1994).

49 Wilson (1987a), 26-28.

50 Ibid., 34-35. The treatment of automobile
expenses was one of the most bitterly
contested provisions of the White Paper.
It received several major revisions before
a truncated version was passed by the
Commons Finance Committee in
August 1988.

51 Minister's speeches, Department of
Finance archives: 20 June, 24 June, 25
June, 26 June, 28 June, 29 June, 2 July, 3
July, 8 July, 11 July, 19 August, 24 August.

52 After the 1988 election, Wilson imposed
a large corporations tax to limit the
pyramiding of tax preferences. However,
it maintained the existing carry forward
of business losses against future tax
liabilities.

53 The last one was the Income Tax Act of
1949, arising out of the work of the Ives
Royal Commission on Taxation.
MacDonald (1985).

The Politics of Sales Tax Reform

The first problem you have in Canada is you do not have a constituency for sales tax reform.... If you do not have a political constituency for reform, it will be seen by the general public as being a tax
grab.... Any time you mix tax reform with revenue raising it has serious political implications.

John Bulloch[1]

Few tax measures in recent years have evoked as much public anger or sustained dislike as the introduction of the Goods and Services Tax. However,
most economists respond that, given Canada's relatively high level of public
spending compared to the United States and other major trading partners,
the GST and general sales taxes as a whole are probably the most practical
and efficient way of raising government revenues without undermining
Canada's international economic competitiveness.[2] They would argue that,
rather than hurting Canada's economy, replacing the old Federal Sales Tax
on manufactured goods with the GST in 1990 helped to stimulate the trade-
driven economic recovery that saw Canadian exports increase by 105 per
cent after inflation between 1989 and 1999, compared to 18 per cent real
growth in Canada's economy during the same period.

The GST debate reflects a profound clash of cultures and outlooks
between much of the Canadian public and the Finance and Treasury
Department policy-makers who shape tax policies at the federal and provincial levels. Governments struggled unsuccessfully for more than 15 years
between 1975 and 1990 to reform the inefficient and uncompetitive Federal
Sales Tax, and then to find alternatives to the new GST that could accommodate public opinion without unduly disrupting either the economy or
their own shaky finances. Finance Department officials found the road to
sales tax reform blocked repeatedly by political and administrative obstacles
until Michael Wilson finally persuaded his cabinet colleagues to risk the

government's accumulated political capital on the introduction of the Goods and Services Tax in April 1989. The Chrétien Liberals, elected in 1993 on a platform of "replacing the GST," struggled unsuccessfully to persuade more than a handful of provinces to coordinate their sales taxes with the new federal tax.

This chapter examines the pressures for sales tax reform, the political and administrative obstacles that repeatedly frustrated it, the decision to force through the Goods and Services Tax in the face of massive public opposition, and its survival and even expansion despite its continuing public unpopularity.

Sales Tax Reform: A Long Time Coming

Excise or "indirect" taxes, sales or "consumption" taxes collected from persons other than the final consumer, are the one major source of Canadian government revenues not shared with the provinces. In 1867, the federal government inherited the right of colonial governments to collect customs duties on imported goods. These taxes were the largest single source of federal revenues until 1934.[3] All provincial governments except for Alberta also impose retail sales taxes on a variety of consumer goods and some business services, although the tax base varies widely from province to province.[✓]

The federal sales tax was introduced in 1920 as a more efficient substitute for the high tariffs and excise taxes on specific products imposed to pay for World War 1.[4] Hidden in the price of manufactured goods (including building materials), the federal sales tax was for many years a major source of federal revenues, but one of which the general public was only dimly aware. This changed dramatically when Finance Minister Michael Wilson decided to extend the tax base to include most of the services sector, to transform the federal sales tax from a traditional excise tax into a Value-Added Tax similar to those imposed by most other industrial countries, and to make it visible with each consumer purchase. Both federal and provincial governments levy a variety of additional consumption taxes on particular products and services, especially alcohol, tobacco, and gasoline. Historically, most provinces have jealously guarded their control over the design and collection of sales and consumption taxes, resisting periodic federal efforts to develop a "harmonized" tax base.

The Carter Royal Commission recycled the idea of a broadly-based national sales tax in the 1960s. However, political and administrative difficulties in designing an alternative sales tax base meant that it would be more than 20 years before the federal government could act on this recommendation. Douglas Hartle, who served as the Commission's research director

Table 8.1 ·· FEDERAL EXCISE TAXES AND DUTIES AS A PERCENTAGE
OF FEDERAL REVENUE

	Goods and Services Tax	Sales Tax	Customs Import Duties	Energy Taxes	Other*	Total Excise Taxes and Duties
1961–62	—	16.2	8.3	—	9.7	34.1
1971–72	—	16.0	6.0	—	6.0	27.9
1981–82	—	10.2	5.7	7.5	2.9	26.3
1986–87	—	13.9	4.9	2.3	3.4	24.5
1991–92	12.4	-1.6	3.3	2.8	3.7	20.6
1996–67	12.8	—	1.9	3.2	2.8	20.7
1999–2000	13.8	—	1.3	2.9	2.0	19.8

* Mainly excise taxes on alcohol and tobacco.

Source: Canada, Department of Finance (2000d), Table 6.

before embarking on a distinguished career in the federal public service, has noted seven major criticisms of the Federal Sales Tax:

➤ its tendency to promote "pyramiding" or "cascading," the imposition of tax upon tax, especially by provincial governments;

➤ its non-neutrality—the taxation of goods at different rates, depending on their countries of origin and methods of distribution;

➤ its invisibility—an invitation to higher taxes and increased government spending;

➤ its arbitrariness—especially in calculating taxes on *notional values*[5] rather than market prices in certain cases;

➤ its discrimination against "brand name" goods in favour of "private brand" goods, generic equivalents to brand name goods used by many retail chains;

➤ its impact on business location decisions, resulting from the different tax treatment of transportation costs before and after manufacture; and

➤ its discrimination against domestic goods and in favour of certain imported goods.[6]

The cumulative impact of these inequities and distortions was to create a strong economic incentive for businesses to reorganize their activities to minimize their federal sales and excise taxes payable. By 1981, increasingly aggressive tax management practices by manufacturers, distributors, and importers were beginning to erode federal revenues. Businesses successfully used the courts to broaden the scope of FST exemptions, preferences, and special rulings in the name of horizontal equity (see Table 8.1).[7]

Sales tax reform had three major technical goals, all of which appeared eminently reasonable to tax theorists. It sought to equalize sales tax rates paid on all goods (and eventually services) sold in Canada, regardless of their country of origin, methods of distribution, or end use within Canada. It was intended to capture the revenue base of the growing services sector—about two-thirds of total consumption—that had previously been exempt from federal sales taxation. In turn, this would permit lower tax rates on manufactured goods, which had risen sharply during the 1980s, and allow the government to compensate manufacturers and other capital-intensive industries for higher taxes resulting from corporate tax reforms in 1985-86. Finally, by exempting exports from taxation, a value-added tax would complement the federal government's emerging trade-based industrial strategy and place Canadian products on a more level playing field in the US and other export markets.

During the 1970s and early 1980s, Canada was becoming an increasingly open, trade-dependent economy. A series of federal efforts to broaden the Federal Sales Tax base between the mid-1970s and the late 1980s bogged down amid growing administrative complexity, rapidly changing business practices, strong political opposition from the organized business community, and the need to increase sales tax rates to stem revenue losses from growing levels of tax avoidance. The ability of Canadian and foreign multinationals to arrange production, marketing, and distribution functions in order to minimize taxes led to a steady erosion of the tax base.[8] Sales tax rates increased from 9 per cent in 1983 to 10 per cent in 1984, 12 per cent in 1986, and 13.5 per cent in 1989. These rate increases helped to restore the sales tax yield to 1980 levels, but also magnified incentives for tax avoidance (see Table 8.2).

Most other industrial countries relied on some form of Value Added Tax for a major portion of their tax revenues. By 1985, only Canada, Australia, New Zealand, Japan, and the United States among industrial countries were without some form of VAT, and all but the US were seriously considering the introduction of such a tax.[9]

Table 8.2 ·· FEDERAL SALES TAX RATES AND REVENUES: 1977-89

	FST Rate		Gross Revenue (in $millions)	Adjusted tax yield ($mm. / 1% FST)**
	GENERAL	BUILDING MATERIALS		
1977-78	12%	5%	$4,427.0	$527.06
1978-79	9%	5%	$4,729.4	$621.52
1982-83	9%	5%	$5,893.9	$542.77
1984-85	10%	6%	$7,592.0	$530.15
1986-87	12%	8%	$12,022.1	$615.69
1989-90	13.5%	8%*	$17,768.2	$628.45

*   Rate on building materials increased to 9% on January 1, 1990.

**   Adjusted for inflation.

Source: *The National Finances: 1977-78 – 1989-90* (Toronto: Canadian Tax Foundation); author's calculations.

Finance Minister Michael Wilson struggled to find a politically acceptable alternative to the Federal Sales Tax, tinkering repeatedly with its tax base before finally plunging ahead with the Goods and Services Tax in 1989-90. However, the huge federal deficit demanded a more reliable source of revenues, and one with a less distorting effect on economic activities. This required fundamental sales tax reform rather than a series of budgetary band-aids.

FALSE STARTS: THE WHOLESALE TAX AND THE BUSINESS TRANSFER TAX

The sales tax reform debate went through four stages. During the first, between 1975 and 1983, Finance Department officials attempted to build a consensus on replacing the federal sales tax on manufactured goods with a tax levied at the wholesale level. This proposal proved to be administratively unworkable and was scrapped following its overwhelming rejection by the organized business community.

The second stage, between 1985 and 1988, saw the Finance Department tinker with the sales tax base in efforts to limit tax avoidance, while attempting to introduce a comprehensive Value Added Tax in some form.

Initially conceived as the Business Transfer Tax, a comprehensive, hidden consumption tax applying to all goods and services, it was repackaged twice, first in the hope of financing significant income tax cuts, and then in the hope of persuading the provinces to agree on a joint federal-provincial VAT or "National Sales Tax." The third stage, between 1989 and 1990, witnessed the political and parliamentary battle surrounding the introduction and passage of the Goods and Services Tax. The fourth stage, from 1993 to 1997, resulted from the federal Liberals' efforts to live up to their campaign promise to "replace" the GST. These efforts led to negotiations for a "Harmonized Sales Tax" that resulted in the combining of provincial sales taxes with the GST in three Atlantic provinces.

The idea of replacing the Federal Sales Tax had been raised as early as the 1956 report of Kenneth Carter's Sales Tax Committee, which recommended a shift in the tax to the wholesale level, that is, the level at which retailers purchase goods for sale to the public. This idea was taken up by Finance Department reports in 1975 and 1977, despite widespread criticism of its potential inequities, costs, and complexity from virtually all sectors affected by the proposed tax.[10]

Efforts to broaden the FST base or, between 1979 and 1981, to extend it to the wholesale level, created as many inequities as they resolved. Finance Department officials responsible for commodity tax policy finally convinced Allan MacEachen that the only practical way out of the morass was to revisit the twice frustrated wholesale tax. The result was a White Paper with draft legislation, tabled in April 1982.[11] MacEachen's officials considered three options to reform the FST: further piecemeal changes, shifting the tax to the wholesale level, or shifting it to the retail level. The piecemeal option was rejected as inadequate, given the administrative problems of generating needed revenues while maintaining horizontal equity in a system with more than 20,000 special provisions for about 60,000 registered vendors. The retail sales tax option was rejected as an invasion of provincial jurisdiction likely to create unmanageable political problems.[12] The "wholesale tax" therefore seemed the "least worst" option available to the federal government.

This round of the sales tax debate took place almost entirely between the business community and its tax advisors and the Department of Finance, with public discussion being limited mostly to the business press. Although the White Paper received strong support from automobile manufacturers, who were placed at a competitive disadvantage by the FST's failure to tax marketing and distribution costs of imported cars within Canada, the vast majority of major business organizations opposed the wholesale tax.[13] A business coalition spearheaded by the Canadian Manufacturers' Association, the Canadian Chamber of Commerce, and the Retail Council of Canada, all strong critics of the White Paper, pressed for an independent review of the sales tax reform proposals, that is, outside the control of the Department of Finance.

By early 1983, Marc Lalonde and his senior officials concluded that the proposed wholesale tax would create as many administrative problems as it resolved, and that the government needed an excuse either to salvage the proposal or to help the government save face in withdrawing it. Following informal discussions with senior business representatives, Lalonde appointed a committee of tax professionals and industry representatives that recommended the withdrawal of the wholesale tax, except for the automotive sector.[14] The Goodman Report of May 1983 also suggested that the federal government explore the replacement of the FST by a broadly-based consumer-level tax, preferably in cooperation with the provinces.[15]

The Goodman Committee suggested two main options for sales tax reform: a joint federal provincial sales tax, and a broadly based federal value-added tax (VAT). The federal VAT was the preferred option of most senior Finance Department officials at the time the Conservatives took office in September 1984. The conventional wisdom, borne out by subsequent negotiations, was that the provinces would never agree to the federal invasion of their tax base or come to a consensus on the rules necessary to administer a joint federal-provincial tax.

The 1985-model version of sales tax reform was the Business Transfer Tax (BTT), a comprehensive, hidden consumption tax applying to all goods and services except for exports. The thousands of often arbitrary distinctions in existing FST rules would be swept away. The BTT differed from the established Value-Added Taxes of Europe in that it would have been a tax calculated from balance sheet information ("the subtraction method"), rather than being calculated on the basis of individual transactions ("the credit-invoice method"). Buried in every transaction, the BTT's invisibility would lessen the political pain of deficit reduction after the initial transition period.

Although these features gave the BTT the appearance of greater simplicity, they also implied a greater political and administrative rigidity. The universal, single rate system left little room for the exclusion of politically sensitive goods or services from the tax base or for the normal trade-offs of the political process.

Wilson's Business Transfer Tax proposal, though enjoying support within much of the highly specialized sales tax policy community, fell victim to the growing public suspicion of federal tax grabs and to the Mulroney cabinet's increasing sense of political isolation in 1985-86. While Wilson introduced a refundable sales tax credit for low-income families in his 1986 budget in response to concerns over tax fairness,[16] the Prime Minister and his cabinet colleagues baulked at the thought of defending sales taxes on food in an upcoming election, despite apparent bipartisan support for the new tax from the Commons' Finance Committee.[17] While basic food products traditionally were exempt from both the FST and provincial sales taxes, the BTT could not be made to work if such a large and ill-defined category of goods were exempted from taxation.

The Commons Finance Committee revisited the debate in 1987, attempting to design a "win-win" proposal that would use the new Value-Added Tax to finance major cuts in personal and corporate income tax rates in response to recent American rate reductions. As a practical politician, Committee Chair Don Blenkarn dreaded the prospect of having to sell the castor oil of sales tax reform without the sweetener provided by major income tax cuts. After taking Committee members to New Zealand to examine the effects of recent tax reforms, Blenkarn succeeded in winning all-party support for the BTT in March 1988.[18]

However, this was too late to convince Mulroney and Wilson of the political and administrative viability of introducing the new tax before the 1988 election. Strong opposition in the government caucus, fuelled by intense small business opposition to the new tax, had persuaded them to defer the battle and to attempt to negotiate agreement on a joint federal-provincial sales tax with the provinces.[19] In the absence of any broadly-based public or interest group support for sales tax reform, Wilson opted for the path of least resistance: deferred sales tax reform and modest income tax reductions. The hard decisions would be put off until after the 1988 elections.

Introducing the GST: The "Least Worst" Option

The Goods and Services Tax became a lightning rod for the unpopularity of the Mulroney government and for the anger of the government's opponents in the aftermath of the bitterly contested free trade election of 1988. Free trade made sales tax reform unavoidable. In the absence of a national sales tax in the United States, Canada could not impose a 13.5-per-cent tax on manufactured exports to its largest trading partner without making its industries seriously uncompetitive.

All major European countries had introduced Value Added Taxes—levied on the difference between the sales prices of goods or services and the costs of the materials and services needed to produce them—during the previous 20 years. The challenge of the GST was not whether to introduce it, or when, but how to mitigate the political backlash resulting from the replacement of a tax largely invisible to (and ignored by) Canadians with one that slapped them in the face with just about every purchase. This backlash was magnified by the resentment of many of its own supporters, especially the organized small business community, most of whose members would face significant costs in accounting and inventory control systems when collecting federal sales taxes for the first time.

The government's problem was magnified by its own internal conflicts over policy goals. Wilson's officials initially had approached sales tax reform as a means of financing larger reductions in income taxes and shifting a larger share of the tax burden onto consumption taxes. Although the White Paper of April 1989 proposed modest income tax reductions as well, this option was undercut by the government's decision to separate Phase I of tax reform, the pre-election cuts to income taxes, from Phase II, the sales tax reform process.

The intractability of the federal deficit, despite continued federal spending restraints, led Wilson to discuss sales tax reform as a means of increasing government revenues and reducing the deficit. While cabinet ultimately decided that sales tax reform would be revenue neutral, the application of the tax to millions of previously untaxed transactions reinforced the public impression that sales tax reform was an ill-disguised tax grab at its expense. The opposition capitalized on this perception to seize control of the public debate. Each time Wilson modified his proposals in response to public concerns (such as his decision of December 1988 to exempt "basic food products" from the GST), the opposition and interest groups were emboldened to demand even more. The now-mandatory process of public consultations revealed that most interest groups and the general public were less interested in fine-tuning the GST than in scrapping it altogether. In the process, the government lost control of the public debate, the legislative agenda, and its own moral authority to implement tax reform.[20]

Wilson faced a no-win decision on the timing of sales tax reform. Parliamentary hearings on sales tax reform before the election indicated that a significant level of political conflict was inevitable, especially since rising interest rates and deficits precluded significant tax cuts to offset the impact of sales tax reforms. Wilson's decision in April 1989 to pursue a stand-alone Goods and Services Tax represented a calculated political decision that the government was more likely to weather the storm that would probably be caused by forcing through sales tax reform early in its mandate than it was to reach a workable consensus on sales tax reform with the provinces. Most provincial governments were reluctant to pay the political price for being associated in the public mind with the new tax. At the same time, the federal government was unwilling to tie its own hands by allowing the provinces to share control over the future tax rate and base. However, in order for Ottawa to implement the complex administrative details of tax reforms involving almost 1.8 million vendors, it had to act by early 1989 to introduce the new tax as planned by January 1991.[21] The 1991 implementation date was intended to allow vendors and taxpayers at least a year to adjust to the new tax before the government expected to call an election. However, rather than garnering political credit for trying to win over the provinces or consulting with Canadians on the implementation of the new tax, the government provoked massive resentment for its "arrogance" in pressing ahead with tax reform in the face of overwhelmingly hostile public and interest group opinion.

The White Paper on Sales Tax Reform, introduced in April 1989, set out the defects of the existing federal sales tax, the benefits of the new tax, and the measures proposed to make the GST fairer and more responsive to public concerns. A refundable sales tax credit would be introduced to ensure that families earning less than $30,000 would be better off after the GST than before it. A range of necessities (food, prescription drugs, residential rents, medical devices) and essential services (day care, health, dental and educational services) would be either tax-free or tax exempt.[22] The narrowing of the tax base from all these measures would have resulted in a tax rate of 9 per cent, compared to the existing 13.5 per cent federal sales tax. However, the technical details of the proposed tax were not introduced until August.

The Commons Finance Committee was at the centre of the public debate, as large corporate and manufacturing interests squared off with a diverse group of interests united only by their opposition to the proposed sales tax. Despite strong support from the Business Council on National Issues, the Canadian Manufacturers' Association, and the Canadian Exporters' Association, overall business support for the Goods and Services Tax turned out to be much weaker than anticipated. A majority of national business groups opposed the concept. Although some were willing to consider a federal VAT exempting food, most advocated a joint federal-provincial sales tax as their preferred option. Labour and social policy groups were almost unanimous in their opposition to sales tax reform and to shifting part of the tax burden from income to consumption taxes.[23] Small business groups, led by John Bulloch of the CFIB, attacked the GST as a potential tax grab, and a costly and complex administrative burden on small businesses. A membership revolt forced the Canadian Chamber of Commerce to withdraw its lukewarm support for the new tax. Unlike the income tax reform debates of 1986-88, the Committee's review of Wilson's GST proposals became polarized along partisan lines. By late August 1989, published polls suggested that public support for the GST had dropped to 23 per cent.[24]

The firestorm of public criticism forced Wilson to make a number of changes to his proposals. Shortly after the release of the Finance Committee's Report in November 1989, Wilson accepted its recommenda-

EIGHT ·· THE POLITICS OF SALES TAX REFORM

tion to cut the GST rate to 7 per cent, scrap proposed reductions in middle-income tax rates from 26 to 25 per cent, and make offsetting reductions to sales tax credits. He also increased the high-income surtax from 3 per cent to 5 per cent to compensate for the revenue losses resulting from these changes.

Although the GST bill easily passed the House of Commons, due to the large Conservative majority, it bogged down in the Senate as the Liberal majority left over from the Trudeau era subjected it to months of public hearings. By September 1990, public support for the bill had dropped to 14 per cent, only slightly ahead of the Mulroney government's plummeting popularity. The Liberal-dominated Senate Banking Committee voted to reject the GST. Only the government's decision to appoint eight new "emergency" senators under Section 26 of the Constitution—the first time this power had been used in the twentieth century—allowed the new tax to pass the Senate in the teeth of an all-out Liberal filibuster.

Although the GST may have been the most practical response to the need for sales tax reform, the government's decision before the 1988 election to separate it from politically popular income tax reductions and force it through Parliament in the face of public opposition that grew until it was almost unanimous, made sales tax reform a fatal political liability. Combined with the 1990-92 recession and Mulroney's failed experiment in constitutional reform, it tarred the government with a public perception of arrogance and unresponsiveness that led to the near-destruction of the Conservative Party in the 1993 federal election. The Liberal government of Jean Chrétien that came to power in that election soon reversed its policy on the GST, just as it later came to adopt virtually every major economic policy reform introduced by the Mulroney government. However, in the short term, although the patient survived the operation, it proved to be fatal (at least, politically) to the "doctors" who performed it.

The Aftermath: "Replacing the GST"–1993-97

The traditional pattern of large-scale tax reforms has been either for governments to retreat from the most controversial elements of these reforms in order to shore up political support (usually after the appointment of a new Finance Minister), or for a newly elected government to roll back some or all of the changes introduced by their predecessors in fulfilment of its election promises. Although all federal opposition parties promised during the 1993 federal election campaign to reduce, review, or replace the GST, the victorious Liberals not only retained the new tax with mainly cosmetic changes, but sought to extend it to replace provincial sales taxes.

The Liberals' 1993 election platform had committed them to "replace the GST with a system that generates equivalent revenues, is fairer to consumers … minimizes disruption to small business, and promotes federal-provincial cooperation and harmonization." In practice, this artful dodge was intended to disguise a planned shift to the Business Transfer Tax considered and rejected by the Mulroney cabinet in 1985-86.[25] However, the rhetorical enthusiasm of many Liberal candidates left many Canadians with the impression that the new government had promised to "eliminate" the GST.[26] Like most newly elected governments in the early 1990s, the Liberals conveniently discovered that the fiscal situation they had inherited was significantly worse than expected, leaving them little room to manoeuvre. Although Deputy Prime Minister Sheila Copps, who had promised to resign her seat during the 1993 campaign if the Liberals did not scrap the GST, eventually was forced to do so (she was subsequently re-elected in a by-election and reappointed to cabinet), the government discovered that most alternatives to the GST lacked significant public support (see Table 8.3).

√Shortly after the 1993 election, Finance Minister Paul Martin referred the problem to the Commons Finance Committee, chaired by veteran Liberal MP Jim Peterson, brother of former Ontario Premier David Peterson. The Committee toured the country, hearing from almost 500 individuals and groups, including a wide range of tax experts. It examined 20 alternatives to the existing GST, and recommended that the federal government try to negotiate the integration of federal and provincial sales tax systems into a single national value-added sales tax with a single administrative bureaucracy. It also recommended a shift to tax-included pricing, in effect burying the cost of the GST in the prices of particular products or services, but requiring that taxes paid be disclosed on sales receipts.[27]

The Committee's report, released in June 1994, largely vindicated the Goods and Services Tax. After examining the trade-offs involved in the GST and most of the alternatives proposed, it concluded that the GST could be fine-tuned, but that the single biggest improvement in the sales tax system could be achieved by extending Wilson's tax structure to replace provincial sales taxes as well. This outcome reflected the preferences of most of the business community, especially small business groups, and of tax professionals, who generally supported the new tax. In response to studies that showed that small businesses face significantly higher GST compliance costs than larger firms,[28] the Committee recommended a further simplification of GST collection and reporting rules for small companies and self-employed individuals.

The Committee's recommendations were broadly consistent with the drift of public opinion that, while not fully reconciled to the new tax, recognized that the government was facing serious problems in the aftermath of the recession. Finance Department polling in July 1994 found that "doing

Table 8.3 ·· PUBLIC SUPPORT FOR SPECIFIC ALTERNATIVES TO THE GST—1994

	Strongly Support	Support	Neither	Oppose	Strongly Oppose
INCLUDE GST IN PRICES	27	47	7	12	6
MERGE FEDERAL & PROVINCIAL TAXES	14	47	10	19	7
LEAVE GST "AS IS"	6	27	16	37	14
CUT GST TO 6%, REMOVE FROM BOOKS	5	33	13	40	6
APPLY THE GST TO ALL GOODS, SERVICES	5	26	6	38	23
REPLACE WITH 5.5% BUSINESS TRANSFER TAX	5	25	14	32	21
LOWER SALES TAXES, RAISE INCOME TAXES	3	26	9	43	18
ELIMINATE GST, "HOPE FOR GROWTH"	6	31	9	37	13
ELIMINATE GST; LET DEFICIT RISE	3	9	7	44	34
ELIMINATE GST, CUT TRANSFER PAYMENTS	5	22	8	40	20
ELIMINATE GST, RAISE OTHER TAXES	2	11	7	46	31

Highlighted type indicates majority support for or opposition to GST reform proposal.

Source: ESG Research & Communications (1994), 25.

something with the GST" was a relatively low priority for most voters compared with economic recovery and deficit reduction, and that most voters would be satisfied if the government were to made the tax simpler and "more efficient."[29]

Martin accepted the Finance Committee's broad recommendations and launched a new round of negotiations with the provinces, but with limited success. Although Quebec had signed a partial sales tax harmonization agreement with Ottawa in 1991 that allowed that province to collect a "GST-like tax" jointly with the federal tax, few other provinces were willing to risk a public backlash by extending their sales taxes to include previously untaxed services.[30] Most provinces also were reluctant to take the political risk of shifting as much as a third of their sales tax burden from businesses to consumers, ignoring economists' arguments that business tax costs eventually were passed on to consumers anyway. The Ontario government estimated that the loss of sales taxes on business inputs would offset virtually all of its revenue gains from aligning its sales taxes with the GST.[31]

Prince Edward Island and Saskatchewan already had withdrawn from previously signed agreements with the federal government, the latter after NDP Premier Roy Romanow won the 1991 election partly on the strength of his promise to scrap the tax. Finally, in 1996, Martin persuaded New Brunswick, Nova Scotia, and Newfoundland to harmonize their provincial sales taxes with the GST, largely by promising a federal subsidy of $961 million, payable over four years, which would enable them to reduce their sales tax rates to 8 per cent (see Table 8.4).

Although recent polls still suggest that much of the public would reduce the GST before any other tax, policy-makers in the Department of Finance and most economists and business groups that dominate the broader tax

Table 8.4 ·· HARMONIZING FEDERAL AND PROVINCIAL SALES TAXES

	Sales Tax Rates		
	1995	1997	2000
FEDERAL GST	7%	7%	7%
NEWFOUNDLAND	12%*	8%**	8%**
NEW BRUNSWICK	11%*	8%**	8%**
NOVA SCOTIA	11%*	8%**	8%**
PRINCE EDWARD ISLAND[†]	10%*	10%*	10%*
QUEBEC	6.5%*	6.5%*	7.5%*
ONTARIO	8%	8%	8%
MANITOBA	7%	7%	7%
SASKATCHEWAN[†]	9%	7%	6%[††]
ALBERTA	no PST	no PST	no PST
BRITISH COLUMBIA	7%	7%	7%

*   Indicates provincial sales tax imposed on prices, including federal GST.

**   Harmonized 15% federal-provincial sales tax since 1997.

[†]   Withdrew from sales tax harmonization agreements, 1991.

[††]   Saskatchewan's 2000 budget announced plans to significantly expand the provincial sales tax base over three years in order to offset revenue losses from income tax reforms.

Source: *Finances of the Nation: 1995-2000* (Toronto: Canadian Tax Foundation).

policy community have reached the firm conclusion that income tax reduction should be the top priority if Canada is to compete internationally for investment and skilled people. (These issues will be discussed further in Chapters 9 and 10.)

Lessons from Sales Tax Reform

The GST debate demonstrated conclusively that majority governments in Canada can impose new taxes on an unwilling public if they are willing to pay the political price for doing so. However, it also demonstrated that much of the public is more concerned about the prospect of paying higher taxes than about theoretical arguments concerning tax fairness or economic efficiency. Consumption taxes on products widely perceived to be "necessities of life"—food, residential rents, health services, public utilities—are likely to prompt strong public resistance.

Many economists have suggested that Canadian governments should increase their dependence on sales and consumption taxes rather than personal and corporate income taxes. However, any such shift in the pattern of taxation is likely to be politically controversial. Sales taxes tend to be regressive, with the greatest relative burden falling on lower- and middle-income earners, although this effect may be offset by a system of refundable tax credits.

The visibility of general sales taxes and their relative intrusiveness into the daily lives of citizens impose a significantly higher degree of political accountability than do excise taxes on specific products, which tend to be hidden in their prices. This consequence has limited the growth of consumption taxes in recent years as a source of government revenues, in sharp contrast to European countries whose hidden Value Added Taxes are often imposed at rates significantly over 20 per cent.

It is conceivable that sales tax reform could have been sold to the Canadian public, as it was in New Zealand, despite the Mulroney government's low standing in public opinion, if it had been accompanied by sizeable reductions in income taxes that left most citizens demonstrably better off. Quebec and Saskatchewan introduced such reforms in their 1998 and 2000 budgets respectively that, although not generally popular, were crafted carefully enough to avoid public outrage. However, the federal government's efforts to find a formula for tax reform that would be acceptable to the majority of provinces, small and large businesses, and consumer groups proved to be largely self-defeating, given the relatively narrow "window" provided by the electoral cycle. This reaction placed the government on the defensive and giving the political initiative to its critics.

During the 1990s, the relative decline in personal and family incomes and the steady growth of personal income and payroll taxes needed to reduce government deficits shifted public attention away from battles over sales tax reform. Instead, public debate over budgetary and tax policies focused first on the challenge of forcing governments to live within their citizens' means, and then on the emerging fiscal dividend and how governments should allocate fiscal surpluses generated by a growing economy and rising employment.

NOTES

1   John Bulloch (1986) Canadian Federation of Independent Business, testimony to Commons Finance Committee, *Minutes and Proceedings*, Issue # 19 (Ottawa, House of Commons, 16 December, 16).

2   Dale W. Jorgenson and Kun-Young Wan, "The Excess Burden of Taxation in the United States," 6 *Journal of Accounting, Auditing and Finance* [Fall 1991], 503-04, cited in Kesselman (1999), 215-16.

3   Gillespie (1991), Appendix B.

4   Ibid., 124.

5   Notional values are estimated prices based on industry averages—more or less arbitrary bureaucratic estimates of wholesale prices rather than actual market prices.

6   Hartle (1985), 214-16.

7   Interview, Eric Owen, Canadian Manufacturers' Association. The CMA provided its members with regular updates on the application of federal sales tax rules.

8   Importers paid FST on duty-valued prices. Domestic manufacturers paid it on their selling prices. A series of court cases increased the freedom of domestic firms to organize distribution channels to reduce sales and excise taxes payable. Goodman (1988b).

9   New Zealand introduced a VAT, the Goods and Services Tax, in 1987, subsequently followed by Australia. Japan's attempt to introduce such a tax lin 1987 was greeted by riots in the streets—a fact not lost on Prime Minister Mulroney's advisors [interview, former PMO official (PMO-1)].

10 Sales Tax Committee (1956) *Report to the Minister of Finance* (Ottawa: Queen's Printer), in Hartle (1985); Canada, Department of Finance (1975); Canada, Department of Finance (1977); A later government report notes that only 10 per cent of submissions received in response to the 1975 Green Paper endorsed the wholesale tax proposal. Wolfe Goodman (1983) *Report of the Sales Tax Advisory Committee* ,"The Goodman Report" (Ottawa: Department of Finance, May), 10.

11 MacEachen (1982b).

12 Goodman (1983), 9-10 (see n. 10 above).

13 Hartle (1985), 226-27.

14 Interviews, Hon. Marc Lalonde, Marshall A. Cohen, business association representative (AE-2).

15 Goodman (1983), 55-58 (see n. 10 above). The general sentiment of the Committee was in favour of federal harmonization with the provinces, either in a Value-Added Tax or a general retail sales tax. Wolfe D. Goodman, correspondence with author.

16 Wilson hoped that the sales tax credit could be integrated with the child tax credit as the beginning of a potential guaranteed annual income delivered through the tax system [interview, former provincial finance minister (PG-1)].

17 Wilson's first attempt at sales tax reform was apparently scuppered by Revenue Minister Elmer MacKay and other cabinet ministers, who bitterly opposed the application of the Business Transfer Tax to food. MacKay, having vacated his seat for Mulroney while the latter was Leader of the Opposition, exerted considerable influence with the Prime Minister [interviews, former cabinet minister (M6), former PMO official (PMO-I); Don Blenkarn, MP, Finance Department officials (FO2, FO3)].

18 Canada, Standing Committee on Finance (1988a, 1988b).

19 Interviews, senior Finance Department official (D4), former PMO official (PMO-I).

20 Campbell and Pal (1991), 347.

21 Campbell and Pal (1991), 377-78; interviews, provincial government officials (PG-I, PG-2).

22 "Tax free" or "zero rated" meant that the GST would not be levied on consumers of such products and services, and that GST paid on business inputs would be refunded to producers, allowing for lower consumer costs. Such refunds would not be available to producers of "tax exempt" products and services, although no GST would be charged to end users.

23 Industries dominated by smaller firms loathed the idea of having to administer two separate sales taxes levied on different bases at different rates. However, support for a federal-provincial tax was a tactical manoeuvre for several groups, some of which wanted a federal VAT, but were unable to persuade their members to swallow the idea; others did not want any kind of VAT, but hoped to use the prospect of a joint federal-provincial tax as a firewall against the BTT [interviews, business association representatives (AE-I, AE-5)]. See also Hale (1996), Chapter 12.

24 The Globe and Mail, 22 August 1989.

25 Interview, federal cabinet minister, 1994 (M5).

26 A July 1994 poll revealed that 42 per cent of respondents believed the government had promised to eliminate the GST and raise money in other ways, 21 per cent to simplify its operation, and 23 per cent to review alternatives to the GST. ESG Research and Communications (1994), 15-16.

27 Canada, Standing Committee on Finance (1994).

28 A study commissioned by the Department of Finance suggested that the administrative cost of collecting GST was over 15 per cent of revenues collected for firms with sales under $200,000 compared to less than 3 per cent for firms with annual sales over $500,000. Plamondon and Associates (1994) "GST Compliance Costs for Small Business in Canada" (Ottawa: Department of Finance), 3.

29 ESG Research and Communications (1994), 10, 19.

30 Hugh Winsor (1996) "Deal to replace GST evades Ottawa," The Globe and Mail, 2 April.

31 Alan Freeman (1995) "Liberal promise on GST creating national discord," The Globe and Mail, 12 August; Manitoba (1997) "Manitoba Government Position: Sales Tax Harmonization" (Winnipeg: Manitoba Finance, September). Similar positions were taken by Ontario, Saskatchewan, and British Columbia.

NINE

Chrétien, Martin, and the Politics of Deficit Reduction

The mid-1990s marked a significant shift in the politics of taxation in Canada, even though the income tax system itself experienced a longer period of relative stability than at any time since the release of the Carter Commission Report in the 1960s. This seeming paradox can be explained by the unprecedented commitment of the federal and most provincial governments to balancing their budgets through a combination of greater spending discipline, increased tax revenues, and the creative use of fiscal illusion.

In sharp contrast to the early 1980s, when the Trudeau government sought to spend its way out of recession, leaving a huge *structural budget deficit*, the Chrétien government dealt with the often-contradictory commitments of its 1993 campaign platform by making the achievement of specific deficit reduction targets the precondition for additional spending on the income transfers and new social programs demanded by many of its supporters. This led to an actual, sustained reduction in the level of federal program spending between 1993 and 1997—the first time this had happened since the 1940s.[1]

The new government also benefited from a series of tax increases and structural tax changes introduced by its predecessors, particularly the partial de-indexation of personal income taxes, to increase its revenues as the economy recovered from the 1990-91 recession. Unlike the newly-elected Mulroney government of 1984, many of whose supporters had long stored up grievances against the tax policies of the Trudeau government, the Chrétien Liberals faced few major pressures to change the tax system. As noted in Chapter 8, their one major commitment—to replace the Goods and Services Tax—generated much political discussion but few tangible results other than the largely symbolic gesture of harmonizing sales taxes with three Atlantic provinces. The Chrétien government's social policy reform initiative generated the other two major changes to the tax system during its first term. These were a restructuring of the Unemployment Insurance system that generated annual surpluses to speed the deficit reduction process, and a major extension of Child Tax Benefits in cooperation with the provinces.[2]

By making deficit reduction the top priority for his first term, Prime Minister Chrétien effectively gave his Finance Minister, Paul Martin, unprecedented control over his government's fiscal agenda. Martin expanded the power of the Department of Finance to coordinate the government's fiscal, economic, and social policies to a degree not seen since the heyday of Keynesian public finance in the 1950s and 1960s. His creative use of the budget process to impose political and policy coherence and firm priorities on the far-flung activities of the federal government, dampen public expectations and cabinet colleagues' demands for more spending or lower taxes, and mobilize public consent and support for the government's policies made him the most powerful and successful Finance Minister since the 1950s.

This chapter examines the factors that enabled Martin to succeed in tackling the deficit where his predecessors had failed. It looks at the effects of tax changes introduced by the Mulroney government in spurring the huge windfall in federal revenues after 1995, and the ways in which Martin succeeded in camouflaging his actual fiscal position while building a political consensus in support of his strong budgetary medicine. The chapter also looks at Martin's creative use of the tax system to coordinate the government's social and economic policy goals as a reflection of the neo-liberal philosophy that enabled the Chrétien government to reconcile its disciplined financial management with a renewal of the Canadian welfare state.

Balancing the Budget: Waking up to Fiscal Realities

Fifteen or twenty years ago, the old-fashioned fiscal orthodoxy that governments should live within their citizens' means might have received lip service from governments, but not much more. Times have changed. Federal and provincial governments of most political persuasions, and most opposition parties with realistic hopes of forming a government, recognize that maintaining fiscal balance over an economic cycle is essential to stable economic growth, improved living standards, and the quality of public services. As a result, Canada's public sector eliminated a $63 billion deficit between 1993 and 1997, its first overall financial surplus in 23 years (see Table 9.1).

In 1993-94, when the Chrétien government inherited the political and financial wreckage of the Mulroney government, the federal deficit had ballooned to $42 billion. Federal spending had grown to an unsustainable 136 per cent of revenues. Unlike the previous government, which warred rhetorically on the deficit for most of its nine years in office with relatively little to show for its efforts, the Liberals soft-pedalled deficit reduction during the 1993 election, pledging to reduce it to 3 per cent of GDP (about $24 billion), marginally better than the Tories' best performance. Yet, faced with many of the same political and economic pressures, it took a sharp turn from fiscal gradualism to serious retrenchment within nine months of taking office, delivering a bal-

Table 9.1 ·· BALANCING THE BOOKS: 1974-99
(MILLIONS OF 1999 DOLLARS, NATIONAL ACCOUNTS BASIS)

	Revenue	% of GDP	Spending	% of GDP	Surplus/ (deficit)	% of GDP
1974 TOTAL GOVERNMENT*	179,381	39.2	164,796	36.0	14,585	3.2
FEDERAL	87,265	19.1	85,354	18.6	1,912	0.4
PROVINCES/TERRITORIES	84,839	18.5	76,901	16.8	7,938	1.7
1984 TOTAL GOVERNMENT	252,340	40.2	289,977	46.2	(37,638)	-6.0
FEDERAL	104,011	16.6	144,251	23.0	(40,240)	-6.4
PROVINCES/TERRITORIES	136,486	21.8	139,167	22.2	(2,681)	-0.4
1988 TOTAL GOVERNMENT	308,694	44.2	330,898	44.5	(22,204)	-3.0
FEDERAL	130,668	17.6	158,183	21.3	(27,515)	-3.7
PROVINCES/TERRITORIES	159,421	21.5	160,256	21.6	(835)	-0.1
1993 TOTAL GOVERNMENT	339,618	44.2	402,475	52.4	(62,857)	-8.2
FEDERAL	138,582	18.1	180,126	23.5	(41,544)	-5.4
PROVINCES/TERRITORIES	174,172	22.7	197,321	25.7	(23,149)	-3.0
1997 TOTAL GOVERNMENT	393,729	44.1	392,920	44.1	809	0.1
FEDERAL	163,462	18.3	163,460	18.3	2	0.0
PROVINCES/TERRITORIES	192,359	21.6	191,499	21.5	859	0.1
1999 TOTAL GOVERNMENT	421,369	44.0	404,321	42.2	17,048	1.8
FEDERAL	173,962	18.2	172,533	18.0	1,429	0.1
PROVINCES/TERRITORIES	210,462	22.0	198,118	20.7	12,344	1.3

* Total government figures also include revenue, spending, and budget balances for local governments and the Canada/Quebec Pension Plans; adjusted by GDP Implicit Price Index.

Sources: Canada, Department of Finance (2000d); Statistics Canada, *National Income and Expenditure Accounts*, Cat. # 13-001.

anced budget at the end of its fourth year in office. Ironically, this abrupt transformation appears not to have resulted from any premeditated political strategy. Rather, it came from Martin's—and Chrétien's—belated realization that only by demonstrating their government's clear control over its finances could they enable the federal government once again to play a creative leadership role in social policy, federal-provincial relations, and its relations with Canadians, the role that traditionally had dignified the Liberal claim to be Canada's natural party of government.[3]

Balancing the budget may have been a means to an end rather than an end in itself, but reaching this goal required a systematic rethinking of contemporary Liberalism, an unprecedented ability to focus the energies of government, the political skill to win the grudging, if not always enthusiastic support of Canadians, and a fair amount of luck. At least seven factors, combining the creative use of ideas, the effective management of institutions, and the astute mobilization of interests, explain how Chrétien and Martin succeeded not only in balancing the budget where Mulroney and Wilson had failed, but in winning re-election and building a renewed public consensus around the role of government as well.

The federal Liberals largely abandoned the interventionist nationalism that had dominated their outlook during the 1980s in favour of a neo-liberal philosophy that embraced the concepts of economic globalization, deficit reduction, and a redefined role for governments which involved the closer integration of economic and social policies. This process was made easier by a fragmented political opposition, much of which was urging even more aggressive deficit reduction measures. A growing commitment from provincial governments of all political stripes to fiscal discipline, deficit reduction, and balanced budgets also provided Ottawa with political "cover" for its own budget reductions.

After a short period of drift, Chrétien imposed a ruthless centralization of power to define and impose the government's agenda. This enabled Martin and the Department of Finance, with the active support of the Prime Minister, to set and enforce fiscal targets, imposing unprecedented spending reductions on cabinet colleagues, provincial governments, and interest groups. At the same time, Martin used Finance's increasingly central position within the government to determine which new spending policies and programs, often delivered through the tax system, would be central to the government's agenda.

Martin also made creative use of "fiscal illusion" to increase his political flexibility in defining and reaching his budget targets. Although this practice can involve the management of budget forecasts to disguise higher than expected spending, Martin set up a series of fiscal firewalls to regain control of the federal government's finances. This forced his cabinet colleagues to accommodate their policy and spending plans to the government's short-term deficit targets, while enabling Martin to capture most of the "windfall" revenues to balance the federal budget without large-scale changes to the tax system.

Successful political leadership, as with other forms of entrepreneurship, often results from identifying opportunities when others are focused on problems and taking advantage of circumstances beyond one's immediate control. Martin used the Mexican peso crisis of 1994, when international financial markets threatened a run on the Canadian dollar, to persuade his colleagues that Canada faced an impending financial disaster unless they abandoned their business-as-usual agenda inherited from the 1993 election. Having built relatively high interest rates into his fiscal projections, Martin reaped a fiscal and economic windfall from falling interest rates during and after 1995, which reduced the burden of interest payments on the public debt and spurred economic growth across North America.

Martin also benefited from tax increases built into the personal and corporate tax systems by his predecessors and record tax revenues generated by economic growth. However, he also took advantage of structural changes to Unemployment Insurance to divert an average of $5.5 billion a year in EI premiums to deficit reduction between 1995 and 2000. Initially this meant passing legislation requiring the government to run EI fund surpluses large enough to finance increased benefits during a moderate recession without the need for rate increases, a total of about $15 billion. EI rates were allowed to drop slowly as employment increased. But this still left huge surpluses to finance other government priorities (see Table 9.2).

Effective leadership requires followers. Martin introduced formal and informal changes to the public, or "external," budget process that helped him to build public support for proposed changes, identify and diffuse potentially damaging political conflicts, and mobilize enough public support for his policies for the government to win re-election in 1997. Each of these changes played a significant role in enabling the Chrétien government to balance its budget more promptly than thought possible by all but the most ideologically committed of its neo-conservative opponents. In doing so, the Chrétien government significantly changed the political environment for tax policy as Canada entered the new century.

Table 9.2 ·· FINANCING THE EI WINDFALL: 1993-2000

	Unemployment Rate	Employee Premium Rate	Break-even Premium Rate	Premium Revenues	Program Costs*	Surplus /deficit**	Balance
1993	11.4%	3.00%	3.23%	18,469	19,678	-1,208	-5,884
1994	10.4%	3.07%	2.71%	19,327	17,044	2,283	-3,601
1995	9.4%	3.00%	2.30%	19,180	14,913	4,267	666
1996	9.6%	2.95%	2.23%	19,091	14,169	4,999	5,665
1997	9.1%	2.90%	1.96%	19,379	13,363	6,295	11,960
1998	8.3%	2.70%	1.76%	19,623	13,012	7,291	19,251
1999	7.6%	2.55%	1.65%	18,648	13,013	6,611	25,862
2000^P	6.8%	2.40%	1.46%	18,868	12,736	7,725	33,586

P   Projected

*   Includes interest on cumulative program deficits

**   Includes interest on notional surpluses in EI fund (in $ millions): 1996: $78; 1997: $278; 1998: $680; 1999: $976; 2000: $1,592.

Source: Canada, Human Resources and Development Canada (2000), 2.

INTELLECTUAL RENEWAL: THE EMERGENCE OF NEO-LIBERALISM

While in opposition and during their first year in office, the leadership of the federal Liberal party went through a significant intellectual renewal, although the extent of this change did not become apparent for some time.

The 1991 Aylmer Conference marked the beginning of the party's accommodation to the realities of economic globalization and the politics of the Mulroney government.[4] Its leading economic policy critics, Paul Martin, John Manley, and Roy MacLaren, argued that economic globalization and the policies derived from it, including trade liberalization, the GST, fiscal discipline, and a mix of market-driven strategies and selective privatization for government-run businesses, were economic facts of life to be accommodated, rather than a partisan conspiracy against Canada's national interest to be fought at every turn. After the 1993 election, Prime Minister Chrétien confirmed this direction by appointing the three to shape the new government's economic policies as Ministers of Finance, Industry, and International Trade respectively.

This accommodation could be seen in the Liberals' prompt adoption of the Mulroney government's major economic policies shortly after taking office. Martin spelled out the central elements of this neo-liberalism in October 1994 in a major paper, *A New Framework for Economic Policy*, colloquially known as "the Purple Paper."[5] The new liberals believed that government, while continuing to provide a degree of security against the uncertainties of the marketplace, has a significant role to play in fostering both economic growth and opportunities for its citizens, and in ensuring that disadvantaged members of society have a chance to share in those opportunities. This approach stood in sharp contrast to contemporary neo-conservatism, with its skepticism—if not hostility—towards the growth of government as a barrier to economic opportunities and individual freedom. Both rejected the tendency of welfare liberals and social democrats of the 1970s and 1980s to promote the state's increased power and control over both market and society and their tendency to subordinate the wealth- and growth-creating activities of the marketplace to the expansion of government programs, services, and regulations.

The new market liberalism identified "getting government right"—a combination of financial self-sufficiency, the efficient management of public services, and the creative use of market forces to complement government policies—as a precondition for governments to play an effective role in both economic and society. Thus, it accepted the need for deficit reduction, balancing the budget, and reducing the size of the national debt relative to the economy, not as ends in themselves, but as a means of ensuring governments' economic capacity to sustain Canada's public services and major income support programs.

The new market liberalism also emphasized the need to make economic and social policy complement one another, rather than functioning in relative isolation or at cross-purposes—applying the same language of economic incentives to social policy and the operations of government as to economic policy. This new "managerialism" sought to accommodate the growing individualism of contemporary society and the growing impatience of its citizens with hierarchy and bureaucracy in any walk of life. Accepting the neo-conservative critique that governments had too often become the captives of narrow special interests—whether the producers of public services or client groups unrepresentative of the broader society—the neo-liberals of the 1990s sought new ways to make governments more flexible and responsive to an increasingly diverse, consumer-oriented society. The language of "rights" and "entitlements" to public services was tempered by a new emphasis on "enabling individual choice," "overcoming dependence," and "shared responsibility" as part of a new "balance" in the relationship between individuals and society, market, and state.

Restoring control over its finances became the condition for the federal government to shape and, if possible, control that balance rather than international bankers, provincial governments, interest groups, or the vagaries of market forces.

A CHANGING POLITICAL ENVIRONMENT

The 1990-91 recession and 1993 federal election fundamentally changed the political balance of power in federal and provincial politics in ways that removed many of the traditional obstacles to deficit reduction. Although the Liberals, while in opposition, had challenged virtually every effort of the Mulroney government to reduce the growth of government spending, the political dynamics of the 1993-97 Parliament provided the Government with an almost free rein in enforcing fiscal discipline and spending reductions, resulting in the elimination or retrenchment of dozens of major federal programs.

Small-l liberals and social democrats in the Liberal caucus were bound by party discipline to support the government's fiscal measures, although not without some grumbling. The solidarity of cabinet ministers' views was reinforced by their participation in the cabinet committee on program review led by Paul Martin and Public Service Renewal Minister Marcel Masse.[6] At the same time, the federal "UI caucus"—MPs from areas of chronically high unemployment who had long blocked reform of the often economically perverse system of regional transfers and incentives—made up a smaller proportion of the government caucus than at any time since the 1950s, despite the Liberals having elected 31 of 32 MPs from Atlantic Canada.[7]

The NDP and PC opposition in Parliament was decimated in the 1993 election. The federal NDP's loss of official party status in Parliament undercut its traditional role as champion of growing social entitlements and critic of public spending restraint. The separatist Bloc Québécois opposition, which assumed the NDP's traditional role as champion of the welfare state and its beneficiaries, failed to attract much media attention or sympathy in its opposition to spending cuts outside Quebec. The Reform Party, the largest opposition party in English-speaking Canada, constantly challenged the government to move even faster to reduce its deficit.

During the early and mid-1990s, similar policies were adopted by provincial governments covering the entire political spectrum. This provided the Chrétien government with political cover for its unprecedented exercise in fiscal discipline. Liberal governments in Atlantic Canada, led by New Brunswick's Frank McKenna and Nova Scotia's John Savage, imposed major budget reductions on their patronage and debt-ridden public sectors.

Table 9.3 ·· ENFORCING SPENDING REDUCTION—OTTAWA IN
COMPARATIVE PERSPECTIVE
TOTAL PROGRAM EXPENDITURES (IN $MILLIONS)

FEDERAL	1993-94	120,014	1996-97	104,820	% Change - 12.7%
ALBERTA	1992-93	16,264	1995-96	12,897	% Change - 20.7%
ONTARIO*	1995-96	49,798	1997-98	47,725	% Change - 4.2%

* Program spending is defined as total budgetary spending less interest payments on the public debt. Ontario reduced its program spending 1.9 per cent in the three years after the 1995 election.

Sources: Canada, Department of Finance (1998a), 15, 33; *1999 Ontario Budget*, 52.

Saskatchewan's NDP government, which inherited a fiscal disaster after the 1992 election, in 1995 became the first province to balance its budget, following a series of tax increases and spending reductions. The anti-government rhetoric of populist, right-wing Conservative governments in Alberta and Ontario, the latter elected after Martin's deficit reduction program began in earnest, made Liberal budget policies seem relatively moderate, although Martin reduced program spending in his first three budgets more than did the Harris government in Ontario (see Table 9.3). Moreover, the Chrétien government's decision to promote its policies as a means of sustaining public services and the welfare state, rather than dismantling them, was vital to reassuring and maintaining public support from centrist voters.[8]

John Richards has noted that, except for Sweden and Finland, social democratic countries whose huge welfare states faced a crisis even greater than Canada's in the 1990s, Canada exercised greater spending discipline than any other OECD country during the 1990s (see Table 9.4). Unlike the 1980s, when a large share of revenues from economic growth were applied to new program spending, the federal and most provincial governments actually reduced program spending during the mid-1990s, both in absolute terms and as a share of the growing economy.[9] Although most provinces subsequently restored these spending cuts, provincial fiscal policies tended to reinforce federal deficit reduction efforts, rather than undercutting them as they had during the late 1980s (see Table 9.5).

Forcing through changes of this magnitude, while maintaining firm control on the growth of spending after governments had balanced their budgets, required both a significant change in political attitudes and a centralization of power over government priorities and budget processes.

THE POLITICAL POWER SHIFT: SETTING AND ENFORCING FISCAL TARGETS

The government's initial goal was to reduce the deficit from $42 billion in 1993-94 to $24 billion, or 3 per cent of GDP, in 1996-97. The rapid growth of foreign-held debt, from $93.6 billion (21.0 per cent of GDP) in 1984 to $304.5 billion (40.7 per cent of GDP) in 1994, made the Canadian economy increasingly vulnerable to pressure from international financial markets.

After a largely stand-pat budget in 1994, Finance Minister Paul Martin came under significant pressure from business and financial markets to take more aggressive measures to reduce the deficit.[10]

Previous Finance Ministers had seen efforts to enforce budgetary targets disappear when other ministers were able to persuade Prime Ministers and cabinets to approve new "budget-busting" spending initiatives, or when they sought to head off new spending through selective tax reductions. These actions prevented them from making much headway against the

Table 9.4 ·· CHANGES IN PROGRAM SPENDING–SELECTED OECD COUNTRIES–1990-99

	MAXIMUM IN 1990-94		MINIMUM IN 1995-99		*Spending Reduction*
	% of GDP	*Year*	*% of GDP*	*Year*	
CANADA	46.0	1992	36.4	1999	-9.6
FINLAND	59.5	1992	45.6	1999	-13.9
SWEDEN	66.9	1993	53.5	1999	-13.4
BRITAIN	43.2	1992-93	36.9	1999	-6.3
IRELAND	34.4	1994	28.1	1999	-6.3
ITALY	44.9	1993	41.0	1997-98	-3.9
UNITED STATES	31.1	1992	27.3	1998-99	-3.8
FRANCE	51.0	1993	49.3	1997-98	-1.7
GERMANY	45.6	1993	44.3	1998	-1.3
JAPAN	34.4	1994	34.0	1997	-0.4

Source: Richards (2000), 3.

Table 9.5 ·· DISTRIBUTION OF BUDGET BALANCES: 1991–92-1998-99

	Budget Balance 1991–92 $MILLION	%	Net Revenue Growth from Own Initiatives* 1991-92–1998-99 $MILLION	%	Ratio of "Own Initiatives" to Own Deficits
FEDERAL GOVERNMENT	- 34,357	60.3	37,461	55.9	0.93
PROVINCES	- 22,654	39.7	29,541	44.1	1.11
ATLANTIC PROVINCES	- 1,087	1.9	324	0.5	0.25
QUEBEC	- 4,301	7.5	5,657	8.4	1.12
ONTARIO	-10,931	19.2	14,461	21.6	1.13
PRAIRIE PROVINCES	- 3,805	6.7	6,748	10.1	1.51
BRITISH COLUMBIA	- 2,531	4.4	2,351	3.5	0.79

Source: Richards (2000), 26.

deficit, since it would have involved politically unpopular decisions to make most Canadians pay higher taxes for fewer transfers and services.

During his first term, Prime Minister Chrétien delegated considerable authority to Martin in the management of fiscal and economic policy. Some observers suggest that this action reflected a managerial style of delegating responsibility to manage major issues to line ministers rather than the centralized, hands-on management by the Prime Minister's Office and Privy Council Office seen often during the Trudeau and Mulroney years. Others suggest that Chrétien maintained a firm, if often hidden, hand on the policy controls, and that Martin skilfully used his relationship with the Prime Minister to centralize budgetary and policy-making authority in the Department of Finance to an extent not seen in more than 30 years.[11]

When, in the wake of the 1994 Mexican financial crisis, rising interest rates threatened to undercut even the relatively cautious fiscal targets in his first budget, the Finance Minister initiated a detailed spending review that forced significant reductions in federal administrative and program spending.[12] Pressures for spending reductions were reinforced by the growing burden of interest charges on the federal debt (see Table 9.6). Martin and his colleagues came to accept the view that failure to reduce the deficit imperilled future efforts to invest in public services, increase productivity, or improve Canadians' standards of living.

Table 9.6 ·· INTEREST CHARGES AS A PERCENTAGE OF FEDERAL SPENDING AND REVENUES

	Interest on public debt (millions of $1995)	Share of federal revenues	Share of federal spending
1980	19,681	16.0%	19.0%
1985	34,369	21.6%	28.7%
1990	46,773	27.1%	32.2%
1995	46,254	39.5%	30.1%
2000	40,538	22.7%	24.7%

Source: Canada, Department of Finance (2001). *Fiscal Reference Tables* (Ottawa); author's calculations.

Martin also forced provincial governments to absorb a major share of the federal government's spending reductions. During the early 1990s, the Mulroney government tried to limit the impact on its budgets of rapid increases in provincial taxes and social spending by unilaterally capping its transfers to the three largest provinces and by limiting deductibility for increased provincial payroll taxes.[13] In 1995, however, Martin went significantly farther, announcing reductions in transfers to the provinces of more than 20 per cent over three years. He replaced "Established Programs Financing" (EPF), in place since 1977, with the Canada Health and Social Transfer. This block grant effectively removed most federal controls over the provincial use of transfers traditionally used for health, education, and social services. Federal transfers dropped on average from 21 per cent of provincial revenues in 1993 to 13 per cent in 1997, although these cuts were partially restored after the 1997 election. Ironically, the cuts ultimately gave Ottawa significantly greater leverage over the provinces than it had enjoyed since the 1960s, by enabling the federal government to balance its budget (and generate surpluses) after 1997.

Although both inflation and nominal interest rates subsided between 1995 and 1997 to the lowest levels since the 1960s, Martin was able to use the spectre of unexpected shocks in global financial markets as part of a broader pattern of "prudent economic assumptions." These assumptions enabled him to dampen public expectations of higher spending or lower taxes, and to enforce a greater measure of budgetary discipline on his colleagues than might otherwise have been possible. The creative use of fiscal illusion provided Martin with the political and financial flexibility he needed to balance the budget in the face of competing expectations and demands.

THE POLITICS OF FISCAL ILLUSION

Previous Finance Ministers had become prisoners of fiscal illusion by projecting rosy, growth-driven scenarios for deficit reduction that were inevitably frustrated by shifting political and economic circumstances. Paul Martin reversed this process, insisting on cautious fiscal and economic forecasts based on figures lower than the consensus of private-sector forecasts in setting budgetary targets, and then forcing his cabinet colleagues to make the spending trade-offs necessary to meet them.[14]

The 1993 Liberal Red Book deficit target of 3% of GDP within three years—about $24 billion—became a non-negotiable floor for budget planning. The volatility of international financial markets in 1994-95 (and again in 1998) allowed Martin to base spending estimates on worst-case economic projections in order to "guarantee" that deficit targets would be met. In this process, Martin fashioned overlapping layers of "fiscal illusion" that enabled him to exceed his deficit reduction forecasts by $15.4 billion in 1996-97 and $20.5 billion in 1997-98, and to eliminate the federal deficit within four years of taking office. These budgetary "cushions" included:

> ➤ deliberately cautious projections of economic growth and interest rates, resulting in forecasts which systematically underestimated revenues and overestimated expenditures, particularly interest payments on the federal debt;[15]

> ➤ an official "contingency fund" of $3 billion as a precaution against unforeseen economic circumstances, which would otherwise be used for deficit reduction (debt reduction after 1997); and

> ➤ the building of a sizeable surplus in the Employment Insurance Fund, designed to maintain fund surpluses through a recession without raising taxes, based on extremely cautious economic projections. After 1996, this surplus was artificially inflated by using worst-case economic scenarios to provide for rate stability in the event of an imminent slide into recession, rather than continued growth in the economy and employment levels.[16]

Appendix 9.1 details the effects of Martin's "prudent economic projections" on his ability first to meet and then to exceed his deficit reduction forecasts. Although he was determined to avoid the massive 1993-94 budget shortfall of his predecessor, Don Mazankowski, Martin's cautious forecasts proved necessary during his first two budgets since revenues fell short of expectations and Finance Department economists failed to anticipate the sharp interest rate increases of 1994. However, the cumulative effects of fiscal prudence (or carefully "fudged" assumptions) allowed him to exceed his initial budget forecasts by $15 billion in 1996-97 and by $20 billion in 1997-98.

These practices, which continued throughout the Chrétien government's second term (1997-2000), enabled Martin to impose more stringent spending restrictions on his cabinet colleagues and provincial governments than traditionally had been considered politically possible. At the same time, the government's substantive efforts to reduce, not just contain, federal spending and to balance the budget kept most business and other groups from demanding substantial tax reductions until it became clear that the bulk of emerging budget surpluses would be used to increase federal spending rather than reducing the federal debt.

THE MARTIN EFFECT: MANAGING THE POLITICAL SPECTACLE

Another major factor contributing to Martin's success in balancing the budget—whether persuading Canadians to accept a gradual 20-per-cent increase in taxes or unprecedented constraints on federal spending—was the changes introduced to the budget process after 1993. Following the MacEachen budget debacle of 1981, Finance Ministers retreated from the rigid doctrine of budget secrecy. Consultation processes involving both ministerial meetings with major interest groups and hearings of the Commons Finance Committee continued as in previous years.

Martin took this process several steps farther, making communications a central part of the budget process.[17] The political marketing of the budget message has taken on a political importance as great as the contents of the budget itself. Since Martin has used his annual budget statements not only to present the government's fiscal agenda but to showcase large parts of its economic and social policy agendas, the budget process has become a year-round public relations effort. Initially, Martin sought to move away from the traditional one-on-one meetings with interest groups, essentially a private, elitist process, preferring instead "multi-stakeholder" consultations with a cross-section of groups with competing outlooks.[18] This approach forced participants to move away from "wish-list" thinking to a broader view of the national interest.

Since 1994, the Commons Finance Committee has taken an increased role in the process by inviting policy experts and major interest groups to present their views and policy proposals in pre-budget hearings three to four months before the budget. Although formally at arm's length from the Minister, the Finance Committee process has allowed him to shape the public dialogue through a group of Liberal MPs broadly sympathetic to his views. The Finance Committee's pre-budget reports have become a fairly reliable indicator of the government's direction in the budget.

Martin also uses extensive public opinion polling for his budgets and major policy initiatives. These play a significant role in shaping the theme and message of the budget, if not its actual contents.[19] However, Martin has been far from passive in his management of public opinion. In contrast to the obsessive secrecy that often characterized budget preparations in the past, even when the formalities of consultation were observed, Martin has made frequent use of both public speeches and trial balloons, launched by "informed sources" through the media, to test various public policy ideas and to suggest to various interests that the government is listening to their concerns. Although these efforts prompted both friendly and hostile feedback from voters, the media, MPs, and various interest groups, they ensured that federal budgets contained few real surprises. The general direction of budgets—if rarely any financially sensitive information—is splashed across the front and business pages of major newspapers days before the budgets themselves are presented in the House of Commons.

Like his predecessors, Martin also uses his budget statements as an occasion to promote the government's agenda in the full glare of the national media, and through a series of subsequent speaking engagements and media events across the country. Although many politicians use these techniques to promote their agendas, Martin has demonstrated a skill and confidence in their use that has helped substantially to restore the political credibility of the federal government and to enhance Martin's own political standing as the government's second most powerful minister next to the Prime Minister himself.

Reaping the Fiscal Dividend: Canada's Tax System as Cash Cow

Noticeably absent from the budgetary upheavals of the 1990s were major changes to federal tax laws—with the modest exceptions already noted. After twenty years of almost constant change or the threat of change, Canadian income tax policies experienced a decade of relative stability after Michael Wilson's income tax reforms of 1988. Although annual budgets have resulted in a number of incremental changes, most were extensions of policy changes introduced between 1985 and 1988.

Several reasons can be advanced for the relative stability of federal tax policies during the 1990s. Unlike the aftermath of previous tax reforms, there was little change in the top leadership of the Department of Finance between 1991 and 1997. Deputy Minister David Dodge, who had led the planning for tax reform as Assistant Deputy Minister—Tax Policy in the late 1980s, retained his position for almost four years after the 1993 election. This enabled an effective and durable consensus on the role and limits of the tax system as an instrument of economic and social policy to solidify among the Department of Finance, senior tax practitioners, and major interest groups in the business and social policy communities. After an initial flurry of efforts to trim tax preferences for businesses and investors, Martin has shown relatively little interest in structural tax reform.[20] Traditional business demands for sectoral tax reductions gave way to the overriding objective of deficit reduction, an objective long sought by most in the business community.

Martin made only minor changes to Conservative tax policies in his 1994 and 1995 budgets, winding up the remains of the capital gains exemption (except for small businesses and family farms), and limiting entertainment write-offs for businesses. However, his efforts to reduce the deficit benefited significantly from tax changes and increases introduced by the previous government. Michael Wilson's partial de-indexation of the personal income tax system after 1985 added almost $10 billion to annual federal revenues between 1988 and 1997.[21] A series of deficit reduction taxes and surtaxes, along with higher payroll taxes, also contributed to personal tax rate increases averaging 20 per cent between 1989 and 1997, a level nearly matched by rising business taxation.[22] The growing reliance of governments on capital, payroll, and other profit-insensitive taxes largely offset the drop in corporate income tax revenues during and after the recession of the early 1990s. The Mintz Task Force on Business Taxation estimated that profit insensitive taxes accounted for 78 per cent of business taxes in 1995.[23] These windfalls, together with Martin's effective power to dictate the federal government's fiscal framework after 1994, the absence of any serious controversies over the workings of the tax system, and the lack of a parliamentary opposition capable of forming an alternative government created the perfect environment for tax stability, so long as Martin could maintain the public perception that Ottawa had little fiscal discretion.

The most significant changes to the federal tax system during this period were the conversion of the Child Tax Credit to a major new national social program, a largely uncontroversial measure, and the restructuring of the Unemployment Insurance system to generate a major fiscal windfall for the government.

THE NATIONAL CHILD BENEFIT: EXPANDING THE TAX TRANSFER SYSTEM

The emergence of the National Child Benefit as the centrepiece of Canada's tax-transfer system for lower- and middle-income families reflects a number of enduring political realities about Canada's tax system.

It is easier to take an existing feature of the tax system and expand or modify it to deal with changing political and economic conditions than it is to invent a new program from scratch. When there is conflict between the Department of Finance and a spending ministry over a major proposal for social spending, Finance is often successful in substituting a tax-based spending measure over which it has some measure of control for a new social policy entitlement that may involve a major expansion in the size of government. The political trade-offs involved in creating a new social program through the tax system lend themselves to targeted social programs. Ultimately, however, they also create pressures to extend the same benefits to the broad middle class.

The National Child Benefit (NCB), introduced in 1997 and subsequently extended, now provides lower-income parents with a refundable tax credit of $2,372 for the first child and $2,172 for each additional child. Lower amounts are available to families earning between $30,754 and $80,000.[24] The NCB emerged from a series of federal-provincial negotiations in 1996-97, following abortive discussions arising from the federal government's social policy review of 1994-95. The NCB combines the former federal Child Tax Benefit, introduced in 1978 and significantly expanded in 1992-93, with a variety of provincial measures. It enables lower-income parents to earn modest incomes from employment without facing punitive tax penalties from the loss of social assistance (welfare) benefits. This addresses the problem of the "welfare wall," the disincentive effect of high tax-back rates on welfare recipients seeking part-time or full-time work.

The original Child Tax Credit was one of the few ideas of the welfare reform campaign of the 1970s to promote a Guaranteed Annual Income to survive contemporary pressures for budget restrictions to curb inflation and growing public resistance to the expansion of the welfare state. Unlike previous tax credits, it was refundable, enabling governments to use the existing Revenue Canada bureaucracy to deliver cheques to lower-income families as a supplement to the then-universal Family Allowance or "baby bonus."

The enormous structural deficits of the 1980s caused both Liberals and Conservatives to look for more cost-effective ways of assisting families through government transfer programs as well as increasing the real and perceived fairness of the tax system. The 1988 tax reform's conversion of tax deductions for dependent family members to credits emphasized the targeting of family tax benefits to lower- and middle-income families. From there, it was a short leap to abolishing family allowances and allocating part of the savings to an expanded child tax credit in 1993.

Social changes, including the entry of a majority of mothers with dependent children into the labour force, prompted calls throughout the 1980s from parts of the social policy community and daycare providers for a national childcare program that would extend federal transfers to the provinces to include a major expansion of subsidies for public and non-profit childcare providers. However, these proposals were political non-starters. Ottawa was trying to slow the rate of growth of its transfer programs to deal with its deficit, not increase it. The Mulroney government was reluctant to increase taxes (except by means of "bracket creep"), let alone to finance a major expansion of social programs. Social conservatives in the Tory caucus strongly resisted universal daycare as a threat to family autonomy, parental choice, and the limited state. Targeted tax credits offered a practical way to accommodate these social pressures, balance competing political demands, and, above all, to maintain control over costs.

Although many activists in the social policy community bemoaned the new trend as a betrayal of the universality of social programs as a rite of citizenship, a few looked for ways to use the ideas of the new liberalism to correct the indignities of the "welfare wall" and to persuade governments it was possible to help the poorest Canadians move towards greater participation in society without creating a financially crushing burden of social entitlements. The most prominent of these activists was Ken Battle, a former government official and Director of the National Council of Welfare, who set up the Caledon Institute in 1992 to champion ideas for a "progressive, pragmatic social policy" through a series of publications and conferences and by persistent lobbying of federal politicians and officials.

Battle was part of the blue ribbon advisory committee appointed by Human Resources Development Minister Lloyd Axworthy that prepared the so-called "Green Paper" on Social Policy Reform in 1994.[25] The review's ambitious proposals to reform Canada's social security system to restructure and target social programs ran aground, owing to the opposition of social activists and provincial governments, and to Finance's insistence on sizeable spending reductions to help it head off a looming fiscal crisis. While EI reform dominated the agenda of the new Department of Human Resources Development (HRD) for almost two years, senior department officials continued to champion the expansion of the Child Tax Credit, in cooperation with the provinces if possible, as the initiative most likely to strengthen the federal government's social policy profile. In this process, Battle worked closely with officials in HRD and Finance, becoming part of a select inner circle of policy-makers, and was extended the rare privilege, as a non-civil servant, of making a presentation to a cabinet committee considering pre-budget policy options.[26]

The Chrétien government, although sympathetic to demands for expanded public services from its caucus's social policy lobby, faced the same trade-offs as did the Mulroney government. Correcting the perverse economic incentives of the welfare system, especially its punitive marginal tax rates, and increasing work incentives for recipients of social benefits and the "working poor" were central to its social policy review and, indeed, to its entire philosophy of neo-liberalism. By focusing on the economic needs of lower-income working families, it managed to convert public frustration with growing levels of welfare dependence into support for significant change in the delivery of social benefits.

The introduction of the National Child Benefit became the first instalment of the long-awaited fiscal dividend from deficit reduction. Although Martin was determined to balance the budget, an election was looming on the horizon. Increasing refundable tax credits for lower-income families could serve several useful political and policy objectives at the same time. The move allowed Martin to trumpet a policy of "targeted tax cuts," benefiting mainly lower- and middle-income Canadians, as a reward for their economic sacrifices in the fight against the deficit. It gave social policy Liberals the opportunity to champion the cause of fighting "child poverty," a catchy slogan developed to popularize an expansion of social spending in the face of populist conservative pressures for large-scale tax cuts and smaller government. It enabled the Liberals, on the eve of an election, to present themselves as the party of "balance," offering a mix of competent financial management and greater parental choice to fiscally and socially conservative voters, while demonstrating to social liberals and lower-income parents a commitment to promote "social justice" and increased social spending. It offered the provinces greater flexibility in their own welfare reform measures (triggered in large measure by cuts in federal transfers) by encouraging them to shift spending from politically unpopular welfare spending to other social services for families and parents seeking to re-enter the workforce. In addition, it provided a practical example, especially in Quebec, that a well-managed federal government could still play a direct and active role in the lives of individual Canadians.

The National Child Benefit has become the cornerstone of the federal government's tax transfer system which seeks to improve the living standards of lower-income families, particularly those often described as the "working poor." Although social policy groups continue to lobby for the expansion of the program, particularly for families earning less than $30,000 a year, the program's very political success has created a new series of challenges.

The targeting of the NCB means that two-thirds of program funding in 1996 went to the 31 per cent of Canadian families earning less than $30,000 a year,[27] with benefits being phased out at a rate of 5 per cent per $1,000 of family income. However, studies have shown that the cumulative effect of tax clawbacks on refundable tax credits has pushed the marginal tax rates of many middle-income families with earnings in the $25,000–$40,000 range above 60 per cent when all federal and provincial taxes are taken into account.[28] This result, in turn, creates pressures either for more generalized tax reductions or for increases in tax benefits for middle-income parents, which would significantly increase program costs and dilute the degree of program targeting. The effects of high marginal tax rates on families with relatively modest incomes were seen as sufficiently unfair by Martin and his officials that the 2000 budget announced plans to reduce the tax clawback by more than half over four years, and to increase the income ceiling for the full benefit to at least $35,000.

At the same time, the NCB's emphasis on channelling tax dollars directly to parents has undercut the efforts of professional childcare providers and public service unions to secure large-scale federal funding for a national daycare program. (Ironically, this may be one cause of the program's relatively broad support among many small-c conservatives as well as liberals.)

As tax policy measures go, the Child Tax Benefit has proven a useful initiative in addressing the income needs of the working poor and the problems of welfare dependence and public resistance to welfare spending. However, it is far from being a magic bullet that can address all the policy issues related to family living standards and the costs of raising children. (These issues will be addressed in greater detail in Chapter 13.)

Conclusion

The federal government's success since 1997 in eliminating its deficit and running a string of balanced budgets has helped to change the terms of political debate in Canada. Federal opinion surveys suggest that Canadians now expect governments to live within their means, set priorities, and focus their spending on key areas of social and economic priority.

However, with federal revenues continuing to grow much faster than most Canadians' standards of living, the rising tax levels that helped to balance the budget are now contributing to a growing level of political controversy. On one side of the debate are those who see themselves as the beneficiaries of the existing welfare state and those who hope to cash in on a growing federal surplus in the form of higher public-sector spending and employment. On the other are those, especially middle- and upper-income earners in the private sector, who see their taxes going up significantly faster than their earnings, and wonder whether they will share in the benefits of the much-anticipated fiscal dividend. Striking a politically and economically appropriate balance between the two is the biggest challenge facing federal and provincial governments as they try to define a new role for governments in the era of post-deficit politics.

Appendix 9.1 ·· FISCAL ILLUSION AS AN INSTRUMENT OF FISCAL DISCIPLINE—
1993-94–1999-2000 FEDERAL BUDGET PROJECTIONS COMPARED TO
FINAL OUTCOMES (IN $ BILLION)

	1993-1994	1994-1995	1995-1996	1996-1997	1997-1998	1998-1999	1999-2000
Budget Balance							
BUDGETED	-29.6	-39.7	-32.7	-24.3	-17.0	0.0	0.0
INTERIM	-45.6	-37.9	-32.7	-19.0	0.0	0.0	0.0
ACTUAL	-42.0	-37.5	-28.6	- 8.9	3.5	2.9	12.3
VARIANCE	-12.4	2.4	4.1	15.4	20.5	2.9	12.3
"Operating Balance" (before interest charges)							
BUDGETED	6.9	1.3	19.2	26.0	32.0	46.5	45.5
INTERIM	- 7.1	6.7	16.8	26.5	41.5	44.4	44.5
ACTUAL	- 4.0	4.6	18.3	36.1	44.4	44.3	53.9
VARIANCE	-10.9	3.3	- 0.9	10.1	12.4	- 2.2	9.4
Budgetary Revenues							
BUDGETED	119.1*	123.9	133.2	135.0	137.8	151.1	156.7
INTERIM	114.7	125.0	130.6	135.5	147.5	156.5	160.0
ACTUAL	116.0	123.3	130.3	140.8	153.2	155.7	165.7
VARIANCE	- 3.1	- 0.6	- 2.9	5.8	15.4	4.7	9.0
Public Debt Charges							
BUDGETED	39.5	41.0	49.5	47.8	46.0	43.5	42.5
INTERIM	38.5	42.0	47.0	45.5	41.5	41.4	41.5
ACTUAL	38.0	42.0	46.9	45.0	40.9	41.1	41.6
VARIANCE	- 1.5	1.0	- 2.6	- 2.8	- 5.1	- 2.4	- 0.9
Projected EI Balance							
BUDGETED	- 1.8	1.0	5.4	4.7	5.8	6.0	4.9
INTERIM	- 0.4	3.6	5.0	6.5	6.7	7.1	6.9
ACTUAL	0.6	4.1	5.0	7.4	7.0	7.5	7.2
VARIANCE	2.4	3.1	- 0.4	2.7	2.2	1.5	2.3

* Adjusted for one-time administrative and policy changes in 1993-94.
"Budgeted" = Initial budget forecast. "Interim" = Subsequent year's budget estimate.
"Actual" = Final budget figures reported in annual financial statement.

Sources: *The Budget Plan*: 1993-2000; Annual Financial Report of the Government of Canada, September 2000.

NOTES

1 Real federal program spending (all activities except debt interest, adjusted for inflation) dropped 10.7 per cent (national accounts basis) between 1993 and 1997. In contrast, real provincial spending dropped 4.3 per cent during the same period. Canada, Department of Finance (1998a).

2 It also succeeded in negotiating a long-overdue agreement with the provinces to fend off the looming bankruptcy of the Canada Pension Plan by phasing in premium increases of 73 per cent between 1996 and 2003, the implications of which will be discussed in Chapter 10.

3 Interview, senior Finance Department advisor (P15).

4 Greenspon and Wilson-Smith (1998), 97-99.

5 Canada, Department of Finance (1994).

6 Greenspon and Wilson Smith (1998), 207-27; Savoie (1999), 172-87.

7 Hale (1998), 438-40.

8 Angus Reid Associates (1994a, 1994b, 1994c, 1996).

9 Richards notes that the provinces, as a whole, financed their deficit reduction programs from their own revenue sources between 1991-92 and 1998-99, but that this process was significantly more pronounced in provinces west of the Ottawa River. Richards (2000), 24-26.

10 Greenspon and Wilson Smith (1998), 153-70.

11 Ibid.; Savoie (1999), 156-92; interviews, Department of Finance, Prime Minister's Office (PMO-11, ADM-12).

12 A senior Finance Department official describes the program review exercise as a partnership between Finance and the Privy Council Office: "We set the targets [for departments' budget reductions]. PCO ran the committee which made their deputies come and tell how they were going to achieve them. PCO was very firm, saying if you don't identify where the savings are, this committee will make the decision for you. I don't think it would have been done if PCO hadn't played such a strong role" (ADM-12).

13 Higher provincial taxes reduced the federal tax base. Increased spending in shared-cost programs financed through EPF reduced Ottawa's ability to control its own finances. Thomas J. Courchene and Colin Telmer (1998) *From Heartland to North American Region-State: The Social, Fiscal and Economic Evolution of Ontario* (Toronto: Centre for Public Management, Faculty of Management, University of Toronto), 78, 165-67.

14 Beginning in the 2000 budget planning cycle, Martin incorporated the consensus forecasts of senior bank economists and selected private economic consultants into the government's own fiscal policy forecasts. Interview, senior Department of Finance official (ADM-12).

15 Budget documents usually compared these forecasts to others of leading private-sector economists, as well as providing other data that enabled informed observers and financial markets to project the government's likely financial position.

16 Finance Department officials note that these "abstract scenarios" were designed by the EI Chief Actuary independently of the Department.

17 Greenspon and Wilson-Smith (1998); interviews, Finance Dept. and advisors (P16).

18 Phillips (1995), 5.

19 Interview, Finance Department advisor (P16).

20 Interview, senior official, Department of Finance (ADM-11).

21 Low inflation rates resulted in no inflation indexing between 1992 and 1999, something only partly remedied by Martin's ad hoc changes to basic tax exemptions in 1998 and 1999. Martin restored full indexation in his 2000 budget (see Chapter 10).

22 Hale (1999).

23 Canada, Department of Finance (1997b).

24 Canada, Department of Finance (2000e), 150-51.

25 Canada, Human Resources Development Canada (1994).

26 Ken Battle, letter to the author.

27 Perry (1999); Statistics Canada (1998a), "Income after tax, distribution by size in Canada, 1996," Cat. # 13-210, June.

28 Brown (1999).

part three

The Politics of Taxation in the Twenty-First Century—Balancing National, Regional, and Global Pressures

Introduction

The balancing of public-sector budgets, especially at the federal level, has changed the context of the debate over tax policy as Canada enters the twenty-first century. Continued economic growth, low inflation, and relatively high levels of employment, especially west of the Ottawa River, have increased the fiscal resources and, with them, the political choices available to most senior governments. However, the political competition to control these surpluses and how they are to be used to set the political agenda has also increased. This competition takes place at four levels: for control over discretionary spending within the federal government; between advocates of large-scale tax reduction and increased federal spending on public services and income transfers; between the federal and provincial governments for control over a larger share of overall government revenues; and between advocates of increased private discretion and state control in the allocation of social spending.

This section examines the major issues and forces currently shaping the politics of taxation in Canada. It considers the effects of balanced budgets and emerging fiscal surpluses—the so-called "fiscal dividend"—on the tax and spending priorities of federal and provincial governments. It assesses the political and fiscal balances that governments are attempting to strike, often in different ways, to meet Canadians' competing expectations of governments as they try to reverse the decline in Canadian living standards that accompanied deficit reduction policies during the 1990s.

The Fiscal Dividend: Balancing Competing Interests and Outlooks

Economist John McCallum defines the fiscal dividend as "the surpluses that would emerge if the federal government put itself on automatic pilot, allowing tax revenues to grow along with the economy and allowing program spending to rise in line with inflation plus population growth."[1] Others argue for a more cautious definition, suggesting that, since voter demands rarely permit democratic governments to run budget surpluses for an extended period, the only genuine fiscal dividend results from sustained reductions in the interest payments to service government debt.

Private-sector economists suggest that expected levels of economic growth could result in a "fiscal dividend" for the federal government of between $120 billion and $150 billion between 2001 and 2006, if tax levels of the 1999-2000 fiscal year were to be maintained and spending levels were to grow in proportion to inflation and population. Of course, the realities of politics have ensured that such a pool of money could not remain undisturbed for long, particularly in the run-up to a federal election.

Governments are not elected to function on autopilot, but to make political decisions and set priorities. The prospect of budget surpluses will always lead politicians, voters, and just about all organized interests inside and outside government to ask "what's in it for us?". The biggest challenge facing all governments and the groups that seek to influence their priorities is to balance these competing expectations and policy goals while trying to create the conditions necessary for continued economic growth in a highly competitive, fast-changing global economy. A fundamental reason for centralized control of budgetary policies, and for the tactics of budgetary prudence and fiscal illusion practised by many Finance Ministers in recent years, is to insulate budgetary decisions from pressures that are intended to serve short-term political interests but that may not be sustainable in the medium and long term without eroding the conditions necessary for continued economic growth.

One of Paul Martin's most significant achievements as Minister of Finance has been to restore his department's ability to dominate the design and implementation of the national agenda, not just in fiscal and economic policies, but in social policy as well. Martin's fiscal agenda, which has been based largely on the strategic vision outlined in his 1994 "Purple Book," has five main elements which help to shape a fiscal framework of balanced budgets and stable medium-term policies:

> ➤ promoting economic growth, minimal inflation, and continued improvement in the living standards of the average Canadian;

> investing in key social priorities, notably health, education, and child welfare, that reinforce or complement the government's economic agenda;

> reducing personal taxation, particularly in areas in which Canada faces a significant competitive disadvantage, or which create significant distortions in Canada's tax system;

> maintaining the competitiveness of Canada's business tax system relative to those of its major trading partners, especially the United States; and

> reducing the federal debt *as a share of the national economy*, and debt interest payments as a share of federal revenues in order to provide the government with greater fiscal flexibility.

A key factor in this policy mix is the encouragement through both tax and spending policies of the emerging "knowledge-based economy," which is rooted in the development and application of new information and computerized technologies.

This outlook, which combines elements of the traditional public finance view described in Chapter 2 with a recognition of the need to set disciplined priorities concerning the size and scope of government, is likely to shape the options considered by future governments in managing the politics of taxation and public finance. These options include maintaining balanced budgets, reducing the debt, limiting spending growth, and implementing sustainable reductions in personal and business taxation that will foster economic growth, social opportunity, and higher living standards.

MAINTAINING BUDGET BALANCE WHILE REDUCING TAXES

At the beginning of the twenty-first century, the federal and most provincial governments appear committed to balancing their budgets and holding spending growth within expected levels of revenue. There seems to be a broad consensus among both political leaders and the general public that governments should live within their citizens' means. Canadians' living standards declined or were stagnant during most of the 1990s. Average after-tax family incomes only recovered to pre-1990 recession levels by 1998. Although rates of economic and income growth have recovered since 1997, many economists, interest groups, and politicians have suggested that continued growth in a highly competitive global economy will require some level of tax reduction in coming years.

Public opinion appears consistently to favour modest tax reductions and selected increases in public spending, particularly on middle-class entitlements such as health care and education. However, there appears to be little support for policies that would lead to a return to deficit spending. The federal government and some provinces have adopted prudent budgeting strategies that explicitly provide for formal contingency funds in the event of revenue shortfalls or interest rate increases, and other forms of fiscal discretion that slow rates of spending growth and protect budgets from external economic shocks. Although such strategies allow governments to respond to short-term spending pressures, they also provide large enough surpluses to finance some level of debt reduction, further reducing the share of taxes spent on interest payments and creating a fiscal cushion against the rising costs of services expected by an aging population.

The October 2000 "mini" budget, which provided several major planks for the Chrétien government's successful re-election campaign, reinforced this agenda in promising individual tax reductions averaging 21 per cent between 2000-01 and 2005-06, selected tax reductions for business and investment income, and close to $50 billion in additional spending, in particular, major increases in federal-provincial transfers.[2] However, some economists have suggested that without continued spending restraint, the federal government may be unable to maintain its commitment to balanced budgets throughout this period, should growth rates falter, particularly in response to a cyclical downturn in the American economy.[3]

Although the cumulative effect of these measures amounts to the largest tax reductions in modern Canadian history, the reductions generally reflect marginal changes to existing policies, carefully balanced for maximum political effect, rather than significant changes to existing tax structures or economic entitlements.

REDUCING THE DEBT

Martin appears to have won broad political support for a slow but steady process of debt reduction, relying on small, regular annual payments for debt retirement, combined with steady economic growth, to reduce the national Debt to GDP ratio to levels comparable to those of other industrial nations (see Table c.1). Much higher than expected growth rates and federal revenues allowed Martin to make extraordinary payments against the federal debt, totalling $29 billion in 2000 and 2001. At projected growth rates, averaging 2.5 per cent over five years, current forecasts suggest that the federal debt could be reduced to below 40 per cent of GDP—roughly the same level as in 1983-84—provided Finance's cautious economic forecasts permit it to allocate its annual $3 billion *"contingency fund"* to debt reduction. Debt repayment also enables government to use a larger share of taxes collected for public services and income transfers, linking tax levels more closely to the actual provision of public benefits. This is a key factor in legitimizing government policies designed to reduce social conflict.

Canada's aging society, which will see the number of pensioners increase by at least 80 per cent relative to the working age population within thirty years, will force governments to reduce levels of public debt, if only to protect their capacity to pay for essential public services without incurring economically crippling levels of taxation or engendering political conflict between an older generation heavily dependent on government transfers and services and a younger generation who will be expected to pay for them.[4]

The federal government already has institutionalized a modest level of annual debt repayment, but is placing a high priority on a growing economy to reduce the relative size of the debt. Although several provincial governments, notably Alberta, Manitoba, Ontario, and New Brunswick, have also provided for consistent debt repayment, using various forms of balanced budget legislation, only Alberta has made debt reduction a major priority.

Table C.1 •• CANADA'S PUBLIC DEBT IN INTERNATIONAL CONTEXT TOTAL GOVERNMENT DEBT: 2000 (AS A PERCENTAGE OF GDP)

	Gross Debt	Net Debt
G-7 AVERAGE	76.2	48.5
ITALY	110.8	98.7
CANADA	104.9	66.0
JAPAN	122.9	50.7
UNITED STATES	58.8	43.0
FRANCE	64.4	42.5
GERMANY	59.7	41.8
BRITAIN	54.4	33.5

Source: *Fiscal Reference Tables* (Ottawa: Department of Finance, September 2001), 64-65.[5]

LIMITING SPENDING GROWTH

The most significant difference between the economic recovery of the 1990s and that of the 1980s was that most Canadian governments, even after balancing their budgets, held their real spending levels at or near the rate of population growth, rather than allowing them to parallel the growth of tax revenues (see Table C.2). At the federal level, spending constraints were reinforced by a mixture of fiscal illusion, centralized control over budgetary pressures, and the use of surplus revenues to finance end-of-year spending

Table C.2 ·· AVERAGE REVENUE AND SPENDING GROWTH (ADJUSTED FOR INFLATION AND POPULATION GROWTH) 1995-96–1999-2000

	Average own source revenue growth	Average total revenue growth	Average annual spending growth	Average budget balance	Budget balance 1995-96	Budget balance 1999-00
	–PER CENT–				–PER CENT OF REVENUE–	
FEDERAL	3.7		– 1.7	– 3.1	– 22.0	7.4
PROVINCIAL/ TERRITORIAL AVERAGE	3.9	2.4	0.0	– 2.8	– 7.4	1.3
NFLD.	-0.3	– 0.5	– 0.2	– 0.3	0.3	– 0.9
PEI	1.6	1.7	1.7	0.1	0.5	0.4
NS	4.1	1.2	1.6	-10.3	– 11.2	– 12.9
NB	0.1	0.4	0.8	0.1	1.2	– 0.4
QUEBEC	5.7	3.4	0.8	– 4.3	– 9.2	0.1
ONTARIO	5.0	– 1.7	– 1.4	– 8.5	– 15.1	1.1
MANITOBA	1.9	1.1	1.6	1.3	2.9	0.2
SASKATCHEWAN	1.2	1.7	1.3	2.1	0.4	1.4
ALBERTA	4.1	3.1	0.9	11.5	7.8	15.6
BC	0.2	0.2	0.1	– 1.4	– 1.8	– 1.6

* Public accounts basis. Inter-provincial comparisons may not be exact because of differences in accounting methods.

Sources: Canada, Department of Finance (2000d); Statistics Canada, Consumer Price Index, Catalogue # 62-010-XIB.

commitments in response to key political priorities. The steady growth of the Child Tax Benefit—which could be reported either under the category of targeted tax reductions or under increases in social spending, depending on the government's political requirements—allowed Martin to maintain firm control over the fiscal framework while easing the burden of rising taxes on the living standards of lower- and middle-income families.[6]

Although six of ten provinces had balanced their budgets by 1995-96, sharp reductions in federal transfers after 1995 imposed constraints on the growth of their spending. The political and ideological commitments of provincial governments also played a major role in this process. Electoral politics and the partial restoration of transfer payments eased these pressures in 1999 and 2000.

However, although political leadership played a vital role, this newfound discipline in public spending would not have been possible except for the shift in public opinion during this period. Most Canadians appear to have recognized that the higher taxes of the previous 10 to 15 years left them with fewer public services and less take-home pay. Although opinion surveys consistently showed public support for targeting available spending increases to health care and education, the specific balance between tax reduction, debt reduction, and increased spending has varied widely from one jurisdiction to another, depending on the resources available to each government and the political priorities of the party in power.

Outline of the Section

Finance's success in reporting consistent budget surpluses has increased public expectations that Ottawa will return a large share of its growing *fiscal dividend* to Canadians in the form of higher spending, lower taxes, and increased transfers to the provinces to finance core social spending. Budget surpluses create a political dilemma for politicians. Polls tell governments that their constituents want *both* lower taxes and higher spending on health, education, and other services dear to the middle class.[7]

A broad consensus has emerged within the tax community on the major elements of this tax reduction agenda.[8] Rather than major changes to Canada's personal tax structure, the agenda involves a mix of broadly-based rate reductions and incremental changes based on existing structures designed to address a series of carefully targeted policy objectives. The federal government and most provinces have increased spending on core social benefits while introducing varying levels of tax reduction, usually targeted primarily to lower- and middle-income families, in order to maintain broad public support for their policies. Chapter 10 evaluates the political and economic trade-offs that have shaped the significant tax reductions announced before the 2000 federal election.

However, although the trade-offs that shape the levels and distribution of personal taxes reflect mainly domestic political and economic considerations, business taxes are heavily influenced by international economic factors. Canada's increased openness to the global economy and the fact that most large Canadian corporations now operate in many countries, locating their investments where they can produce the greatest after-tax return, place effective limits on the levels of taxation governments can place on corporate incomes. A broad consensus among economists has emerged that, if Canada is to be successful in attracting investment and jobs, effective corporate income tax rates must be comparable with those in the United States and Canada's other major trading partners.

At the same time, the political ability of Canadian governments to reduce business tax rates to internationally competitive levels depends on their ability to deliver lower tax rates to individuals and families, while business is seen to pay its "fair share" of the tax burden. Chapter 11 examines the politics of business taxation in the twenty-first century and governments' growing use of "benefit-related taxes" that attempt to link tax levels with benefits received and to maintain the cash flow of federal and provincial governments while increasing the competitiveness of corporate income taxes in international markets.

As discussed in Chapter 3, the federal government's ability to introduce major changes to the tax system often depends on the acquiescence or support of provincial governments that share jurisdiction with Ottawa over almost 90 per cent of Canada's tax base. Canada's tax system is unique in the industrial world in allowing provincial (or "sub-national") governments to collect almost as large a share of overall tax revenues as the federal government. The parallel efforts of federal and provincial governments during the 1990s to balance their budgets led to a growing decentralization of federal and provincial tax policies, and to pressures on Ottawa to allow the provinces to set their own tax rate structures independently of federal tax rates. Chapter 12 addresses the factors that led to the overhaul of the federal-provincial tax collection systems. The series of provincial tax reforms that resulted and are continuing to emerge from these changes are among the most significant changes to Canada's personal tax system in almost 30 years.

Canada's tax system is also a major and growing factor in the delivery of social policy. Governments are facing a series of choices that will affect the relationship between governments and "civil society." These choices will affect the ways in which governments assist families in fulfilling in their social responsibilities. They will also determine whether governments will further empower individuals, families, and community organizations to make their own decisions and set their own priorities, or attempt to channel and control the delivery of services in these areas through direct government spending. These choices will help to shape the nature and direction of Canadian society for many years. Chapter 13 reviews the growing debate over the role of government in assisting families and community organizations in carrying out their social responsibilities, and the underlying political agendas that help to shape this debate.

These economic and social realities, combined with the ongoing emergence of a knowledge-based economy that is global in scope and changes the ways in which people and communities relate to one another and to the state, suggest that, although radical changes to basic tax structures are unlikely in the foreseeable future, Canada's tax system will continue to evolve in response to changing social and economic conditions.

NOTES

1   McCallum (1999), 2.

2   These figures include tax reduction and spending commitments from the February 2000 budget which were extended and accelerated in the October 2000 budget. Targeted tax reductions and increased tax transfers under the Canada Child Tax Benefit are included as tax reductions in this calculation. Yalnizyan (2000), 8.

3   Drummond (2001).

4   Canada, Department of Finance (2000c), *Annex*, 7-8; Robson (2001).

5   Subsequent to changes in international accounting practices, Canada (and other countries) has allocated both assets and liabilities related to public-service pension plans to the public sector, resulting in significant increases in both gross and net debt levels for most G-7 countries.

6   Hale (2001).

7   Earnscliffe Research and Communications (2000a); Ekos Research Associates (1999); John Gray, "Tax less, spend more, Canadians say," *The Globe and Mail*, 17 March 2000, A7.

8   Major exceptions to this consensus were the Canadian Alliance proposal before the 2000 federal election for the phased introduction of a "single rate tax" based on the Alberta model, and the NDP's proposal for tax increases for corporations and upper-income Canadians.

Living Standards and the Politics of Personal Taxation

> The world of politics is not an academic seminar, but a political world
> of interests whose advocates focus on the short run. To them analysis
> is good or bad, depending on its utility for their goals.
>
> *Alan Cairns*[1]

Canada's income tax system has always reflected trade-offs between the desire of politicians and governments to promote economic growth and wealth creation, redistribute incomes from more to less prosperous citizens, and generate enough revenues to pay the ongoing costs of public services. The tax reduction strategy of the Chrétien government, tabled before the 2000 federal election, and the provincial tax reforms announced by several provincial governments in recent years have been broadly consistent with this approach. These changes reflect a series of trade-offs in the distribution of taxes and benefits, and the targeting of both tax and spending measures to ensure that members of all income groups can anticipate higher standards of living. As such, the changes are rooted in both political and fiscal pragmatism. At the federal level, they reflect the federal government's determination to maintain control of both its political agenda and its fiscal framework in the face of political competition to distribute a growing fiscal dividend.

The realities of election year politics, the need to balance the demands of competing social and economic interests, and the opportunities created by record federal surpluses combined to give large-scale tax reductions priority over proposals for the reform or restructuring of the personal income tax system. These changes respond to growing pressures from inside and outside the tax policy community to address the rising tax burdens of middle-income families and the disparities between personal tax levels in Canada and the United States, especially for Canadians at higher income levels. Although the proposed extent and timing of tax relief have been accelerated as a result of intensified pre-election political competition, these changes are entirely consistent with the existing structures and principles of Canada's tax system.

Public discussion of tax levels and tax policies has focused mainly on the taxation of personal and family incomes. Personal income taxes are the largest source of federal and provincial revenues and affect the largest number of voters. Payroll taxes on labour income have also risen rapidly in recent years. The prospect of continuing economic growth and budget surpluses—the growing "fiscal dividend"—have made it possible for federal and most provincial governments to provide the prospect of significant personal tax relief to most Canadians for the first time in more than a decade.

Proposals for more fundamental change, such as the single rate tax proposal floated by the Canadian Alliance and the experience rating of Employment Insurance premiums suggested by some business groups, generally have failed to evoke enough enthusiasm from tax policy experts or the general public to catch fire politically. Indeed, Finance Minister Paul Martin's large-scale tax reductions clearly were intended to head off opposition and business proposals for much bigger changes to the tax system or reductions in the size of government.

This chapter examines the political and economic factors influencing the evolution of tax policies, tax levels, and the distribution of personal taxation as Canada enters the twenty-first century. It examines the major ideas that are shaping current debates over personal taxation and the efforts of Finance Ministers and their officials to control the policy process and to develop strategic plans that would enable them to maintain, or possibly enhance, public services while reducing taxes.

The Tax Policy Debate in 2000: Tax Reform vs. Tax Reduction

One of the challenges of managing economic policy, including tax policies, in a democracy is to balance good politics and good policy. As Canada enters the twenty-first century, public debates over personal taxation are taking place at three different levels. The first focuses on overall levels of taxation: What share of their incomes should Canadian be paying in taxes, and what goals and principles should be considered in answering this question? The second assesses the distribution of taxation and the principles of "fairness" that determine how the costs of government services and the benefits of tax reductions should be assigned to particular groups of Canadians or sources of income. The third is preoccupied with the competitiveness of Canada's tax system, not merely in comparison to other countries, but in terms of its ability to promote or limit economic growth and Canadians' living standards over the medium and long term.

Balancing these often-competing objectives requires a balancing of interests. Finance Ministers and their officials look for specific policy tools that can bring together economic and social policy goals in a politically saleable fashion. This process has been described as "triangulation": combining policy proposals in ways that balance and bring together different and sometimes competing political interests into a viable political coalition.

A number of academic economists have argued that growing federal surpluses provide an unprecedented opportunity to finance major structural reforms to the tax system. A common theme of these proposals is to shift a greater share of the tax burden from the taxation of income to consumption-based taxation, whether through a mix of lower income taxes and higher sales taxes or expanded provisions for tax sheltered savings.[2] However, there appears to be little political support for tax reform, as opposed to lowering overall levels of taxation. Much of the tax reform debate has focused on the role of the tax system in encouraging savings and investment, the equitable taxation of families, and the degree to which the progressivity of Canada's personal income tax structure should be reduced.[3] However, only the third issue lends itself to a discussion of the broad political principles that engage politicians, interest groups, and the news media.

Most public discussion of taxation has focused instead on overall levels of taxation and the degree to which the fiscal dividend should be applied to lowering taxes as opposed to increasing public spending or reducing the debt.

THE PUBLIC DEBATE—TAX REDUCTION: HOW MUCH, AND FOR WHOM?

The political battle for the fiscal dividend—and how it should affect the level and distribution of taxes—reflects both a contest among competing ideas and the efforts of competing interests inside and outside government to recoup their losses after the sacrifices occasioned by deficit reduction between 1992 and 1998. It also reflects the efforts of Finance and Treasury Department officials to maintain control over their government's budgetary priorities, while balancing policies conducive to the promotion of economic growth with other social and political objectives in an increasingly open economy. In some cases, especially in federal politics, the pressures of impending elections have also played a significant role.

The contest of ideas reflects competition among different social and economic interests for a larger share of the economic pie, while protecting their existing shares against the political demands of other groups. Political parties compete for the support of these groups, translating these ideas into competing policy agendas. The contest also includes competing ideas about the most effective ways to promote economic growth and wider participation by Canadians in its benefits.

Market-oriented economists, business groups, journalists, and politicians who share their views want governments to reduce taxes as the most effective way of promoting economic growth, higher living standards, and international competitiveness. Economists link higher living standards to continued economic growth, increased employment, and investments in innovation and technology to enhance economic productivity, and a tax system that allows individuals to keep a larger share of their earnings.[4]

Rising personal and payroll taxes effectively wiped out most of the gains in Canadians' real, pre-tax earnings in the 1990s. The tight monetary policies designed to squeeze inflation out of the Canadian economy resulted in a relatively slow recovery from the recession of the early 1990s. Although Canada's economy grew by a slim 6.2 per cent during the 1990s, after discounting for inflation and population growth, disposable family incomes, a reasonable gauge of living standards, only returned to their pre-recession levels in 1998.[5] Average tax rates paid by Canadians increased by 20 per cent between 1989 and 1997, as federal and provincial governments reduced their deficits and financed the increasing costs of social programs, especially the Canada Pension Plan (CPP). Table 10.1 notes that, even when rising transfer payments are taken into account and the effects of other taxes are ignored,

Table 10.1 ·· TRENDS IN FAMILY* INCOME: 1989-98

| | – constant 1998 dollars – | | | *Percentage change* | |
	1989	1993	1998	1989-98	1993-98
AVERAGE MARKET INCOME	54,508	49,329	55,224	1.3	12.0
AVERAGE TOTAL INCOME	60,480	56,615	62,116	2.7	9.7
INCOME TAXES	11,673	10,887	12,490	7.0	14.7
AVERAGE INCOME AFTER TAX	48,807	45,728	49,626	1.7	8.5

* Economic families, two people or more.

Source: Statistics Canada (2000) *Income in Canada, 1998*, Cat. # 75-202-XIE (Ottawa, June).

income taxes grew faster than the income of the average Canadian household during the 1990s. The paradox of rising incomes combined with stagnant or lower take-home pay for most working Canadians, has created a political environment receptive to demands for lower taxation, especially among Canadians with average and above-average earnings.

Many social liberals and social democrats have argued that tax reduction should be subordinated to increased spending on public services and income transfers. In their view, absolute levels of taxation are less important than their net effects, i.e., the value of services received relative to taxes paid for the majority of households.[6] Between 1992 and 1998, there were significant reductions in public-service employment and sizeable reductions in most areas of federal and provincial spending, apart from the quasi-protected areas of health care and education.[7] Groups dependent for their incomes, status, and security on high levels of government spending and transfers contend that the budget restrictions of the 1990s have undermined the quality of public services Canadians expect and demand. Although some of these groups, especially the leadership of organized labour, call for a return to greater state control over the economy, most argue simply that increased public spending should take priority over tax reduction.[8]

Not surprisingly, opinion polls commissioned by the Department of Finance indicate that support for tax reduction tends to increase with income.[9] Upper-income groups pay a disproportionate share of the tax burden, far more than most receive in public services or benefits (see Tables 10.2, 10.3). Before 2000, the top federal tax rate in Canada took effect at the relatively modest income of $63,000, compared to about $420,000 in the United States. Changes introduced in the October 2000 economic statement increased the top marginal income tax threshold to $100,000 in 2001.

Lower-income groups, who benefit disproportionately from the expanded use of refundable tax credits to deliver income transfers and social benefits, and employees of the broader public sector are most likely to support increased public spending and resist broadly-based tax reductions which, in the short-term, reduce funds available for the expansion of public services. Middle-income groups tend to be ambivalent, having seen little improvement in their standard of living in recent years, as relatively modest income tax reductions have been offset by bracket creep and higher taxes and user fees in other areas. However, some of the strongest pressures for middle-income tax reduction have resulted from the relatively high tax levels of single-income families and the sharp clawbacks on tax benefits paid to parents of dependent children.

Most Finance Ministers claim to be striking a balance between the two approaches, although this "balance" usually reflects the political leanings of their governments. Since balancing its budget in 1997-98, the federal

Table 10.2 ·· DISTRIBUTION OF TAXPAYERS, INCOME, AND FEDERAL
INCOME TAXES—LOWER-, MIDDLE-, AND UPPER-INCOME TAXPAYERS:
1993, 1997

1993	Under $25,000	$25,000–$50,000	Over $50,000
NUMBER OF TAXPAYERS	45.0%	39.2%	15.8%
TOTAL INCOME ASSESSED	21.3%	40.8%	37.8%
FEDERAL TAX PAYABLE	11.8%	37.8%	50.3%
1997	Under $25,000	$25,000–$50,000	Over $50,000
NUMBER OF TAXPAYERS	41.7%	39.2%	19.1%
TOTAL INCOME ASSESSED	18.3%	37.9%	43.8%
FEDERAL TAX PAYABLE	9.6%	32.8%	57.6%

Sources: Revenue Canada (1995) *1995 Taxation Statistics on Individuals* (Ottawa: Revenue Canada); Canada Customs and Revenue Agency (1999), *1999 Taxation Statistics on Individuals* (Ottawa: Canada Customs and Revenue Agency); author's calculations.

government has sought to minimize ideological conflicts over the distribution of emerging budget surpluses by promising to divide them "50-50" between increased program spending and tax relief and debt repayment. However, close observers of the process suggest that the "50-50" principle was more a means of packaging the government's policy decisions than of shaping the priorities of senior budget decision-makers. One senior official comments that the policy had "no importance for (specific) policy decisions," but was used primarily to show how the government's actions lived up to it after the fact.[10]

Unlike the 1980s, when the federal and provincial governments spent most of the windfall revenues resulting from increased economic growth, the federal government, after balancing its budget in 1997-98, kept tight control over its spending. This approach lent itself to a series of incremental policy changes during most of the Chrétien government's second mandate between 1997 and 2000.[11] However, the success of these policies in generating huge budget surpluses, combined with the political pressures of an impending federal election, prompted the federal government to pre-empt opposition proposals for substantial tax reductions before the 2000 election. (Those measures will be addressed later in this chapter.)

The debate over the fiscal dividend has been influenced by many of the same principles as the successful introduction of tax reforms or the restructuring of public finances during the 1990s. The outcome of the debate depends on the capacity of the federal government to build public support for policies that are economically feasible and sustainable, and which convince a large enough cross-section of voters that they will be economically better off.

THE POLICY DEBATE: MANAGING WITHIN THE FISCAL FRAMEWORK

The parallels in the deficit fight and the tax fight are exactly the same.

Hon. Paul Martin[12]

Canada's political culture and the incentives it provides for politicians, policy-makers, and interest groups are heavily weighted toward the redistribution of incomes and economic opportunities by governments rather than toward broadly-based tax and debt reduction. Many Canadians look to governments for status, security, and opportunities rather than to the marketplace or to the emerging orthodoxies of neo-liberal economies. However, without sustained economic growth, government-driven redistribution of incomes and opportunities can easily become a zero-sum or even a negative-sum game, in which

Table 10.3 ·· RELATIONSHIP BETWEEN TAXES AND TRANSFERS: 2000 (PRE-BUDGET)

Family Income	Net Tax Burden	Taxes as % of Income	Difference	Transfers as % of Income	Taxes–Transfers as % of Income
$13,500	- 4,571	0%	—	-34%	-34%
$20,000	- 3,130	7%	7%	-23%	-16%
$30,000	1,233	13%	6%	- 9%	4%
$40,000	5,879	19%	6%	- 4%	15%
$50,000	10,253	22%	3%	- 2%	20%
$60,000	14,663	26%	4%	- 1%	25%
$75,000	21,988	29%	3%	0%	29%
$100,000	33,152	33%	4%	0%	33%

Source: Canada, Privy Council Office (1999a).

society is no better off, or even worse off. Therefore, governments must balance demands for increased spending with economic policies that foster the increased productivity, competitiveness, and higher income levels that result from economic and employment growth.

Paul Martin has compared his current effort to manage the fiscal dividend and to accommodate competing pressures for tax reduction and new social spending to his campaign of 1994-97 against the entrenched budget deficits that had defeated the best efforts of his predecessors.[13] The federal government's medium-term strategy continues to reflect many of the objectives outlined in its 1994 "Purple Book" on fiscal and economic policy. Martin's strategy can be summarized under four major headings:

> ➤ reducing federal debt as a share of national income, while making small, regular payments from budget contingency funds when they are not needed to finance existing services;

> ➤ improving the living standards of most Canadians through sustainable, incremental tax reductions and the promotion of economic growth;

> ➤ encouraging and assisting Canadians to compete in the "new economy" of information, environmental and bio-technologies, and other rapidly growing industries; and

> ➤ maintaining public services while targeting increased revenues to improving access to education, research, and innovation, and the lowering of barriers to the full participation of poor families and other disadvantaged groups in Canadian society.[14]

Debates over the mix of policies required to achieve these goals and the priorities for using discretionary tax dollars take place primarily within the economic and tax policy communities centred in the Department of Finance, although the timing and marketing of policy decisions are more likely to be the product of political calculations than economic ones.

Martin and his advisors have largely accepted the principle that tax reduction is more likely to promote economic growth and higher living standards than large increases in public spending, provided governments continue to balance their budgets. However, such tax reductions must take into account distributive considerations and political pressures for increased spending on priority services. Since these pressures increase with the amount of money seen to be available, setting clear multi-year tax reduction targets is one way of imposing spending discipline and forcing the government to set priorities in dealing with the almost open-ended wish-lists of cabinet, the Liberal caucus, and many interest groups. This strategy also seeks to deflect business and opposition pressures for more aggressive tax reduction strategies.

This strategy presumes certain attitudes toward the role of government and its relationship to the well-being of individuals and society as a whole. Martin has been more explicit than any Liberal Finance Minister since John Turner in the early 1970s in stating that "tax dollars belong to taxpayers," who, he implies, can make better use of them than politicians or governments. A less clearly stated assumption—although one that emerges in interviews with senior "business Liberals" and government officials—is that budgeting within revenue limits forces government departments to be more efficient and disciplined in spending money and setting priorities. By using a tax-cut strategy to reduce projected revenues, Finance officials hope to head off proposals for large, new spending programs that may not be sustainable in the long run, given Canada's rapidly aging population.

Several other factors appear to be influencing the policy outlook of the Department of Finance. Martin and his officials are committed to a policy of balanced budgets and modest debt repayment as long as the economy continues to grow. Most economists agree that, under normal economic circumstances, increasing levels of employment and economic growth are more important in reducing the share of tax revenues needed to finance debt interest charges than is the level of debt repayment. However, institutionalizing annual budget rules, such as Ottawa's annual "contingency funds" of $3 billion for debt repayment, provides a useful cushion against the effects of an unforeseen economic downturn or higher interest charges on government finances. Martin's control over the fiscal framework is demonstrated by his ability to take advantage of unexpectedly high growth and revenues in 1999-2000 and 2000-01, applying a record $27 billion from budget surpluses to debt reduction over the two years. The emergence of the conservative Canadian Alliance under the leadership of former Alberta Treasurer Stockwell Day, a strong advocate of debt reduction, as the federal Liberals' biggest challengers made it easier for Martin to take this action than might otherwise have been possible, given the ambivalence of public opinion.[15]

The capacity of governments to reduce taxes without resorting to deficit spending is directly linked to their ability to control the growth of their spending. Most governments have attempted to keep spending growth rates below those of the economy as a whole. When growth rates exceed their forecasts, they then can allocate some or all of the higher-than-expected revenues to offset key political pressure points later in the fiscal year.[16] Such end-of-year spending measures—about $6 billion at the federal level alone in fiscal year 1999-2000—have become the equivalent of a consolation round for spending departments (see Table 10.4). Alternatively, a significant share of unbudgeted revenues could be used for debt reduction, although relatively few governments have the fiscal discipline to do so.

The biggest difference between the politics of tax reduction in the late 1990s and the early twenty-first century compared to the previous era of sustained tax-cutting initiatives during the 1970s is that persistent budget surpluses and the budgetary processes used to protect them have enabled the federal government and most provinces to enforce their policy priorities while retaining the flexibility to respond to political and economic circumstances beyond their immediate control. This process can be seen in four specific sets of changes to the federal tax structure introduced over the past five years: tax measures to promote increased savings and investment; changes to the progressivity of tax rates and the overall distribution of tax relief; family-related tax measures; and changes to federal payroll taxes.

Tax policies are shaped not only by domestic economic and political considerations, but by international economic factors as well. The realities of North American and global economic integration force Canada to compete in international markets for investment capital and for highly skilled professional and technical employees. Although the impact of these forces on the savings and investment decisions of most individual Canadians is indi-

Table 10.4 ·· BUDGET "CONSOLATION ROUNDS"–1998-2000 (IN $ BILLIONS)

	1997-98		1998-99		1999-00	
	PRELIM.*	FINAL*	PRELIM.	FINAL	PRELIM.	FINAL
IN-YEAR "SPENDING INCREASES"	3.2		5.4		5.9	
IN-YEAR "TAX REDUCTIONS"	0.2		0.3		0.3	
PERCENTAGE OF NEW IN-YEAR SPENDING REALLOCATED FROM EXISTING SPENDING	100%	100%	0%	0%	42%	100%
PERCENTAGE OF UNBUDGETED REVENUE SURPLUSES ASSIGNED TO NET GROWTH OF IN-YEAR SPENDING	0%	0%	101.8%	102.1%	70.5%	0%

* Preliminary—based on figures released with subsequent year's budget; final—based on Annual Financial Report, usually released 6-7 months after the subsequent year's budget.

Sources: Canada, Department of Finance (1997-2000) *The Budget Plan*; Canada (2000) *Annual Financial Report: 1999-2000*; author's calculations.

rect at best, economists suggest that tax levels on savings and investment can have a disproportionate effect on levels of economic activity over the medium and long term.

Relative tax levels are not the only factor in this competition. Political and social stability, a relatively transparent, pro-growth regulatory environment, a skilled, productive labour force, access to reliable, creative financial and supplier networks, and a well-developed physical infrastructure are also major factors contributing to increased productivity, competitiveness, and growth. However, since most major industrial nations possess these advantages to some degree, a well-designed, competitive tax system can be a major factor in promoting economic growth.

Recent debates on tax competition have focused on three main issues: the sizeable gap between top marginal tax rates (MTRs) and capital gains taxes in Canada and the United States: the impact of high marginal tax rates on savings, investment, and entrepreneurship: and the contribution of tax differentials (among other factors) to the emigration to the United States of managers, professionals, and skilled technology sector workers (the "brain drain").

REDUCING TAX DISPARITIES WITH THE UNITED STATES

Current research suggests that overall levels of taxation may be less important to the promotion of economic growth and higher living standards than the mix of taxes levied and their impact on savings, investment, job creation, and work effort.[17] Although high levels of taxation can hinder economic growth, higher tax rates on personal and business income have a greater negative effect than higher consumption taxes.[18]

Canada relies more heavily on income taxes for government revenues than any of its major industrial competitors. At the same time, payroll taxes on employment are below those in other G-7 nations. Kesselman notes that overall Canadian income taxes, including the employee share of payroll taxes, are about 20 per cent higher relative to GDP than comparable taxes in the US. The income levels at which top marginal tax rates (MTRs) take effect are also much lower in Canada than in the United States for most forms of income.[19] Including payroll taxes in tax-rate comparisons between the two countries is important because high payroll tax rates and ceilings in the United States result in most middle-income families and a majority of upper-middle-income families paying more in payroll taxes than in income taxes.[20]

Wolfson and Murphy note that, although effective tax rates for low-income families are comparable in Canada and the United States, income tax rates on middle- and upper-income families are significantly higher in

Canada (see Table 10.5). This comparison, in itself, does not pose a significant political problem. Relatively few Canadians are either inclined or able to move to the United States in search of greener pastures. Those most likely to do so are young, relatively well-educated people with greater mobility, fewer emotional or financial commitments, and greater earnings opportunities.[21] Available research suggests that Canadians evaluate their tax burden according to whether they are financially better or worse off than in the recent past, and whether they have reliable access to expected levels of key public services.

Economic concerns over personal income tax differentials between Canada and the United States are most clearly focused on their effects on savings, investment, and entrepreneurship. However, although upper-income earners in the private sector are often bitterly critical of high marginal tax rates, their political leverage is limited by public expectations that a disproportionate share of any tax savings will be directed toward the far larger number of lower- and middle-income earners, and that core public services will not be neglected. This is a key trade-off in designing tax reduction proposals that will sell politically and be sustained long enough to produce the desired economic results.

Table 10.5 ·· AVERAGE EFFECTIVE TAX RATES* BY FAMILY INCOME GROUP–CANADA AND THE UNITED STATES–1997 (IN PER CENT)

Income (1997 C$)**	Proportion of Families		Average tax rate	
	CANADA	US	CANADA	US
ALL FAMILIES	100.0	100.0	16.4	13.8
LESS THAN $10,000	7.3	10.9	1.0	2.3
10,000–24,999	24.8	21.1	6.2	6.2
25,000–49,999	30.4	27.3	17.3	12.9
50,000–99,999	29.9	26.5	24.3	19.0
100,000–149,999	5.9	8.6	27.9	24.1
150,000 OR MORE	1.8	5.7	32.8	27.6

* Effective tax rates–the ratio of personal and payroll taxes paid to total income (including transfers) for each family averaged over all families in the income group.

** Based on 1997 purchasing power parity of $US 0.79 = $C 1.00.

Source: Michael Wolfson and Brian Murphy (2000) "Income Taxes in Canada and the United States," *Perspectives on Labour and Employment*, Cat. # 75-001-XPE (Ottawa: Statistics Canada).

PROMOTING INCREASED SAVINGS AND INVESTMENT

Savings and investment rates are a major component of medium- and long-term economic growth. Higher investment rates tend to increase the productivity and, subsequently, the incomes of workers, while increasing business competitiveness. Although most Canadians benefit from the wide range of tax measures intended to encourage capital formation through retirement savings, pension funds, small business ownership, and gains-sharing with employees through stock options, most discussion of these issues tends to take place within the tax policy community rather than the general public.

A growing body of research suggests that high taxes on investment (or capital) income have a more negative impact on economic growth than other forms of taxation (see Table 10.6). Even so, effective tax rates on income from savings and investments in Canada are often over 50 per cent, especially when the effects of inflation on earnings are taken into account. Mintz has suggested that this is a major reason Canada had one of the lowest savings rates among major industrial nations during the late 1990s.[22]

Another major challenge facing governments in the medium to long term is enabling Canadians to "save for our collective old age."[23] Providing social and economic security for an aging population requires significantly increased savings and investment rates. These are needed not only to finance economic growth, but also to grow the pensions and retirement savings pool necessary to protect future generations against crushing tax increases and the social conflict likely to accompany them. The cost of pensions, health, and other services for Canada's aging population is expected to rise from 13 per cent of GDP in 1995 to 23 per cent in 2030, while in the absence of major demographic shifts, the ratio of workers to pensioners is likely to decline from 4:1 to 2:1 over the next thirty years. Recent studies commissioned by Canada's pension industry suggest that, if these cost increases were to be fully financed by taxes on future taxpayers, revenues from all sources would have to rise about 30 per cent in real terms. Although other studies suggest that governments can sustain higher spending on services to the elderly without major tax increases, this outcome is conditional on increased productivity, continued economic growth, and an ongoing commitment to budget surpluses and public-sector debt repayment.[24] Understanding these principles in theory is one thing; balancing competing pressures for tax reduction and increased public spending, while maintaining enough political and fiscal flexibility to run the regular budget surpluses needed to pay down public debt *and* accommodate unforeseen economic circumstances, is another.

Table 10.6 ·· MARGINAL EFFICIENCY COSTS* OF ALTERNATIVE
TAX INCREASES

Tax Base	MEC per $1 of tax
SALES VALUE (CONSUMPTION)	0.262
LABOUR INCOME	0.376
ALL TAXES TOGETHER	0.391
CAPITAL INCOME AT CORPORATE LEVEL	0.448
CORPORATE PLUS INDIVIDUAL INCOME	0.497
INDIVIDUAL INCOME (LABOUR PLUS CAPITAL)	0.520
ALL CAPITAL INCOME	0.675
CAPITAL INCOME AT INDIVIDUAL LEVEL	1.017

* Marginal Efficiency Costs: the costs to the economy resulting from the collection of an additional dollar of tax on a specified tax base. Calculations based on tax bases resulting from US Tax Reform Act of 1986.

Source: Dale W. Jorgenson and Kun-Young Yun, "The Excess Burden of Taxation in the United States," *Journal of Accounting, Auditing and Finance* 6 (Fall 1991), 503-04, cited in Kesselman (1999).

Since the mid-1990s, both federal and provincial governments have introduced a number of policy changes in order to build up Canada's overall savings rate and make personal tax rates on long-term investments comparable with those in the United States. Some of these, particularly increases in payroll taxes to rebuild the investment base of the Canada Pension Plan, have been defensive strategies designed to avoid larger tax increases when the baby boom generation begins to retire in larger numbers after 2011. Other policy changes have been responses to sustained political pressure from the financial community and high technology firms that are a critical part of the government's effort to promote Canada's adaptation to the emerging "knowledge-based economy."

The growing integration of international financial markets and the increasing number of savings and investment options available to Canadians have led to demands from the financial services industry that Ottawa raise or eliminate the 20-per-cent ceiling on foreign investments by Canadian pension and retirement savings funds.[25] This action would enable Canadians to take advantage of historically higher returns in international financial markets, while increasing future incomes and tax revenues to governments. Martin's February 2000 budget increased the "foreign property" limit to 30 per cent, effective in 2001. A number of business groups and many academic economists have called also for lower capital gains taxes. Between 1990 and 2000, capital gains—the profits from the sale of capital or financial assets—were taxed at 75 per cent of the individual or business's marginal tax rates, compared to 50 per cent between 1971 and 1988.

Mintz and Wilson note that the higher the corporate income tax rate, the lower the *inclusion rate* should be for the taxation of capital gains, in order to ensure the *integration* of personal and corporate taxation. This principle of tax design is intended to ensure that income from capital is taxed at the same level whether retained by corporations or paid in dividends to shareholders, thus avoiding double taxation of investment income.[26] Lower tax rates on capital gains also encourage more frequent turnover of investment portfolios, significantly offsetting revenue losses to governments, although the growing popularity of mutual funds somewhat reduces this phenomenon.[27]

In recent years, several foreign countries have reduced their tax rates on investment income and/or capital gains. US capital gains tax rates, which have fluctuated since the early 1980s, are subject to five different rates, the most general one being 20 per cent for assets held by individuals for more than one and a half years.[28] Sweden and other Nordic countries have introduced a two-tier tax system that taxes investment income at lower rates than other income in order to reduce international tax avoidance and increase national revenues. Before the 2000 federal election, the federal Progressive Conservatives went even further, proposing the elimination of capital gains taxes altogether. However, other observers have suggested that this might lead the federal government to reimpose estate taxes, which were abolished in 1971 as a political trade-off for the introduction of capital gains taxes.[29]

The February and October 2000 federal budgets reduced the capital gains tax inclusion rate from 75 per cent to 67 per cent, and subsequently to 50 per cent, as suggested by Mintz and Wilson.[30] Martin also changed the tax treatment of *stock options* to defer their taxation (as capital gains) until employees sell their shares. This measure is part of the government's broader strategy of encouraging the development of high technology firms. These actions make capital gains tax rates in most Canadian provinces comparable to those on long-term gains in the United States.

During the 1990s, the emergence of strong secondary markets for the sale of shares in smaller companies enabled many firms to raise capital in financial markets more easily than ever before. Many of these companies, especially emerging technology firms, use stock options as a form of compensation for managers and technical personnel. However, until recently,

Canadian tax laws taxed stock options when they were received by employees, rather than subjecting them to capital gains tax when they were sold, as in the United States, undermining the ability of Canadian firms to compete for skilled employees with larger firms or with those operating in the United States.

Martin's changes to the taxation of stock options also were intended to address the heated public debate over growing migration levels of Canadian managers, professionals, and recent university graduates to the United States, the so-called "brain drain." The Canada-US Free Trade Agreement of 1988 reduced barriers to the movement of professionals and skilled workers to the United States, particularly in response to the recruiting efforts of American companies. Many Canadian business-people and some economists have blamed tax differentials between the two countries for a significant part of this migration. Much of the debate over the relative scale and significance of migration to the United States is driven by ideology, particularly the preferences of advocates for tax reduction or increased government spending.

A more balanced approach to the issue suggests that numerous factors are involved, including greater levels of professional and economic opportunity in some sectors, significantly higher pay scales for some professions in the United States, and the short-term constraints on public funding in Canada during the mid-1990s, especially for health care and academic research professionals. Although these factors do not discount the effects of tax differentials, they do suggest that a more wide-ranging approach to creating a culture of opportunity is necessary to address issues of competitiveness for businesses and talented individuals.[31]

Quebec, which controls its own personal income tax system, unlike the other provinces, has taken the unique step of offering some university professors and other "strategic workers" from other countries a five-year holiday from provincial income taxes as an incentive to move to and work in that province.[32] However, since there is no guarantee that such an incentive will not encourage mobile professionals to take advantage of offshore employment opportunities in order to benefit from such generous tax holidays on their return, it is unlikely that the federal government (or other Canadian provinces) will imitate Quebec's example.

PAYROLL TAXATION: A MINIMUM TAX FOR THE WORKING CLASS?

Payroll taxes are another significant factor in the tax mix of most working Canadians. These taxes normally are levied on employment income in order to finance specific social benefits. Employers pay half the cost of Canada and Quebec Pension Plan (CPP/QPP) premiums and 1.4 times the employee premium rate for Employment Insurance "premiums." Four provinces— Ontario, Quebec, Newfoundland, and Manitoba—also levy payroll taxes, usually on larger businesses, to pay for a variety of social programs. Two others—Alberta and British Columbia—finance a portion of health spending from insurance premiums whose costs are often split between employers and employees. Payroll taxes are generally credited against income taxes payable. However, since 1989, the federal government has served notice on provincial governments that, in order to limit the effects of provincial tax competition on federal revenues, increases in their general payroll tax levels will not be deductible against federal taxes payable.

CPP premiums are "dedicated" revenues intended to pay for current pensions and to allow the creation of an investment fund capable of financing most ongoing benefits. However, a growing share of EI revenues is diverted from program-related costs to finance other government activities. As noted in Chapter 9, the federal government now uses about one-third of EI revenues to finance other tax and spending priorities. Some observers have suggested that this diversion to other purposes of tax revenues ostensibly levied on employers and workers to finance social benefits could be open to a constitutional challenge by provincial governments for violating the principle that "the Crown cannot tax the Crown."[33]

Table 10.7 ·· TURNING AROUND THE CANADA PENSION PLAN

	"PAYGO" Rate*	Contribution Rate**	CPP Receipts– Expenditures ——(IN $ MILLIONS)——	Investment Income	CPP Assets: Expenditure Ratio
1983	3.73%	3.60%	– 124	2,494	6.22
1993	7.79%	5.00%	– 5,106	4,479	2.72
2000[f]	8.16%	7.80%	– 879	3,763	1.94
2003[f]	8.06%	9.90%	5,230	4,313	2.56
2010[f]	8.27%	9.90%	7,015	9,724	4.12
2030[f]	11.09%	9.90%	–12,912	42,137	5.07

[f] = Forecast

* PAYGO Rate: Contribution rate required to finance current CPP benefits.

** Contribution rate by employers (50%) and employees (50%).

Sources: Canada, Office of the Superintendent of Financial Institutions (1997) *Canada Pension Plan: Sixteenth Actuarial Report* (Ottawa, September); Canada (1998) *Canada Pension Plan: Seventeenth Actuarial Report* (Ottawa, December).

The federal-provincial agreement in 1965 that created the Canada Pension Plan gave provincial governments a veto over changes to its rate structure. Concerns that the costs of CPP benefits to Canada's aging population might lead to huge program deficits or payroll tax increases in the early twenty-first century led to a joint decision to raise premiums from 5.6 per cent of pensionable income in 1996 to 9.9 per cent in 2003. Although this has resulted in major payroll tax increases for working Canadians earning less than $37,400, it has also allowed the creation of an investment fund whose earnings are expected to keep premium rates stable when the baby boom generation begins to retire in large numbers after 2011 (see Table 10.7). CPP premium increases have been offset to some degree by reductions in EI premiums in recent years (see Table 10.8).

Some tax experts have suggested that, rather than continuing in its current form, EI premiums above the level needed to finance current program costs should be converted to a general payroll tax on all employment income, rather than the rather spurious "insurance" payment that is increasingly difficult to relate to the unemployment benefits it is supposed to finance. Others have suggested that applying the tax to all employment earnings, not just wages and salaries under $39,000 as at present, would enable the government to lower premium rates for all workers, while eliminating the linkage between payroll taxes and the financing of specific social

Table 10.8 ·· FEDERAL PAYROLL TAXES

	CPP Rate*	Maximum Payable	EI Rate**	Maximum Payable	Total
1995	2.70%	850.50	3.00%	1,271.40	2,121.90
1996	2.80%	893.20	2.95%	1,150.76	2,043.96
1997	3.00%	969.00	2.90%	1,131.00	2,200.00
1998	3.20%	1,068.80	2.70%	1,053.00	2,121.80
1999	3.50%	1,186.50	2.55%	994.50	2,181.00
2000	3.90%	1,329.90	2.40%	936.00	2,265.90
2001	4.30%	1,496.40	2.25%	878.00	2,374.40

* Employee rate only; self-employed persons pay twice the employee rate on pensionable earnings, but do not pay EI premiums. CPP employee premium rates will peak at 4.95 per cent in 2003.

** Employee rate; employers pay 1.4 times this rate on insurable earnings.

Sources: EI Chief Actuary's Report, 1998; *Finances of the Nation*, 1995-99; Canada, Department of Finance (2000f).

benefits. It would also dispense with the fiction that unemployment benefits are based on "insurance" principles.[34]

However, adopting any of these proposals raises both major technical problems of implementation and the potential for intense political resistance from groups that would be hurt financially. The federal government and most business groups are reluctant to eliminate the link, however tenuous, between EI premiums and benefit levels. The federal government may lack constitutional authority to impose payroll taxes on provincial public-sector employers which are unrelated to specific social benefits.[35] Raising taxes on employment income while eliminating EI premiums for employers whose layoff decisions directly affect program costs would be politically controversial and economically questionable. However, "experience rating" the employer share of any tax—that is, relating premiums to benefit costs triggered by employers' layoff decisions—would be highly controversial in Atlantic Canada and other regions that are heavily dependent on seasonal employment.[36] The growing number of self-employed, who already pay both the employer and employee share of CPP premiums, but who do not qualify for EI benefits, would strongly resist a new tax from which they would derive little or no benefit.

The cumulative effect of these objections was to make Martin and his senior officials reject the restructuring of EI taxes as "the Liberal equivalent of the Conservatives' GST."[37] As a result, changes to EI taxes are likely to be limited to their phased reduction of around $2 per $100 of payroll over the next few years, unless an economic slowdown significantly increases program costs.

Whatever the priorities of economists, the political agenda for personal tax reduction is far more directly affected by distributive concerns—the ways in which proposed tax cuts are shared among different income groups. The political benefits of using surplus EI revenues, much of which are financed by employers, to finance personal income tax cuts for all Canadians heavily outweigh the potential benefits of restructuring payroll taxes, a process in which there are likely to be as many losers as winners. This process can be clearly seen in the federal government's use of growing surpluses to introduce major personal tax reductions as it approached the 2000 federal election.

Priorities for Policy Change: Managing Distributive Concerns and Maximizing Political Support

Following its re-election in 1997, the federal government took a cautious, step-by-step approach to tax reduction in its first two budgets. However, a number of political, economic, and policy factors combined to trigger the largest tax reduction plan in Canadian history. The government faced growing pressure to reduce marginal income tax rates, especially for economically mobile upper-income professionals, managers, and technical employees. Noting the political success of promised provincial tax cuts in the 1995 and 1999 Ontario elections, both Canadian Alliance and Progressive Conservative opposition parties pursued similar strategies by promising major tax reductions in the run-up to the federal election anticipated for 2001.

However, political realities, and the Liberal government's own commitments, dictated that governments should target the bulk of tax relief to the majority of lower- and middle-income earners whose after-tax incomes had stagnated during most of the 1990s. To be politically viable, any tax reduction plan needed to make a majority of all income groups significantly better off in order to satisfy competing views of "fairness." At the same time, a broad consensus emerged within the tax policy community over the basic changes needed to remove economic distortions in the tax system that had grown since Michael Wilson's tax reform package of 1987-88.

Some of these measures, while benefiting all or most taxpayers, would be of greatest benefit proportionally to lower- and middle-income earners. These included restoring inflation indexing to tax rates and brackets, which added between $8 and $9 billion to personal tax bills during the 1990s, increasing basic tax exemptions and thresholds, and increasing family-related tax credits for both lower- and middle-income families. A late addition to this list was the reduction of the lowest income tax bracket, as political parties engaged in electoral one-upmanship to win voter support. Another batch of measures was aimed at reducing tax rates for middle- and upper-middle income families. These included sizeable reductions in the "middle income" tax bracket, payable by individuals earning $30,000 to $60,000, and increases in the threshold in the top tax bracket from about $60,000 to $100,000. The intended impact of these measures was cumulative, in response to the pyramiding of various taxes and tax clawbacks on middle-income families.

Finance Department officials and many academic economists had become increasingly concerned in recent years over the high marginal tax rates paid by taxpayers earning between $25,000 and $60,000 a year.[38] In the late 1990s, many families with incomes below the national average were paying marginal tax rates of over 60 per cent, thanks to the combined effects of bracket creep, sharply rising payroll taxes, high clawback rates for refundable tax credits (especially the Child Tax Benefit), and sharply progressive federal and provincial tax rates. These tax increases gave Canada one of the most sharply progressive tax rate structures in the industrial world for taxpayers earning less than the average employee's earnings (about $32,300 in early 2000), raising fundamental questions both about the fairness and the economic efficiency of the tax system.[39]

The Chrétien government attempted to maintain control over both the tax cut agenda and its fiscal framework by promising in its February 2000 budget to phase in annual tax reductions over four years of $2 to $5 billion—more if fiscal circumstances permitted.[40] Although the cumulative effect of these tax cuts totalled a record $58 billion over five years, higher than expected economic growth and record budget surpluses triggered a bidding war among the opposition parties to distribute the fiscal dividend. In response to opposition proposals for much greater tax cuts, Finance Minister Paul Martin accelerated the government's tax reduction plan in a pre-election "budget update" of October 2000, calling for cumulative tax reductions of $100 billion–including about $16 billion in 2001-02. The Canadian Alliance plan called for about $115 billion in tax reductions over the same period, and the Conservatives' plan proposed tax cuts of more than $122 billion.[41]

Martin's decision to accelerate the federal government's proposed tax reduction plan reflected the politically competitive environment of a pre-election year in which middle-class Ontario voters, who had supported tax cut agendas of the provincial Conservative governments in two successive elections, were perceived to be the largest group of potential swing voters. Like the far more modest tax reductions used to sweeten Michael Wilson's tax reform program of 1988, Martin's agenda was carefully crafted to offer net benefits to virtually every income group.

Unlike Wilson, however, Martin enjoyed the luxury of rapidly growing federal surpluses that enabled him to offer a mix of higher spending and lower taxes to virtually every income group over a number of years. Under these circumstances, although a number of academic economists repeatedly suggested the desirability of using the surpluses to finance major structural changes in Canada's personal and business tax systems,[42] the political dynamics of an election year argued strongly for avoiding the complexities and potential pitfalls of tax reform in favour of a simpler, more saleable tax cut agenda.

MARTIN'S 2000 TAX CUT AGENDA: BALANCING POLITICAL AND ECONOMIC GOALS

The federal tax reduction budgets of 2000 balanced four major objectives intended to win broad political support: removing large numbers of lower-income Canadians from the tax roles; reducing income tax rates for all income groups; reducing the overall progressivity of the tax system, while visibly targeting the largest proportional tax reductions to lower- and middle-income earnings; and increasing direct tax benefits available to the vast majority of lower- and middle-income families.

Increasing Basic Tax Exemptions
In 2000, personal income taxes applied to all individual income above $7,231. Increasing this exemption and the related non-refundable tax credit for spouses with limited incomes reduced the number of low-income individuals and families who pay income taxes while benefiting all taxpayers to a lesser extent.

The 2000 report of Manitoba's Lower Tax Commission recommended that income tax exemptions be set at levels to offset the basic non-discretionary living expenses of individuals and families—approximately $11,000 for a single individual and $28,600 for a family of four.[43] Alberta's tax reforms, which exempt the first $12,900 of individual and spousal income from provincial taxation, are based on this principle.[44] However, while all three national opposition parties proposed significantly higher tax thresholds in their 2000 election platforms, the newly formed Canadian Alliance found that Alberta's single-rate tax proposal had limited political appeal outside Western Canada.

Ontario's Conservative government has emphasized a more conventional approach to tax reduction: targeting its tax cuts to families earning less than the average provincial income of $60,000, with most families earning $35,000 or less paying little or no provincial income tax.[45] As a result, although overall Ontario tax levels have dropped to the second lowest of any province, its tax system is still one of the most sharply progressive in Canada for individuals earning more than the average industrial wage. The Harris government's policies, which gave tax reduction priority over deficit reduction until balancing the provincial budget in 1999-2000, have greatly influenced the policies of the federal Progressive Conservative Party.

Expanding Refundable Tax Credits
The federal government has chosen to target a larger share of tax reductions to lower-income families by increasing its refundable child tax credit in several steps between 2000 and 2005, while increasing income levels on which

the full benefit is payable, from about $25,921 to $35,000. This approach benefits families without taxable incomes. It also gives the federal government increased visibility by allowing it to send income transfer cheques to more voters. Given its flexible reporting systems, such payments may be reported as higher spending or lower taxes at the government's discretion.[46]

Reducing the 17-Per-Cent Marginal Tax Rate

Cuts in the lowest marginal tax rate benefit all taxpayers, but they provide the greatest benefit to the 40 per cent who earn less than $30,000 a year. Some provinces have also introduced low-income tax credits targeted specifically to low-income earners. Until 2000, federal income taxes on the first $30,000 of taxable income were levied at a rate of 17 per cent. The October 2000 budget responded to opposition tax cut proposals by reducing this rate to 16 per cent.

Restoring Inflation Indexing / Increasing Tax Bracket Thresholds

The effects of bracket creep and other stealth taxes have fallen disproportionately on lower- and middle-income earners in recent years, forcing many into higher tax brackets and largely offsetting the benefits of the modest tax reductions introduced by Martin between 1997 and 1999. Martin's restoration of full inflation indexing in his February 2000 budget

Table 10.9 ·· REDUCING THE EFFECTS OF BRACKET CREEP

	1988	1999	2000	2004 (proposed)
BASIC PERSONAL CREDIT:				
Current $	6,000	6,794	7,231	"at least" 8,000
$ 1988		8,071	8,200	8,876*
FIRST BRACKET THRESHOLD				
Current $	27,500	29,590	30,004	"at least" 35,000
$ 1988		36,990	37,582	40,680*
UPPER INCOME THRESHOLD				
Current $	55,000	59,180	60,009	106,102*†
$ 1988		73,981	75,165	81,361*

* Assumes projected inflation rate of 2%

† Upper income threshold increased to $100,000 in October 2000; new 26% tax bracket introduced for incomes between $60,000 and $100,000.

Sources: Canadian Taxpayers' Federation, 1999; *The Budget Plan* 2000; author's calculations.

eliminated automatic annual tax increases of close to $900 million at current inflation rates, benefiting all taxpayers to some extent. Planned increases in basic exemptions and tax bracket thresholds announced in the February 2000 budget will begin the process of restoring them to their 1988 purchasing power (see Table 10.9).

Reducing the Middle-Income Tax Rate / "Redefining Middle Income"
A major factor in Canada's sharply progressive tax rate structure between 1988 and 2000 was the sizeable jump in marginal tax rates facing individuals with taxable incomes over $30,000. The gap between the 17-per-cent "lower-income" tax rate and the 26-per-cent "middle-income rate" was significantly greater than that between the "middle-" and "upper-income" tax rate of 29 per cent, particularly when the cumulative impact of payroll taxes and tax clawbacks are added into the mix (see Table 10.10).

The February 2000 federal budget cut the "middle-income" tax rate from 26 per cent to 24 per cent, while announcing plans to reduce it to 23 per cent and increase its "ceiling" to $70,000 by 2004. It also eliminated the 5 per cent "deficit reduction" surtax for Canadians earning between $63,000 and $85,000, while promising to phase out the remaining surtax over 5 years. These measures respond to criticism that the gap between the "lower-income" and "middle-income" tax rates is too great, and that the top federal tax rate takes effect at relatively modest income levels, considered "middle class" by many Canadians. The measures were also an attempt to blunt the political appeal of much sharper tax cuts proposed by the conservative opposition parties. An anticipated surplus of $15 billion in 2000-01 and a looming federal election prompted Finance Minister Martin to reduce the middle-income rate to 22 per cent in his October 2000 budget, and to create a new 26-per-cent tax bracket for upper-middle income taxpayers earning $60,000 to $100,000 a year.

Table 10.10 ·· MARGINAL TAX RATE STRUCTURES

	1988	2001 Feb. 2000 Budget	2001 Oct. 2000 Budget	
FIRST BRACKET	17%	17%	16%	
SECOND BRACKET	26%	24%	22%	
THIRD BRACKET	29%	29%	26%	($60,000 threshold)
FOURTH BRACKET	...	...	29%	($100,000 threshold)

Increasing Middle-Class Children's Benefits
Canada is the only major industrial country that does not provide universal recognition of the costs of raising children, either through direct income transfers to parents or through the tax system, although some child care expenses are deductible from income. Martin has two major options in responding to this critique. He could increase the Child Tax Benefit for middle-income parents by reducing the tax clawback rate on benefits payable to families earning more than the $25,900 threshold or by increasing the threshold. Alternatively, he could restore the universal tax deduction or credit for dependent children in addition to or as a partial substitute for the Child Tax Benefit.

The 2000 federal budget announced plans to reduce the tax clawback rate by more than half over the next four years, to 2.07 per cent for one child and 4.14 per cent for two or more children, and to phase in increases in the threshold to $35,000. These moves allow Martin or his successors to implement the proposal as quickly or slowly as fiscal conditions allow or political conditions require. These measures more than double the share of the Canada Child Tax Benefit going to middle-income families, and provide some tax relief to families earning up to $85,000. Martin's tax reduction plan effectively deprived the opposition parties of their most effective campaign issue when the government called a snap election for November 27, 2000. In the election, the Liberals overwhelmed their opponents, especially in urban Ontario, and retook a number of urban and suburban Quebec seats from the Bloc Québécois.

Conclusion: Taxation, Redistribution, and the Politics of Tax Reduction

The changes to tax policy and overall tax levels contained in the government's pre-election budgets of 2000 reflected an emerging consensus within much of the tax policy community. The government was careful not to attack the entrenched rights or expectations of any significant social or economic group. Indeed, the government packaged its fiscal program as a "win-win" exercise designed to diffuse criticism from virtually all major political, economic, and social interests.

The government carefully balanced a series of tax measures designed to target benefits toward lower- and middle-income taxpayers and families in the name of "fairness" with measures intended to reduce tax levels on savings and investment, increased incentives for education and research, and substantial increases in federal transfers to support major social programs.

The technical policy goals addressed by Martin's budget—expanding tax preferences for families, increasing income thresholds and reducing progressivity, and making capital gains tax rates competitive with long-term rates in the United States—were consistent with the emerging consensus among tax policy professionals and economists.

Proposals for the replacement of the traditional progressive tax rate structure by a single rate tax, such as those advanced by the Canadian Alliance opposition before the 2000 election, were too radical a departure from existing taxation practices to win broad political support beyond the party's existing supporters. However, as with many previous changes to Canadian tax policies, the political pressures created by the Alliance's campaign for large-scale tax reduction created an environment conducive to significant tax cuts and a number of piecemeal changes to the tax structure by the Chrétien government.

The government's initial promises of tax reduction in its February 2000 budget received an enthusiastic welcome from the media, business groups, and most of the general public. Its decision to accelerate and expand its tax cuts in its pre-election budget of October 2000 cut the political ground from under both the Canadian Alliance opposition and the federal Progressive Conservatives in the November 2000 federal election. Criticisms of a "sell-out to business interests" from the New Democratic Party and some social policy activists generated virtually no political traction as the NDP was reduced from 19 to 13 seats.

These results should not be terribly surprising. The government clearly signalled its general intentions, engaged key interest groups through parliamentary consultations, conducted extensive opinion polling to fine-tune its message, and took numerous steps to win the confidence of independent economic forecasters and other opinion-shapers in the private sector. It also took advantage of the political benefits that result from sustained prosperity, rising living standards, and high levels of employment in an election year.

These outcomes are quite consistent with the "pragmatic" approaches to tax reform discussed earlier and with the government's commitment to incremental changes within the existing context of Canada's economic constitution now that it has put its fiscal house in order. Although the scale of proposed tax cuts has effectively limited the future growth of federal spending and economic intervention, unless the government were to renege on its commitments or revert to deficit spending, there are indications that this outcome was quite consistent with Martin's policy goals as Minister of Finance and with those of most major elements of the tax policy community. At the same time, the canny Finance Minister's restructuring of federal-provincial fiscal relations has forced the provinces to accept increased responsibility for managing the trade-offs between their own tax

Table 10.11 ·· PROJECTED COSTS OF VARIOUS TAX REDUCTIONS—1999

Broadly-based tax reductions

INCREASING BASIC PERSONAL EXEMPTION (THRESHOLD ON WHICH NO TAX IS PAYABLE) BY $100	$ 250 million
INCREASING BASIC SPOUSAL/EQUIVALENT TO MARRIED EXEMPTION BY $100	$ 40 million
REDUCTION OF 26% PERSONAL INCOME TAX RATE (ON TAXABLE INCOMES BETWEEN $29,000 AND $59,180) BY 1 PERCENTAGE POINT	$ 1.1 billion
REDUCTION OF ALL PIT RATES BY 1 PERCENTAGE POINT	$ 3.7 billion
REDUCTION OF EI PREMIUMS BY 10C PER $100 OF INSURED PAYROLL	$ 700 million

Changing tax rate thresholds

RESTORING INDEXATION OF ALL BRACKETS AND CREDITS AT 1.5% INFLATION	$ 840 million
INCREASING 29% TAX RATE THRESHOLD FROM CURRENT $59,180 TO $100,000	$ 860 million
TO $250,000 (CURRENT US TOP TAX RATE THRESHOLD)	$ 1.4 billion

Targeted tax reductions

ELIMINATION OF 5 PER CENT INCOME SURTAX (ON TAXABLE INCOMES OVER $63,000)	$ 665 million
REDUCTION BY 1 PERCENTAGE POINT	$ 130 million

Source: Canada, Standing Committee on Finance (1998), Chapter 4.

and spending levels, while using the federal spending power and promises of increased transfers to address the concerns of interest groups engaged in the social policy debate.

Although Martin's tax reduction plan was introduced before the election of US President George W. Bush, the latter's proposals for tax reduction reflect many of the same principles,[47] although the major differences between the tax systems of the two countries make precise comparisons difficult. Depending on the precise form in which these tax cuts obtain

Congressional approval, they may increase the political pressure to raise the thresholds for upper-income tax rates in Canada. However, if past history is any guide, Canadian governments are unlikely to cut top marginal tax rates without offering tax relief to lower- and middle-income earners.

Even more than Michael Wilson's politically successful income tax reforms in 1987-88, Paul Martin's changes to Canada's personal tax system have been carefully designed to provide the basis for a sustained political consensus and the economic prosperity needed to maintain it. The changes have also provided Martin and his successors with the political cover necessary to restructure Canada's business tax system as part of the larger challenge of helping Canada compete effectively in the rapidly changing North American and global economies.

NOTES

1 Cairns (1986), 83.

2 Kesselman (2000); Jack Mintz (2001) "Smart Sovereignty: Canadian Prosperity in an Integrating World Economy," speech to Canadian Club (Toronto: C.D. Howe Institute, April 2); Don Drummond (2001) *The Penny Drops* (Toronto: TD Economics, April 24).

3 Poschmann and Richards (2000); Robson, Mintz, and Poschmann (2000); Duclos and Gingras (2000); Mintz (2000c); Kesselman (2000).

4 For example, see Fortin (1999); Robson, Mintz, and Poschmann (2000).

5 Statistics Canada (2000), *Income in Canada, 1998*, Catalogue # 75-202-XIE (Ottawa, June); CANSIM Matrix 6548.

6 Jackson (2000); Rowe (2000), "The 'tax dollars are scarce and should only be spent on the most needy' fallacy," *Policy Options* 21:8 (October), 32-35.

7 Hale (2000b), 241. Total employment in public administration at all levels declined from a peak of 903,000 in 1993 to 774,000 in 1999; by contrast, overall employment in "educational services" and "health and social services" increased from 927,000 to 983,000 and from 1,312,000 to 1,444,000 respectively during the same period. Statistics Canada, Cat. # 71F004XCB.

8 Sandra Cordon (2000) "Social groups say Liberals spent too little; business wants deeper tax cuts," *Ottawa Citizen*, 12 October.

9 Earnscliffe Research and Communications (1999b, 1999c).

10 Correspondence, senior Finance Department official (ADM-12).

11 For a more detailed discussion, see Hale (2001).

12 Hon. Paul Martin, Interview with Author (August 1999).

13 Ibid.

14 Rt. Hon. Jean Chrétien (1999) "Response to the Speech from the Throne" (Ottawa: Prime Minister's Office, 13 October); Martin (1999a); Canada, Department of Finance (2000b).

15 Finance Department and other published polls sent mixed messages on the subject of debt reduction, with significant regional differences apparent. Council for Canadian Unity (2000); Winsor (1999); Compas, Inc. (2000) "The policies, politics and principles of taxing and spending," *National Post* (February); Earnscliffe Research and Communications (2000a, 2000b); Ekos Research Associates (2000).

16 For a discussion of the "multi-stage" budgeting practices of the federal government, see Hale (2001).

17 Fortin (1999), Table 1; Kesselman (2000), 47-52; Bruce Little (2000) "Smart tax mix crucial for economic health," *The Globe and Mail*, 18 December, B8.

18 Kesselman (1999).

19 This comparison is based on a purchasing power parity (PPP) exchange rate of 84 cents US to $C1, as opposed to a market exchange rate of 64-67 cents in 2000. The biggest distinction in tax levels is between state and local governments in the United States, where there are huge variations in regional tax levels, and provincial governments in Canada. Differences in provincial and state tax rates mean that two-income families earning less than $120,000 in provinces such as Alberta, Saskatchewan, and Ontario may face lower MTRs (including payroll taxes) than residents of higher-taxed American states. A key factor

reducing the discrepancy between overall Canadian and US tax rates is that the latter's 7.65 per cent social security tax rate applies to individual incomes up to $76,000 (US)—more than double the ceilings for EI and CPP taxes in Canada. Kesselman (2000), 6-21.

20 In 1999, 74 per cent of American families with incomes between $US40,000 and $50,000 paid more in payroll taxes than income taxes; 55 per cent of families with incomes between $US75,000 and $100,000 paid more in payroll taxes than income taxes—compared with 5 per cent in 1979. Andrew Mitrusi and James Poterba (2000).

21 Wagner (2000). A November 2000 survey by the Council on Canadian Unity indicates that 32 per cent of Quebecers and 37 per cent of Canadians outside Quebec would be willing to move to the United States to "take a job that is better than the one they have now." This compares with 45 and 65 per cent respectively willing to move to another part of Canada, and 39 per cent of non-Quebecers willing to move to Quebec. By contrast, 61 per cent of 18- to 24-year-old respondents from outside Quebec would be willing to move to the United States. Council on Canadian Unity (2000), 16-17.

22 Mintz (2000c), 691-95.

23 Dodge (1998).

24 Association of Canadian Pension Management (2000); Robson (2001); King and Jackson (2000).

25 Keith P. Ambachtsheer (1995) "Canada's 20% Foreign Property Rule: Why and How It Should be Eliminated" (Toronto: Pension Investment Association of Canada, September); Fried and Wirick (1999).

26 Mintz and Wilson (2000), 3, 13-14.

27 Mutual funds report capital gains on asset sales annually to unit holders. Portfolio turnover depends on investment managers' strategies, not the tax consequences to unit holders. Eichner and Sinai (2000).

28 Mintz and Wilson (2000), 1, 12.

29 Drache (2000).

30 The larger reduction followed a sharp federal-provincial dispute after Ontario announced plans in its 2000 budget to reduce its capital gains tax rate to 50 per cent. This has raised issues of federal-provincial and inter-provincial tax competition that raised serious concerns in some parts of the tax community. Ontario (2000); G. Gherson (2000) "Ottawa warns of collapse of tax system," National Post, 15 June.

31 "The Brain Drain," Policy Options 20:7 (September 1999); Helliwell (2000); Wagner (2000).

32 Shearmur (2000); Andrew McIntosh (2001) "Quebec offers profs tax freedom," National Post, 16 January, A1.

33 Tom Flanagan and Ken Boessenkool (2001) "Politics and pogey," National Post, 16 February, A14.

34 Beausejour, Sheikh and Williams (1998); Kesselman (1998); Boessenkool, Finn Poschmann, and William B.P. Robson (1998) "Solving the EI Conundrum" (Toronto: C.D. Howe Institute, 13 October). This issue has been debated lat length within the Department of Finance (interview, senior Finance Department official).

35 Mintz and Poschmann (1999), 18.

36 Canada (1997b); Beausejour, Sheikh, and Williams (1998).

37 Interview, senior Finance Department official (ADM-12).

38 Interviews, Department of Finance; Davies (1998); Brown (1999).

39 Canada, Privy Council Office (1999a), 5.

40 Hale (2000a), 77.

41 Yalnizyan (2000).

42 Kesselman (1999); Duclos and Gingras (2000); Mintz (2000c). Significantly, while most business groups have supported broadly-based tax reduction, there has been no organized effort by business groups to promote major structural changes to the tax system.

43 Manitoba, Lower Tax Commission (2000) *Final Report* (Winnipeg: Ministry of Finance, January), 95-97.

44 Alberta's tax reforms, which took effect in January 2001, exempt families from provincial taxation on at least their first $25,800 of taxable income, and tax the remaining income at a single rate of 10.5 per cent. Alberta, Legislative Assembly (2000a) *Bill 18–Alberta Personal Income Tax Act 2000*, as amended (Edmonton, June).

45 Ontario (2000), 74; Alberta (2001), 128.

46 Canada, Department of Finance (2000b), 154.

47 United States, Executive Office of the President (2001). President Bush's proposal, which must be negotiated with Congress, recommends marginal tax rate reductions targeted towards lower and middle-income individuals and families, increased tax credits for children and families, and expanded R&D tax credits—all features of Canadian tax reductions. It also proposes the elimination of the federal Estate Tax, which was eliminated in Canada after the introduction of capital gains taxation in 1971.

ELEVEN

Globalization, Domestic Politics, and Business Taxation

"Don't tax you, don't tax me, tax that guy behind the tree."
Former US Senator Russell Long (D-Louisiana)

Business tax issues have taken a relatively low profile in recent years, in sharp contrast to the bitter debates over the levels and fairness of business taxes during the tax reform debates of the 1970s and 1980s. The rising level of business taxation paralleled the steady growth of personal tax rates during the 1990s, yet without sparking the kind of conflict between business and governments typical of the 1970s.

Conflicts over the growth of government and who should pay for it, which were the main focus of earlier ideological battles, gave way during the 1990s to more technical arguments about how best to promote economic growth and safeguard public services within the global economy. With few highly publicized tax injustices to provoke an anti-business backlash in recent years, the complexities of business taxation, which are usually beyond the understanding of all but a few private- and public-sector specialists, also tended to limit public debate. Proposals for a more extensive restructuring of corporate taxation contained in the 1997 report of the Technical Committee on Business Taxation gave way to the politically and technically simpler process of incremental tax reduction and a narrowing of the differences in tax rates between different industrial sectors.

Most Canadian business groups, although urging the federal government to allow them a larger share of the emerging fiscal dividend in the form of lower taxes, supported the general direction of federal economic and tax policies during the 1990s. In practice, this meant accepting the tax increases necessary, along with temporary reductions in government spending, first to curb the growth of deficits and then, between 1994 and 1998, to balance federal and provincial budgets. Since then, despite ongoing efforts by major business groups to promote personal and business tax reduction, there has been little evidence of the systematic mistrust or ideological grievances that shaped organized business attitudes towards federal policies during most of the Trudeau era. However, recent international trends towards reduction of corporate income tax (CIT) rates have increased pressures on Canada to follow suit in lowering CIT rates as well as pursuing policies supportive of research, innovation, and entrepreneurship.[1]

The Canadian left traditionally has championed high taxes on business and capital to finance social programs and the redistribution of income. However, the left has been deeply divided by the effects of globalization and the trade-offs necessary for governments to balance their budgets during the 1990s. Many social activist groups and much of organized labour remain bitterly critical of the neo-liberal, market-oriented policies of most Canadian governments. But most NDP-led provincial governments effectively have come to terms with the market economy as the main instrument of economic growth and high employment, albeit with far higher levels of regulation, spending, and taxes than most business leaders would prefer.

Neo-liberal governments, seeking to build public support for their policies of balancing budgets and smaller, more efficient governments, initially focused their attention on restoring individual living standards through modest personal tax reductions, especially for lower- and middle-income

Table 11.1 ·· CORPORATE TAXES AND THE BUSINESS CYCLE
1999 CONSTANT DOLLARS (IN $ MILLIONS)

	1985	*1989*	*1992*	*1995*	*1999*
CORPORATION PROFITS BEFORE TAXES	72,915	74,610	35,336	79,862	101,032
% OF GDP	10.4	9.2	4.9	9.3	10.5
FEDERAL DIRECT TAXES ON CORPORATIONS	17,070	15,063	11,029	14,180	23,868
% OF PROFITS	23.4	20.2	31.2	17.8	23.6
TOTAL DIRECT TAXES ON CORPORATIONS	22,929	23,051	16,041	23,476	36,869
% OF PROFITS	31.4	30.9	45.4	29.4	36.5

Sources: Statistics Canada, "Economic and Financial Accounts, Catalogue 13-001-X1B; Canada, Department of Finance (2000d).

families. At the same time, they have reaped a long-deferred windfall from the rising corporate profits of the late 1990s (see Table 11.1).

Published polling data have consistently confirmed that there is little public support in Canada for lower business taxes. However, since the growing activity of transnational corporations has made corporate income one of the most mobile tax bases in today's economy, major changes in business taxation are far more likely to reflect competitive pressures from Canada's major trading partners—especially the United States—than domestic political forces.[2]

At the same time, domestic politics, especially distributive issues, continue to play a major role in federal and provincial business tax policies. The political capacity of federal and provincial governments to reduce corporate income tax rates without triggering a voter backlash is closely linked to their ability to reduce personal income taxes, increase tax transfer payments to lower- and middle-income families, and ensure that the small business sector shares in the benefits of business tax reduction. Recent federal and provincial announcements of phased tax reductions on business, although quite significant in some cases, have been preceded by sizeable tax cuts on personal incomes and, to a lesser degree, on small businesses.[3]

This chapter reviews the main elements of the business tax system and examines the competing pressures that have shaped its evolution, and suggests the trade-offs between domestic political pressures and global economic competition that are likely to shape the evolution of Canada's business tax system as it enters the twenty-first century.

Major Elements of Canada's Business Tax System

Most of the political rhetoric surrounding the taxation of business and whether business is paying its "fair share" of the costs of government is related to the corporate income tax. However, taxes on profits accounted for only 21 per cent of business taxes paid in Canada in 1995.[4] The cyclical nature of business profits has forced both federal and provincial governments to look for more reliable sources of revenue from business. At the provincial level, this process is reinforced by wide disparities in provincial economic structures, corporate profitability, and tax bases (see Table 11.2). There has also been a long-term trend toward lower business profits as a share of economic activity, although this is partially disguised by wide swings in the business cycle.[5]

The Technical Committee on Business Taxation, chaired by economist Jack Mintz, reported in 1997 that businesses contributed about 30 per cent of

Table 11.2 ·· CORPORATE PROFITS AND PROVINCIAL DIRECT TAXATION:
1992-97

| | CORPORATE PROFITS | | DIRECT PROVINCIAL CORPORATE TAXES* AS | | | |
	% of GPP	vs. national average	% of profits	vs. national average	% of provincial own-source revenues	vs. national average
ALL PROVINCES	7.86	100.0	12.6	100.0	5.8	100.0
NFLD.	4.94	62.9	11.1	88.1	2.8	49.2
PEI	7.69	97.9	9.1	72.2	3.9	68.1
NS	5.34	68.0	10.3	81.7	3.5	60.6
NB	6.29	80.1	14.0	111.1	4.6	79.7
QUEBEC	6.95	88.5	12.7	100.8	4.1	71.1
ONTARIO	8.43	107.2	12.6	100.0	7.6	132.2
MANITOBA	4.70	59.8	13.6	107.9	3.5	60.4
SASK.	9.56	121.6	7.4	58.7	3.7	63.5
ALBERTA	11.47	146.0	11.4	90.5	8.1	140.2
BC	5.76	73.4	16.7	132.5	4.9	84.0

* Includes direct taxes paid by government business enterprises.

Source: Statistics Canada (1999) *Provincial Economic Accounts*, Cat. # 13-213; Annual Estimates, 1998 (Ottawa); author's calculations.

the revenues of federal and provincial governments in 1995. Most sources of business taxation—taxes on business profits and capital, payroll taxes, sales taxes, and a wide range of business license and user fees—are divided between federal and provincial governments or, in the case of business property taxes, between provincial and municipal governments (see Table 11.3).

The Mintz Report notes that, despite the long-term decline of corporate income taxes as a share of government revenues, business taxes as a whole have remained a relatively stable part of economic activity.[6] Governments have increased their reliance on sources of business revenues that are less likely to fluctuate with the level of economic activity. Both federal and provincial governments since the mid-1980s have made increased use of payroll taxes on employment income, despite criticism that these serve as "taxes on job creation." Declining federal and provincial revenues from resource royalties have been offset by increased taxes on gasoline and other motive fuels, which fall heavily on business.

Taxes on capital—the total amount invested by businesses, regardless of profit—have come to serve as a form of minimum tax for large corporations, especially financial institutions. Provincial capital taxes accounted for almost one-third of direct corporate taxes in British Columbia, before its new Liberal government promised to phase out its capital tax on non-financial institutions by September 2000, and actually previously exceeded provincial CIT revenues in Saskatchewan in 1999-2000.[7] Alberta, previously the only large province without a general capital tax on business, draws a major part of its revenues from resource royalties, which fluctuate with oil, gas, and other commodity prices.

However, these tax increases have been offset by several factors. The replacement of the 13.5-per-cent manufacturers sales tax by the Goods and Services Tax in 1990, although bitterly resented by many small service businesses, has greatly eased the adjustment of many Canadian businesses to free trade with the United States by lowering taxes on exported goods and most business inputs, the non-labour costs of producing goods and services. Most business groups strongly supported government deficit reduction programs during the 1990s, even when it meant significant cuts to business subsidies and some increases in business taxes. The Bank of Canada's success in reducing inflation has led to significantly lower borrowing costs, offsetting higher tax costs and making it easier for many businesses to expand.

Table 11.3 ·· DISTRIBUTION OF BUSINESS TAXATION–1995 ($ BILLIONS)

	Federal	Provincial	Local	CPP/QPP	Total
CORPORATE AND CAPITAL TAXES	15.6	10.1			25.7
PAYROLL TAXES	8.2	9.2		5.2	22.6
PROPERTY TAXES		1.6	13.5		15.1
SALES AND EXCISE TAXES	1.8	9.2			11.0
INDIRECT TAXES AND FEES*	1.8	10.1	4.3		16.2
TOTAL	27.4	40.2	17.8	5.2	90.6
PERCENTAGE	30.4%	44.4%	19.6%	5.7%	100.0%

* Includes resource royalties.

Source: Canada, Department of Finance (1997b). Modified to include provincial resource royalty revenues.

Some observers have suggested that Canada's business tax system, although still a patchwork quilt of policies often working at cross-purposes to one another, has moved toward a system of benefit-related taxation in which the taxes paid by businesses are more closely related to the benefits they derive from society.[8] Although many business groups and economists argue that this is a worthy objective, business taxation is as much the product of competing political and business interests within the political marketplace as it ever was, reflecting a process that is still far more responsive to political appearances and pressures than to any coherent set of economic theories.

The Politics of Business Taxation

All forms of taxation are influenced, to some degree, by competition between a large number of governmental, community, and private interests in the political marketplace.[9] Business taxation is no exception. Historically, the level and distribution of business taxes have reflected a political balancing act involving at least four major considerations:

➤ the redistribution, real or symbolic, of income and wealth from owners of capital to other citizens;

➤ business taxes as instruments of federal and provincial industrial strategies intended to promote economic development and innovation;

➤ the construction of broadly-based political coalitions of stakeholders in government economic policies with a vested interest in the maintenance of the economic system.

➤ payment for the direct and indirect benefits received by businesses from public services.

These factors continue to shape the political environment for business taxation. However, growing North American and global economic integration are increasing pressures to tie business taxes more closely to economic factors—the efficient distribution of resources by the market economy, and direct payment for services provided directly to businesses by governments—and less to overtly political factors, particularly the redistribution of wealth and income.

BUSINESS TAXES AND THE POLITICS OF REDISTRIBUTION

Most economists contend that, appearances to the contrary, businesses do not really pay taxes. They merely collect them for governments and pass them along to other people.[10] Consumers may be asked to pay higher prices than would otherwise be the case, unless foreign competition makes this impossible. Shareholders may be asked to accept lower profits, dividends, and share values, unless international competition for capital forces governments to offer investors similar after-tax rates of return to those available in other countries. Workers may be asked to accept lower wages and benefits, an outcome that can be achieved through either hard-nosed collective bargaining or the depreciation of national currencies.[11]

However, corporate income taxes serve a useful political purpose in providing the appearance that large corporations and prosperous small businesses are paying a fair share of the costs of public services, thus either reducing the visible tax burdens of ordinary citizens or expanding the public services governments can afford to provide. The political importance of business taxation increases when governments are providing significant subsidies to businesses to pursue their policy goals or when individual living standards are declining. Voters may resent groups perceived not to be "paying their fair share," especially if they feel they have been "left behind" during times of general prosperity and business expansion.

Corporate income taxes peaked as a share of federal revenues during World War II and the Korean War. Since then, all governments have introduced new taxes on business to compensate for the slow decline in corporate profits and tax revenues as a share of the national income. As was the case with individual taxation, it has proven easier to finance the growing costs of government and repay the debts incurred in previous years by expanding the number of activities subject to taxation than to impose high rates of taxation on one or two major revenue sources.[12]

The Carter Royal Commission suggested that the main economic argument for a corporate income tax is as a withholding tax, ensuring payment of taxes on investment income, especially by investors from outside Canada. Poddar and English have suggested that even this function is largely symbolic since personal income taxes are deferred on as much as 75 per cent of investment income earned by Canadians, much of it through tax sheltered pension plans and RRSPs.[13] However, politicians from all parties have shown a keen sensitivity to the symbolic value of corporate income taxes.

Insistent attacks by the federal New Democratic Party and its supporters on corporate tax preferences as a form of "corporate welfare"[14] helped shape Allan MacEachen's ill-fated tax reform budget of 1981, which attempted to eliminate many business tax breaks or replace them with direct government subsidies subjected to greater bureaucratic control. The NDP attacks also prompted the expansion of federal and provincial capital taxes as de facto minimum taxes in the mid- and late 1980s. Tory Finance Minister Michael Wilson's decision to finance the short-lived personal income tax cuts of 1987-88 through increases in corporate income taxes displayed a clear concern for the "optics" of business taxation. So did sharp increases in provincial payroll taxes on business in most provinces, some of them to replace health insurance premiums on individuals, during the late 1980s.

The Chrétien government has displayed a similar concern for the appearance of "tax fairness" during the 1990s, broadening the corporate tax base and reassuring voters that "the corporate income and capital tax burden has not declined," despite the sharp drop in corporate income tax revenues as a share of government revenues and GDP in the early 1990s.

> Comparison of the ratio of corporate income taxes to total government revenues or to GDP can create the misperception that the total tax burden on corporations is falling. The major reasons these ratios fell, particularly in the early 1990s, is that corporate profits have fallen as a percentage of Canada's GDP. In fact, the corporate income and tax burden has not declined. It has ranged, on average between 32 and 41 per cent of pre-tax earnings since 1965.... Over the years, payroll taxes paid by employers for EI, CPP/QPP, Workers' Compensation and other provincial payroll taxes increased significantly from 1.4 per cent of total payroll in 1961 to 7.8 per cent in 1993.[15]

The balancing of federal and provincial budgets and the emergence of surpluses in some jurisdictions have made the distribution of prospective tax reductions and new spending the focal point of budget debates since 1997, rather than whether particular industries or social groups are paying their fair share of the tax load.

Finance Minister Martin announced plans to reduce corporate income tax rates on relatively highly taxed, large service businesses from 28 per cent to 21 per cent over five years, as part of the "fiscal dividend" announced in his February and October 2000 budgets. However, corporate tax relief is carefully packaged alongside far larger tax reductions for lower- and middle-income Canadians and significant increases in federal spending. Federal tax reductions are expected to reduce effective personal tax rates by an average of 21 per cent, 27 per cent for families with children (see Chapter 10).[16] This move reflects government polling data that suggest Canadians are more likely to think business taxes are too low than too high, and that business tax cuts provide a disproportionate benefit to business executives rather than to the people who work for them or the economy as a whole[17] (see Table 11.4).

Table 11.4 ·· PUBLIC OPINION ON BUSINESS TAXES

Do you think the taxes on Canadian Businesses are too low, too high or about right?

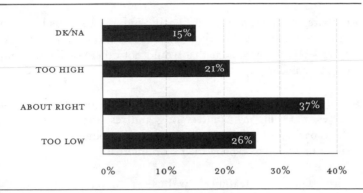

Source: Earnscliffe Research and Communications (1999c).

Distributive issues have also been vital to the packaging of business tax changes at the provincial level. Most provinces have chosen to reduce personal income and sales taxes to a much greater extent than business taxes during the 1990s. Except for Quebec, which controls its own CIT system, provincial corporate tax reductions during this period tended to be targeted at small businesses. Ontario and Alberta, while proposing major tax reductions for large corporations between 2000 and 2005, have also provided proportional tax reductions to smaller firms. However, although income redistribution has always been a major objective of the corporate tax system, it has also placed a heavy emphasis on the redistribution of income among different types of businesses as expressions of industrial and economic development policies, not only on redistribution from rich to poor or from the owners of capital to consumers of public services.

INDUSTRIAL STRATEGY AND BUSINESS TAXATION

The modern Corporate Income Tax (CIT) system has always balanced relatively high marginal tax rates, intended to project the impression that businesses are paying much of their profits in taxes with a wide range of exemptions, credits, and deductions that are intended to promote various forms of economic development as part of a broader industrial strategy. As a result, average tax rates—the ratio between taxes paid and business profits—vary widely from one industry sector to another and between businesses in the same sector.

This result is the product of four overlapping sets of policies intended to promote business investment and access to capital for purposes of investment and job creation:

➤ encouraging the expansion of specific industrial sectors by means of lower tax rates and/or the expansion of tax preferences to promote levels of investment that would not otherwise be economically sustainable;[18]

➤ maintaining the international competitiveness of Canadian businesses, especially in manufacturing and resource industries, and the capacity of Canadian businesses both to obtain access to foreign capital and to expand their own international operations;[19]

➤ encouraging job creation, new business development, and the maintenance of a strong Canadian-controlled small business sector;[20] and

➤ encouraging investment and economic development in underdeveloped regions of Canada through the use of regionally targeted tax preferences, as well as direct subsidies.

As a result, the design of the corporate tax system has often resembled a patchwork quilt of political and economic objectives intended to balance the often-competing interests of various business sectors and of the regional economies that have depended on investment by specific industries as the mainstay of their economic development.

However, the changing economic conditions of the 1990s led both governments and business groups to rethink these objectives. Traditional arguments for favouring particular industries through an "industrial strategy" approach to business taxation and subsidies are giving way gradually, if often grudgingly, to policies that reduce both corporate subsidies and targeted tax breaks in favour of lower tax rates that apply more consistently across industry sectors.

RETHINKING THE CORPORATE TAX SYSTEM

The "industrial strategy" argument—promoting economic development by providing particular business sectors with a mixture of government subsidies and preferential tax treatment—has been a mainstay of economic policies in Canada since the colonial era.[21] Business groups have often found it easier to lobby governments for specific tax concessions that improve their cash flow or to defer taxes payable than to promote changes that increase the system's overall efficiency or competitiveness.

Governments have introduced a wide range of tax preferences—or *tax expenditures*, where these represented explicit alternatives to direct government subsidies—to support investment in specific sectors: manufacturing, resource development (especially oil and gas drilling), construction, research and development, agriculture, underdeveloped regions, small business, and often, a combination of the above. Some of these measures are "structural," in the sense of being "built in" to the definition of income, such as allowing the depreciation (or "write off") of business assets over their normal use lives as normal costs of doing business, or taking normal patterns and fluctuations of business activity into account when deciding when to "recognize" income or business losses for tax purposes.[22] Other measures provide incentives for companies that engage in particular activities that support economic development by providing bigger (or faster) write-offs and lower effective tax rates. The federal government has tended in recent years to move away from such incentives, except for its encouragement of Research and Development (R&D) activities. Federal and provincial measures that encourage R&D as a key component of Canada's engagement with the new "knowledge-based economy" have given Canada the "most generous R&D tax environment" among major industrial nations[23] (see Table 11.5).

Both Quebec and Ontario—two of three provinces that administer their own corporate tax systems—also provide a wide range of special incentives for businesses in selected industry sectors.[24] In 2000, Quebec provided a qualified 10-year income, capital, and payroll holiday for companies whose major investments result in significant job creation. These measures were extended to include a blanket tax holiday for small and medium-sized manufacturers in regions of high unemployment in Quebec's 2001 budget.[25]

Table 11.5 ·· COMPETITIVENESS OF R&D TAX SYSTEMS*–1998

CANADA	0.7
UNITED STATES	0.9
AUSTRALIA	0.9
FRANCE	0.9
KOREA	0.9
MEXICO	1.0
UNITED KINGDOM	1.0
JAPAN	1.0
SWEDEN	1.0
ITALY	1.0
GERMANY	1.1

* "The B-index represents a ratio of the after-tax cost of a $1 expenditure on R&D divided by 1 less the corporate tax rate. A lower B-index indicates a more competitive R&D system."

Source: Conference Board of Canada, June 1999; Martin (2001), *Canada's New Economy*, 10.

With the exception of R&D measures and the changes to capital gains taxation (discussed in Chapter 10), federal tax changes since the mid-1980s have reduced the value of business tax expenditures significantly, narrowing the gap between "book profits" and "taxable profits." However, there are still major differences in the tax treatment of different industries[26] (see Table 11.6). Fiscal constraints led the Mintz Report of 1997 to propose tax increases for manufacturing and resource sectors in order to finance lower tax rates for service businesses. However, this recommendation was a political non-starter. Instead, Ottawa's burgeoning surpluses made it possible to avoid a "zero-sum" approach to corporate tax reform.

Economists have developed the concept of "Marginal Effective Tax Rates" (METRs) to provide a clearer basis for comparison—and competition—between corporate tax structures.

Table 11.6 ·· EFFECTIVE TAX RATES ON MARGINAL INVESTMENTS, BY SECTOR, 1997

	Large Businesses	*Small Businesses**
AGRICULTURE, FISHING, TRAPPING	—	7.9%
OIL AND GAS	5.5%	—
MINING	8.7%	—
MANUFACTURING	17.9%	7.6%
COMMUNICATIONS	23.9%	20.2%
OTHER SERVICES	27.6%	10.1%
TRANSPORTATION	27.9%	15.7%
FORESTRY	28.8%	12.6%
PUBLIC UTILITIES	30.3%	14.7%
WHOLESALE TRADE	32.1%	15.5%
RETAIL TRADE	33.8%	16.4%
CONSTRUCTION	37.0%	17.5%
SUB-TOTAL	27.0%	13.3%

* Small businesses are Canadian-controlled private corporations paying the low corporate tax rate.

Source: Canada, Department of Finance (1997b), Table 3-1.

Table 11.7 ·· MARGINAL EFFECTIVE TAX RATES, INTERPROVINCIAL AND
INTERNATIONAL COMPARISONS–2000

	Alta.	Ont.	Que.	UK	Italy	Germany	France	Japan	US
MANUFACTURING	19.9	22.1	22.5	17.2	18.1	19.8	22.7	22.6	23.6
SERVICE	29.1	31.5	29.5	17.2	21.4	19.6	25.3	24.0	24.8

Source: Alberta Business Tax Review Committee (2000), 15.

> The METR ... measures the difference between the before and after
> tax rate of return on an additional or incremental capital project.
> METRS take into account not only differences in statutory tax rates,
> but also differences in the tax base due to different write-off rates and
> deductions, differences in tax credits, and the presence of some other
> taxes such as direct taxes on capital.[27]

A comparison of combined federal-provincial METRs with those in other G-
7 countries shows that, although effective tax rates on Canadian
manufacturers are competitive with those of Canada's major trading partners, tax rates on large service firms are substantially higher (see Table 11.7).

In his 2000 budgets, Finance Minister Paul Martin announced plans to
reduce CIT rates between 2000 and 2004 on relatively highly taxed service
sector firms, from 28 per cent to the manufacturers' tax rate of 21 per cent.
Ontario and Alberta also plan to reduce their general CIT rates, from 15.5
per cent to 8 per cent over six and four years respectively (4 and 3 per cent
for small businesses), providing the same tax rate for manufacturing and
service businesses.[28] Taken together, these measures will reduce Canada's
marginal corporate and capital tax rates to levels generally below those in
the United States. These trends reflect growing international competitiveness for corporate investment and the ability of many corporations to shift
income among divisions in different countries.[29]

Some tax policy experts have suggested that provincial governments
reduce potential for tax competition between provinces by replacing their
existing corporate income and capital taxes with a new "Business Value
Tax" on operating profits, wages, and salaries generated within each
province.[30] Such a move might contribute to greater economic efficiency in
tax collection. However, since this change would entail replacing existing
corporate taxes with an explicit tax on business exports and other major
administrative adjustments, the likelihood of such a radical change to the
tax system winning broad political acceptance is probably small.

GLOBALIZATION AND BUSINESS TAXES: COMPETING FOR
CAPITAL AND MARKETS

Canada has long depended on foreign investment to develop its economy.
This has led to the shaping of tax rules that encourage direct foreign investment and provide Canadian firms adequate access to foreign capital
markets. As a result, Canada's corporate tax system is shaped by market
pressures to provide a competitive rate of return on capital for both
Canadian and foreign-owned businesses and a positive investment climate
so that investors will reinvest their profits, while providing them with
opportunities to repatriate their dividends if desired.

Canada's emergence since the 1970s as a major exporter of capital reinforces the importance of a rules-based system of international finance. This
policy ensures Canadian companies a relatively level playing field in international markets, while limiting opportunities for large-scale (legal) tax
avoidance and (illegal) tax evasion (see Table 11.8). Although Canada
imposes a 25-per-cent withholding tax on the corporate income of foreign-
controlled corporations, this tax is effectively waived for companies based in
any of the more than 100 countries with which Canada has negotiated tax
treaties. Since more and more corporations pursue international expansion
strategies, it has become increasingly important that the complex technical
details of tax policy provide Canadian firms with a level playing field when
they invest outside Canada, while applying the same principles to foreign
firms in Canada.

As early as 1963, Canada's growing integration into the North American
economy forced the withdrawal of Walter Gordon's proposal for a 30-per-
cent "takeover tax"[31] and subsequent efforts to remove the deductibility of
interest on money borrowed to finance corporate takeovers. Economic
integration has also undercut recent efforts to promote a "financial transactions tax"—the so-called "Tobin Tax"—to discourage the rapid
movement of short-term capital across national borders unless adopted as
a collective strategy by most industrial nations.[32] The Mintz Report notes
that the introduction of a financial transactions tax in Sweden reduced
local trading of bonds by about 85 per cent and trading in futures by 98 per
cent within one week.[33]

At the same time, international investment strategies have led to the creative use of transfer pricing techniques and inter-corporate transactions
involving the use of "tax havens" that contribute to large-scale tax avoidance, and to equally complex rules to combat these techniques. Research
commissioned by the Department of Finance suggests that Canada's relatively high tax rates have led many multinational corporations to shift a

Table 11.8 ·· FOREIGN INVESTMENTS AND CANADIAN INVESTMENT ABROAD
(IN BILLIONS OF 1999 DOLLARS)

	1969	1989	1999
CONTROLLING INVESTMENTS IN CORPORATIONS			
foreign direct investment in canada	$ 119.0	152.8	240.0
canadian direct investment abroad	$ 24.6	104.7	257.4
RATIO OF FOREIGN TO CDN. DIRECT INVESTMENT	4.85	1.46	0.93
PORTFOLIO INVESTMENTS (STOCKS, CORPORATE AND GOVERNMENT BONDS)			
foreign portfolio investment in Canada	$ 73.2	240.4	495.5
Canadian portfolio investment abroad	$ 14.2	51.8	163.7
RATIO OF FOREIGN TO CANADIAN HOLDINGS	5.17	4.64	3.03

Source: Statistics Canada, *Canada's International Investment Position* (Cat. # 67-202); CANSIM, Matrix 4180.

larger share of debt financing to their Canadian operations in order to reduce their overall tax burden.[34]

The complexities of such issues as the design of Foreign Accrued Property Income (FAPI) rules,[35] the "thin capitalization" rules which allow Canadian firms to obtain financing from non-resident firms,[36] transfer pricing, non-resident-owned investment corporations, and a wide range of other technical tax rules relating to international investments are the subject of ongoing discussion between Finance Department officials and tax advisors of major corporations and business associations. However, only when national governments attempt to coordinate their tax policies through organizations such as the OECD are rules likely to emerge to limit the aggressive use of discriminatory tax shelters to attract investment or prevent the aggressive use of tax havens to avoid taxes on corporate income.

PROMOTING JOB CREATION AND A STAKEHOLDER SOCIETY

The corporate tax system's generous treatment of small businesses[37] has led to the development of a "two-tier" economy in which small business corporations—most with fewer than 20 employees—account for more than half of all private-sector employment.[38] Corporate income tax rates on small businesses are significantly lower than those for large firms, federally and in most provinces (see Table 11.9).

Technical tax rules allow for business investment losses to be written off, within certain limits, against personal income. Small businesses and family farms enjoy a generous exemption from capital gains. As noted in Chapter 10, the federal budgets of 2000 created and expanded provisions for capital gains "rollovers" for entrepreneurs who sell one eligible small business and, within four months, invest in another. Other tax preferences may be enriched for small firms (see Table 11.10).

These tax preferences partly reflect political considerations, partly the traditional difficulty experienced by most small, owner-managed firms

Table 11.9 ·· CORPORATE INCOME TAX RATES–2001

	Small Business Corporate Tax Rate	General Corporate Tax Rate	Corporate Tax Rate—Manufacturers
CANADA (INCLUDING SURTAXES)	13.12%	28.12% 22.12% (2005)	22.12%
BRITISH COLUMBIA	4.5%	16.5% 13.5% (2002)	16.5% 13.5% (2002)
ALBERTA	5.25% 3.0% (2003)	14.0% 8.0% (2004)	14.0% 8.0% (2004)
SASKATCHEWAN	6.0%*	17.0%	17.0%
MANITOBA	6.0%	17.0% 15.0% (2005)	17.0%
ONTARIO	6.5% 4.0% (2005)	14.0% 8.0% (2005)	12.5% 8.0% (2005)
QUEBEC	9.15%	9.15%	9.15%
NEW BRUNSWICK	4.0%	16.0%	16.0%
NOVA SCOTIA	5.0%	16.0%	16.0%
PRINCE EDWARD ISLAND	7.5%	16.0%	7.5%
NEWFOUNDLAND	5.0%	14.0%	5.0%

* Effective July 1, 2001.

Sources: Provincial Budgets, 2001-02; British Columbia, *Economic and Fiscal Update*, (Victoria, Ministry of Finance, July 30, 2001).

Table 11.10 ·· SMALL BUSINESS TAX SUPPORT, 1997

	$ millions	percentage
SMALL BUSINESS DEDUCTION	2,620	64
LIFETIME CAPITAL GAINS EXEMPTION	685	17
SCIENTIFIC R&D TAX CREDIT	455	11
ALLOWABLE BUSINESS INVESTMENT LOSSES	117	3
LABOUR-SPONSORED VENTURE CAPITAL CREDIT	105	3
EMPLOYEE STOCK OPTIONS	93	2
TOTAL	4,075	100

Source: Canada, Department of Finance (1997b), Chart 5A.6

in raising capital, and partly the importance of small business in job creation. Since the 1970s, small businesses have created the vast majority of new jobs, even after job losses from business failures are taken into account. Much of this job creation has taken place in newly-formed companies, despite their high failure rate, while many large firms have shed significant portions of their work forces in response to growing competition, technological change, and the contracting out of many business services.

Small business tax rules are heavily influenced by political factors. Small business emerged as a self-conscious political force during the debate over the federal White Paper on Tax Reform in 1969-71, which resulted in the formation of Canada's largest small business lobby group, the Canadian Federation of Independent Business. A tax system favourable to small business tends to broaden the number of stakeholders and beneficiaries of the capitalist system, particularly in smaller communities that would otherwise be largely dependent on outside corporate interests for investment and employment. Lower tax rates for small businesses are also a way for provincial governments to favour home-grown firms, whose owners and close relatives account for 20 per cent or more of voters in most provinces, over large national or multinational concerns.

The expansion of the small business sector during the 1970s and 1980s was a major factor in absorbing a rapidly growing labour force, thus helping governments with the pressing problem of high unemployment. During the 1990s, a similar role was played by the rapid growth of self-employment businesses, as new technologies allowed many people to build successful businesses as independent contractors.[39] For these reasons, the persistence of an extensive small business sector in an era of global capitalism is a major factor in the preservation of communities and social cohesion and in the building of social capital.

At the same time as politicians rush to enrich the tax preferences available to small businesses, their officials have warn against enriching incentives to the point of creating artificial inducements for individuals to incorporate purely for tax purposes. The ongoing battle to collect (and avoid) taxes between Revenue Canada (now the Canada Customs and Revenue Agency) and small business owners (and their advisors) has contributed to increased complexity in the administration of tax laws. Periodic efforts to "clean up" the proliferation of tax preferences inevitably lead to conflict, as governments seek to expand their revenue base to reduce deficits or expand public services, while businesses fight to maintain overall business taxes at existing levels.[40]

The Mintz Report criticized the small business tax system for hindering rather than promoting small business growth, particularly for the minority of fast-growing firms most likely to consider going public. The report also challenged the failure to link most small business tax preferences directly to job creation or new investment.[41] However, Canada's highly developed system of tax measures to assist small businesses is likely to be politically untouchable for the foreseeable future, given the considerable public support for the idea of "being your own boss" and the huge number—almost 2 million—of self-employed Canadians and small business owners. However, international trends in business taxation may result in significant changes to the overall pattern of business taxation.

The Changing Face of Business Taxation

> It is possible to view corporate taxes as compensation for the many services corporations obtain from the public sector, such as education of its workers, public-sector infrastructure, and the protection of property rights.... It would be difficult, however, to design satisfactory tax policy on the basis of this rationale.[42]

Proposals for business tax reform tend to fall into three categories. One addresses business taxation as a form of user-pay. The second emphasizes the importance of maintaining effective corporate income tax rates at levels competitive with those of Canada's major competitors, and of reducing the differences between tax rates on different industry sectors. The third attempts to deal with more technical issues of tax design, particularly the integration of corporate and personal income taxes and the use of the corporate income tax as a "withholding tax" on investment income.

BENEFIT-RELATED TAXES: THE POLITICS OF USER-PAY

The fastest growing areas of business taxation during the 1980s and 1990s were taxes linked to the provision of particular benefits and services to businesses and their workers. Most of these taxes are not "pure" benefits taxes, since it is difficult to link the provision of particular services to individual taxpayers in proportion to the level of taxes paid. However, to the extent that taxes rise roughly in step either with usage or liability for future services, politicians often attempt to make the connection between tax levels and benefits received.

This connection is particularly true for a wide range of *profit-insensitive taxes* levied on businesses—taxes unrelated to a business's profits or ability to pay. These include payroll taxes that are often levied to finance social insurance programs such as the CPP, Employment Insurance, Workers' Compensation and other social services. They also may include consumption taxes on specific products, such as gasoline or automobile air conditioners, to finance public infrastructure or to compensate for environmental costs imposed on society. Oil and gas and forestry firms pay resource royalties for business exploitation of provincially owned resources. Most business pay a wide range of user charges and regulatory fees related to business use of public services. Such taxes totalled approximately $43.2 billion in 1995, about 48 per cent of overall business taxes (see Table 11.11).

Federal and provincial governments tend to champion the user-pay principle when it serves their interests. This tendency can be seen in the rapidly increasing use of user fees and other forms of cost recovery in major areas of federal regulation, increases in federal and provincial gasoline taxes to offset revenue losses resulting from falling oil and natural gas prices in the late 1980s and early 1990s, and the 73-per-cent increase in premiums to finance the Canada Pension Plan between 1996 and 2003.[43] Indeed, the Mintz Report has recommended a more systematic application of the user-pay principle to two major federal taxes—employer contributions to Employment Insurance and taxes on gasoline and other energy sources—in order for business tax levels to be more directly and transparently related to the costs of related programs and services borne by governments.[44]

However, Richard M. Bird, a leading authority on Canadian public finance, suggests that "much of what is currently going on across Canada under the banner of 'user charges' makes little sense."[45] Existing financial

Table 11.11 ·· SOCIAL INSURANCE AND OTHER "BENEFIT"-RELATED TAXES ON BUSINESS: 1995[46] (IN $ BILLION)

	Federal	Provincial	Local	CPP/QPP	Total	Percentage of business tax
PAYROLL TAXES	8.2	9.1		5.2	22.5	25
FUEL EXCISE TAXES	1.8	2.6			4.4	5
OTHER INDIRECT TAXES AND FEES*	1.8	3.9	4.3		10.0	11
RESOURCE ROYALTY FEES		6.2			6.2	7
TOTAL	11.8	21.8	4.3	5.2	43.2	48

* Include federal import duties, excise taxes on alcohol and tobacco, provincial motor vehicle licences, liquor commission profits, and other indirect taxes and fees.

Source: Canada, Department of Finance (1997b); author's calculations.

management systems transfer all government revenues, except for legislated exceptions such as the Canada Pension Plan and provincial Workers' Compensation funds, to a Consolidated Revenue Fund which effectively removes any relationship between taxes or fees paid and services provided.

When programs supposedly funded on a user-pay basis generate surplus revenues, these often are transferred to finance other government priorities. For example, despite federal legislation in 1996 that provided for Employment Insurance rates to be set on a cost-recovery basis through a normal business cycle, EI premiums have become a cash cow, generating between $5 and $7 billion more in annual revenues than are needed to run the program on a break-even basis, even after taking into account provisions for a sizeable reserve fund.[47] When a 1998 Supreme Court decision ruled that probate fees charged to transfer the estates of deceased Canadians were de facto taxes, levied unconstitutionally as administrative user charges bearing no relationship to benefits provided, most provincial legislatures passed retroactive legislation to reinstate these fees.[48] In addition, the federal government has successfully curbed the growth of provincial payroll and capital taxes as a form of tax competition by refusing to allow the deduction of future increases in these taxes from federal taxable income.[49]

A number of government reports have recommended the study and possible introduction of "green taxes" to encourage energy conservation and the responsible use of renewable and non-renewable resources, and to discourage the discharge of pollutants into the air and water by businesses, farmers, and consumers.[50] However, in the absence of a clear relationship between these taxes and public policies or services designed to improve environmental quality, they run the risk of becoming like Ontario's tax on automobile tires, which was diverted into the province's general revenues while different ministries squabbled over its use.

The political credibility of user fees and other benefit-related taxes as a means of financing public services depends largely on the willingness of governments to be open and transparent in raising and spending these funds, and on the ability of independent third parties, such as the Auditor General or Provincial Auditors, to evaluate and comment on the methods used to link user fees with the benefits received by various taxpayers. Although some governments have made significant progress in achieving these goals, the use and misuse of user fees by others often resemble the bait-and-switch techniques used by disreputable businesses to exploit unwary consumers.

KEEPING BUSINESS TAX RATES "INTERNATIONALLY COMPETITIVE"

The most visible changes in Canadian business taxation are driven by forces effectively outside the control of Canadian governments. The globalization of the international economy has contributed to the emergence of capital markets and transnational corporations (TNCs) that effectively transcend the efforts of national governments to tax and regulate them as national entities. Although national governments retain the power to impose corporate income taxes, the capacity of TNCs to manage the incidence of taxation through a wide variety of legal means limits the capacity of governments to impose corporate tax rates that are significantly above global norms. In Europe and Australia, this has led to a shifting of the tax base from taxes on capital income to taxes on less mobile factors of production such as consumption, wages and salaries, and to a more extensive use of benefit-related taxation on businesses.

However, national governments are not helpless in the face of such trends. The Organization for Economic Cooperation and Development, which represents 29 major industrial states, has developed conventions on taxation which attempt to limit "predatory" tax policies, or TRIMS (tax-related investment measures) that attempt to divert investment from one country to another by creating special tax preferences for offshore investors or export-related activities. More recently, OECD members have been attempting to force "tax havens," such as Barbados, Liechtenstein, Panama, and Bahrain, to change their tax laws and provide for greater financial transparency, or face economic sanctions.[51]

However, the broader question facing Canadian governments is whether Canada should seek to parallel the corporate tax rates of its major trading partners or to pursue Ireland's strategy of setting its CIT rates slightly below those of its major industrial neighbours—in Canada's case the United States—in order to promote investment-driven growth patterns. This policy is advocated by economist Jack Mintz, recently appointed as President of the influential C.D. Howe Institute, and has been explicitly adopted by the governments of Ontario and Alberta as they attempt to cut their corporate income taxes to levels below those of neighbouring American states. The federal government's decision to phase in lower CIT rates on large service-sector firms complements this policy, without firmly committing it to one approach or the other.

Some economists have suggested that reducing tax rates further in this way would be economically feasible if Canada were to follow Britain's lead in integrating personal and corporate income taxes so that the corporate income tax becomes more explicitly a withholding tax on the capital income of individuals and businesses. However, the decision of the United States not to apply withholding taxes to the investment income of foreign-based investors places significant limits on Canada's ability to shift its tax policies in that direction without undermining its ability to compete for foreign investment in global markets.[52]

Another factor influencing international tax competition is the spread of internet-based commerce, which makes it difficult to enforce and collect locally-based sales taxes when internet servers may be located beyond the reach of state or national jurisdictions. The United States, already the only major industrial country without a national sales or value-added tax, has chosen not to tax internet-based transactions in order to make itself a focal point for the spread of "e-commerce." Although Canadian sales taxes, including the GST, are supposed to be payable on internet-based transactions, the inability of the Canada Customs and Revenue Agency (CCRA) to monitor the millions of small shipments which yearly cross the Canada-US border limits the capacity of Canadian governments to expand their sales tax revenues—although no one can accurately predict the extent of such revenue losses. This trend will prompt more provinces to contract with the CCRA to collect provincial sales taxes, if only to step up tax enforcement.

Conclusion: The Politics of Business Taxation in the Twenty-first Century

For years, think tanks, interest groups, academics, and civil servants have discussed the levels, objectives, and distribution of business taxes while looking for ways to balance governments' traditional objective of raising sufficient revenues to finance public services with the demands of financing continued business expansion in an economy with few limits on the movement of capital. Recent events suggest future patterns in the evolution of business tax reform. Canadian governments are likely to reduce corporate income and capital taxes as sources of revenue to the extent they can do so without triggering a public backlash. This process will be smoothed by periodic reductions in personal income taxes, so that business tax reduction will take place in the shadow of a broader fiscal dividend.

These trade-offs will be heavily tested by the decisions of Ontario and Alberta to make deep cuts in their corporate income tax rates, not just small business taxation. Although corporate income and capital tax revenues account for a relatively small share of their revenues, most provinces have maintained wide tax rate differentials between large and small corporations in order to encourage the development of locally-owned small businesses.[53] Several provinces have increased the annual profit ceiling on their small business tax rates from $200,000 to $300,000 in recent budgets–the first major changes to this level in more than 20 years.

Further reductions in general corporate tax rates are less likely to result from the efforts of Canadian business groups than from international economic forces. Governments will attempt to offset international limits on corporate tax rates by working across national boundaries to coordinate international tax policies and by expanding the use of "benefit-related" taxation and user fees for services provided. The greater the role that transnational corporations—particularly Canadian-based firms—play in the economies and tax bases of individual provinces, the greater the likelihood that international economic factors will play a significant role in their corporate tax structures and rates. However, the significant differences in business tax policies implemented by the governments of Quebec, Ontario, Alberta, and British Columbia in recent years suggest that these decisions are affected as much by domestic political factors as by the desire of governments to attract and retain corporate and head office investments.

The introduction of environmental taxes will likely be debated at length. However, given the limitations of cold winters and the need for many Canadians to travel long distances, such changes are likely to take place slowly and to emphasize incentives for the adoption of energy-efficient technologies rather than punitive measures.

The most unpredictable element in business taxation is the relationship between federal and provincial tax policies. The last several years have witnessed the growing decentralization of Canadian fiscal and tax policies, as provincial governments take different approaches to balancing their budgets and changing their tax policies. These changes, and their broader implications for the future of Canadian tax policies, are the subject of the next chapter.

NOTES

1 Chwialkowska (1999a); Avi-Yonah (2000); Mintz (2000a); Thomas J. D'Aquino (2000) "Global Champion or Falling Star: Canada Must Lead to Succeed in the Global Economy" (Ottawa: Business Council on National Issues, 5 April).

2 Support for business tax reduction as a "priority" ranged from 2 to 7 per cent in opinion polls published between August 1999 and February 2000. The federal government's decision to lower the inclusion rate for capital gains taxes from 75 to 50 per cent of taxable income in its 2000 budgets was a direct response to American cuts in tax rates on long-term capital gains, as well as to technical arguments advanced by tax experts. Ekos Research Associates (1999); Compas, Inc. (2000b), "The 2000 Federal Budget: A report prepared for the *National Post* on public opinion about taxes and spending," *National Post*, 19 February; Mintz and Wilson (2000).

3 Since tax rate differentials between large and small businesses were typically much greater at the federal level than in most provinces, a larger share of business tax reductions has been targeted to small firms in most provinces. This trend is probably reinforced by political considerations, notably the fact that the number of small business owners is significantly greater than the number of corporate executives.

4 Canada, Department of Finance (1997b), 2:6; modified to include provincial resource royalties.

5 Canada, Department of Finance (1997b), 2:10.

6 Canada, Department of Finance (1997b), 2:12-15.

7 British Columbia (2001). *Fiscal and Economic Update* (Victoria: Ministry of Finance and Corporate Affairs); Saskatchewan (2000) *Public Accounts: 1999-2000* (Regina, September), 11.

8 Nancy Olewiler (1998); Mintz and Sargent (1998), 2:22.

9 Gillespie (1983, 1991).

10 Boadway and Kitchen (1999), 213-20.

11 For a detailed discussion of corporate tax incidence, see Boadway and Kitchen (1999); for a discussion of tax incidence in an international context, see Avi Yonah (2000).

12 Bird (1970).

13 Poddar and English (1999), 1280-87. The imputed rental value of owner-occupied housing—the expected rental value if homeowners were to rent out their properties rather than live in them "rent-free"—accounts for 30 per cent of Poddar and English's estimate of tax-sheltered investment income. Given currents levels of residential property taxation, it may be an overstatement to describe such investments as "tax exempt." Poddar and English's article was written before the federal government reduced capital gains taxes in 2000.

14 Lewis (1972); Brooks (1979); Brooks (1981).

15 Canada, Department of Finance (1997) *1997 Budget* (Ottawa, February), 157.

16 Hon. Paul Martin (2001) "Canada's New Economy: Winning the World Over" (Ottawa: Department of Finance, January), 13.

17 Earnscliffe Research and Communications (1999c). A review of published polling data suggests these views are deeply entrenched in Canadian public opinion (see n. 2).

18 Michael Bliss (1985) "Forcing the Pace: A Reappraisal of Business-Government Relations in Canadian History," in V.V. Murray, ed., *Theories of Business-Government Relations* (Toronto: Trans-Canada Press), 106-17.

19 Thirsk (1993).

20 For a comprehensive discussion of small business taxation in Canada, see Canadian Tax Foundation (1983).

21 For discussions of the mercantilist economic strategies of Canadian governments from different perspectives, see Bliss (1987); Brooks and Stritch (1991).

22 For more detailed explanations of these concepts, see Krishna (1993).

23 Martin (2001), 10.

24 Deborah L. Ort and David B. Perry (2000) "Provincial Budget Roundup," *Canadian Tax Journal* 48(3), 722.

25 Bertrand Marotte (2001) "Quebec to spend $800 million on remote regions," *The Globe and Mail*, 30 March.

26 Mintz defines the "effective tax rate on marginal investments" as the tax rate "paid on income earned by investing in a marginal project," a rate at which after-tax profit is "just sufficient to attract funds from investors in the form of equity and bond financing," given alternative investments in the marketplace. Canada, Department of Finance (1997b), 2:5.

27 Alberta Business Tax Review (2000), 13.

28 However, Ontario has also introduced a wide range of tax preferences for specific industries in what appears to be a hybrid of the old "industrial strategy" approach with equalization of marginal CIT rates. Ontario (2000); Alberta Business Tax Review (2000).

29 Mintz (2000c), 692-94.

30 Bird and Mintz (2000); Alberta Business Tax Review (2000), 19.

31 Peter C. Newman (1968) *Distemper of Our Times* (Toronto: McClelland & Stewart), 18-29.

32 Tobin (1997); Michalos (1999).

33 Canada, Department of Finance (1997b), A-2.

34 Jog and Tang (1998); Conklin and Robertson (1999); Avi-Yonah (2000); KPMG (1999).

35 Brian S. Arnold, Jinyan Li, and Daniel Sandler (1996) "Comparison and Assessment of the Tax Treatment of Foreign Source Income in Canada, Australia, France, Germany and the United States," Working Paper # 96-1 (Ottawa: Department of Finance, December)

36 Barry Critchley (2000) "Mr. Martin Changes His Mind," *Financial Post*, 20 June; Hon. Paul Martin, *The Budget Plan 2000*, 311-12.

37 Formally "Canadian Controlled Private Corporations," under Section 125 of the *Income Tax Act*.

38 Hendricks, Amit, and Whistler (1997).

39 "Between 1980 and 1989, 66% of the growth in self-employment has been among business owners with paid help (employers).... In sharp contrast, employers account for very little (10%) of the net growth in self-employment between 1989 and 1996; 90% of the growth in self-employment in the 1990s has come from entrepreneurs who work alone (own account)." Statistics Canada (1997) "A Profile of the Self-Employed," *Canadian Economic Observer*, Cat. # 11-010-XPB, 3:12-22, November.

40 Hale (1996).

41 Canada, Department of Finance (1997b), Chapter 5; Mintz (2000c), 698-99.

42 Boadway and Kitchen (1999), 244.

43 Blair Consulting Group (1999) "User Fees: Where does the Buck Stop?" (Ottawa: Alliance of Manufacturers and Exporters Canada, January); James, et al. (1995). In Alberta in 1999, user fees were collected under the authority of 80 separate pieces of legislation. Alberta (1999a) *Bill 35: Government Fees and Charges Review Act* (Edmonton, Legislative Assembly).

44 Canada, Department of Finance (1997b), Chapters 8, 9.

45 Bird and Tsiopoulos (1997) "User Charges for Public Services: Potentials and Problems," *Canadian Tax Journal* 45:1, 26.

46 Canada, Department of Finance (1997b), Tables 2:1, 2:6—modified for inclusion of resource royalties. Since these are a tax paid by businesses to exploit provincially owned resources for profit, usually related to the volume or value of production, they should be considered a form of benefit-related taxation.

47 See Table 9.2; also Hale (2000a); Canada, Human Resources Development Canada (2000).

48 Re Eurig Estate [1998] 2 s.c.r. 565; Kaye (1999); LeBreux (1999). Alberta has been the exception to this rule, reducing specific user fees that exceeded costs of providing particular services by about $60 million out of total user fee revenues of $1.3 billion. Alberta (2000) *Budget 2000: New Century, Bold Plans* (Edmonton: Alberta Treasury, 24 February).

49 Seven provinces levy corporate capital taxes at different rates and with different thresholds. Capital tax revenues were higher than corporate income tax revenues in Saskatchewan in 1999-2000. They also accounted for about one-third of direct corporate taxes collected by British Columbia.

50 Canada, Department of Finance (1997b), Chapter 9; Taylor, Jaccard, and Olewiler (1999); Perrin (2000) "Options to Reduce Light Duty Vehicle Emissions in British Columbia" (Victoria: Ministry of Finance and Corporate Relations, 20 October).

51 Scoffield (2000).

52 Avi Yonah (2000).

53 See Chapter 12.

Taxation, Federalism, and the Provinces

> Multi-tiered governments in principle work best when taxes and the
> benefits of public spending are as closely related as possible ... that is,
> when the citizens ... residing in a particular political jurisdiction both
> pay for what they get from the public sector and benefit from the
> expenditures made by the taxes they pay.[1]

Most studies of the politics of taxation since World War II have focused on
the federal government. This reflects Ottawa's historic dominance of fiscal
policy, its power to define the tax bases of most major sources of revenue,
especially the personal and corporate income taxes, and the usual willingness of most provinces, other than Quebec, to defer to federal leadership.
The provinces traditionally have been viewed as "policy takers," rather than
trend-setters whose tax policies have relatively little influence beyond their
own borders.

These relationships are beginning to change. The "own-source" revenues
of most provinces are covering a steadily increasing share of provincial
spending. Total provincial revenues, excluding federal transfers, are now
larger than those of the federal government.[2] Unilateral reductions in federal transfers to the provinces during the 1990s have made most provinces
reluctant to depend on Ottawa's fickle largesse, despite promises to restore
past transfer cuts by 2005. Provincial budgetary policies diverged during the
1990s, as governments with different political priorities took different
approaches to deficit (and debt) reduction, reflecting their provinces' different political cultures. Provincial governments are taking the initiative,
introducing significant innovations in tax policies.

Most importantly, the renegotiation of the federal-provincial tax collection agreements has enabled the provinces to define their own tax rate
structures independently from those of the federal government and to make
a variety of other changes to their tax systems. These changes have triggered

the most significant changes to the Canadian tax system since the signing of the 1962 federal-provincial tax collection agreements and the federal tax reform bill of 1971. They continued what Dyck and Dahlby have called the continuing "provincialization of the Canadian fiscal system," while preserving a common personal income tax base and a shared tax collection system as central elements of the Canadian economic union.[3]

These changes reflect several trends in federal-provincial fiscal and economic relations. The pursuit of different political agendas and economic strategies by provincial governments has resulted in the growing decentralization of fiscal and economic policies in Canada. A number of provinces are increasing their use of the tax system to facilitate policy innovations in response to changing social and economic conditions. In addition, the federal government has demonstrated an increased willingness to accommodate provincial autonomy in fiscal and tax policies.

This chapter examines proposed changes to provincial income tax systems following recent revisions to the federal-provincial tax collection agreements. It considers the factors that have contributed to diverging provincial fiscal and tax policies and to the dynamics of federal-provincial relations. It also reviews the different approaches to provincial tax policies that are emerging with the introduction of the "tax on income" concept in designing provincial tax policies.

The Trend to Fiscal Decentralization

The adoption of the "tax on income" model, which enables provincial governments to design rate structures for their provincial income tax (PIT) systems independently of the federal PIT structure while maintaining a common definition of income and a unified system for tax administration and collection, reflects a broader trend towards the decentralization, or "provincialization," of Canadian fiscal policy.[4]

The rapidly growing cost of provincial welfare states and of related federal transfers to the provinces have forced Ottawa repeatedly to change its policies governing transfers to the provinces in order to control its own finances. In 1977, Ottawa replaced a number of shared-cost programs with the so-called "Established Programs Financing" program. At the same time, it shifted personal and corporate income tax points in order to make the wealthier provinces more fiscally self-sufficient by enabling them to finance a larger part of their spending from their "own source" revenues. As a result, provincial revenue sources have continued to grow marginally faster than those of the federal government, and federal transfers have declined as a share of the revenues of most provinces[5] (see Table 12.1).

Since both senior levels of government share most major sources of revenues, the integration of federal and provincial tax systems makes each vulnerable to unilateral policy shifts by the other. Federal tax increases and bracket creep after 1985 allowed the provinces to reap windfall revenues. However, most provinces raised their own taxes to offset the tax cuts that accompanied the Mulroney government's tax reforms in 1987-88. Ottawa responded to the growth of provincial payroll and capital taxes, which cut into its own tax base, by warning the provinces that future increases in these areas would not be deductible from federal taxes. It also imposed a series of unilateral reductions in federal transfers to the provinces between 1989 and 1997.

However, there have been two significant exceptions to this pattern of federal-provincial competition. In 1985, federal Finance Minister Michael Wilson allowed Saskatchewan to experiment with the introduction of a flat tax on net income, in effect, a provincial minimum tax applied on a rela-

Table 12.1 ·· FEDERAL TRANSFERS AS A PERCENTAGE OF PROVINCIAL REVENUES

	1980-81	*1989-90*	*1997-98*	*1999-2000*
CANADA	23.3	20.6	14.9	14.9
NEWFOUNDLAND	49.4	48.7	52.1	43.8
PRINCE EDWARD ISLAND	50.6	44.4	37.1	39.3
NOVA SCOTIA	47.9	40.5	39.5	37.2
NEW BRUNSWICK	43.2	39.7	37.1	38.6
QUEBEC	26.6	21.3	14.3	13.4
ONTARIO	20.1	13.0	9.7	9.4
MANITOBA	42.4	36.0	32.8	32.6
SASKATCHEWAN	17.5	29.6	10.7	20.6
ALBERTA	8.3	15.1	6.6	8.1
BRITISH COLOMBIA	18.0	15.5	9.1	11.9

Source: Canada, Department of Finance (2000d); author's calculations.

tively broad base. Manitoba and Alberta were allowed to create their own flat taxes in 1987. In 1996, Ottawa agreed to facilitate British Columbia's creation of a refundable child tax credit. This became the model for the 1997 federal-provincial agreement on the creation of the National Child Benefit.

Economist John Richards notes that, as a whole, "the provinces have mattered nearly as much as Ottawa in terms of both contributing to deficits early in the 1990s and restoring fiscal balances in subsequent years." Provincial revenues increased at more than four times the rate of spending, despite the decline in federal transfer payments experienced by provinces west of the Ottawa River.[6] Under such circumstances, it is not surprising that provinces have demanded greater autonomy in the management of their own fiscal and tax policies.

Since balancing its budget in 1997-98, the federal government has changed its approach to federal-provincial fiscal relations, negotiating a number of general and bilateral agreements with provinces to link increased transfer payments to the achievement of specific federal objectives. This approach reflects the federal Liberals' clearly expressed desire to increase their political credit for tax and spending measures, while maximizing the federal Finance Department's flexibility in balancing the many demands of the government's broadly-based political coalition.[7]

DECENTRALIZING PROVINCIAL FISCAL POLICIES

The decentralization of Canadian tax policies in recent years has resulted from more than just the federal government's declining financial leverage over the larger provinces. It also reflects the growing diversity of provincial economies, the provinces' different business cycles, and the effects of Canada's growing integration into continental and global economies.[8] Provinces have responded to these changes in different ways, reflecting different economic or "province-building" strategies and the different effects of regional economic competition, differing electoral cycles, and the relative dependence of individual provinces on federal cash transfers.

Province-building is not a new phenomenon. However, Canada's growing integration into the continental and global economies has shifted the emphasis of most provincial economies from inter-provincial to international trade. Most provinces now export more to other countries than to other parts of Canada. In 1998, international exports accounted for 42 per cent of Canada's GDP, ranging from a high of 52 per cent in Ontario to a low of 30 per cent in British Columbia.[9]

Provincial governments have sought to diversify their economies and develop economic strategies emphasizing regional comparative advantages.

Some provinces, particularly New Brunswick, Quebec, and British Columbia, have sought to attract or retain business investment with a variety of incentives that can withstand challenges under WTO and NAFTA rules, including a wide range of corporate tax incentives. Others, notably Ontario and Alberta, have significantly reduced their business subsidies and have sought to make their provincial tax systems more competitive with those of neighbouring American states and other international competitors.

A number of provinces, including New Brunswick, British Columbia, Alberta, Prince Edward Island and, more recently, Ontario, have centralized control over property taxes levied to finance primary and secondary education costs. In most cases, this has been intended to balance greater budgetary control over provincial education costs, equity in funding between urban and rural areas and, in some cases, the perceived need to limit the growth of property tax rates in the name of economic development.[10] Many of these changes were closely linked to budgetary pressures, as provincial governments struggled to balance their budgets in the mid-1990s.

Most provinces, regardless of ideological outlook, have reduced tax rates for lower-income taxpayers, raised the income thresholds at which provincial income taxes are applied, and increased the progressivity of their provincial tax systems. These changes were usually justified on the grounds of fairness, particularly in sharing the burdens of deficit and debt reduction policies. However, the extent and speed of tax reduction have been closely tied to the political outlook of individual provincial governments and their relative emphasis on promoting private sector wealth creation rather than income redistribution and the extension of public services.

Most provinces also used deficit reduction as an excuse to change their tax systems by altering rate structures and the mix of revenue sources. Most increased the progressivity of their provincial tax systems, adding surtaxes on middle- and/or upper-income earners. Top marginal tax rates in all ten provinces rose significantly between 1988 and 1995. Since then, however, all provinces have cut their personal tax rates to varying degrees (see Table 12.2).

After 1996, most provinces relaxed their spending controls and introduced modest tax cuts to "reward" taxpayers for the sacrifices resulting from deficit reduction. Ontario and Alberta were "outliers" in this process. The Harris government sharply cut basic provincial income tax rates by 30 per cent to offset provincial spending cuts between 1996 and 1998. It also announced plans to cut PIT rates by a further 20 per cent over four years before winning re-election in 1999, and finally balanced its budget in 2000. Alberta's Klein government ran large surpluses after 1994-95, deferring tax cuts and applying 75 per cent of its surpluses to debt reduction.[11]

Governments have also resorted to the expansion of other revenue sources to reduce their deficits or offset tax reductions in other areas. Most

Table 12.2 ·· PERSONAL INCOME TAXES–TOP MARGINAL TAX RATES BY
PROVINCE: 1988-2001 (PERCENTAGES)

	1988	1995	2000	2001
NEWFOUNDLAND	47.3	51.3	51.3	48.64
PRINCE EDWARD ISLAND	47.7	50.3	48.8	47.37
NOVA SCOTIA	46.3	50.3	48.8	47.34
NEW BRUNSWICK	47.3	51.4	48.8	46.84
QUEBEC	51.1	52.9	50.7	48.71
ONTARIO	46.1	53.2	47.9	46.41
MANITOBA	47.5	50.4	48.1	46.50
SASKATCHEWAN	48.4	51.9	49.7	45.00
ALBERTA	44.9	46.1	43.7	39.00
BRITISH COLUMBIA	44.8	54.2	51.3	45.70

notably, during the 1990s governments of all political complexions have aggressively expanded revenues from various forms of gambling. Gambling revenues now account for between 6 and 10 per cent of provincial incomes in eight of ten provinces (see Table 12.3).

Provincial deficit and tax reduction strategies have tended to reflect the political philosophies of provincial governments and the political cultures of individual provinces rather than external economic pressures. For example, Ontario's high profile emphasis on tax cuts before balancing its budget reflected an ideological commitment to smaller government as much as to increasing economic competitiveness.

Faced with a low tax regime in neighbouring Alberta, Saskatchewan's Romanow government emphasized sales tax reductions rather than lower income taxes after balancing its budget in 1994-95, while allowing overall provincial tax levels to grow relative to those of its neighbours (see Table 12.4). Quebec's decision to rely more on tax increases than spending reductions to balance its budget suggests that its social democratic political culture greatly outweighed competitive pressures from Ontario's tax cuts in shaping the province's recent budgetary priorities, although it too has reduced taxes since balancing its budget. The same could be said for British Columbia's NDP governments of the 1990s. However, BC's newly-elected

Liberal government has promised that "British Columbians in the two lowest tax brackets" (below $61,000 in 2001) "will pay the lowest income tax rate in Canada" and that "the top marginal rate will be the second lowest in Canada."[12] Provincial budget priorities are also affected by the electoral cycle and the imminence of an election. Governments tend to concentrate painful economic news in the early years of their mandates, while relaxing their purse strings—or in some cases, the rigours of proposed budget reductions—as they approach an election.[13]

Now that most provincial governments have balanced their budgets, their citizens can look forward to a growing fiscal dividend. Finance

Table 12.3 ·· DISTRIBUTION OF PROVINCIAL OWN SOURCE REVENUES BY REVENUE SOURCE—1999 (IN PER CENT)

	Personal Income Tax	Corporate Income, Capital Taxes	Sales Taxes	Social Insurance Taxes*	Liquor and Gambling	Resource Income	Property Taxes**
CANADA	35	11	18	6	6	4	2
NFLD.	33	7	27	4	10	2	0
PEI	29	6	28	0	6	0	6
NS	37	6	27	0	11	0	0
NB	34	4	24	0	3	5	10
QUEBEC	41	9	18	12	4	1	0
ONTARIO	34	15	23	6	6	1	0
MANITOBA	35	9	20	5	9	1	0
SASKATCHEWAN	30	9	16	0	9	13	0
ALBERTA	30	11	0	4	8	15	7
BC	30	9	17	5	6	10	7

*   Social Insurance taxes include general payroll taxes on employers in Newfoundland, Ontario, Quebec, and Manitoba, and health insurance premiums payable by individuals in Alberta and British Columbia.

**   Property taxes collected by provinces as part of consolidated revenues. Other provinces may or may not collect property taxes on behalf of municipalities and school boards. Most local government spending is financed either by property taxes or provincial transfer payments.

Sources: Provincial Budgets 1999-2000; Ontario Economic Outlook and Fiscal Review, November 1999.

Table 12.4 ·· PROVINCIAL OWN SOURCE REVENUES AS SHARE OF
GROSS PROVINCIAL PRODUCT (IN PER CENT)

	1992	*1996*	*1998*
NEWFOUNDLAND	20.1	20.3	18.4
PEI	19.9	19.4	18.3
NOVA SCOTIA	16.4	16.1	16.2
NEW BRUNSWICK	18.3	20.1	19.1
QUEBEC	20.0	20.1	21.2
ONTARIO	13.7	13.9	14.5
MANITOBA	17.5	18.5	18.6
SASKATCHEWAN	18.4	18.4	19.2
ALBERTA	15.8	14.8	14.8
BRITISH COLUMBIA	18.9	21.6	20.0

Source: Statistics Canada, *Public Sector Finance, Cat. 68:212.*

Minister Paul Martin's announcement in his 2000 budgets of a multi-year personal income tax reduction plan would have had a significant effect on provincial revenues in the absence of further changes to provincial income tax systems. Before recent revisions to the federal-provincial tax collection agreements, the federal government could not reduce its taxes without also reducing the flexibility of provincial governments in setting their own priorities. To offset this problem, the provinces have persuaded Ottawa to give them greater flexibility in managing their own tax systems by allowing them to set their own rate structures on a common definition of income, the so-called "Tax on Income" system.

The "Tax on Income"

Like most ideas for tax reform, recent provincial tax changes reflect years of discussion and debate between federal and provincial government officials.[14] The "tax on income" concept, or TONI, is intended to allow the nine provinces that have participated in the federal-provincial tax collection agreements since 1962 to set their own tax rates and brackets on a common definition of taxable income, while continuing to contract with the federal government for the collection and administration of personal income taxes.

Several provinces, mainly in Western Canada, asked the federal government to accommodate their revenue needs and differing tax policy objectives by implementing a "tax on income" system as early as 1987.[15] During the early 1990s, federal and provincial officials worked together to develop options for resolving technical issues. A joint discussion paper relating to these issues was released in 1991.[16] However, growing deficit pressures and the strong opposition of many tax professionals and business groups sidetracked further action on the tax on income for several years.[17]

During the mid-1990s, provincial tax officials, especially in Alberta and Manitoba, continued to work out the details of a feasible tax-on-income proposal, although the proposal languished in the absence of political support.[18] One senior tax policy observer, noting the effects of unilateral federal actions on federal-provincial relations during the period, comments that "if the provinces were not simply to be subject to the whims of the federal tax base and tax rates, they had to gain somewhat greater control over the provincial tax situation."[19] However, the provinces also recognized the political and economic benefits to their citizens of maintaining a common tax base and a common tax collection system with the federal government, including:

> "a common definition of what constitutes income for tax purposes";

> "a common set of deductions that recognizes the importance of certain expenditures such as child care expenses, medical expenses, education costs and retirement planning";

> "a common definition of residency, ensuring that taxpayers will be taxed fairly"; and

> "a common tax administration, allowing provincial residents to file only one tax return and follow a common set of tax rules."[20]

The tax on income proposal resurfaced in 1997. The federal government, having balanced its budget, could look forward to the prospect of lowering its income taxes, with a corresponding impact on provincial tax revenues. The tax on income proposal allowed the provinces to protect their tax bases against erosion by federal tax cuts.[21] Moreover, the growing complexity of provincial tax systems during the 1980s and 1990s, resulting from the introduction of separate surtaxes, flat taxes, and a variety of tax credits in different provinces, argued in favour of a shift to the tax on income, if only in the interests of greater transparency and tax simplification.[22]

Federal and provincial Finance Ministers agreed in principle on the proposed changes in December 1997. The details of the new system emerged from a federal-provincial committee of senior officials in October 1998.[23] Although allowing provincial governments to set their own tax rates, the new system maintains several features of the present system that are central to Canada's economic union. These include a common definition of taxable income, to be set by the federal government, a core system of tax preferences and expenditure based on federal law, and a centralized tax collection system to avoid the creation of separate provincial bureaucracies.

The federal government agreed to accommodate provincial tax reform proposals consistent with the consensus "Tax on Income" report, with provisions for implementation by January 1, 2001. In response, several provincial governments announced public consultations on provincial tax reforms, Alberta following its 1998 budget, and four other provinces during 1999. By the end of the 2000 provincial budget cycle, all provinces had indicated their intentions to switch to some form of the new system. However, they have done so in very different ways.

PROVINCIAL TAX REFORM INITIATIVES

The introduction of the tax-on-income system has led most provinces to restructure their tax systems. Provincial debates over provincial tax reforms hinge on two main factors: the trade-offs between tax reductions and other priorities, such as increased spending and debt reduction (mainly in Alberta), and the degree to which the tax system should emphasize the redistribution of income and wealth rather than incentives for wealth creation.

Alberta and Ontario have placed the strongest emphasis on pro-growth policies of tax reduction, but in very different ways. Ontario has sharply reduced its tax rates for all taxpayers, but most significantly for lower- and middle-income families. At the same time, it is reducing taxes on investment and business income significantly below the levels of other provinces. By introducing its "single rate tax" on personal incomes over $12,900, Alberta has broken with the North American tradition of progressive tax rates and set clear limits on the redistribution of income through the tax system. Saskatchewan has "flattened" its personal tax rate structure in response to Alberta's tax reforms, while shifting part of its tax load to provincial sales taxes.

Most other provinces continue to maintain sharply progressive tax systems, while attempting to reduce taxes for lower- and middle-income individuals and families through a mix of targeted tax reductions and increased tax credits for children and families (see Table 12.5). These changes point to the likelihood of an increasingly diverse set of provincial tax systems whose futures are likely to depend more on the vagaries of provincial politics than on external economic forces.

Table 12.5 ·· PROVINCIAL TAX THRESHOLDS AND BASIC RATES—2001

	Basic Personal Exemption	Spousal credit	Per child allowance	Basic tax rate	Middle-income top rate	Top tax rate	Threshold for top tax rate
BC*	8,000	6,850	n/a	7.3%	10.9%	16.7%	85,000
ALBERTA	12,900	12,900	2,353	10.0%	10.0%	10.0%	12,900
SASK.**	8,000	8,000	1,500	11.5%	13.5%	16.0%	60,000
MANITOBA†	7,412	6,294	300 (tc+c)	10.9%	16.2%	17.4%	61,089
ONTARIO††	7,412	6,294	309 (tc+c)	6.2%	9.24%	17.41%	61,430
QUEBEC‡	5,900	5,900	2,600/2,400	16.0%	20.0%	24.0%	52,000
NB	7,412	6,294	n/a	9.68%	14.82%	17.84%	59,181
NS	7,231	6,140	low-income	9.77%	14.95%	18.34%	92,000
PEI	7,412	6,294	n/a	9.8%	13.8%	16.7%	61,510
NFLD.	7,412	6,294	n/a	10.57%	16.16%	19.64%	60,009

* British Columbia personal income tax rates are 13.7% on taxable income between $60,670 and $70,000, and 15.7% on income between $70,001 and $85,000. Effective in 2002, BC's indexed five-tier system will have the following rates:

Taxable income	<$34,484	34,484-60,969	60,969-70,000	70,000-85,000	>85,000
2002 rate	6.05%	9.15%	11.7%	13.7%	14.7%

** Saskatchewan will reduce tax rates to 11, 13, and 15 per cent, increase the top rate threshold to $100,000, and increase the tax credit for each child to $2,500 by 2003.

† Manitoba will reduce middle and upper tax rates to 15.4% and 17.4% respectively and the top tax rate threshold to $65,000 in 2002; (tc+c)–tax reduction for each child, reduced by "clawback" rate.

†† Ontario has announced plans to reduce income tax rates by an average of 15 per cent by 2004.

‡ Effective July 2001. Quebec provincial taxes are offset by a reduction of 16.5 per cent of basic federal tax in calculating federal taxes payable; Quebec's non-refundable tax credit rate was reduced to 20 per cent in July 2001 to offset tax rate reductions.

ONTARIO: TAX CUTS, TAX BREAKS, TAX CONFLICTS

Since its election in 1995, Ontario's Conservative government has defied fiscal orthodoxy and challenged the conventional political wisdom in its fiscal and tax policies. As promised, the Harris government reduced personal income tax rates by an average of 30 per cent during its first term, while eliminating its inherited $11.3 billion deficit over five years. This fiscal stimulus offset the effects of spending cuts during Harris' first two years in office. Tax cuts targeted at lower- and middle-income earners undercut the efforts of public-sector unions to mobilize large-scale public opposition to the new government, which was re-elected in 1999. Payroll taxes on small employers were replaced by income surtaxes on taxpayers earning more than $50,000, partially offsetting the effects of lower PIT rates.

Harris' "Common Sense Revolution" did not reverse the growth of government, but after its initial spending cuts between 1995 and 1997, it did allow public spending to grow slightly faster than inflation and population. However, the Harris government clearly gave the financial needs of citizens and the private-sector economy priority over those of the public sector, even though this meant allowing the provincial debt to grow faster than in most other provinces. This marked a sharp departure from the Liberal and NDP policies of the previous decade.

The Harris government's second term also emphasized an agenda of tax cuts and limited government growth. Personal income taxes were to be reduced by a further 20 per cent by 2004. Corporate and small business tax cuts announced in the 2000 budget were intended to cut the general CIT rate from 15 to 8 per cent, halve the 8-per-cent small business tax rate from 8 to 4 per cent, and double the value of the small business tax rate ceiling from $200,000 to $400,000 over 5 years.[24] Over the past several years, Ontario also has introduced a wide range of targeted tax preferences for both individuals and businesses.

These changes, which recall the federal government's active use of the tax system during the 1970s to stimulate a wide variety of specific activities, have drawn the Ontario government into a series of conflicts with federal Finance and Revenue officials who are responsible for managing the design and administration of the tax system. Because it administers its own corporate tax system, Ontario has unfettered discretion when introducing corporate tax expenditures. However, federal Finance Department officials have been reluctant to accommodate the Harris government's activist approach to the tax system. This has led to threats that Ontario will secede from the tax collection agreements and set up its own tax collection system.

Although Ontario governments have made such noises for almost twenty years, there appears to be little popular or interest group support for balkanizing Canada's provincial tax systems in this way. However, the provincialization of Canada's tax system has been able to accommodate other, more significant changes, particularly Alberta's decision to replace its progressive tax rate system with a single rate tax.

ALBERTA'S SINGLE RATE TAX

Alberta has been the catalyst for much of the provincial tax reform process. Along with Manitoba, it played a leading role in negotiations leading to the introduction of the tax-on-income system. Alberta was the first to announce specific proposals for provincial tax reform. Its approach to tax reform reflects a mixture of home-grown issues and concerns for the competitiveness of both the Albertan and Canadian tax systems compared to those of neighbouring American states.[25]

Despite its conservative political culture, Alberta's oil and gas revenues consistently allowed the government to record the highest tax and spending levels of any province during the 1980s. However, the collapse of energy prices in the mid-1980s and again during the 1990-91 recession saddled the province with a huge deficit. Premier Ralph Klein's government cut provincial spending by almost 20 per cent during its first term. Economic recovery resulted in large budget surpluses during the late 1990s, most of which were applied to reducing the province's debt. As a result, Alberta lagged behind other provinces in reducing taxes, despite balancing its budget in 1994-95.

Alberta's tax reforms emerged from the report of a provincial Tax Review Commission appointed in 1998. During its consultations, the Committee found broad support for a single rate tax system, especially from the province's business community. This represented a major departure from the existing progressive tax rate structure that has long been the norm for federal and provincial income tax systems, and reflected the conservative populism of Alberta's political culture. Consultations also revealed strong support for measures to reduce the tax differences between single- and dual-income families in order to provide parents with greater choice in balancing the trade-offs between work and family needs.[26]

Alberta Treasurer Stockwell Day accepted the Committee's recommendation to shift to a tax-on-income system, a single rate tax of 11 per cent on all income over a basic personal exemption of $11,620 (compared to the existing federal threshold of $6,456), and an equal spousal credit in October 1998. The increased tax threshold was vital to ensure that the proposed system would result in a net tax reduction for most Albertans, a critical condition for winning broad public support for the proposed changes. These changes replaced Alberta's existing flat tax and "deficit reduction" surtaxes.

Subsequent tax reductions have increased the income threshold to $12,900 per spouse and cut Alberta's tax rate to 10 per cent, effective in 2001.

Alberta's proposed tax reforms have been relatively uncontroversial within the province. Efforts by opposition parties to challenge the single rate tax structure fell flat during the 2001 election campaign, which resulted in the re-election of the Klein Conservatives with an increased majority. The Alberta reforms also provided direct inspiration for the 2000 federal election platform of the Canadian Alliance—which initially proposed a single 17-per-cent tax rate on family incomes over $20,000. They have also provoked a major restructuring of Saskatchewan's tax system.

SHIFTING AND CUTTING TAXES: SASKATCHEWAN'S TAX REFORMS

Table 12.6 ·· AVERAGE PROVINCIAL PERSONAL INCOME TAX RATES (PERCENTAGE)–1999*

ONTARIO	43.5
ALBERTA	48.4
BRITISH COLUMBIA	53.7
MANITOBA	56.6
NOVA SCOTIA	57.2
PRINCE EDWARD ISLAND	59.7
NEW BRUNSWICK	60.8
SASKATCHEWAN	66.8
NEWFOUNDLAND	70.3**

* Ratio of provincial to federal income tax revenues collected in each province.

** Newfoundland has announced plans to reduce its basic tax rate, while introducing a system of graduated surtaxes.

Source: Saskatchewan Finance, Saskatchewan Personal Income Tax Review Committee Report (1999), 9.

Saskatchewan's NDP government has long supported the "tax on income" concept as the basis for provincial tax reforms. However, until recently, it has preferred to reduce sales taxes and rely mainly on a sharply progressive income tax system for increased revenues. This has given it the second highest personal income tax rate among the provinces (see Table 12.6).

Saskatchewan set up a Tax Review Committee, composed exclusively of tax experts, to review the tax-on-income proposal and make recommendations on possible implementation. Its mandate was to recommend changes to the province's tax system to promote "fairness in the tax system; support for the family; simplicity for both the tax filer and the Government; and competitiveness in attracting jobs and investment to Saskatchewan."[27] Premier Romanow promised tax reductions of up to $200 million, about 4 per cent of the provincial tax base, during the 1999 election. This made it possible for the Tax Review Committee to recommend much larger reductions in PIT rates than would otherwise have been the case in order to make Saskatchewan's tax system more competitive with Alberta's.

The Committee's report was clearly influenced by Alberta's proposed tax reforms and by concerns raised during consultations that many upper-income taxpayers already were moving to Alberta for tax-planning purposes. It recommended that the province's basic tax rate match the proposed Alberta rate of 11 per cent, albeit with a lower income threshold. Concerns over work/family trade-offs were to be accommodated by equalizing the basic personal and spousal exemptions and by eliminating the 2 per cent flat rate income tax on net income over $10,000. Concerns over high marginal rates and taxpayer flight were to be addressed by increasing the ceiling on the new middle-income tax bracket to $100,000 (from the current $63,438), and by matching Alberta's capital gains tax rate of 11 per cent on profits from the sale of small businesses and family farms. As a result, Saskatchewan would sharply reduce the personal income tax gap with Alberta and have the second lowest top marginal rate among Canadian provinces.[28] Apart from some limited tax competition in Atlantic Canada, Saskatchewan is the only province to date whose tax reforms have been directly influenced by competitive pressures from neighbouring provinces.

Since the price tag of the proposed reforms—about $427 million—was well outside the Committee's fiscal terms of reference, it recommended offsetting increases in the sales tax base. Most of these recommendations were accepted in Treasurer Eric Cline's 2000 budget. These changes, while not excessively popular,[29] demonstrated that tax reforms that shift part of the tax burden from income to sales taxation can be politically viable, as long as they result in net tax reductions for most citizens and they directly address related fairness issues.

OTHER PROVINCES: MINOR CHANGES TO THE STATUS QUO

Manitoba has less fiscal flexibility in implementing provincial tax reforms than either Alberta or Saskatchewan. The province currently depends on both personal income taxes and sales taxes for a larger share of its revenues than either of its Prairie neighbours. Its sales tax base is significantly broader than Saskatchewan's, precluding major revenue gains from base-broadening.[30] Balanced budget legislation requires a province-wide referendum before increasing tax rates on several major taxes. Although Manitoba's overall personal taxes on lower-income individuals and families are comparable to Alberta's pre-reform tax levels, Manitoba's tax rates are more sharply progressive.[31]

Manitoba's 2000 budget, which confirmed the adoption of a provincial tax-on-income, emphasized increases in a number of personal exemptions and credits which are of greatest benefit to lower- and middle-income taxpayers, rather than general rate reductions. NDP Premier Gary Doer effectively shelved the report of a "Lower Tax Commission," appointed by his Conservative predecessor and chaired by former PC Finance Minister Clayton Manness, which borrowed heavily from changes previously proposed in Alberta and Saskatchewan. The Doer government also introduced further middle-income tax reductions in its 2001 budget.

British Columbia's sizeable budget deficits of the 1990s left little room for tax reduction. Most tax cuts have been targeted to lower- and middle-income taxpayers and small businesses. BC's NDP governments of the 1990s gave the province the highest tax rates and spending levels of any province in Western Canada, while targeting modest tax reductions to lower- and middle-income taxpayers and small businesses. However, the Liberal government elected in 2001 followed Ontario's early example in cutting most tax rates by 25 per cent or more over two years at the expense of larger short-term deficits. These changes reflect a mixture of ideological changes and growing concerns over the growing tax gap with Alberta and its impact on British Columbia's prospects for economic growth.

Provincial governments in Atlantic Canada have used the adoption of the "tax on income" system to insulate provincial tax rates from the federal tax cuts announced in Ottawa's 2000 budgets. Newfoundland and New Brunswick have announced plans to reduce provincial tax rates over several years. Nova Scotia, faced with significant budget deficits, is the one province that has yet to restore indexing to personal income tax rates or brackets.

Quebec, as the one province that has administered its own personal income tax system since the 1960s, has been only marginally affected by other provinces' shift to the tax on income. Despite modest tax reductions announced in its 2000 and 2001 budgets, Quebec continues to have the highest tax rates in Canada. Although recent opinion surveys suggest that Quebecers are showing signs of tax fatigue, it would take an unprecedented shift in Quebec's political culture for it to follow Ontario, Alberta, and Saskatchewan in the direction of competitive tax reductions.

Conclusion

Recent changes to the tax collection agreements that provide for the decentralization of provincial tax systems have resulted in one of the most significant amendments to Canada's "fiscal constitution" in more than thirty years. By giving provincial governments increased autonomy in designing their income tax systems, the agreements recognize the provinces' increasing fiscal and political weight, along with the growing diversity of their economic policies. The agreements also demonstrate the continued flexibility of Canadian federalism by allowing the new Canada Customs and Revenue Agency to administer provincial tax initiatives which differ slightly from federal policies on a cost recovery basis.

This flexibility will be an advantage in dealing with the next major challenges to fiscal federalism within Canada: the development of tax-sharing agreements between federal and provincial governments and the emerging system of aboriginal governments. These negotiations, which are proceeding at varying rates in different provinces, are sufficiently complex and diverse to be beyond the scope of this study.[32] Just as the existing system of fiscal federalism has evolved slowly in response to changing political and economic circumstances, the emergence of partially self-sustaining aboriginal governments is likely to take place gradually, in response to the very different circumstances of native communities in different provinces and to the growing expectations of native communities for greater internal accountability in the use of their fiscal resources.[33]

The "tax-on-income" system allows for the introduction of creative approaches to tax policy, such as Alberta's adoption of a proportional tax system and Saskatchewan's innovative efforts to protect its tax base from aggressive tax competition from its rapidly growing neighbour. Changes announced to date suggest that, in most provinces, politics trump economics or issues of inter-provincial competition when it comes to setting personal income tax rates. It will be up to the voters of these provinces, and the political leaders they elect, to determine whether the politics of redistribution continue to take priority over the economics of growth.

NOTES

1 Bird and Mintz (2000), 268-69.

2 Measured on a National Accounts basis, provincial and territorial own-source revenues first exceeded federal revenues in 1993. Canada, Department of Finance (2000d), Tables 35, 38.

3 Dyck and Dahlby (1999). The so-called "five province report" was published as *Federal Administration of Provincial Taxes*, "Annex 4" [Canada, Department of Finance (2000a).] The federal-provincial consensus agreement is outlined in Canada, Department of Finance (1998c).

4 Dyck and Dahlby (1999); Courchene (1999).

5 Canada, Department of Finance (1999).

6 Richards (2000), 24-25.

7 Hale (2000a).

8 Courchene (1999), 862.

9 Bruce Little (1999), "Q. Who supplies Canada's trading muscle? A: Ont....," *The Globe and Mail*, 13 December, A10.

10 In Alberta, this has included elimination of the provincial business property tax on machinery and equipment in 1996-97, introduction of a uniform provincial education tax rate, and recommendations to average and cap property tax increases arising from rapid increases in property values. Alberta (1997) *Treasury Annual Report for the fiscal year ended March 31, 1997* (Edmonton, Alberta Treasury); Alberta (1999b) Education Property Tax Committee, *Interim Report* (Edmonton, Alberta Treasury, 4 October). In Ontario, the 1998 budget introduced phased reductions of education taxes on commercial and industrial properties over average provincial rates. Ontario (1998) *1998 Ontario Budget* (Toronto, Ministry of Finance, May), 90-93, 98.

11 Canada, Department of Finance (1999d), 33. Alberta amended its *Fiscal Responsibility Act* late in 1999 to allow for spending of more than 25 per cent of projected revenue windfalls for in-year spending initiatives.

12 British Columbia (2001).

13 This truism is confirmed by Kneebone and McKenzie's (1999) analysis of the discretionary fiscal stance of nine provinces during the early and mid-1990s.

14 Interviews, current and former Finance/Treasury officials of Manitoba, Saskatchewan, and Alberta governments (PG-12, PG-13, PG-18, PG-22).

15 Saskatchewan (1988) *Tax on Income: Discussion Paper* (Regina: Ministry of Finance, March).

16 Canada, Department of Finance (1991).

17 Interviews, federal Department of Finance and Alberta Treasury. Explanations for the breakdown in negotiations between federal and provincial officials reflect the rather different perceptions of federal and provincial officials.

18 Interview, Government of Alberta.

19 Interview, member, Alberta Tax Review Committee. This theme surfaced again and again in interviews with provincial officials.

20 Saskatchewan (1999a). A senior federal official notes that most provincial officials assumed a shared tax base as an effective condition of decentralizing control over tax rates (ADM-12).

21 Giles Gherson (1999) "Martin to tell provinces he needs surplus," *National Post*, 9 December, A7; Toulin (1999). Provincial officials interviewed for this chapter suggest that federal officials after 1996 tacitly encouraged the development of provincial tax on income proposals.

22 Interview, senior Finance Department official (ADM-12).

23 Canada (2000a).

24 Ontario (2000), 97-98.

25 Interviews, Alberta Tax Review Committee.

26 Interviews, Alberta Tax Review Committee.

27 Saskatchewan (1999a).

28 Saskatchewan (1999b).

29 Gerry Klein (2000) "Divided over tax changes," *Regina Leader Post*, 17 May.

30 Interview, Government of Manitoba.

31 Saskatchewan (1999b), Tables 1, 2, 15, 16.

32 Austin (2000); Jules (2000). For an extended discussion of tax issues related to aboriginal self-government, see Canadian Tax Foundation (2000).

33 Assembly of First Nations (2000) AFN-CGA Task Force on Financial Accountability, (www.afn.ca); *First Nations National Accountability Coalition Report*, mimeo, 1999; David Roberts (2001) "Taxpayers footed bill for cruise, judge finds," *The Globe and Mail*, 9 February.

THIRTEEN

Taxation, the Family, and Civil Society

Tax policies play an important role in economic growth, the distribution of disposable income, and the financing of public services across Canada. However, they also play a significant role in the shaping of civil society—the voluntary, private, and community institutions and organizations through which individuals cooperate to pursue common goals apart from the commercial, profit-driven institutions of the marketplace and from state institutions financed and controlled by governments. The persistence and health of civil society, including the family, non-profit organizations, the religious sector, private charitable and educational organizations, and other autonomous community organizations, are widely considered to be essential elements for continuing democratic renewal in liberal democratic societies.[1]

Strong institutions of civil society help to broaden the choices available to individuals and communities and assist them in mobilizing resources to make those choices effective. They also provide important social and economic buffers for the accommodation of different values, priorities, and social and political outlooks within society. A number of studies also suggest links between family attitudes and structures, the moral-cultural dimensions of citizenship and civic responsibility, and levels of participation in civic organizations.[2]

Canada's tax system traditionally has empowered the institutions of civil society in a number of ways. It has acknowledged and accommodated the responsibilities of parents in raising children, caring for other dependent family members, and offsetting the costs of their education above and beyond services financed by direct public expenditures. The tax system enables individuals to finance a secure retirement through their employers and other organizations. It accommodates charitable giving and philanthropy, along with the performance of religious obligations and community services. It also provides significant incentives for donations to support political parties, and more restricted allowances for other forms of political engagement.

One element of the current debate over tax reduction and the use of the fiscal dividend relates to the balance governments should strike in providing services directly to families and children and the accommodation of greater parental discretion and choice through tax cuts targeted to families.[3] Many of the same issues are at stake in continuing debates over the ways in which governments should accommodate and support the activities of charitable and other non-profit organizations, or should allow citizens to do so through their charitable giving.

This chapter examines the ways in which competing concepts of civil society and the role of government have entered into issues of tax policy and government spending. It summarizes the major options available to governments, both in assisting families and in expanding the private resources available for charitable and educational activity.

Competing Visions of Civil Society

The voluntary institutions of civil society are part of a broader system of checks and balances that includes the institutions of democratic choice, the division of power within and between governments, and judicial guarantees of the rule of law. The institutions of civil society are vital elements in preserving and renewing the capacity of citizens for responsible self-government. They do this by enabling citizens to take responsibility for the management of their own lives and by helping to create the shared values, interests, and identities of communities. Voluntary institutions often are able to accommodate social diversity and value differences more effectively than governmental institutions.

Susan Phillips notes three key functions performed by voluntary organizations in contemporary Canadian society: service delivery; "citizenship engagement," through volunteering and providing other opportunities for civic participation; and "advocacy" or "representation" in influencing public opinion and/or the formation of public policy.[4] Another significant function, performed not only by voluntary organizations but by nuclear and extended families as the nurseries of civil society, is that of socialization, equipping current and future citizens with the habits and attitudes of responsible citizenship in which rights are typically accompanied by responsibilities toward other members of the group, the broader community, and society.

The liberal-pluralist tradition emphasizes the role of civil society as voluntary, autonomous institutions and organizations through which individuals cooperate to pursue common goals apart from both the profit-driven institutions of the marketplace and from state institutions which are primarily financed and controlled by governments. This tradition is based on the firm belief that, in a diverse, pluralistic society, the public interest cannot be defined only by governments, political parties, or interest groups. A healthy civil society requires that individuals and groups have both the freedom and the capacity to protect their own interests and to contribute according to their own values to the well-being of the broader community through both private choices and cooperative actions, without undue restrictions by governments.

The social democratic tradition emphasizes the interpenetration of state and society and the interdependence of voluntary organizations and those of the state. This is more than just an observation of empirical reality. It is also a means of enlisting the resources of the state to enable disadvantaged groups and their representatives to compete more effectively with other social and economic interests in order to influence and sometimes control government policies vital to their interests.[5] However, to the extent that certain interests succeed in obtaining control of government policies through collective action, they also may attempt to use the state's administrative power to convert institutions of civil society from largely autonomous social agents to vehicles for the projection of state power and the policy preferences of state actors within the broader society.[6] This is consistent with John Stuart Mill's warning that "the very principle of constitutional government requires it to be assumed that political power will be abused to promote the particular purposes of the holder; not because it always is so, but because such is the natural tendency of things, to guard against which is the especial use of free institutions."[7] Public choice analyses of interest group politics have suggested that such approaches to public policy, while increasing the responsiveness of different parts of government to particular interests, may also undermine the ability of governments to respond to changing circumstances or to the changing priorities of the broader electorate.[8] They may also lead to the systematic exclusion from effective influence over the policy process of non-institutionalized or politically disfavoured groups.

Three other major conceptual challenges in defining civil society and voluntary organizations are related to problems of determining which associations are effectively "autonomous," "non-governmental," and "noncommercial."

The dependence of many voluntary organizations on direct government funding calls into question the ability of many groups to preserve the autonomy necessary to be effective members of civil society, rather than extensions of state policy. Recent research shows that 57 per cent of overall voluntary sector revenues, compared with 35 per cent in the United States, come directly from governments. This figure is much higher in some sectors.[9] The conditions attached to the receipt or renewal of direct government funding may impair the capacity of groups to define their own mandates or govern themselves according to their own values. This issue frequently arises in the funding of organizations that are actively engaged in advocacy activities or that seek to define their mandate in terms of particular religious values.[10]

Fiscal retrenchment has led also to a shift in some of the functions traditionally carried out by governments to voluntary and non-profit organizations.[11] This shift has blurred even further the distinction between non-profit organizations as autonomous groups responsible for the delivery of particular services to different publics, independent advocacy organizations, and client groups dependent on government funding and supportive government policies.[12]

Many "voluntary" organizations also depend for much of their revenues on the sale of goods or services in the marketplace. This often involves significant employment. Overall, the voluntary sector receives 32 per cent of its revenues from the sale of goods and services, ranging from small-scale fundraising activities to the widespread use of organized gambling and large-scale quasi-commercial activities.[13] The tax exemptions and preferences enjoyed by non-profit organizations carrying out charitable and other activities of public benefit provide significant financial support for their fund-raising activities.[14] Recent studies suggest that the arts sector depends on such activities for more than half of its revenue.[15] Although voluntary fund-raising is usually necessary to offset the deficits of such groups, there is no consensus on how to distinguish between non-profit commercial organizations that depend primarily on the sales of goods and services and those that are primarily voluntary, non-commercial institutions of civil society.

FAMILIES AND CIVIL SOCIETY

In recent years, there has been renewed interest in the role of families as part of civil society. This is not a new concept. Family and kinship structures have long been vital to the ordering of society, as well as providing stability, security, and identity, and transmitting values. Although social, economic, and cultural changes have resulted in a growing diversity of family structures and roles, families continue in contemporary Canadian society to be a principal source of personal identity and attachment, transcending social class, occupational status, and political ideology.[16] The role of family as part of civil society, not merely a reflection of private or transient individual choices, is recognized in common, statute, and even international law, including tax laws. These laws provide for the sharing and transmission of

344

property, parental responsibility for the education and welfare of children, the maintenance of a sphere of parental autonomy in value choices related to child rearing and the sharing of family responsibilities, and an acknowledgement in public policy that the state and society as a whole both have a vital interest in the stability and well-being of families. Indeed, parental involvement and example are increasingly acknowledged as a central factor in child development and the maturing of children to become responsible and productive citizens.[17]

The family is also recognized increasingly as a vital institution that provides a fundamental role in the development and engagement of citizens.[18] Families play a vital role in the socialization of children, training them to accept personal responsibility for their own lives and the well-being of the society around them, reflected in an ethic and the example of volunteer activities of many kinds.

The decision to assist the activities of families, voluntary organizations, and other elements of civil society as a matter of public policy may be exercised through direct government spending,[19] through more or less intrusive forms of regulation, or through the use of tax preferences which may attempt to make private choices conform to the preferences and priorities of government policy-makers. Alternatively, governments may seek to maintain or enhance citizens' freedom and the autonomy of civil society by leaving greater discretionary income to individuals and families. This income can be used to support voluntary institutions of community according to individuals' preferences and priorities. Governments may also create regulatory frameworks with provisions for greater transparency, internal and/or public accountability in the operations of voluntary organizations, rather than subjecting them to direct government control.

The following section examines the role of the tax system in balancing these approaches as they apply to families, and voluntary charitable and non-profit organizations in Canadian society.

Taxation and Civil Society

The tax system has long recognized that certain obligations of responsible citizenship precede obligations to the state. These include the obligation to provide oneself and one's family with the basic necessities of life, recognized in the basic personal and spousal exemptions, additional provisions for the support of dependent children, and the deductibility of expenses incurred for the purposes of earning income, contained in the Income Tax Act of 1917 and subsequent revisions.[20] They also include the effective exclusion from taxable income of contributions to charitable, religious, and other activities of recognized public benefit, first recognized in the tax system in 1930.[21] Based on the same principle, property owned by churches and other registered charitable organizations usually is exempt from municipal and educational property taxes unless used for commercial purposes.

Although the size of government grew steadily during the twentieth century, state provision has not replaced either the voluntary personal or financial support of community and charitable organizations or traditional concepts of family responsibility for most Canadians. Although charitable giving is subject to (counter-)cyclical fluctuations, it increased by at least 24 per cent relative to after-tax income between 1971 and 1995, even before sizeable increases in the tax preferences available for charitable giving in 1996-97 (see Table 13.1).

Table 13.1 ·· CHARITABLE GIVERS AND DONATIONS: 1972-97

	Taxpayers reporting charitable donations on tax returns				Charitable donations as a percentage of after-tax incomes (TAXABLE RETURNS ONLY)	
	ALL RETURNS		TAXABLE RETURNS			
	%	Average ($ 1997)	%	Average ($ 1997)	All taxpayers	Pro-rated Donors only[††]
1997	25.2%	$797	36.3	$715	0.91	2.50%
1996*	26.4%	$754	35.6	$777	0.98	2.76%
1995	26.7%	$663	37.2	$667	0.89	2.39%
1984**	25.6%	$684	34.3	$693	0.79	2.30%
1983	12.1%	$1,276	16.2	$1,322	0.79[††]	4.32%
1979	9.2%	$1,481	12.5	$1,535	0.79[††]	4.74%
1972	3.1%	$4,376	n/a	n/a	0.67[††]	n/a

* The limit on charitable tax credits increased from 20 per cent to 50 per cent of taxable income (75 per cent in 1997). Allowable tax deductions were converted to tax credits in 1988, increasing their relative value to taxpayers earning less than the maximum federal tax rate threshold ($55,001 in 1988 dollars).

** $100 standard deduction eliminated

† Assumes that the 13.2 per cent increase in donations relative to after-tax income between 1983 and 1984 reflects reporting of donations previously covered by the $100 standard deduction; the same ratio applied to actual 1972 and 1979 donation levels (0.60%, 0.70%).

†† Assumes that donors' after-tax incomes are comparable to those of non-donors within and across income groups. Actual figures may be higher, since analysis suggests an inverse relationship between donation levels as proportion of after-tax income and total incomes below $150,000 (1996 dollars).

Source: Revenue Canada, *Taxation Statistics: 1971-1997* (Ottawa, 1973-1999); author's calculations.

Families and voluntary organizations can and will continue to exist without tax preferences. Relatively few citizens consult tax professionals prior to having children. Only 77,000 of Canada's approximately 175,000 voluntary organizations are registered charities enjoying preferential tax status.[22] Opinion surveys suggest that Canadians support provisions for the child-rearing responsibilities of families through the tax-transfer system. However, they are ambivalent and significantly divided over the extent and means by which governments should provide publicly-funded services to families.[23]

Government policies will play a major role in determining whether support for families and children is delivered in ways that enhance family choices or through the expansion of public and quasi-public services. These choices will have major implications both for the autonomy of families in carrying out their responsibilities towards their children and for the diversity of family arrangements and child-rearing choices accommodated by public policies.

These choices will also influence the degree to which voluntary organizations, many of which are playing an increased role in the delivery of public services, will compete not only with one another for government funding and private donations, but also with a growing range of advocacy organizations which seek to influence the direction of public policy and public opinion. This section examines a number of major options available to governments in dealing with these issues, and their implications for the autonomy and civic capacity of families and voluntary organizations.

FAMILIES, TAXATION, AND CIVIL SOCIETY

Historically, the primary responsibility of parents to care for their children has also been recognized by the tax system. The current debate over the design and financing of family and children's benefits is closely related to the question of the relative priority that should be given to the delivery of government support for families and children through expanded public services, the expansion of family-related tax preferences for parents, or a combination of both.

Federal and provincial tax systems and related government transfer programs recognize, accommodate, and support the needs of families and children in several ways. These have changed significantly since the 1971 income tax reform added the child care expenses deduction to the traditional system of deductions for dependent family members.

Deductions and non-refundable credits for dependent children were phased out between 1988 and 1991, when they were replaced by an expanded Child

347

Tax Benefit targeted to lower- and middle-income families. This change resulted from efforts to reduce the deficit by replacing a number of universal social benefits with targeted measures "so that benefits could be concentrated in those families where they were most needed."[24] The National Forum on Health in 1996 noted that Canada is "the only Western industrialized country that does not take into account the cost of raising children when determining how much tax families with children should pay, compared to those without children."[25]

Spousal and equivalent to spouse exemptions/credits recognize the costs of supporting dependent spouses and family members with a tax credit of up to $6,293 (in 2001). Other credits, including medical and education costs and charitable donations, may be transferred from one family member to another. Recent tax reforms in Alberta and Saskatchewan increased these credits to match the basic personal exemption as a way of providing more equal tax treatment to one- and two-income families.

Child Care Expense Deductions. Introduced in 1971, the child care expense deduction (CCED) is intended to offset additional costs of child-rearing resulting from participation in the workforce and, more recently, from pursuit of education or training. Originally $2,000 per child under the age of 14 to a maximum of $8,000 per family ($8,722 and $34,892 in constant 1998 dollars), the CCED is now $7,000 per child under 6 and $4,000 per child under 16.[26] Davies notes that only about 17 per cent of parents with children are able to claim child care expenses on their tax returns, and that these restrictions apply to both single- and dual-income families. CCED claimants are disproportionately middle- and upper-income families.[27]

Refundable tax credits for lower income families. The Child Tax Credit, introduced in 1978, was expanded in 1991 to replace both the universal tax credit for dependent children and the family allowance with an income-tested credit, phased out for families with annual incomes between $20,000 and $40,000. It was replaced in 1997 by a greatly expanded Canada Child Tax Benefit, targeted mainly at families earning less than $25,921. As discussed in Chapter 9, the 2000 budget further expanded the CCTB, and expanded benefits for "middle-income" families earning $30,000 to $75,000. Several provinces also offer "earned-income tax credits," targeted at low-income working families, along with a range of services financed from savings realized from the consolidation of some provincial spending on family benefits with the National Child Benefit.

In recent years, the integration of the personal income tax and social transfer systems has helped to blur the distinction between direct government spending and tax preferences for families. Table 13.2 summarizes the costs in foregone government revenues and direct expenditures of measures delivered through the income tax system. Of course, the benefits listed above constitute only a small share of federal and provincial expenditures on services to families and children.

THE CHILDREN'S AGENDA AND THE FISCAL DIVIDEND

The National Child Benefit and the Canada Child Tax Benefit have been the two most significant elements introduced to date as part of the so-called National Children's Agenda (NCA). The NCA is one of several major changes to federal social policies arising from Ottawa's social security review of 1994-95.[28] Although it has a number of political and bureaucratic parents, the NCA reflects the strong desire of many "social Liberals" to restore a more active federal role in providing social transfers and services directly to Canadians.

The NCA has become the central focus of efforts to expand government services and benefits to children and families as part of an expanded role for the federal government in Canadian society. Much of the debate over the children's agenda centres on three overlapping issues:

Table 13.2 ·· VALUE OF FEDERAL TAX PREFERENCES, CHILD-RELATED TAX TRANSFERS FOR FAMILIES

	1989	2000[P]	1989	1997
	(2000 constant dollars)		(% of families claiming)	
MARRIED EXEMPTION/CREDIT	$1,405	$1,375	36.6	36.2
EQUIVALENT TO MARRIED CREDIT	$605	$475		
BASIC CHILD EXEMPTION/CREDIT	$490	n/a	44.0	n/a
CHILD CARE DEDUCTION	$337	$515	8.6	11.5
CANADA CHILD TAX BENEFIT*	$2,627	$6,930	31.6	38.0
FAMILY ALLOWANCES	$ 2,633	n/a	44.0	n/a
TOTAL	$8,097	$9,295		

[P] = Projected.

Source: *Personal and Corporate Tax Expenditures* (Ottawa, Dept. of Finance, 1993); 2000 *Tax Expenditures and Evaluations* (Ottawa, Dept. of Finance, 2000); *Tax Statistics for Individuals*, (Ottawa, 1991, 1999).

> the mix of policy instruments that should be used to channel government support to children and their parents;

> the degree to which the projected fiscal dividend should be used to expand public services and income transfers, rather than reversing the trend towards higher taxes which have eliminated virtually all income gains for middle- and upper-income Canadians during the 1990s; and

> the degree to which any net tax reductions should be broadly-based or targeted to particular constituencies in order to maximize their political impact.

Some policy-makers and interest groups view children's and family issues from a social services and therapeutic perspective that believes that the majority of children and families require external assistance and direction in order to discover their potential and to escape social problems that result from socially "at-risk," ill-equipped, or overextended families. This approach has led to proposals to direct the major share of new resources towards the provision of a broad range of child care, "early childhood development," and parent support services that would largely socialize the responsibilities and costs of child-rearing.[29] Quebec's $5 per day system of subsidized child care is the most ambitious example of such an approach in Canada.[30]

This approach would reduce child-care costs for the majority of working parents with pre-school children. However, it is likely to transfer significant discretion from parents and taxpayers as a whole to government policy-makers and providers of children's services. While Mustard and others contend that early childhood development services cannot and should not be provided on the basis of a "one size fits all" model in order to be able to meet the highly diverse needs of parents and children, government provision and public service unionization lend themselves to standardization, producer control over services, and limits on consumer choice, except for those families with high enough incomes to purchase services outside the public system.

Creating a large and growing constituency for increased public spending likely would reduce the flexibility of families in balancing work and family choices by increasing overall levels of taxation. Although such an approach might reduce the burden of child-rearing for many parents, contributing to greater individual autonomy in many cases, it would tend to undermine the autonomy of families by shifting control over services and the terms on which they would be provided to governments and service-providers. Since parental decisions to participate in the labour force do not vary significantly with family income levels, as suggested by Shillington,[31] universal, publicly-funded child care services may result in a sizeable subsidy to upper-income parents that would increase tax levels for the entire population.

The past history of monopoly government provision of public services (and of federal shared-cost transfers to the provinces) suggests that there would be an initial honeymoon as services are expanded, followed by gradual public disillusionment as governments impose greater financial controls and limit choices available to the public, and as services are politicized by producers struggling to insulate themselves against budgetary, managerial, and political restrictions. An alternative approach that is more sensitive to the capacities of families to make their own choices and to their role in civil society would be to place greater emphasis on federal tax preferences and income transfers, while allowing provincial governments to provide a variety of subsidies and services supportive of child care and early child development which reflect differing public demands and philosophies of government.

The initial political success of the Canada Child Child Benefit in channelling increased benefits to lower- and lower-middle-income families with children (see Table 13.3), and the absence of any requirement for provincial consent or cooperation in the delivery of increased benefits have reinforced calls in some quarters for expanding the CCTB as the major vehicle to finance the National Children's Agenda.[32]

To this end, the Commons' Finance Committee has suggested the introduction of a new refundable tax benefit under the CCTB to all parents

Table 13.3 ·· DISTRIBUTION OF FAMILY INCOMES, CANADA CHILD TAX CREDIT (BASED ON 1997 INCOMES)

Family income*	% of families	% of families receiving CCTB	% of benefits paid
UNDER $30,000	24.3%	49.0%	69.5%
$30,000—50,000	25.2%	28.1%	21.9%
$50,000—70,000	21.7%	20.2%	7.6%
$70,000—100,000	18.7%	2.6%	1.0%
OVER $100,000	10.7%	0.1%	<.1%

* Income distributions for "all families" and "CCTB recipients" may vary slightly due to minor differences in definitions of income.

Sources: Canada Customs and Revenue Agency (1999), *Income Statistics 1999 (1997 Tax Year)*; Statistics Canada (1999), *Income Distribution in Canada, 1997*, Cat. # 13-207-XPB.

providing "direct parental care of children." The Committee also recommends policies to accommodate both parents' primary role as caregivers and the growing diversity of parental situations requiring accommodations by government policies.

> Parents ... are in the best position to determine what constitutes the best possible care arrangement for their children. Our policy should provide flexibility, options and choices which will make it feasible for either parent to be the caregiver or to be in the paid workforce. Our policy should be inclusive and responsive to the social realities, circumstances and preferences of parents and their children.... Our policy should be fair and equitable and neither encourage nor penalize caregiving choices.[33]

The 2001 extension of family leave entitlements under Employment Insurance from 26 to 52 weeks was another response to this recommendation.

Recent controversy over the relative tax treatment of single-income and dual-income families reflects the value conflict inherent in the targeting of tax preferences to families and children based on different approaches to the balancing of work and family responsibilities. The controversy also demonstrates the difficulty of defining "horizontal equity" when income taxes are levied on *individual* incomes, while many tax preferences and transfers apply to *family* incomes. No single tax measure can adequately compensate for the costs of professional child care, the relief of poverty, and the income trade-offs resulting from the choice of one parent to work at home or accept part-time instead of seeking full-time paid employment.

The gradual extension of a universal child tax credit to supplement existing measures may be the most effective way for governments to avoid socially divisive debates over tax preferences and increased services to families, The federal government's proposed reduction in the tax clawback on the Child Tax Benefit, which would extend limited CTB benefits to families earning more than $80,000 by 2005, reflects the preference of the Chrétien government for building on existing programs rather than introducing major new initiatives. Since the provinces have jurisdiction over most social and family services, the existing model of bilateral agreements on employment training is probably the most practical for the federal government to use to encourage the provision of a flexible, varied range of public, nonprofit, and quasi-commercial services which respect Canada's social diversity and the heterogeneous character of our civil society.[34]

Tax Laws, Civil Society, and the Capacity of Charitable Organizations to Influence Public Policy and Public Opinion

The capacity of citizens to influence the political process through voluntary associations and organizations is a vital element of political pluralism and democracy. Political parties may provide useful avenues for citizens to influence the political process. However, as organized appetites for power, they rarely lend themselves to the promotion of causes that may offend key stakeholders or divert attention from their main agenda. Political and advocacy activity by voluntary organizations thus provides an important means for citizens to influence public opinion and public policy, to promote a healthy pluralism in civil society, and to enable societal groups to transcend political partisanship in attempting to identify their particular concerns with a broader view of the public interest.

The tax system accommodates the efforts of Canadians to influence public opinion and public policy through voluntary organizations in at least four ways. It gives generous, non-refundable tax credits to political parties at both federal and provincial levels. It allows the deduction of dues or contributions to professional or business associations and trade unions as an expense of earning income. It extends tax credits for contributions to registered charitable organizations, but only to the extent that "political activities of a non-partisan nature" as defined by the Canada Customs and Revenue Agency or the courts are "ancillary or incidental," and that "substantially all" (90 per cent or more) of their annual revenues are applied to charitable purposes.[35] The tax system also provides tax credits for contributions to registered charitable organizations engaged in public education, as long as the direct purpose of this activity is to provide "information and non-partisan views" to the media and the public—unless these objectives "can only be achieved by legislative reform."[36]

The tax system also provides extensive tax exemptions to non-profit organizations carrying out business activities for purposes of charitable fund-raising. These exemptions are similar to those available to non-profit or intermediate organizations in Western Europe, which has a much less developed tradition of philanthropy or charitable giving and far less accommodation of charitable giving in national tax systems than do Britain or North America.[37]

TAXATION, CHARITIES, AND NPOs—LEGAL AND ECONOMIC STATUS

The level of marginal tax rates on most Canadians earning more than a subsistence income gives charitable organizations a significant competitive advantage in fund-raising over non-profit organizations without charitable status. The ceiling on charitable contributions eligible for the tax credit was increased from 20 per cent of taxable income to 50 per cent in 1996, and to 75 per cent in 1997. This change led to increased donation levels, particularly from upper-income donors.[38] Donations above this ceiling can be carried forward against future income for up to five years. These measures are considered important in encouraging the "philanthropic impulse" and in increasing overall levels of charitable giving, although this view has been contested in some quarters.[39]

Buildings owned by charitable, educational, and religious organizations are generally exempt from property taxes under provincial laws, whether or not they are owned, operated, or partly financed by the government. The treatment of charitable organizations may vary, depending on whether they are specifically committed to the relief of the poor or to the receipt of public funding, or whether they are beneficiaries of special exemptions. The traditional exemption given to churches and other religious organizations was intended to avoid preferential treatment of minority religious communities during an era when most citizens were associated with some form of organized religion. Some studies have suggested that, in an era of growing secularization, this exemption should be withdrawn.[40]

Table 13.4 ·· ESTIMATED BENEFIT OF TAX PREFERENCES FOR CHARITABLE DONATIONS, PROFESSIONAL AND UNION DUES, AND POLITICAL CONTRIBUTIONS (IN 2000 CONSTANT $)

	Charitable Donations TOTAL BENEFIT	*Deduction of union,* PROFESSIONAL DUES*	*Political Contributions* (THREE YEAR AVERAGE)**
1989	$994 million	$ 451 million	$ 12.7 million
2000	$1,365 million	$ 555 million	$ 16.7 million

*   Includes representational functions for individuals; does not include value of membership fees and assessments for business representation.

**   Federal tax credits only; Elections Canada's direct reimbursement of political parties and candidates for allowable election expenses totaled $24.0 million for the 1997 general election.[41]

Source: Canada, Department of Finance (1993, 2000g).

Canadians reported $4.25 billion in charitable donations on their income tax returns in 1997, not counting contributions by corporations, about 10 per cent of revenues reported by registered charitable organizations.[42] The federal Department of Finance estimated the value of non-refundable charitable tax credits at $1.3 billion in 1998, more than 80 times the value of individual tax credits for contributions to political parties (see Table 13.4). This total does not include the value of tax credits for contributions to registered provincial political parties provided by eight provinces or the direct subsidies provided by federal and provincial governments.

The common law definition of charitable activity covers four primary purposes: the relief of poverty, the advancement of education, the advancement of religion, and "other purposes beneficial to the community not falling within any of the foregoing heads."[43] Section 149.1(1) of the Income Tax Act distinguishes between registered charities which are eligible to issue tax receipts and non-profit organizations, which are not. It also establishes criteria for public and private foundations, which may raise and disperse money for charitable activities performed by other groups, including some in the broader public sector, such as hospitals and educational institutions.

Canadian rules distinguishing between "education" and "political advocacy," although consistent with common law precedents, are considerably more restrictive than those governing non-profit organizations registered as "501(c)(3)" corporations in the United States. A recent Canada Customs and Revenue Agency (CCRA) information bulletin defines advocacy as "the act of speaking or of disseminating information intended to influence individual behaviour or opinion, corporate conduct, or public policy and law." At present, the CCRA limits charities' political advocacy, defined as "promotion of a particular point of view or political orientation, or to persuasion, indoctrination or propaganda,"[44] to incidental activity that accounts for less than 10 per cent of a charity's annual expenditures.

Policy advocacy in the United States is actively encouraged by federal legislation. Internal Revenue Service guidelines allow non-profit organizations to spend up to 20 per cent of their first $500,000 on lobbying or political activities, with an annual expenditure ceiling of up to $1 million per organization.[45] However, the definition of political activities by charities not restricted by this ceiling is significantly broader than in Canada, and may include public statements in support of or in opposition to proposed legislation (within certain limits), private meetings of charity officials with executive branch officials and legislators, and "self-defence lobbying" on legislation which may directly affect the material interests of particular charities.[46]

The CCRA defends the current rules by arguing that, under common law, political advocacy by charities is a privilege subject to administrative regulation by governments under the terms of their incorporation rather than a constitutional right.[47] The tax treatment of voluntary organizations that engage directly or incidentally in advocacy has become a matter of growing public debate in recent years. The CCRA appears to have taken a more aggressive approach to the screening of advocacy and educational organizations seeking charitable status and to the attempted deregistration of charities that engage in advocacy.[48] Boyle notes that

> even when organizations feel that the guidelines set out by Revenue Canada ... are fair and reasonable, there is widespread (though not unanimous) concern that the supposedly objective yardsticks are being applied in a subjective and sometimes arbitrary or discriminatory fashion.... The result is uncertainty. It can have the effect of silencing debate which, in a free and democratic society, is worth preserving.[49]

These issues raise fundamental questions of freedom of speech and association, the degree to which political speech exercised by groups other than political parties or occupational associations should be accommodated or penalized by the tax system, and whether efficiency issues related to fiscal constraints and the competition among groups for public support should be a major factor for policy-makers who are attempting to balance competing views of the public interest. There are enough inconsistencies in the application of rules governing charitable status, and in the relative availability of tax measures to assist occupational and advocacy organizations in their fund-raising activities, to raise significant questions of equity in the application of the laws. CCRA rules restricting governing political activity by charities include activities "designed essentially to sway public opinion on a controversial social issue."[50] The courts have also applied a "reverse onus" test, effectively forcing charities to prove that their advocacy activities are not controversial. Drache and others have noted that this effectively "creates a muzzle on charities which are involved in any activity which may not find 100 per cent support within the community—whether that activity involves environmental work, tobacco distribution, birth control, prison reform, or a host of other issues which are debated in the pages of Canada's newspapers."[51]

Rulings effectively designate as "charitable" the educational activity of any organization supporting policies recognized and authorized by existing laws. However, should these laws be changed by Parliament or the courts, these activities would be rendered "political" and, therefore, ineligible for continued tax support through the issuing of receipts for charitable donations. Ironically, the willingness of the courts to accommodate advocacy activity by charities is closely related to their receipt of government funding for these activities, creating a double-standard by which politically favoured charities are effectively "untouchable," doing "what they will in terms of lobbying while smaller, more vulnerable organizations are under constant threat."[52]

The dependence of many charitable and non-profit organizations on various forms of public funding for the delivery of core services already contributes to a chilling of public discussion on many issues. At the same time, many members of the public are deeply ambivalent about funds donated for ostensibly charitable purposes that are then diverted to the purchasing of advocacy advertising, the hiring of lobbyists, or the solicitation of public funds to further the interests of the charitable organizations themselves.

One way of reconciling these different values may be for governments to provide legal recognition and sanction to a complementary category of educational and advocacy or "public benefit" organizations comparable to those recognized under American 501(c)(3) legislation, while maintaining the current 10 per cent limit on "ancillary" expenditures for traditional charities. This move would limit cross-subsidization or diversion of funds given in support of charities' "service" activities for other purposes. However, the practical challenges of distinguishing between these categories and of regulating non-arm's-length dealings between related organizations involved in "charitable" and "advocacy" activities resist easy solution.

EQUITY ISSUES

Existing rules governing access to charitable status and charities' freedom to engage in advocacy activities raise significant issues of both horizontal equity, the equal treatment of individuals and groups in similar situations, and vertical equity, the relative capacity of individuals and groups with unequal means to participate in civil society. Fees or donations paid to occupational groups—business and professional associations, labour unions, and other representative interest groups, all of which engage in some advocacy activities as part of their *raison d'être*—have long been deductible by individuals and businesses as expenses of earning income. Some of these costs are discretionary, but others are either mandatory or unavoidable in the normal course of doing business or earning an income. There are enough such organizations to provide representation and choice for most Canadians, regardless of their income levels or political outlook.

Although some have criticized the deductibility of such expenses, few Canadians of any political persuasion would wish governments to have the untrammelled right to change the terms by which they earn their livelihood without the right to defend themselves or to seek changes in public policy without incurring crippling financial expense. Furthermore, most organizations have limits on their financial capacity to engage in political activity.

Conspicuous consumption in lobbying and advocacy may be politically counterproductive, since politicians or voters may resent what they perceive as political overkill or the efforts of advocacy organizations to buy political or public favour.[53] The greater flexibility of American tax laws in dealing with advocacy organizations reflects a conscious effort by Congress to balance explicit restrictions on political activity by businesses and unions—effectively turning them into a dead letter.[54]

Some observers have suggested that, instead of changing the law to facilitate advocacy activity by charitable organizations, the federal government should create a specific category of educational or advocacy organization entitled to issue "charitable tax receipts" for activities of public benefit. Arthur Drache takes this position even further in a recent paper, arguing for a free market in the provision of goods, services, and ideas that serve significant public purposes:

> People will vote with their wallets. Newly designated organizations will not be able to exist if there is not enough popular support. Thus, the expansion can be viewed as an exercise in fiscal participatory democracy with a major increase in eligible candidates. In our view, the widest possible spectrum of organizations should qualify to issue receipts for donations which give tax relief—provided only that (they) can meet the broad test of improving the quality of life in Canada or abroad. Those which cannot command enough public support to operate will fall by the wayside—but they will have been given a fair opportunity to compete.[55]

However, Drache suggests also that, in return for increased flexibility in charitable fund raising, the preferential tax exemptions enjoyed by many non-profit organizations to finance charitable activity should be scaled back, reversing trends of recent years. Many organizations are so dependent on quasi-commercial activities that a sounder policy might be to distinguish between "charitable" and "advocacy" activities in ways that enable citizen and consumer choices, without unduly restricting freedom of speech and association. In recent years, the most significant cleavages in political attitudes and advocacy activity have not been defined by income levels or access to private funding so much as by relative dependence on public spending and protective regulations.[56] The formidable advocacy activities of unions and related social movements, or of advocates of expanded social and health care spending at the federal level, suggest that there is no shortage of institutionalized activism or lobbying among self-proclaimed advocates for the disadvantaged.

Groups outside existing advocacy networks continue to face an uphill climb in influencing public opinion or competing with larger institutionalized groups. However, the spread of information technologies has democratized much of the process of disseminating information and gathering support without large financial investments.[57] Persistence, dedication, and the capacity to demonstrate a degree of professionalism in dealing with governments, the media, and the broader public remain important elements for outsider groups seeking to gain influence and credibility with governments. Although access to charitable status may help to accelerate this process, it is no substitute for it.

Equity issues raised by property tax exemptions for properties owned by religious and other charitable organizations could be addressed effectively by the use of itemized bills for public services consumed, a practice already used by many municipalities. At the same time, this method would avoid the difficult problem of market value assessment of church and other properties that may have few alternative uses without huge expenditures on renovations.

ECONOMIC EFFICIENCY AND AFFORDABILITY

The accommodation within the tax system of advocacy activities by charitable and non-profit organizations, and even of charitable activity, is sometimes challenged on the basis of economic efficiency and affordability. Some have suggested that both governments and individuals could make more effective use of the funds saved by reducing tax preferences for charitable giving, and that existing tax measures to support charitable giving in effect undermine both equity and efficiency by providing a "coerced subsidy" to activities favoured by particular individuals, at the expense of non-givers and society as a whole.[58] Others contend that reducing tax incentives for charitable giving would enable governments to reduce overall tax levels, increasing economic efficiency, personal incomes, and the capacity of those inclined to support charitable causes to do so from increased disposable incomes.[59] To support this argument, Francis and Clemens cite revenue statistics, noting that both the likelihood and average level of charitable giving declared on tax returns increases with disposable income.

However, a closer study of these figures suggests that although the tendency to give increases with income, there is no clear relationship between disposable income and the level of charitable giving. This finding, which is confirmed by other recent studies, suggests that motivations for giving are complex, not unidimensional or purely economic, but reflect strong social and ethical motivations as well.[60] Other groups suggest that, with a growing number of organizations approaching businesses and individual donors for financial support, governments must defend the existing definition of charitable status in order to limit fund-raising competition. They also cite the increasing need of many community organizations to raise private donations to supplement or replace government funding. In recent years, this competition has resulted in the annual registration of more than 4,000 new charities by the CCRA, not including the many groups whose applications for charitable status are refused.[61]

These arguments strike a supportive chord with governments, which have encouraged extensive private fund-raising by large, institutionalized charities in order to offset public funding constraints and to encourage greater responsiveness to community priorities. Both federal and provincial governments increasingly use the rhetoric of "partnership," speaking of increased cooperation between governments and non-profit and community organizations in the delivery of public services. Whether such partnerships, fuelled by mutual dependence, are an expression of civil society, as claimed by its advocates, or a substitute for it, given the level of government direction and control which usually accompany government funding of any endeavour, they do increase pressures on governments to make their fund-raising policies consistent with their rhetoric.

SEEKING A BALANCE

The *Working Together* report of 1999, which reflects the views of senior government officials and the representatives of major institutionalized charities, has suggested a number of measures that attempt to balance these concerns for the autonomy and accountability of charitable and non-profit organizations, within the context of fiscal capacity (or "affordability") of governments.

The report's recommendations are similar to Drache's proposal for the extension of charitable status to public benefit organizations, "substantially all the resources of which are devoted to public benefit activities ... [defined as] actions which are intended to improve the quality of life of the community or a group within the community".[62] However, the highly selective list of activities qualifying for this designation suggests an inordinate fear of groups whose advocacy activities might be politically inconvenient to governments of the day, or to the public-sector elites whose biases usually govern the distribution of public funding to such organizations. The report also presents a highly restricted view of "public benefit" that excludes many parts of civil society that do not enjoy the wholehearted endorsement or participation of contemporary economic or public-sector elites.

Representatives of the voluntary sector have made a strong case that the administration and enforcement of such rules should be carried out at arm's length of government. This approach is required both to avoid the potential politicization of these rules, and to maintain non-profit organizations' administrative autonomy from governments.[63]

Conclusion: Recognizing the Diversity of Civil Society

Recent changes to tax laws that affect families, charitable organizations, and other segments of civil society generally have been incremental in nature, rather than the products of basic structural reform. The largest single exception, in response to the fiscal crisis of the early 1990s, was the gradual replacement of universal family allowances and tax credits with larger refundable tax credits targeted at lower-income families.

Any changes made to tax laws with the intention of promoting civil society should be inclusive rather than exclusive in its definitions. Public purpose should not be synonymous with *raison d'état* or with the use of preferential government legislation to favour particular social interests or ideological agendas. This does not mean that the tax treatment of families or the charitable and non-profit sectors should impose a stifling uniformity. Indeed, such uniformity may result in a significantly unequal impact on different groups, given the diversity of family circumstances and the different activities and resources available to different charities.

Much of the political controversy over the tax treatment of families and the accommodation of political activities by charitable and non-profit organizations through the tax system reflects the widespread perception or fear that such policies lend themselves to a zero-sum game in which the gains of one group automatically result in losses to other interests. This approach promotes political conflict between advocates for lower-income families, families reliant on professional child care, and those that forego additional market incomes to raise children at home. Although the state has a vested interest in the generation of additional revenue, as high taxes force parents to expand their hours of work to maintain or improve stagnant living standards, one wonders whether the tax system should not provide greater accommodation of parental choices and values in raising their children.

Should the federal government choose to modernize its definition of charitable activity, particularly by means of establishing a public purpose test which includes particular criteria, these criteria should be sufficiently broad to preclude politicians, bureaucrats, or judges from picking and choosing among "socially friendly" and "socially unfriendly" elements, according to their political interests or ideological orientations. The federal government should avoid the temptation to restrict eligibility for charitable status to groups whose activities and objectives are consistent with its own political or ideological objectives. This approach would accelerate the politicization of tax laws, and increase the likelihood that successive governments would repeatedly change the rules in order to assist their political supporters and penalize their perceived opponents.

NOTES

1   Alexis de Tocqueville, *Democracy in America*, trans. George Lawrence (New York: Perennial Library, 1988); Wuthnow, ed. (1991); Robert D. Putnam (1993), *Making Democracy Work: Civic Traditions in Modern Italy* (Princeton, NJ: Princeton University Press); Don E. Eberly, ed. (1994), *Building a Community of Citizens: civil society in the 21st century* (Lanham, MD: University Press of America); Putnam (1995, 2000); Peter L. Berger and Richard J. Neuhaus (1996) *To Empower People: From State to Civil Society* (Washington, DC: American Enterprise Institute).

2   Peter L. Berger and Richard J. Neuhaus (1977) *To Empower People: The Role of Mediating Structures in Public Policy* (Washington, DC: American Enterprise Institute); Ben Schlesinger, (1998) "Strengths in Families: Accentuating the Positive" (Ottawa: Vanier Institute for the Family); Statistics Canada (1998a), *Caring Canadians, Involved Canadians: Highlights from the 1997 National Survey of Giving, Volunteering and Participating*, Cat. # 71-542-XIE (Ottawa, August); Gary Caldwell and Paul Reed (1999) "Civic Participation in Canada: Is Quebec Different," *Inroads* (Ottawa, Statistics Canada), 215-22; Gary Caldwell (1999), "The Decay of Civil Society in Contemporary Quebec: Causes and Consequences," *Inroads* 7 (Ottawa, Statistics Canada), 176-84.

3   Allen and Richards, eds. (1999); Stewart (1999); "Family Matters," *The Globe and Mail*, 11-18 September 1999; interviews, Department of Finance, Human Resources Development Canada, John Godfrey, MP (ADM-11, ADM-13, ADM-14).

4   Phillips (1995).

5   This concept of civil society is implicit in Torjman (1997) and Phillips (1995); see below nn. 6 and 12.

6   Nordlinger (1981); Ware (1989); Mark Neoclous (1996) *Administering civil society: towards a theory of state power* (New York: St. Martin's Press); Torjman (1997).

7   John Stuart Mill (1862) *Considerations on Representative Government* (New York: Harper & Bros.)

8   Olsen (1982); Hartle (1988a); Hartle (1993); William D. Coleman and Grace Skogstad (1990) *Policy communities and public policy in Canada: a structural approach* (Toronto: Copp Clark Pitman).

9   Cappe (1999), 3. André Picard (1999) "Citizen groups new agents of change," *The Globe and Mail*, 20 September, A3. A recent study of 72 non-profit social service agencies in 1998-99 found that government funding accounted for 81 per cent of sector revenues, and that volunteer activity, although important, was frequently a secondary source of funding and leadership. McFarlane and Roach (1999).

10 Phillips (1995) notes the effects of dependence on government funding on many non-profit organizations; see also Salamon (1994), 109-22; Francis and Clemens (1999a); and the ongoing debate over government's role in funding advocacy organizations and various publicly funded arts organizations. Laurence Jarvik (1997) "Ten Good Reasons to Eliminate Funding for the National Endowment for the Arts," Backgrounder # 1110 (Washington, DC, The Heritage Foundation, 29 April); John L. Hiemstra (1999) "Government Relations with Religious Non-Profit Social Agencies in Alberta: Public Accountability in a Pluralist Society" (Calgary: Canada West Foundation, January).

11 Panel on Accountability and Governance in the Voluntary Sector (1998).

12 Ibid.; Bryden (1994); Boyle (1995); Francis and Clemens (1999a).

13 Statistics Canada (1998a); Cappe (1999).

14 Partial GST exemptions provide charities and NPOS with a benefit estimated at $150 million in 1999. Canada, *Tax Expenditures: 1999* (Ottawa, Dept. of Finance, June). Most provinces have a variety of full or partial rebates for sales and property taxes.

15 Luffman (1999), 2.

16 Graves, with Dugas and Beauchamp (1999).

17 Hon. Margaret Norrie McCain and J. Fraser Mustard (1999) *Reversing The Real Brain Drain, Early Years Study, Final Report* (Toronto: Children's Secretariat, Government of Ontario, April); Sean Fine (1999) "Child development more affected by parenting than social class," *The Globe and Mail*, 4 October, A3.

18 See above n. 2.

19 Transfer programs to individuals may be designed as universal entitlements exempt from government control, although fiscal constraints and predispositions toward the targeting of transfers and tax preferences as part of a general philosophy of redistributive taxation have made these less frequent in recent years. Direct government spending on the activities of private organizations usually requires a measure of financial accountability that links the activities to the fulfillment of specific policy objectives defined by the government.

20 The responsibility of providing for one's own retirement, subject to an individual's means, has also been recognized within limits through a variety of tax and other policy measures that have effectively converted the Personal Income Tax system from an income-based tax to a hybrid income-consumption tax system.

21 Drache (1999), 25-46.

22 Statistics Canada (1998a), *Caring Canadians, Involved Canadians*; Cappe (1999).

23 Angus Reid Group (1999); *Family Matters* (Toronto, 27 September); Compas, Inc. (1997), "Make Family Life a Priority (Ottawa, 5 December); Compas, Inc. (1998), Multi-Audience Research (Calgary, NFFRE, 7 November); Ekos Research Associates, Inc. (1999), *Rethinking Government: Understanding Conflicting Priorities on Tax Cuts, Social Spending and Productivity* (20 August).

24 Standing Committee on Finance (1999), *For the Benefit of our Children: Improving Tax Fairness*, Report # 19 (Ottawa, House of Commons, June).

25 Ibid.

26 Ibid.

27 James B. Davies (1999), "Why we need a universal child deduction...," Testimony to Sub-Committee on Tax Equity for Canadian Families with Dependent Children (Ottawa, House of Commons, May). Only 5.4 per cent of Canadians reporting taxable income claimed the child care deduction in 1996, the last year for which statistics are currently available. This is about one-quarter of the number who received the National Child Benefit. [Revenue Canada, (1998), *Tax Statistics for Individuals, 1998*, 1996 tax year (Ottawa).]

28 Ken Battle, Caledon Institute, Letter to author, Aug. 1999. Federal officials interviewed for this paper noted that some policy and programming initiatives contained in the National Children's Agenda were initiated by the Mulroney government. However, current policies, initiated as part of ongoing discussions on the social union, reflect an effort to coordinate policies and programming related to children across departmental lines and, to some extent, with provincial

government services as well (interview, HRD Canada).

29 McCain and Mustard (1999); House of Commons, Sub-Committee on Children and Youth at Risk (1999), *Interim Report*, June; Tom Blackwell (1999) "$12B child-care program on Liberals' children's agenda, *National Post*, 29 July, A1, 2; Sheldon Alberts (1999) "Social Liberals demand universal daycare plan," *National Post*, 17 August, A1, 7.

30 André Picard (1999) "A working parent's paradise," *The Globe and Mail*, 14 September. The French Government has taken comparable measures to socialize the costs of child-rearing. Alan Freeman (1999) "Two nations divided along family line," *The Globe and Mail*, 17 September.

31 Standing Committee on Finance (1999).

32 Battle (1999, see n. 28 above); Ken Battle, Sherri Torjman, and Michael Mendelson (1999) *The Social Fundamentals* (Ottawa, Caledon Institute, February); House of Commons, Sub-Committee on Children and Youth at Risk (1999); Paul Wells (1999), "Social siblings lose their cool," *National Post*, 14 April.

33 Standing Committee on Finance (1999), *For the Benefit of our Children: Improving Tax Fairness*, Report #19 (Ottawa, House of Commons, June).

34 An alternative approach, suggested in the recent Throne Speech, would expand funding to local community groups that provide services directly to parents through the Community Assistance Program (Children) [CAP(c)], although such programs are vulnerable to politicization.

35 Revenue Canada (1987), "Registered Charities—Ancillary / Incidental Political Activities," Interpretation Circular 87-1 (Ottawa).

36 Ibid, 1-2.

37 Ware (1989), *Between Profit and State*; Drache (1999), 55.

38 Revenue Canada (1998), "Taxation Statistics for Individuals: 1996 Taxation Year" (Ottawa). Total donations declared on tax returns increased 14.4 per cent between 1995 and 1996. This total is about three times the level of growth expected had reported donations remained at their average 1991-95 levels relative to after-tax incomes.

39 Francis and Clemens (1999b).

40 Ontario, Fair Tax Commission (1993), 729-45.

41 Elections Canada (1999) "Contributions and Expenses Reported by Registered Political Parties" (Ottawa).

42 Corporate contributions account for about 1 per cent of charities' incomes. Cappe (1999).

43 *Income Tax Special Purpose Commissioners v. Pemsel* [1891], AC 531, cited in Boyle (1997).

44 Canada, Privy Council Office (1999b), 50.

45 Smucker (n.d.), 51-62.

46 Ibid.

47 Canada, Privy Council Office (1999b).

48 Boyle (1997); Drache (1999).

49 Boyle (1997); Drache (1999).

50 Revenue Canada (1987).

51 Drache (1999), 65; see also Boyle (1997); Canada, Privy Council Office (1999b).

52 Drache (1999), 66-67.

53 Les Whittington (1999) *The Banks* (Toronto: Stoddart); strategic voting campaigns mounted by major unions displaced relatively few PC incumbents in the 1999 Ontario election.

54 Smucker (n.d.); interview, Department of Finance.

55 Drache (1999), 24.

56 Compas, Inc. (1997); Ekos Research Associates (1999).

57 Salomon (1994); Robert O. Keohane and Joseph S. Nye, Jr. (1998) "Power and Interdependence in the Information Age." *Foreign Affairs* 77:5 (September-October), 81-94.

58 This argument is often raised by radical individualists and collectivists from opposite ends of the political spectrum. See Diane Francis (2000) "Certain tax exemptions are no longer valid," *National Post*, 28 September, c3; Bill Tieleman (2000) "It's time the Fraser Institute stopped taking taxpayers' charity," *National Post*, 31 August, c7.

59 Francis and Clemens (1999b).

60 Statistics Canada (1998a); Statistics Canada (1998b); Reed and Selbee (2000).

61 Canada, Privy Council Office (1999b), 47.

62 Drache (1999), 73-74.

63 Panel on Accountability and Governance in the Voluntary Sector (1998).

The Politics of Taxation and the New Economy

The future of taxation in Canada is likely to be one of gradual evolution rather than radical change. Tax levels and the distribution of taxes among different social and economic groups are the product of a wide range of political and economic trade-offs that defy radical restructuring, whether in the name of ideology or economic rationalism. Just as its evolution in recent years has usually resulted from incremental changes to existing rules rather than the introduction of radical innovations, Canada's tax system is likely to accommodate continuing social and economic changes through piecemeal adaptation, rather than root-and-branch tax reforms.

At least four key factors suggest that overall tax levels will continue to drift lower in coming years, although regional political dynamics and the workings of fiscal federalism suggest that tax reduction will be a higher priority in some provinces than others. The pressures to reduce tax rates reflect the ongoing roles of ideas, institutions, and interests in shaping fiscal and tax policies.

1. The politics and economics of neo-liberalism will continue to shape fiscal and tax policies, including the role of the tax system in delivering social policies and programs in most parts of Canada.

Canada is far too dependent on international trade and investment to return to the principles of economic nationalism and protectionism that motivated many liberals and most social democrats in the 1970s and 1980s. Canada's growing integration into North American and global markets is likely to impose fiscal and economic discipline on politicians, and set limits on differences between overall tax levels in Canada and the United States. At the same time, the political freedom of politicians and governments to pursue neo-liberal economic policies will depend on their ability to ensure that their benefits are distributed broadly across Canadian society.

Federal and provincial governments may choose to distribute these benefits through the tax-transfer system or through direct spending on social programs. However, as about one-third of Canadian tax filers are currently exempt from income taxes—a figure that is likely to grow in coming years—middle- and upper-income Canadians are unlikely to receive further tax reductions unless comparable benefits are made available to their neighbours who live below the tax threshold.

Continuing debates over tax rates and policies are likely to take place within the limits of this neo-liberal consensus. The trend of recent years is toward a flattening of progressive income tax rates so that the combined weight of multiple taxes does not discourage work effort, economic innovation, savings, and entrepreneurship, or encourage the channelling of resources into economically unproductive efforts at tax avoidance. This applies not only to top tax rates, but to tax thresholds for lower- and middle-income earners as well. In one sense, Alberta's new "single rate tax," which allows its citizens to earn enough to pay for the necessities of life tax-free, with a single rate of tax beyond that threshold, is the ultimate application of this principle.

However, given the vested interest that many Canadians have in a heavily redistributive tax system—a trend enhanced in recent years through the expansion of refundable tax credits for families—Saskatchewan's model of tax reform suggests a more likely direction for the future of Canada's tax system. This approach maintains a progressive tax rate structure, but reduces the differences in tax levels between different income groups in response to competition from its larger, more dynamic low-tax neighbour, Alberta. This change may also be accompanied by a shifting of the tax mix towards other forms of taxation, so long as most citizens are financially better off. Income tax rates on the broad middle class will gradually apply to all but the top 1 or 2 per cent of income earners, while lower-income earners are likely to be taxed primarily on their consumption and through payroll taxes to finance social insurance programs. This trend will be accentuated should governments choose to pre-fund a portion of the unfunded liability for health services to Canada's aging population through a new social insurance fund or medical savings accounts. At the same time, this approach reduces taxes on savings and long-term investments, including family farms and small businesses, in order to discourage capital flight and to promote business investment. In effect, the capacity to maintain social democratic social policies will become even more dependent on the pursuit of neo-liberal tax policies.

2. Governments that expect to define their own economic and social priorities, rather than react to events beyond their borders, must continue to

exercise centralized control over budgetary policies and spending levels if they hope to foster the economic growth needed to finance the social services demanded by an aging society.

The politics of fiscal discipline pursued by most Canadian governments in recent years are rooted in a paradox of democracy. The pursuit of major priorities, such as fiscal accountability, economic growth, and the preservation of core social programs, is increasingly detached from traditional forms of representation through parliament, legislatures and interest groups. For many governments, balancing economic and social priorities has come to depend on the unprecedented centralization of power in the hands of Prime Ministers or Premiers, a few senior cabinet ministers, and the officials of their central agencies.

Public opinion may accommodate or restrict changes to tax levels or the tax system. But, unless governments try to introduce radical changes, the complexities of the economy, the tax system, social policy, and the trade-offs needed to make them work together ensure that public opinion will be only a secondary factor in shaping these policies.

The capacity of any government, federal or provincial, to move toward a more aggressive policy of redistributing income or wealth through the tax system, or to engage in the politics of class warfare, is likely to be hindered by the growing mobility of capital and the increased ability of most Canadians to protect the value of their savings by investing them elsewhere. At the same time, the political reality that more than 40 per cent of Canadians—most of all, the growing population of seniors—receive significantly more in benefits than they pay in taxes guarantees the continuation of a sizeable welfare state.

Limits on labour mobility allow Canadian governments to impose higher taxes on personal income and consumption than their American neighbours to pay for higher levels of government spending, as long as taxpayers are getting reasonable value for their tax dollars. But, although an aging population creates spending pressures in both countries, it will also force sensible governments to run balanced budgets or small surpluses, pay down debt, and promote increased savings and investment in order to sustain valued social programs over the long term.

These realities, which transcend political ideologies, will force most governments to exercise fiscal prudence as a condition of continued economic growth and social cohesion. Implementing these policies will require a high degree of political skill and the ability to engage voters and interest groups in ways that allow political leaders to appear responsive to short-term political pressures and voter concerns without losing control over public finances.

The ongoing commitment of conservative governments in Alberta and Ontario, and of their counterparts in federal politics, to increasing spending on middle-class entitlements and sharp tax reductions for lower-income earners reflects this reality. Any government perceived to stray too far beyond the limits of this balance is likely to trigger an aggressive political reaction and corrective policies.

3. The ability of governments to combine the promotion of economic growth and higher living standards with the maintenance of existing social programs will be closely linked to their ability to develop a workable division of responsibilities among federal and provincial governments and with other national governments.

The steady growth of provincial governments, whose overall spending levels now exceed those of the federal government, and the ability of most provinces to pursue distinctive economic and social policies will make it difficult for the federal government to impose "one-size-fits-all" policies on an increasingly diverse and decentralized federation.

This suggests that the federal government will continue to emphasize increases in transfers to individuals in its social policies, either directly or through the tax system, while provincial governments will exercise greater control over the actual delivery of social programs such as health care, education, and children's services. The growing ability of most provinces to finance public services through their own revenues and the recent decentralization of the tax system point to greater diversity in tax and social policies. These changes may also lead to the cooperative development of national standards, based on federal-provincial consensus rather than the unilateral decisions of federal politicians. This process is likely to result in increased experimentation and some conflict, since provincial priorities may clash with those of the federal government. However, it may also facilitate the development of creative new policies that enable governments to respond to changing social conditions and the competing expectations of their citizens.

The continued progress of globalization, the internationalization of most significant Canadian companies and of markets for financial services, means that tax rules governing businesses and investment increasingly will be shaped by a combination of market forces and international agreements. Although these developments may reduce access to tax havens and other vehicles for creative tax avoidance, they may also force governments to depend on benefit-related taxes for a larger share of their revenues from business.

4. The spread of new technologies will continue to transform national and regional economies, while giving individuals greater opportunities to avoid government regulations that run contrary to their perceived interests and values.

The greatest, and most unpredictable, challenge in managing these pressures will come from the continuing development of technologies that allow both individuals and businesses to transcend international borders in their economic, social, and political activities. In recent years, both federal and provincial governments have used the tax system to foster the growth of Canada's "knowledge-based" economy through increased support for education and skills development, research and innovation, incentives for venture capital investment, and greater flexibility in the taxation of capital gains and tax-sheltered investment income. These trends are likely to continue, since more and more Canadians depend directly or through their long-term savings on new technologies and the capacity to use them for their economic and social well-being.

However, Canadians would be unwise to take these developments for granted. A previous generation that did so, during the late 1960s and 1970s, seriously overestimated the capacity of governmental and academic elites to predict and manage economic and social processes for the public good. Effective political leadership has been defined as the ability to sell the future to the present while living up to the commitments of the past. Many of Canada's economic problems during the past generation, and the inability of political leaders to sustain a political consensus on tax and spending policies except through the short-sighted expedient of chronic deficits, suggest that such leadership cannot be taken for granted.

Rather, the successful management of fiscal and tax policies requires a capacity to set priorities, adapt to changing circumstances, and build a consensus that enables competing economic, social, and regional interests to identify their own well-being with a broader national interest greater than the sum of its parts. Although economists, tax accountants, public servants, and interest groups can and should contribute to building this consensus, any set of policies that can sustain the test of public opinion and the democratic process ultimately is the product of political leadership and debate. Therefore, it should not be surprising if our tax system—and the taxes we pay—stubbornly refuses to conform either to economic theories or to political ideologies, but reflects past decisions and the policy trade-offs of the political process.

ACCRUED CAPITAL GAINS: the increase in the nominal value of a capital property. Most accrued capital gains are not subject to taxation.

ACCRUED INCOME: income or revenue legally owing to a taxpayer, but not yet received in cash. Historically, business income and taxation have been calculated on an accrual basis; individual and farm income have been calculated on a cash basis. Accrued capital gains (growth in nominal asset values) are not subject to taxation until assets are sold.

CAPITAL GAINS: the profit on the sale of a capital property, including securities (e.g., shares, mutual funds) land, buildings, and equipment. Capital gains were first subjected to income taxes as a result of the 1971 tax reforms. cf. *Inclusion rate of capital gains*

CAPITAL GAINS EXEMPTION: tax measure introduced in 1985 to exempt the first $500,000 of capital gains from income taxation. It was never fully implemented, except for owners of small businesses and family farms.

CAPITAL GAINS ROLLOVER: the deferral of capital gains taxes on profits from the sale of an eligible business when they are invested in another eligible business within a defined time period. This measure, introduced in 2000, is intended to promote venture capital investment and entrepreneurship.

COMPREHENSIVE INCOME TAXATION: inclusion of all forms of income, defined as the growth of "comprehensive net worth," in the tax base, with a minimal number of exemptions or deductions. This differs from comprehensive tax reform, which is a complete overhaul of one or more major elements of the tax system, but which may involve the rationalization rather than the wholesale elimination of tax preferences. Comprehensive income taxation was central to the tax reform proposals of the Carter Royal Commission in 1967.

CONSTITUTIONALIZATION OF INTERESTS: the transformation of interests, subject to the trade-offs of the political system, to "rights" and "entitlements" that are considered politically "untouchable." Governments attempt to reduce the benefits provided to particular groups by such policies at their political peril, unless they are able to obtain stakeholder consent for these changes, usually at the price of effective compensation for their losses.

CONSUMPTION-BASED TAX SYSTEM: System of taxation that exempts or defers savings, investment, and investment income from income taxes. However, interest payments on money borrowed to finance investments are not deductible from income. This approach to tax reform, advocated by US economists Robert Hall and Alvin Rabushka in *The Flat Tax*, has become the basis for some tax reform proposals in the United States. Canada's deferral of taxation on pension and retirement savings (e.g., RRSPs) and related investment income, until received by individuals as pension income, is a variant of the consumption-based tax system.

EFFECTIVE TAX RATE: taxes paid, as a percentage of total income or profit.

ECONOMIC EFFICIENCY: principle of tax design that taxes should have minimal impact on economic decision-making, so that economic resources are allocated to their most efficient uses in the marketplace. Economic research strongly suggests that the objectives of efficiency and growth are best served by low tax rates applied consistently on a broad tax base with minimal exemptions.

FEDERAL-PROVINCIAL TAX COLLEC-TION AGREEMENTS: originally signed in 1962, the tax collection agreements provide for the federal government to collect personal income taxes on behalf of nine provinces (Quebec being the one exception). Until 2000, provincial taxes were levied as a percentage of the federal tax payable. Changes introduced in 2001 allowed provinces to set their own tax rate structures, and to introduce tax credits and preferences consistent with the federal government's definition of taxable income (see Chapter 12). The federal government also collects corporate income taxes on behalf of seven provinces (all except Ontario, Quebec, and Alberta), and general sales taxes on behalf of Newfoundland, New Brunswick, and Nova Scotia.

FISCAL ILLUSION: the use of creative economic forecasting, budgeting, and accounting methods to disguise government taxation and spending decisions, or to enable Finance Ministers to exert greater control over the budgetary process.

FLAT TAXES: a tax system based on a single tax rate for income above a fixed threshold, rather than a progressive tax rate structure. During the late 1980s, three western provinces introduced flat taxes of 0.5 per cent to 2 per cent, which applied to taxable income and were not subject to tax credits, *in addition to* conventional progressive rate structures. Alberta's single rate tax, introduced in 2001, replaced both its supplemental flat tax *and* its traditional progressive rate structure which parallels the federal rate system. This system, which retains all deductions and credits from the existing federal tax system, is very different from the Hall-Rabushka model of *The Flat Tax*, which was the basis for US Presidential candidate Steve Forbes's tax reform proposals of 1996 and 2000. The Hall-Rabushka model is a form of comprehensive tax reform that would replace the existing *hybrid income-consumption tax system* with a *consumption-based tax system*.

HORIZONTAL EQUITY (also known as *neutrality*): the principle that taxpayers in similar circumstances should be subject to similar levels of taxation, and that taxpayers in different circumstances should be subject to different levels of taxation. A major challenge in applying this principle is to define the terms of comparison with other taxpayers.

HYBRID INCOME-CONSUMPTION TAX SYSTEM: Tax system that combines elements of traditional income taxation, which taxes all income when received by individuals and corporations, with elements of a *consumption-based tax system*, in which taxes on savings and investment income are deferred until this income is "consumed" by the taxpayer.

IMPUTED INCOME: income calculated on the basis of a formula imposed by law, rather than actual market values, cash or accrued income; income "which would have been received" if certain circumstances had occurred. Sometimes applied in law to tax income received "in kind" or subject to artificial transfer pricing techniques intended to avoid tax. Economist Henry Simons suggested its application to the "imputed" rental value of family homes and other assets which are used personally by the owner rather than to generate rental income.

INCLUSION RATE OF CAPITAL GAINS: The percentage of capital gains (and losses) subject to taxation or deduction from income (under limited circumstances). Inclusion rates on capital gains were 50 per cent between 1971 and 1988, 75 per cent between 1990 and 1999, and 50 per cent after October 2000. The partial taxation of capital gains is meant to offset the effects of inflation on long-term investments, and to provide for partial *integration* between personal and corporate income tax systems.

INDEXING: the regular adjustment of tax rates, brackets, deductions, and/or credits according to the annual change in the consumer price index (cpi) or other approved measurement of inflation in order to maintain consumer purchasing power, and to ensure that "governments do not profit from inflation at the expense of taxpayers." Full indexation of personal income tax rates was first introduced in 1973; indexation was scaled back in 1985 to apply only to annual inflation levels over 3 per cent. Full indexation was reintroduced in 2000.

INFLATION-RELATED TAX MEASURES: measures intended to reduce the effect of inflation on different aspects of taxation. Major inflation-related tax measures include full or partial *indexation* of tax rates, brackets, deductions, and credits, a *tax-based incomes policy,* and the inflation adjustment of investment income, proposed in a 1983 Finance Department discussion paper.

INTEGRATION OF PERSONAL AND CORPORATE INCOME TAXES: The principle that income should be taxed at the same rate whether retained by a corporation or transferred to shareholders. In Canada, taxes on small business corporations traditionally have been integrated with personal income taxes so that their owners are taxed more or less equally on income received as salaries, dividends, and capital gains. The *capital gains exemption* is an exception to this principle. There is partial integration in the taxation of large corporations. This is intended to provide more or less equal tax rates on capital gains and dividends earned by shareholders. However, taxes paid by large corporations are not credited against shareholder taxes payable. Similarly, there is no requirement that dividends eligible for the dividend tax credit be paid out of a corporation's tax-paid income, as would be required under a system of full integration.

MARGINAL TAX RATE: the tax rate imposed on each additional dollar of income.

NATIONAL ENERGY PROGRAM (NEP): Introduced in 1980, the NEP was part of the Trudeau government's so-called Third National Policy. It replaced existing federal energy *tax preferences* with a system of grants intended to give the federal government greater control over energy development and which favoured Canadian-owned oil companies over multinationals. Revised in 1981 and 1983 following agreements with Alberta and other energy-producing provinces, it was effectively eliminated in 1986 following the collapse of international oil prices.

NEUTRALITY: see *Horizontal equity.*

NOTIONAL VALUES: estimated incomes or prices based on industry averages or more-or-less arbitrary bureaucratic estimates rather than actual market incomes or prices. Used in income tax administration to estimate the levels of income collected in cash businesses (e.g., servers' tips in restaurants) and in sales tax administration to estimate sales levels in cases of "transfer pricing" between different divisions of the same company.

PIECEMEAL TAX REFORM: see Tax reform

POLICY INSTRUMENTS: term used to describe different types of policies used by governments to achieve their objectives. These may include direct government spending, including grants, loans and subsidies for individual or business activities; tax incentives or penalties for particular activities; different approaches to regulation, government ownership, or administration of business or service; and a wide range of other activities.

RETROACTIVE TAXATION: tax measures which are applied to economic activity (income or sales) which took place before these measures are presented to Parliament for its approval.

RETROSPECTIVE TAXATION: tax measures which have the effect of imposing higher taxes on investments and continuing transactions for which pricing commitments have already been made based on previous tax rules; for example, a fixed-price contract for the delivery of goods or services both before and after the coming into effect of the new tax measures.

REVENUE NEUTRALITY (IN TAXATION): policy changes which do not disguise an overall tax increase. In practice, this often means a reduction in overall tax revenues, in order to err on the side of political caution.

STOCK OPTIONS: The option to purchase a company's shares at a predetermined price. Often used as a means of compensating executives and employees which link compensation to the growth of shareholder value. The timing of taxes on stock options can render them of much greater or lesser value to their recipients.

STRUCTURAL BUDGET DEFICIT: The budget deficit estimated to remain when the economy is performing at its full capacity, in contrast to "cyclical" deficits that accompany periods of recession or slow economic growth. Full capacity is sometimes defined as non-inflation-inducing levels of "full employment." Economists generally warn against structural deficits since they force future generations to pay higher taxes to finance services that current governments (and taxpayers) are unwilling to pay for, thus subsidizing current consumption at the expense of future economic growth and living standards.

TAX-BASED INCOMES POLICY: Tax policy intended to discourage inflationary increases in personal incomes and corporate profits by imposing high surtaxes on disproportionate increases in incomes; considered and rejected by Department of Finance on several occasions between 1976 and 1982 due to difficulties in implementation and administration (e.g., distinguishing between "inflationary" rises in incomes or profits and those due to increased productivity, work effort, innovation, special circumstances, etc.)

TAX EXPENDITURES: reductions in tax rates or in definitions of taxable income which confer benefits on taxpayers relative to tax levels that would apply if all sources and forms of income were subject to the same, economically neutral definitions under a normative or idealized tax system, based on the assumption that taxes not collected from a taxpayer are the equivalent of a direct government expenditure. The federal Department of Finance has published periodic tax expenditure studies since 1979, using somewhat different concepts of normative taxation.

TAX PREFERENCES: reductions in tax payable relative to normal rules of taxation.

TAX REFORM: Major structural changes to the tax system, or a major rebalancing of government revenue sources. It may involve *comprehensive* or system-wide attempts at restructuring the rules and principles of major taxes (e.g., income taxes or sales taxes), or *piecemeal* approaches dealing with particular aspects of the tax structure.

TRANSITIONAL MEASURES: legal provisions to reduce negative economic effects of tax changes, usually by exempting existing economic commitments ("grandfathering") or by phasing in the new measures over a period of time. The failure of the 1981 tax reform budget to include transitional measures for many of its tax changes resulted in *retrospective taxation* for many taxpayers.

VERTICAL EQUITY: principle of taxation that tax liabilities should increase with income so that the necessary expenses of government will be distributed among individuals roughly in proportion to the economic advantages derived from their membership in society. Often associated with the idea of a progressive tax rate structure. Related to, but not synonymous with, the principle of "ability to pay."

S E L E C T E D

B I B L I O G R A P H Y

PRIMARY SOURCES

Alberta, Alberta Business Tax Review (2000) *Report and Recommendations* (Ottawa: Alberta Treasury, 13 September)

Alberta (2001) *Budget 2001: Fiscal Plan* (Edmonton: Ministry of Finance, April 24)

Angus Reid Associates (1988) *Canadians' View of Selected Public Policy Issues: The Results of a National Public Opinion Survey* (September)

Angus Reid Associates (1994a) "A Report on Public Attitudes towards Social Security Reform" (Ottawa: Angus Reid Associates)

Angus Reid Associates (1994b) "Social Security Reform: Wave II" (Ottawa, July)

Angus Reid Associates (1994c) "Social Security Reform: Wave III" (Ottawa, December)

Angus Reid Associates (1996) Public Opinion on Employment Insurance Initiatives (Ottawa, January)

Angus Reid Associates (1999) "Family matters" (Toronto, 27 September)

Angus Reid Associates (2000) "Views on the Federal Budget and How to Allocate Any Budget Surplus" (19 February)

Association of Canadian Pension Management (2000) *Dependence or Self-reliance: Which way for Canada's Retirement Income System* (Toronto, January)

Beatty, Perrin, Chairman (1984) *Report of the Task Force on Revenue Canada* (Ottawa: PC Party of Canada, 8 April)

Benson, E.J. (1970) "Letter to Chairman of House and Senate Finance Committees," House of Commons, *Debates*, 11 June, 8023

Benson, Hon. Edgar J. (1969) *White Paper on Tax Reform* (Ottawa: Department of Finance)

British Columbia (2001) "Government Honours Tax Cut Promise," release # 13/01 (Victoria: Ministry of Finance, 6 June)

Canada (1981) *Memorandum of Agreement between the Government of Canada and the Government of Alberta relating to the pricing and taxation of energy*, 1 September

Canada, Department of Finance (1994) *Agenda: Jobs & Growth–A New Economic Strategy for Canada* (Ottawa, October)

Canada, Human Resources Development Canada (1994) "Agenda: Jobs and Growth–Improving Social Security in Canada," (Ottawa, October)

Canada, Department of Finance (1997b) *Report of the Technical Committee on Business Taxation* (Ottawa, December)

Canada, Human Resources Development Canada (2000) Report of EI Chief Actuary (Ottawa, December)

Canada, Commission of Inquiry on Unemployment Insurance (1986) *Report* (Ottawa: Supply & Services Canada)

Canada Customs and Revenue Agency. *Income Statistics* (annual, since 1999)

Canada, Department of Energy, Mines and Resources (1980) *The National Energy Program* (Ottawa, October)

Canada, Department of Finance (1975) *Discussion Paper: Federal Sales and Excise Taxation* (Ottawa, June)

Canada, Department of Finance (1977) *Report of the Commodity Tax Review Group* (Ottawa, June)

Canada, Department of Finance (1981a) *Analysis of Federal Tax Expenditures for Individuals* (Ottawa, 12 November)

Canada, Department of Finance (1981b) "Notes on Transitional Arrangements and Adjustments Relating to Tax Measures Announced November 12, 1981"

Canada, Department of Finance (1986) *Guidelines for Tax Reform in Canada*, 23 October

Canada, Department of Finance (1991) *Personal Income Tax Coordination: The Federal-Provincial Tax Collection Agreements* (Ottawa, June)

Canada, Department of Finance (1996a) *Economic Reference Tables* (Ottawa, August)

Canada, Department of Finance (1996b) *Harmonized Sales Tax: Technical Paper* (Ottawa, 23 October)

Canada, Department of Finance (1997) *Budget Plan: 1997* (Ottawa, 18 February)

Canada, Department of Finance (1998a) *Fiscal References Tables* (Ottawa, November)

Canada, Department of Finance (1998b) *Tax Expenditures, 1998* (Ottawa)

Canada, Department of Finance (1998c) *Tax on Income, Report prepared by the Federal-Provincial Committee on Taxation for presentation to Ministers of Finance* (Ottawa, October).

Canada, Department of Finance (1999) *The Fiscal Balance in Canada* (Ottawa, 10 December)

Canada, Department of Finance (2000a) *Federal Administration of Provincial Taxes* (Ottawa, 25 January)

Canada, Department of Finance (2000b) *The Budget Plan 2000* (Ottawa, 28 February)

Canada, Department of Finance (2000c) *The Fiscal Balance in Canada* (Ottawa, August)

Canada, Department of Finance (2000d) *Fiscal Reference Tables* (Ottawa, September)

Canada, Department of Finance (2000e) *Economic Statement and Budget Update* (Ottawa, October)

Canada, Department of Finance (2000f) "Impact of Federal Income Tax Cuts on Families and Individuals–Update," Release # 2000-094 (Ottawa, 14 December)

Canada, Department of Finance (2000g) *Tax Expenditures and Evaluations* (Ottawa, September)

Canada, Department of Finance (2001) *Fiscal Reference Tables* (Ottawa, September)

Canada, Prime Minister's Office (1978) Transcripts "Notes for the Prime Minister's Address on National Television, " August 1

Canada, Privy Council Office (1999a) "Medium-Term Policy Planning: Canadian Taxation," August 31 [unpublished, document obtained under Access to Information Act]

Canada, Privy Council Office (1999b) *Working Together: A government of Canada/Voluntary Sector Initiative* (Ottawa, September)

Canada, Revenue Canada *Taxation Statistics* (annual to 1998)

Canada, Royal Commission on the Economic Union and Development Prospects for Canada (1985) *Report*, 3 vols. (Ottawa: Supply & Services Canada)

Canada, Royal Commission on Taxation (1967) *Report*, 5 vols. (Ottawa: Queen's Printer)

Canada, Standing Committee on Finance (1988a) "The GST in New Zealand," *Fifteenth Report, Minutes and Proceedings*, Issue # 147 (Ottawa: House of Commons, 15 March)

Canada, Standing Committee on Finance (1988b) "Stage II of Sales Tax Reform," *Sixteenth Report, Minutes and Proceedings*, Issue # 148 (Ottawa: House of Commons, 24 March)

Canada, Standing Committee on Finance (1994) *Replacing the GST: Options for Canada*, Ninth Report (Ottawa: House of Commons, June)

Canada, Standing Committee on Finance (1998) "Facing the Future: Challenges and Choices for a New Era," Report # 11 (Ottawa: House of Commons, December)

Canada, Standing Committee on Finance (1999) *Budget 2000: New Era ... New Plan* (Ottawa: House of Commons, December)

Canada, Task Force on Program Review (1986) *Report*, 21 vols. (Ottawa: Supply & Services Canada)

Council for Canadian Unity (2000) "Portraits of Canada 2000" (Ottawa, 27 November)

Crosbie, Hon. John C. (1979) *Budget Speech* (Ottawa: Department of Finance, 11 December)

Decima Research Ltd. (1985) *Report to the Department of Finance on Qualitative and Quantitative Research* (March-April)

Decima Research Ltd. (1987) *Nation-Wide Survey* (Ottawa: Department of Finance)

ESG Research and Communications (1994) "Attitudes towards the GST: Report to the Department of Finance" (Ottawa: Department of Finance, July)

Earnscliffe Research and Communications (1998) *Pre-Budget Survey, Presentation to Department of Finance*, February

Earnscliffe Research and Communications (1999a) *Pre-Budget Survey, Presentation to Department of Finance*, February

Earnscliffe Research and Communications (1999b) "Policy Priorities and Economic Assumptions, Presentation to Department of Finance," June

Earnscliffe Research and Communications (1999c) "Themes: Taxes and Productivity–Presentation to the Department of Finance" (Ottawa, August)

Earnscliffe Research and Communications (2000a) *Pre-Budget Survey, Presentation to Department of Finance*, February

Earnscliffe Research and Communications (2000b) "Post Budget Reaction" (Ottawa: Department of Finance, March)

Ekos Research Associates (1999) *Rethinking Government: Understanding conflicting priorities on tax cuts, social spending and productivity* (Ottawa, 20 August)

Ekos Research Associates (2000) *Rethinking Government: Canadian View of Emerging Issues* (Ottawa, 30 August)

Goodman, Wolfe (1983) "The Goodman Report" *Report of the Sales Tax Advisory Committee* (Ottawa: Department of Finance, May)

Lalonde, Hon. Marc (1982) *NEP Update* (Ottawa: Energy, Mines & Resources Canada, May)

Lalonde, Hon. Marc (1983) *Budget Speech* (Ottawa: Department of Finance, 19 April)

Lalonde, Hon. Marc (1984a) "Address to Canadian Club of Toronto," Release # 84-8 (Ottawa: Department of Finance, 23 January)

Lalonde, Hon. Marc (1984b) *Budget Speech* (Ottawa: Department of Finance, 15 February)

Lalonde, Hon. Marc (1984c) *Gains Sharing for a Stronger Economy* (Ottawa: Department of Finance, February)

MacEachen, Hon. Allan J. (1980) *Budget Speech* (28 October)

MacEachen, Hon. Allan J. (1981a) "Address, Conference Board of Canada" (Ottawa: Department of Finance, 6 May)

MacEachen, Hon. Allan J. (1981b) "Address to Vancouver Board of Trade" (Ottawa: Department of Finance, 6 July)

MacEachen, Hon. Allan J. (1981c) *Budget Speech* (Ottawa: Department of Finance, 12 November)

MacEachen, Hon. Allan J. (1981d) *Debates*, House of Commons (18 December), 14236-8

MacEachen, Hon. Allan J. (1982a) *The Budget Process: A paper on budget secrecy and proposals for broader consultation* (Ottawa: Department of Finance, April)

MacEachen, Hon. Allan J. (1982b) *Proposal to Shift the Federal Sales Tax to the Wholesale Trade Level* (Ottawa: Department of Finance, 30 April)

MacEachen, Hon. Allan J. (1982c) *The Budget* (28 June)

Manitoba, Lower Tax Commission (2000) *Final Report* (Winnipeg: Ministry of Finance, January)

Martin, Hon. Paul (1999a) "A Presentation to the House of Commons' Standing Committee on Finance" (Ottawa: Department of Finance, 2 November)

Martin, Hon. Paul (1999b) *Fiscal and Economic Update* (Ottawa: Department of Finance, 2 November)

Martin, Hon. Paul (2001) "Canada's New Economy: Winning the World Over" (Ottawa: Department of Finance, January)

Ontario, Fair Tax Commission (1993) *Fair Taxation in a Changing World* (Toronto: Queen's Printer)

Saskatchewan (1988) *Tax on Income: Discussion Paper* (Regina: Ministry of Finance, March)

Saskatchewan (1999a) "Redesign of Provincial Income Taxation," in *1999 Saskatchewan Budget* (Regina: Ministry of Finance, March)

Saskatchewan, Personal Income Tax Review Committee (1999b) *Report* (Regina: Ministry of Finance, November)

Statistics Canada (annual) *Income after tax, distributions by size in Canada*, Cat. # 13-210XPB (Ottawa)

Statistics Canada (1998a) *Caring Canadians, Involved Canadians: Highlights from the 1997 National Survey of Giving, Volunteering and Participating*, Cat. # 71-542-XIE (Ottawa, August)

Statistics Canada (1998b) "Charitable donors," *The Daily* (Ottawa, 3 December)

Statistics Canada (2000) *Income in Canada, 1998*, Cat. # 75-202-XIE (Ottawa, June)

Task Force on Taxation Policy (1986) *Taxation Policy Reform in Canada* (Ottawa: Business Council on National Issues, 1 October)

Turner, Hon. John N. (1973) *Budget Speech* (Ottawa: Department of Finance, 19 February)

United States, Executive Office of the President (2001) "The President's Agenda for Tax Relief" www.whitehouse.gov, 8 February

Wilson, Hon. Michael H. (1984) *Economic and Fiscal Statement* (Ottawa: Department of Finance, 8 November)

Wilson, Hon. Michael H. (1985a) "Address to National Economic Conference" (Ottawa, 22 March)

Wilson, Hon. Michael H. (1985b) *Budget Speech* (Ottawa: Department of Finance, 23 May)

Wilson, Hon. Michael H. (1987a) *The White Paper: Tax Reform 1987* (Ottawa: Department of Finance, 18 June)

Wilson, Hon. Michael H. (1987b) *Tax Reform, 1987: Sales Tax Reform* (Ottawa: Department of Finance, 18 June)

SECONDARY SOURCES

Aaron, Henry J., Harvey Galper, and Joseph A. Pechman, eds. (1988) *Uneasy Compromise: Problems of a hybrid income-consumption tax* (Washington, DC: The Brookings Institution)

Allan, J.R., D.A. Dodge, and S.N. Poddar (1974) "Indexing the Personal Income Tax: A Federal Perspective," *Canadian Tax Journal* XXII(4) (July-August), 355-69

Allan, J.R., S. Poddar, and N. LePan (1978) "The Effects of Tax Reform and Post-Reform Changes in the Federal Personal Income Tax," *Canadian Tax Journal* 26:1 (Jan-Feb.), 1-30

Allen, Douglas W., and John Richards, eds. (1999) *It Takes Two: The Family in Law and Finance* (Toronto: C.D. Howe Institute)

Asper, I.H. (1967) *The Carter Commission Report on Taxation—An Objective View* (Equitable Income Tax Foundation)

Aucoin, Peter (1986) "Organizational Change in the Machinery of the Federal Government: from rational management to brokerage politics," *Canadian Journal of Political Science* (January), 3-17

Aucoin, Peter (1995) *The New Public Management: Canada in Comparative Perspective* (Montreal: Institute for Research in Public Policy)

Austin, W.J.R. (2000) "Self-Government and Fiscal Relations: Fundamental Changes in the Relationship," *Canadian Tax Journal* 48(4), 1232-51.

Avi-Yonah, Reuven S. (2000) "Globalization, Tax Competition and the Fiscal Crisis of the Welfare State," 113 *Harvard Law Review* (May)

Axworthy, Thomas A., and Pierre Elliott Trudeau, eds. (1990) *Towards a Just Society: The Trudeau Years* (Markham, ON: Penguin Canada)

Bakvis, Herman (1991) *Regional Ministers* (Toronto: University of Toronto Press)

Beausejour, Louis, Munir Sheikh, and Baxter Williams (1998) "Experience Rating Employer EI Contributions," *Canadian Public Policy* XXIV:3 (September), 388-93

Bell, Daniel (1974) "The Public Household," *The Public Interest* 37 (Fall), 29-68.

Benson, Hon. Edgar J. (1988) "Attempts to Further the Goals of the Carter Report: The White Paper on Tax Reform," in *The Quest for Tax Reform*, ed. W. Neil Brooks (Toronto: Carswell)

Bercuson, David, J.L. Granatstein, and W.R. Young (1986) *Sacred Trust? Brian Mulroney and the Conservative Party in Power* (Toronto: Doubleday Canada)

Bird, Richard M. (1970) "The Tax Kaleidoscope: Perspectives on Tax Reform in Canada," *Canadian Tax Journal* (September-October), 444-73

Bird, Richard M., and Jack M. Mintz, eds. (1993) *Taxation to 2000 and Beyond*, Canadian Tax Paper # 93 (Toronto: Canadian Tax Foundation)

Bird, Richard M., and Jack M. Mintz (2000) "Tax Assignment in Canada: A Modest Proposal," in *Towards a New Mission Statement for Fiscal Federalism: State of the Federation, 2000-2001*, ed. Harvey Lazar (Kingston: Institute for Intergovernmental Relations, Queen's University), 263-89

Bird, Richard M., and Thomas Tsiopoulos (1997) "User Charges for Public Services: Potentials and Problems," *Canadian Tax Journal* 45:1

Blair Consulting Group (1999) "User Fees: Where does the Buck Stop?" (Ottawa: Alliance of Manufacturers and Exporters Canada, January)

Bliss, Michael (1987) *Northern Enterprise: Five Centuries of Canadian Business* (Toronto: McClelland and Stewart)

Boadway, Robin W., and Paul A.R. Hobson (1993) *Intergovernmental Fiscal Relations in Canada*, Canadian Tax Paper # 96 (Toronto: Canadian Tax Foundation)

Boadway, Robin W., and Harry M. Kitchen (1999) *Canadian Tax Policy*, 3rd ed, Canadian Tax Paper # 103 (Toronto: Canadian Tax Foundation)

Boskin, Michael J. (1978) *Federal Tax Reform: Myths and Realities* (San Francisco: Institute for Contemporary Studies)

Bossons, John (1969) "The Objectives of Taxation and the Carter Commission Proposals," *Canadian Public Administration* XII (Summer), 137-65

Bossons, John (1980) "The Effect of Inflation-Induced Hidden Wealth Taxes" (Toronto: Canadian Tax Foundation), 16-41

Boyle, Eleanor J. (1995) "The Education–Information–Propaganda Continuum" in *'Charitable Activity' under the Canadian Income Tax Act* (Ottawa: Voluntary Sector Roundtable)

Boyle, Francis J. (1997) "'Charitable Activity' Under the Canadian Income Tax Act: Definition, Process and Problems" (Ottawa: Voluntary Sector Roundtable, January)

Bradford, Neil (1998) *Commissioning Ideas: Canadian National Policy Innovation in Comparative Perspective* (Toronto: Oxford University Press)

Brennan, Geoffrey, and James M. Buchanan (1980) *The Power to Tax: Analytical Foundations of a Fiscal Constitution* (Cambridge: Cambridge University Press)

Brittan, Samuel (1977) "Can Democracy Manage an Economy?" in *The End of the Keynesian Era*, ed. Robert Skidelsky (London: Macmillan Press)

Brooks, Neil (1981) "Making Rich People Richer," *Saturday Night* (July), 30-35

Brooks, Stephen, and Andrew Stritch (1991) *Business & Government in Canada* (Toronto: Prentice-Hall)

Brooks, W. Neil, ed. (1979) "Tax Expenditure Analysis," *Canadian Taxation* 1(2) (Summer)

Brooks, W. Neil, ed. (1988). *The Quest for Tax Reform: The Royal Commission on Taxation Twenty Years Later* (Toronto: Carswell)

Brown, Robert D. (1987) "Tax Reform: Can we do better the second time around?" in *Report of Proceedings of the Thirty-Eighth Tax Conference, 1986* (Toronto: Canadian Tax Foundation) Brown, Robert D. (1999) "Tax Reform and Tax Reduction: Let's Do the Job Right," 47 *Canadian Tax Journal* (2), 182-205

Brown, Robert D. (2000) "The Impact of the U.S. on Canada's Tax Strategy," *Isuma* 1:1 (Spring), 70-78

Bryce, R.B. (1988) "Implementing the Report: Processes and Issues," in *The Quest for Tax Reform*, ed. W. Neil Brooks (Toronto: Carswell), 39-42

Bryden, John, MP (1994) "Special Interest Group Funding" (mimeo, November)

Buchanan, James M. (1980) "Rent Seeking and Profit Seeking," in *Towards a Theory of a Rent-Seeking Society*, ed. James M. Buchanan, Robert Tollison, and Gordon Tullock (College Station, TX: Texas A&M University Press), 3-15

Buchanan, James M. (1985) *Liberty, Market and State: Political Economy in the 1980s* (New York: New York University Press)

Buchanan, James M. (1991) *The Economics and Ethics of Constitutional Order* (Ann Arbor: University of Michigan Press)

Buchanan, James M. (1999) "Politics without Romance," in *The Logical Foundation of Constitutional Liberty, Collected Works*, Vol. 1 (Indianapolis: Liberty Fund), 45-59

Buchanan, James M., and Richard A. Musgrave (1999) *Public Finance and Public Choice: Two Contrasting Visions of the State* (Cambridge, MA: MIT Press)

Bukovetsky, M.W. (1975) "The Mining Industry and the Great Tax Reform Debate," in *Pressure Group Behaviour in Canadian Politics*, ed. A. Paul Pross (Toronto: McGraw Hill), 87-114

Bukovetsky, Meyer, and Richard M. Bird (1972). "Tax Reform in Canada: A Progress Report," *National Tax Journal* 25 (March), 15-41

Cahill, Jack (1986) *John Turner: The Long Run* (Toronto: McClelland & Stewart)

Campbell, Robert M., and Leslie A. Pal (1991) "Game, Set and Tax: The Advent of the GST," in *The Real Worlds of Canadian Politics*, 2nd ed., (Peterborough, ON: Broadview Press), 346-416

Canadian Tax Foundation (1983) *Symposium on the Simplification of the Small Business Provisions of the Income Tax Act*

Canadian Tax Foundation (2000) "Special Report: Proceedings of a Policy Conference on Aboriginal Tax, Treaties and Self-Government," *Canadian Tax Journal* 48(4) and 48(5)

Cappe, Mel (1999) "Building a New Relationship with the Voluntary Sector," Speech to Association of Professional Executives (Ottawa: Privy Council Office, 31 May)

Chrétien, Jean (1994). *Straight from the Heart*, 2nd ed. (Toronto: Key Porter)

Chwialkowska, Luiza (1999a) "Canadians Want Relief Targeted to Poorest," *National Post*, 16 April, A1

Chwialkowska, Luiza (1999b) "Canada to have second-highest business tax rate in OECD: report," *National Post*, 5 November

Cnossen, Sijbren (1988) "Comment," in *World Tax Reform, A progress report*, ed. Joseph Pechman (Washington, DC, The Brookings Institution)

Cohen, Marshall A. (1978) "The Budget Process and Income Tax Changes," in *Report of Proceedings of the Twenty-Ninth Tax Conference, 1977* (Toronto: Canadian Tax Foundation)

Coleman, William D. (1988) *Business and Politics: A Study in Collective Action* (Toronto: University of Toronto Press)

Conklin, David W., and Darroch A. Robertson (1999) "Tax Havens: Investment Distortions and Policy Options," *Canadian Public Policy* xxv(3) (September), 333-44

Corak, Miles, ed. (1998) *Government Finances and Generational Equity* (Ottawa: Industry Canada, February)

Courchene, Thomas J. (1991) "Towards the Reintegration of Social and Economic Policy," in *Canada at Risk?*, ed. G. Bruce Doern and Bryne B. Purchase (Toronto: C.D. Howe Institute), 125-67

Courchene, Thomas J. (1999) "National vs. Regional Concerns: A Provincial Perspective on the Role and Operation of the Tax Collection Agreements," *Canadian Tax Journal* 47:4, 861-89

Crozier, Michel, et al. (1975) *The Crisis of Democracy, Report on the Governability of Democracies to the Trilateral Commission* (New York: New York University Press)

Davies, James B. (1998) *Marginal Tax Rates: High and Getting Higher* (Toronto: C.D. Howe Institute)

Dicey, A.V. (1915) *Introduction to the Study of the Law of the Constitution*, 8th ed. (London: Macmillan)

Dodge, David A. (1989) "Economic Objectives of Tax Reform," in *The Economic Aspects of Tax Reform*, ed. J. Mintz and J. Whalley (Toronto: Canadian Tax Foundation), 37-41

Dodge, David A. (1998) "Reflections on the Role of Fiscal Policy," *Canadian Public Policy XXIV:3* (September), 275-89

Doern, G. Bruce (1982) "Liberal Priorities: The Limits of Scheming Virtuously," in *How Ottawa Spends: National Policy and Economic Development 1982* (Toronto, Lorimer)

Doern, G. Bruce, ed. (1985). *The Politics of Canadian Economic Policy* (Toronto: University of Toronto Press)

Doern, G. Bruce, and Brian W. Tomlin (1991) *Faith and Fear: The Free Trade Story* (Toronto: Stoddart)

Doern, G. Bruce, and Glen Toner (1985) *The Politics of Energy, The Development and Implementation of the National Energy Program* (Toronto: Methuen)

Drache, Arthur B.C. (1999) "Charities, Public Benefit and the Canadian Income Tax System," mimeo

Drache, Arthur (2000) "Beware the resurrection of death duties," *Financial Post*, June 28, 10

Drummond, Don (2001) "Ottawa's Fiscal Risks," *Financial Post*, 21 February, c15

Duclos, Jean-Yves, and Julie Gingras (2000) "A Roadmap for Federal Tax Reform," *Canadian Tax Journal* 48(2), 303-39

Dyck, Dagmar, and Bev Dahlby (1999) "Alberta and the Provincialization of the Canadian Fiscal System," (Edmonton: Institute for Public Economics, University of Alberta, 17 September), mimeo

Eichner, Matthew, and Todd Sinai (2000) "Capital Gains Realizations and Tax Rates: New Evidence from Time Series," *National Tax Journal* LIII(3), Part 2 (September), 663-81

Feldstein, Martin (1976) "Compensation in Tax Reform," *National Tax Journal* 29(2) (June), 123-30

Fortin, Pierre (1999) *The Canadian Standard of Living: Is there a way up?* (Toronto: C.D. Howe Institute, 19 October)

Fortin, Pierre (2000) "Less Taxes and Better Taxes: Principles for Tax Cuts and Tax Reform," *Canadian Tax Journal* 48:1, 92-100

Francis, Johanna, and Jason Clemens (1999a) "Public and Private Charities: Ontario as a Case Study," *Fraser Forum* (June)

Francis, Johanna, and Jason Clemens (1999b) "Charitable Donations and Tax Incentives," *Fraser Forum* (June)

Freeman, Alan (1992) "The department that counts," *The Globe and Mail*, 1 June, A1, 5.

Freeman, Alan (1995) "Liberal promise on GST creating national discord," *The Globe and Mail*, 12 August

Fried, Joel, and Ron Wirick (1999) "Assessing the Foreign Property Rule: Regulation without Reason," *Commentary # 133* (Toronto: C.D. Howe Institute, December)

Fuller, Lon L. (1969) "Human Interaction and the Law," *American Journal of Jurisprudence* 14, 1-38

Gallup Canada (1990) "72% believe tax system is less fair," *Toronto Star*, 10 December, A15

Gillespie, W. Irwin (1983) "Tax Reform: the Battlefield, the Strategies, the Spoils," *Canadian Public Administration* 26(2) (Summer), 182-202

Gillespie, W. Irwin (1991) *Tax, Borrow and Spend* (Toronto: Oxford University Press)

Good, David A. (1980) *The Politics of Accommodation* (Ottawa: School of Public Administration, Carleton University)

Goodman, Wolfe D. (1988a) "The Importance of Balance in the Tax System," in *The Quest for Tax Reform*, ed. W. Neil Brooks (Toronto: Carswell), 139-42

Goodman, Wolfe D. (1988b) Submission to Commons' Finance Committee, *Minutes and Proceedings*, Issue # 161A (Ottawa: House of Commons, 4 May)

Gourevitch, Peter (1989) "Keynesian Politics: The Political Sources of Economic Policy Choices," in *The Political Power of Economic Ideas*, ed. Peter A. Hall (Princeton: Princeton University Press)

Graves, Frank L., with T. Dugas and P. Beauchamp (1999) "Identity and National Attachments in Contemporary Canada," in *Canada: The State of the Federation 1998-99*, ed. Harvey Lazar and Tom McIntosh (Kingston: Institute of Intergovernmental Relations)

Greenspon, Edward, and Anthony Wilson-Smith (1998) *Double Vision: The Inside Story of the Liberals in Power* (Toronto: Doubleday Canada)

Hale, Geoffrey (1984) "Reforming Revenue Canada," *Policy Options* 5(5) (September), 56-62

Hale, Geoffrey E. (1996) *The Politics of Canadian Tax Policy: 1978-88*, Ph.D. Dissertation, University of Western Ontario

Hale, Geoffrey E. (1997) "Learning from the Past: Mark Lalonde's Pension Reforms of 1982-4," in *The Welfare State in Canada: Past, Present, Future*, ed. R.B. Blake et al. (Toronto: Irwin), 156-70

Hale, Geoffrey E. (1998) "Reforming Employment Insurance: Transcending the Politics of the Status Quo," *Canadian Public Policy* XXIV:4 (December), 429-53

Hale, Geoffrey (1999) "Living Standards and the Politics of the Fiscal Dividend," paper presented to Canadian Political Science Association, June

Hale, Geoffrey E. (2000a) "Managing the Fiscal Dividend: The Politics of Selective Activism," in *How Ottawa Spends: 2000-2001*, ed. Leslie A. Pal (Toronto: Oxford University Press)

Hale, Geoffrey E. (2000b) "The Tax on Income and the Decentralization of the Personal Income Tax System," in *Canada: State of the Federation 2000*, ed. Harvey Lazar (Kingston: Institute for Intergovernmental Relations, Queen's University), 235-62

Hale, Geoffrey E. (2001) "Priming the Electoral Pump: Framing Budgets for a Renewed Mandate," in *How Ottawa Spends: 2001-02*, ed. Leslie A. Pal (Toronto: Oxford University Press), 29-60

Hall, Peter A., ed. (1989) *The Political Power of Economic Ideas: Keynesianism Across Nations* (Princeton, NJ: Princeton University Press)

Hall, Robert E., and Alvin Rabushka (1985) *The Flat Tax* (Stanford, CA: Hoover Institution Press).

Hartle, Douglas (1982) *The Revenue Budget Process of the Government of Canada* (Toronto: Canadian Tax Foundation)

Hartle, Douglas (1985) *The Political Economy of Tax Reform*, Discussion Paper # 290 (Ottawa: Economic Council of Canada)

Hartle, Douglas (1988a) *The Expenditure Budget Process of the Government of Canada: A Public Choice-Rent Seeking Approach* (Toronto: Canadian Tax Foundation)

Hartle, Douglas (1988b) "Some Analytical, Political and Normative Lessons from Carter," in *The Quest for Tax Reform*, ed. W. Neil Brooks (Toronto: Carswell)

Hartle, Douglas (1993) *The Federal Deficit*, Discussion Paper # 93-30, Government and Competitiveness Series (Kingston, ON: School of Policy Studies, Queen's University)

Head, John G., and Richard M. Bird (1983). "Tax Policy Options in the 1980s," in *Comparative Tax Studies*, ed. Sijbren Cnossen (Amsterdam, North Holland)

Heard, Andrew (1991) *Canadian Constitutional Conventions: The Marriage of Law and Politics* (Toronto: Oxford University Press)

Helliwell, John F. (1970) "Inflation and Tax Reform," *Canadian Tax Journal* 18(2) (March-April), 124-30

Helliwell, John F. (2000) *Globalization: Myths, Facts and Consequences* (Toronto: C.D. Howe Institute, 23 October)

Hendricks, Kenneth, Raphael Amit, and Diana Whistler (1997) "Business Taxation of Small and Medium-sized Enterprises in Canada," Working Paper 97-11 (Ottawa: Department of Finance, October)

Hoy, Claire (1987) *Friends in High Places* (Toronto: Key Porter)

Huggett, Donald R. (1986) "The Minimum Income Tax," in *Report of Proceedings of the Thirty-Seventh Tax Conference, 1985* (Toronto: Canadian Tax Foundation)

Jackson, Andrew (2000) "Tax Cuts: the implications for growth and productivity," *Canadian Tax Journal* 48:2, 276-302

James, Steven, Chris Matier, Humam Sakhnini, and Munir Sheikh (1995) "The Economics of Canada Pension Plan Reforms," Working Paper 95-09 (Ottawa: Department of Finance, November)

Jenkins, Glenn P. (1977) *Inflation: Its Financial Impact on Business in Canada* (Ottawa: Economic Council of Canada)

Jog, Vijay, and Jianmin Tang (1998) "Tax Reforms, Debt Shifting and Corporate Tax Revenues: Multinational Corporations in Canada," Working Paper 97-14 (Ottawa: Department of Finance, February)

Johnston, Donald (1986) *Up the Hill* (Montreal: Optimum)

KPMG (1999) "Transfer Pricing–Time for Action on Canada's New Rules," *Canadian Tax Letter*, October

Kaye, Philip (1999) "The Distinction Between a Fee and a Tax: The Case of *Re Eurig Estate*," Backgrounder 33, Legislative Research Service (Toronto: Ontario Legislative Library, July)

Kesselman, Jonathan R. (1988) "Direct Expenditures vs. Tax Expenditures for Economic and Social Policy," in *Tax Expenditures and Government Policy*, ed. Neil Bruce (Kingston: John Deutsch Institute for the Study of Economic Policy)

Kesselman, Jonathan R. (1998) "Economics vs. Politics in Canadian Payroll Tax Policies," *Canadian Public Policy* XXIV:3 (September), 381-87

Kesselman, Jonathan R. (1999) "Base Reforms and Rate Cuts for a Revitalized Personal Tax," *Canadian Tax Journal* 47:2, 210-41

Kesselman, Jonathan R. (2000) "Flat Taxes, Dual Taxes, Smart Taxes: Making the Best Choices," *Policy Matters* 1:7 (Montreal: Institute for Research in Public Policy, November)

King, Phillip, and Harriet Jackson (2000), "Public Finance Implications of Population Ageing," Working Paper 2000-08 (Ottawa: Department of Finance)

Kneebone, Ronald D., and Kenneth J. McKenzie (1999) "Fiscal Policy in Canada," *Canadian Public Policy* XXV:4 (December)

Krishna, Vern (1993) *The Fundamentals of Canadian Tax Law*, 4th ed. (Toronto: Carswell)

Kristol, Irving (1974) "On Taxes, Poverty and Equality," *The Public Interest* 37 (Fall), 3-28

LeBreux, Paul (1999) "Eurig Estate: Another Day, Another Tax," *Canadian Tax Journal* 47(5), 1126-63

Lewis, David (1992) *Louder Voices: The Corporate Welfare Bums* (Toronto: James Lorimer)

Lipsey, Richard G. (1996) *Economic Growth, Technological Change and Canadian Economic Policy* (Toronto: C.D. Howe Institute, November)

Lipsey, Richard, and Douglas Purvis (1985) "The Poll-icies of Mulroney's reign," *The Financial Post*, 2 March, 9

Luffman, Jacqueline (1999) "The Gift and the Giver: Individual Giving to Culture Organizations in Canada," *Focus on Culture* 11(2), Cat. # 87-004-XPE (Ottawa: Statistics Canada, August)

Lush, Patricia (1981) "Soft cost deduction changes jeopardize 20,000 rental units," *The Globe and Mail*, 17 November, B2

MacDonald, Les (1988) "Why the Carter Commission Had To Be Stopped," in W. Neil Brooks, *The Quest for Tax Reform* (Toronto: Carswell)

Macdonald, Leslie T. (1985) *Taxing Comprehensive Income: Power and Participation in Canadian Politics: 1962-1972*, Unpublished Ph.D. Dissertation (Carleton University)

Macpherson, C.B. (1978) "The Meaning of Property," in *Property: Mainstream and Critical Positions* (Toronto: University of Toronto Press)

Maslove, Allan M. (1989) *Tax Reform in Canada: Its Process and Impact* (Halifax: Institute for Research in Public Policy)

Maslove, Allan M., ed. (1993). *Fairness in Taxation* (Toronto: University of Toronto Press)

Maslove, Allan M., and Heidi I. Eicher (1987) "Reforming Taxes: Where to go and how to get there," in *How Ottawa Spends: 1987*, ed. Michael Prince (Toronto: Methuen), 176-210.

Maslove, Allan M., Michael J. Prince, and G. Bruce Doern (1986) *Federal and Provincial Budgeting* (Toronto: University of Toronto Press)

McCall-Newman, Christina (1980) *Grits: An Intimate Portrait of the Liberal Party* (Toronto: Macmillan of Canada)

McCall-Newman, Christina, and Stephen Clarkson (1994) *Trudeau and Our Times*, Vol. 2, *The Heroic Delusion* (Toronto: McClelland and Stewart)

McCallum, John (1999) "Towards a Medium-Term Fiscal Anchor for Canada" (Toronto: Royal Bank Economics, August)

McDougall, John N. (1985) "Natural Resources and National Policies," in *The Politics of Canadian Economic Policy*, ed. G. Bruce Doern (Toronto: University of Toronto Press), 163-219

McFarlane, Susan, and Robert Roach (1999) *Making a Difference: Volunteers and Non-Profits* (Calgary: Canada West Foundation)

McMahon, Fred (2000) *The Road to Growth* (Halifax: Atlantic Institute for Market Studies)

McQuaig, Linda (1987) *Behind Closed Doors: how the rich won control of Canada's tax system and ended up richer* (Toronto: Viking/Penguin)

Meade, J.D., Chairman (1978) *The Structure and Reform of Basic Taxation* (London: George Allen & Unwin)

Michalos, Alex C. (1999) "The Tobin Tax: A good idea whose time has *not* passed," *Policy Options* (October), 64-67

Milne, David (1986) *Tug of War* (Toronto: James Lorimer)

Mintz, Jack M. (1999) "Why Canada Must Undertake Business Tax Reform Soon" (Toronto: C.D. Howe Institute, November)

Mintz, Jack M. (2000a) "Competitiveness and Economic Growth in Ontario," (Toronto: C.D. Howe Institute, 12 February)

Mintz, Jack M. (2000b) "The February 2000 Federal Budget's Business Tax Measures" (Toronto: C.D. Howe Institute, 23 March)

Mintz, Jack M. (2000c) "Reforming the Tax Cut Agenda," *Canadian Tax Journal* 48(3), 689-709

Mintz, Jack M., and Finn Poschmann (1999) "Tax Reform, Tax Reduction: The Missing Framework," *Commentary # 121* (Toronto: C.D. Howe Institute, February)

Mintz, Jack M., and John Sargent (1998) "The Business Tax Structure and Canada's Economic Performance," *Business Tax Review: 1998 Corporate Tax Management Conference* (Toronto: Canadian Tax Foundation)

Mintz, Jack M., and Thomas A. Wilson (2000) "Capitalizing on Cuts to Capital Gains Taxes," *Commentary # 137* (Toronto: C.D. Howe Institute, February)

Mitrusi, Andrew, and James Poterba (2000) "The Distribution of Payroll and Income Tax Burdens," *National Tax Journal* LIII:3, Part 2, (September), 765-94

National Council of Welfare (1976) *The Hidden Welfare System* (Ottawa, November)

The National Finances (Toronto: Canadian Tax Foundation, annual)

Nordlinger, Eric A. (1981) *On the Autonomy of the Democratic State* (Cambridge, MA: Harvard University Press)

O'Connor, James (1973) *The Fiscal Crisis of the State* (New York: St. Martin's Press)

Olewiler, Nancy (1998) "Let's Use Benefit Taxes More," *Policy Options* (December), 24-27

Olson, Mancur (1982) *The Rise and Decline of Nations* (New Haven, CT: Yale University Press) Osberg, Lars (1993). "The Problem of Equity in Taxation," in *Fairness in Taxation*, ed. Allan M. Maslove (Toronto: University of Toronto Press)

Panel on Accountability and Governance in the Voluntary Sector (1998) *Helping Canadians Help Canadians: Improving Governance and Accountability in the Voluntary Sector, A Discussion Paper* (Ottawa, May)

Panitch, Leo (1993) "Beyond the Crisis of the Tax State: From Fair Taxation to Structural Reform," in *Fairness in Taxation*, ed. Allan M. Maslove (Toronto: University of Toronto Press), 135-59

Peacock, Anthony A., ed. (1996) *Rethinking the Constitution: Perspectives of Canadian Constitutional Reform, Interpretation and Theory* (Don Mills, ON: Oxford University Press)

Perry, David B. (1999) "The Shadow Tax System," *Canadian Tax Highlights* 7:1, 19 (January), 3

Perry, J. Harvey (1982) *Background on Current Fiscal Problems*, Canadian Tax Paper # 68 (Toronto: Canadian Tax Foundation)

Perry, J. Harvey (1989) *A Fiscal History of Canada–The Postwar Years*, Canadian Tax Paper # 85 (Toronto: Canadian Tax Foundation), 151-65

Perry, J. Harvey (1990) *Taxation in Canada*, 5th ed., Canadian Tax Paper # 8 (Toronto: Canadian Tax Foundation)

Peters, B. Guy (1991) *The Politics of Taxation: A Comparative Approach* (Cambridge, MA: Blackwell)

Phillips, Susan D. (1995) "Redefining Government Relationships with the Voluntary Sector: On Great Expectations *and* Sense and Sensibility" (Ottawa: Voluntary Sector Roundtable, November)

Poddar, Satya, and Morley D. English (1999) "Canadian Taxation of Personal Investment Income," *Canadian Tax Journal* 47:5, 1270-1304

Poddar, Satya, Tom Neubig, and Morley English (2000) "Emerging Trends: The Tax Mix and the Taxation of Capital," *Canadian Tax Journal* 48:1, 101-23

Poschmann, Finn, and John Richards, (2000) "How to Lower Taxes and Improve Social Policy: A Case of Eating Your Cake and Having It Too," *Commentary # 136* (Toronto: C.D. Howe Institute, February)

Putnam, Robert D. (1995) "Bowling alone: America's declining social capital," *Journal of Democracy* 6:1 (January), 65-78

Putnam, Robert D. (2000) *Bowling Alone: The Decline and Recovery of Civil Society* (New York: Simon & Schuster)

Reed, Paul B., and L. Kevin Selbee (2000) "Patterns of Citizen Participation and the Civic Core in Canada," mimeo, prepared for presentation at the 29th ARNOVA Annual Conference, New Orleans, Louisiana, 16-18 November

Richards, John (2000) "Now That the Coat Fits the Cloth...," *Commentary # 143* (Toronto: C.D. Howe Institute, June)

Robertson, Ronald (1988) "The House of Commons Committee and the Aftermath of the Royal Commission on Taxation," in *The Quest for Tax Reform*, ed. W. Neil Brooks (Toronto: Carswell)

Robson, William B.P. (2001) "Will the Baby Boomers Bust the Health Budget," *Commentary # 148* (Toronto: C.D. Howe Institute, February)

Robson, William B.P., Jack M. Mintz, and Finn Poschmann (2000) "Budgeting for Growth: Promoting Prosperity with Smart Fiscal Policy," *Commentary # 134* (Toronto: C.D. Howe Institute, February)

Russell, Peter H. (1993) *Constitutional Odyssey*, 2nd ed. (Toronto: University of Toronto Press)

St. Hilaire, France, and John Whalley (1985) "Reforming Taxes: Some Problems of Implementation," in *Approaches to Economic Well-Being*, ed. David Laidler (Toronto: University of Toronto Press)

Sargent, John (1988) "Introduction," in *Tax Expenditures and Government Policy*, ed. N. Bruce (Kingston, ON: John Deutch Institute for the Study of Economic Policy, Queen's University)

Savoie, Donald J. (1990) *The Politics of Public Spending in Canada* (Toronto: University of Toronto Press)

Savoie, Donald J. (1999) *Governing from the Centre: The Concentration of Power in Canadian Politics* (Toronto: University of Toronto Press)

Sawatzky, John (1991) *The Politics of Ambition* (Toronto: Macfarlane, Walter and Ross)

Scoffield, Heather (2000) "OECD tells tax havens to change or face sanctions," *The Globe and Mail*, 27 June, B1, 12

Shearmur, Richard (2000) "Quebec signs on to *The New Barbarian Manifesto*," *Policy Options* 21:10 (December), 42-44

Sheppard, Anthony (1986) "Taxation Policy and the Canadian Economic Union," in *Fiscal Federalism*, ed. Mark Krasnick (Toronto: University of Toronto Press), 154-59

Simpson, Jeffrey (1980) *The Discipline of Power* (Toronto: Personal Library)

Smiley, Donald V. (1987) *The Federal Condition in Canada*, (Toronto: McGraw-Hill-Ryerson)

Smith, Roger S. (1988) *Tax Expenditures, Tax Expenditures and Government Policy* (Kingston, ON: John Deutsch Institute for the Study of Economic Policy, Queen's University)

Smucker, Bob, *The Non-Profit Lobbying Guide*, 2nd ed. (Washington, DC, Independent Sector, n.d.)

Stanbury, W.T. (1986) *Business Government Relations in Canada* (Toronto: Methuen)

Stein, Herbert, ed. (1988) *Tax Policy in the Twenty-First Century* (Toronto: Wiley & Sons)

Steinmo, Sven (1989) "Political Institutions and Tax Policy in the United States, Sweden and Britain," *World Politics* XLI(4) (July), 501-35

Stewart, Edison (1999) "Taxing Families: What's fair?" *Toronto Star* (21 March)

Stewart, Ian A. (1990) "Global Transformation and Economic Policy," in *Towards a Just Society: The Trudeau Years*, ed. Thomas A. Axworthy and Pierre Elliott Trudeau (Markham, ON: Penguin Books Canada), 107-25

Surrey, Stanley B. (1973) *Pathways to Tax Reform* (Cambridge, MA: Harvard University Press)

Surrey, Stanley, and Paul R. McDaniel (1985) *Tax Expenditures* (Cambridge, MA: Harvard University Press)

Tarchys, Daniel (1983) "The Scissors Crisis of Public Finance," *Policy Sciences* 15, 205-24

Taylor, Amy, Mark Jaccard, and Nancy Olewiler (1999) "Environmental Tax Shift: A Discussion Paper for British Columbians" (Victoria: Ministry of Finance and Corporate Relations, October)

Thirsk, Wayne (1993) *Fiscal Sovereignty and Tax Competition,* Discussion Paper 93-08, Government and Competitiveness (Kingston, ON: School of Policy Studies, Queen's University)

Thorburn, Hugh (1985) *Interest Groups in the Canadian Federal System* (Toronto: University of Toronto Press)

Tobin, James (1997) *Good Taxes: The Case for Taxing Foreign Currency Exchange and Other Financial Transactions* (Science for Peace and Dundurn Press)

Torjman, Sherri (1997) *Civil Society: Reclaiming our Humanity* (Ottawa: Caledon Foundation, March)

Toulin, Alan (1999) "Ministers seek tax cuts that won't affect their revenues," *National Post* 9 December, A7

Treff, Karin, and David B. Perry *Finances of the Nation,* annual (Toronto: Canadian Tax Foundation, 1995)

Velk, Tom, and A.R. Riggs (2000) "Brian Mulroney and the Economy: Still the Man to Beat," (Montreal: North American Studies Program, McGill University, unpublished manuscript)

Vercheres, Bruce, and Jacques Bernier (1987) "Rights and Freedoms in Tax Matters," in *Proceedings of the Thirty-Eighth Tax Conference* (Toronto: Canadian Tax Foundation)

Vermaeten, Frank, W. Irwin Gillespie, and Arndt Vermaeten (1994) "Tax Incidence in Canada," Canadian Tax Journal 42(2), 348-416

Wagner, Don (2000) "Do tax differences cause the brain drain?" *Policy Options* 21:10 (December), 33-41

Ware, Alan (1989) *Between Market and State: Intermediate Organizations in Britain and the United States* (Princeton, NJ: Princeton University Press)

Walker, Michael (1999) "Why polls don't tell the whole truth on tax cuts," *Financial Post,* 7 December, C7

Walkom, Thomas (1981) "Return of tax breaks allows Dome to proceed with HBOG share bid," *Toronto Star,* 19 November, B1

Watson, William (1998) *Globalization and the Meaning of Canadian Life* (Toronto: University of Toronto Press)

Wells, Paul (2000) "How the cabinet neutered itself," *National Post,* 19 February, F3

Weyman, David (1986) "Restructuring the Corporate Income Tax: Directions for Change," in *Report of Proceedings of the Thirty-Seventh Tax Conference, 1985* (Toronto: Canadian Tax Foundation)

Wilson, Thomas A. (1999) "On Tax-Transfer Integration: Let Us Return to the Ability-to-Pay Principle," *Canadian Tax Journal* 47:5, 1258-62

Wilson, Thomas A., and D. Peter Dungan (1993) *Fiscal Policy in Canada: An Appraisal,* Canadian Tax Paper # 94 (Toronto: Canadian Tax Foundation)

Winsor, Hugh (1996) "Deal to replace GST evades Ottawa," *The Globe and Mail,* 2 April, A10

Winsor, Hugh (1999) "Tax cut views within the Liberal caucus appear to be polls apart," *The Globe and Mail,* 17 September, A4

Wolfe, David A. (1988) "Politics, the Deficit and Tax Reform," *Osgoode Hall Law Journal* 26(2)

Woodside, Kenneth (1983) "The Political Economy of Policy Instruments," in *The Politics of Canadian Public Policy,* ed. Michael M. Atkinson and Martha A. Chandler (Toronto: University of Toronto Press), 173-97

Wuthnow, Robert ed. (1991) *Between States and Markets: the voluntary sector in comparative perspective* (Princeton, NJ: Princeton University Press)

Yalnizyan, A. (2000) "What would they do with the surplus?" (Ottawa: Canadian Centre for Policy Alternatives, November)

INTERVIEWS

Dr. Thomas Axworthy
Jim Bennett
Don Blenkarn, M.P.
Dr. Neil Brooks
James R. Brown, Q.C.
Robert D. Brown, C.A.
Gary Campbell
Marshall A. Cohen, Q.C.
Robert Couzin, Q.C.
Hon. Bud Cullen
Mark Daniels
Robert Dart, C.A.
Dr. David A. Dodge
Robert Dowsett
Dr. Don Drummond
Hon. John Evans
Jock Finlayson
Joe Fontana, M.P.
Jean Fournier
Hon. Douglas Frith
Thomas S. Gillespie
Dr. James Gillies
John Godfrey, M.P.
Frederick A. Gorbet
Sandy Grant
Brien G. Gray
Stanley Hartt, Q.C
David Herle
Hon. Thomas A. Hockin
Dr. David Laidler
Hon. Marc Lalonde
Robert Lindsay, Q.C.
Hon. Roy MacLaren
Hon. Paul Martin
Dr. Charles J. McMillan
Dennis Mills, M.P.
T.C. Morris
Dr. E.D. Neufeld

William Neville
Dr. Peter Nicholson
Hon. Robert F. Nixon
Hon. Gordon F. Osbaldeston
Eric Owen
Hon. Jim Peterson
Satya Poddar
Richard Remillard
Dr. Grant Reuber
Steven A. Richardson
Dr. Roger Smith
Dr. Ian A. Stewart
Dr. Jack Vicq
Andrea Vincent
James E. Welkoff
Hon. Michael H. Wilson
James S. Witol

The author also wishes to acknowledge the generous cooperation of a number of senior managers of federal and provincial Departments of Finance (or Treasury) and other government departments who generously shared their time and expertise on the condition of confidentiality. References to their comments are coded as follows:

Ministers, Ministers of State (7)
= M plus numeral.

Deputy Ministers (8)
= D plus numeral.

Assistant Deputy Ministers (10)
= ADM plus numeral

Other Finance Department Officials (14)
= F plus numeral.

Officials of Prime Minister's Office (5)
= PMO plus numeral.

Provincial Government Ministers, Officials (13) = PG plus numeral.

Association Executives (6)
= AE plus numeral.

Private sector and academic advisors to federal and provincial governments (12)
= P plus numeral

Energy taxation 158-62, 173, 186,
205n. 36
Epp, Jake 187
Equalization 69
Established Programs Financing 236, 322
Estate taxes 30, 34n. 21, 50, 83, 149,
275, 291n. 47
Excise Tax Act 78, 86
and cigarette smuggling 85
See also Federal Sales Tax

Fairness in taxation 26, 39-40, 75-76,
127, 141, 147, 175, 262, 300, 334,
357-59
Family farms, taxation of 74, 83, 308,
335
Federal Sales Tax 15, 54, 73, 78, 141,
142, 181, 189, 207
introduction 208
major criticisms of 209-10
proposal to convert to Wholesale
Tax 167-68, 179n. 76, 211-13
proposed replacement by Business
Transfer Tax 189, 205n. 35, 212-
14, 218, 224n. 17, n.23
proposed replacement by "National"
Sales Tax 199, 212
reform as trade-off for higher corporate taxes 193-94, 205n. 37
repeated efforts at reform 207,
212-14
See also Goods and Services Tax
Federal-Provincial Committee on
Taxation 94, 330
Federal-Provincial Tax Collection
Agreements 23, 25, 69-71, 84,
258, 328-30
Fiscal crisis 27, 51, 138, 140, 152
Fiscal dividend 16, 33, 251-53, 257, 261-
62, 266-67, 300, 350
Forbes, Steve 49
Forget, Claude 188, 204n. 23
Fraser Institute 126

Galbraith, John Kenneth 44
General Anti-Avoidance Rules
(GAAR) 81

Good, David 55, 92-93, 98
Goodman, Wolfe 179, 213
Goods and Services Tax (GST) 16, 48,
54, 78, 124, 135, 142, 181, 183, 186,
190, 208-22, 314, 364n. 14
conversion to "Harmonized Sales
Tax" 62n. 47, 78, 212, 218-19
impact on business 297
introduction of (1989-90) 27, 32, 59,
64, 105, 199
proposed "replacement" after 1993
124, 208, 217, 225
public opposition to 34n. 20, 127,
132n. 45, 199, 201, 207, 214-17
response to globalization, free trade
73, 85, 141, 207
Gordon, Walter 306
"Green" taxes 312-13
Guaranteed annual income 86, 223n.
16, 241

Hall, Peter 47, 92
Harris, Mike 332
Hartle, Douglas 66, 100, 208
Hartt, Stanley 205n. 37
Hayden, Salter 125, 131n. 35, 178
Hood, William 178n. 32
House of Commons 68
role in deficit reduction 232
role of government caucus 124
role in tax policy process 123-25
Human Resources Development
Canada 79, 242

Income Tax Act 39-40, 77, 86, 149, 152,
345
Indian and Northern Affairs,
Department of 122
Interest groups 116, 120-23, 128-29, 136,
140-41, 149, 171, 238, 291n. 42, 332-
33, 357-59, 369
consultation in 1987-88 reforms 194,
196-98
lobbying for tax preferences 115, 117-
18, 120, 121-22, 140, 153-54, 166,
302-03
pressures for tax reduction 293